Between Worlds
Access to Second Language Acquisition

Second Edition

David E. Freeman

and

Yvonne S. Freeman

HEINEMANN
Portsmouth, NH

Heinemann
A division of Reed Elsevier Inc.
361 Hanover Street
Portsmouth, NH 03801–3912
www.heinemann.com

Offices and agents throughout the world

Library of Congress Cataloging-in-Publication Data
Freeman, David E.
  Between worlds : access to second language acquisition / David E. Freeman and
Yvonne S. Freeman.
    p.   cm.
  Includes bibliographical references and index.
  ISBN 0-325-00350-5
  1. Second language acquisition.   I. Freeman, Yvonne S.   II. Title.

P118.2 .F74 2001
418'.0071—dc21   00-054045

Editor: Lois Bridges
Production: Vicki Kasabian
Cover design: Cathy Hawkes/Cat and Mouse
Manufacturing: Louise Richardson

Printed in the United States of America on acid-free paper
  06 07 08   RRD   7 8 9 10

We dedicate this book to our daughters, Mary and Ann, and to our son-in-law, Francisco, who have provided us with very personal lessons about acquiring a second language and learning to live between worlds.

Contents

Section Three: Bringing the Worlds Together

Acknowledgments

This book, like the first edition of *Between Worlds: Access to Second Language Acquisition*, is a result of our experiences with teachers who are committed to improving the lives of their students. The response to our first edition has been gratifying and humbling. We know that there are many more stories to tell and better ways to tell them.

We have based the revisions of this text on the response of teachers and colleagues who have read and used our book, and we wish to thank them for their insights. As in the first edition, our examples come from the experiences of creative teachers, who provide contexts that make success possible for all their students. We wish to acknowledge the teachers with whom we have worked, and especially the following outstanding educators whose work we share in this book.

Maureen Anderson, Gayleen Aoki, Loretta Aragón, Kay Armijo, Katie Bausch-Ude, Claudia Beymer, Sharon Borgstadt, Christa Bryan, Paulina Castañeda, Carolina Cervantes, Janie Chapman, Pat Cheek, Paulette Clement, Darrin Cook, Andrea DeBruin-Parecki, Lonna Deeter, Kathy DerMugredechian, Leny de Ruijter, Rusty DeRuiter, Cándida Dillon, Mary Durazo, David East, Jeannette Erickson, Steve Ewert, Jean Fennacy, Kushnuma Ferzandi, Linda Friberg, Ann Freeman, Kim Fuzco, Linda Gage, Fermín Garza, Bobbi Jentes Mason, Toni Gerbrandt, Tammy González, Melissa Greer, Mary Gustafson, Shelly Hernández, Elaine Huene, Jane Jones, Charlene Klassen-Endrizzi, Maryann Lambarén, Mary Ann Larsen-Pusey, Elena López, Mike Lebsock, Xueguang Lian, Desiree McDougal, Debbie Manning, Lisa Marasco, Miriam Marquardt, Eva Mauch, Sandra Mercuri, Marjorie Miller, Cheryl Milligan, Helen Milliorn, Xe Moua, Belinda Naso, Sam Nofziger, Lisa Pierro, Roxie Pires, Sharon Porter, Michelle Ramírez, Denise Rea, Gerard Rivas, Susanne Roberts, Bunny Rogers, Jill Rojas, Jerry Sánchez, Sue Scott, Henrietta Siemens, Yolanda Shahbazian, Kathy Smith, Pam Smith, John Sorber, Francisco Soto, Megan Stoehr, Lea Tafolla, Cheryl Timion, Rhoda Toews, Patty Trask, Yvette Vásquez, Kristene Vaux, Doua Vu, Vince Workmon, Marta Yoshimura, Denette Zaninovich.

In addition, we would like to thank our first editor, Dawn Boyer, and our present editor, Lois Bridges. Working with Lois and the staff at Heinemann on this second edition has been a unique and special privilege. All have managed uncomplainingly to overcome the obstacles created in the process of working with authors who move between worlds. Questions have been answered and help given immediately. Karen Chabot has been especially helpful, answering questions, organizing events, and providing assistance. With this second edition, in particular, we have needed support from our production editor, Vicki Kasabian, and production chief, Abby Heim. As always, Maura Sullivan has provided us with personal and caring promotion plans, making us feel that our books are important to her and to Heinemann.

We also wish to thank those who continually support us with a sense that our work matters. Our university student assistant, Veronica Manzo, has efficiently and affectionately helped with collecting permissions, finding references, and supplying contact information.

Finally, we wish to thank our Maine island neighbors—Fran and Fred, Linda and George, and Karen and Bob—who keep reminding us that while work is important, it is equally valuable to enjoy the beauty of nature and the company of good friends.

Introduction

"I was amazed. I had no idea!"—these were the words John kept repeating as he told fellow teachers in his second language acquisition (SLA) class about an experience he had while trying to choose one of his students for a case study, a major class assignment. John teaches choral music, and he began by polling his small class of eleven students:

> First I asked, "Do any of you speak English as a second language?" All raised their hands. To be sure they understood, I asked, "Does anyone speak Spanish?" Again, all raised their hands. I was amazed. I had no idea.

John is a new teacher, trying to prepare himself to work effectively with his students. He recently earned his teaching credential, and now he is returning to graduate school to take the courses for his English as a Second Language (ESL) endorsement. He knew that the student population had changed in recent years, but he "had no idea" that so many of his students speak English as a second language. John's teacher-education classes gave him a good foundation for his teaching assignment, but he now knows that he needs additional information about second language learning if he is to reach all his students.

In his graduate class, John is beginning to learn that the academic success of English learners depends on many factors inside and outside the classroom. Students learning in a new language and in a new culture have unique needs. In a school like John's, the students and the teachers are worlds apart—almost literally. It is critical that teachers, resource specialists, paraprofessionals, administrators, teacher educators, parents, and the general public understand that many elements interact to influence the school performance of students who are acquiring English as another language.

Why a Second Edition?

Responses from teachers like John convince us that teachers who want to do what is best for English learners need to know more about them. We have updated this text because we want to provide teachers with current trends and continue to address the many issues related to teaching multilingual students. The schooling of English language learners has become more complex and more political since the writing of the first edition of this book.

Our schools reflect an increasingly rich linguistic diversity, and this brings with it a challenge for teachers, because many more students at all grade levels have limited English proficiency. Since we wrote the first edition of this book in 1994, the number of students in U.S. schools who have been identified as limited English proficient (LEP) has grown from just over three million to over four million. During this period, the second language population grew by 25 percent, while the total K–12 school population actually declined slightly from about 47.7 million to 46.1 million (NCBE 2000).

The five states with the greatest number of LEP students are California, Florida, Illinois, New York, and Texas. All five of these states have identified more than 100,000 students as LEP. While the population of LEP students for these states may not seem surprising, there has also been increased diversity in states like Alaska, Arkansas, Idaho, Kansas, Nebraska, Oklahoma, and Oregon. All of these states have had an increase in English learners of over 200 percent in the last ten years.

As we have worked with educators in different states, we have seen many more teachers working to earn certification to prepare them to work more effectively with ESL students. Teachers in small communities as well as cities in Iowa, Nebraska, Oregon, Alaska, Alabama, and Kansas are studying SLA and learning about effective approaches to teaching their multilingual/multicultural students.

While teachers are becoming better informed, misconceptions among the general public about new immigrants and their needs have also grown. Immigrants have been blamed for economic and social ills, and there have been strong movements to limit immigration to the United States. In California, a movement against bilingual education resulted in the passage of Proposition 227, which has severely curtailed bilingual programs. It mandated sheltered English immersion, a program with no research base that has never been tried before. Other states have considered similar legislation. We believe that it is perhaps more important now than ever before for educators to be aware of the many issues affecting the academic performance of immigrant students in our schools, so that they can be advocates for all their students.

Certainly, no magic formula will ensure the academic success of any group of learners, and while this book offers examples of practices that have proved effective with a variety of students, we are aware that each learning situation is different. What works in one classroom may not apply down the hall, much less in another part of the country. We hope, however, that by identifying and discussing the social and psychological factors that impact students who are learning academic content in their second or third languages, we can help professionals like John to examine their programs and their classroom practices to ensure that they are providing what is best for all their students.

The approach we develop here recognizes that any student's second language development and academic-content learning are the result of many interacting forces. No one factor determines success or failure for a particular student or group of students. Yet, in the past, some educators relied on single-cause explanations to account for students' progress. For example, some have focused on English proficiency. However, learning English is not the only key to academic achievement. English proficiency, by itself, does not determine success or failure. Cummins (1989) expresses this clearly:

> [U]nderstanding why and how minority students are failing academically requires that educators dig a little deeper than superficial linguistic mismatches between home and school or insufficient exposure to English. Underachievement is not caused by lack of fluency in English. (33–34)

Even when lack of English is not seen as the cause of failure, the students themselves or their backgrounds are sometimes blamed. Such single-cause explanations are often based on social or cultural stereotypes. For example, some teachers might say that Hispanic students lack motivation, so they do not do well in school, but that Asians get good grades because they are influenced by high parental expectations. We would like to suggest that the question of school success and failure is much more complex than most people think.

Our Title

The title for this book, *Between Worlds*, reflects our conviction that providing the best education for second language students requires that as we plan educational experiences, we take into account factors from two worlds, the school and the larger society. In a sense, school is a place that is between two worlds for all students. Students entering school are leaving the smaller world of their home and entering the larger world of their community. For English language learners, these two worlds are often very different. In school, language minority students are often taught by teachers like John, whose experiences have been limited to the mainstream culture and whose attitudes and values have been shaped by mainstream views. John and teachers like him benefit from examining their attitudes and values and also by considering the values and attitudes that their second language learners bring to school. By doing this they can help all their students fully experience the best of both worlds.

Some students are unable to move successfully between worlds because they never fully enter the mainstream school community. They are marginalized by the instruction they receive and the attitudes they encounter. Eventually, many of them drop out or are pushed out of school. Unfortunately, these students often lack a sense of belonging in their home community. They may be in a state of cultural ambivalence, not completely accepted either at school or at home. When this happens, increasing numbers of students turn to alternate communities, such as gangs. Rather than experiencing the best of both worlds, they cannot participate fully in either one.

Other students succeed in school, but in the process they become alienated from their home community. These are students who enter school as monolingual Spanish or Korean speakers and leave school as monolingual English speakers. They are unable to communicate with family and friends in the home community. These students may reject their heritage language and culture in order to become part of the mainstream. Rather than experiencing the best of both worlds, they simply trade one world for another.

We have chosen *Access to Second Language Acquisition* as the subtitle for this book because we believe that a number of psychological and social factors interact to permit or deny students access to the acquisition of a new language. However, the subtitle also has another purpose. We hope that this book gives those involved with English language learners access to language learning theories and effective classroom practice. We hope to bring the theories alive for the readers of this book by providing numerous examples of classroom practice. Educators who understand these theories and their implications can provide English learners with access to their new language.

Teachers have the responsibility for developing not only language but academic content. We provide a number of examples that demonstrate that language is learned best when students are focused on content-area studies rather than on aspects of language itself (see also Freeman and Freeman 1998). We learn language as we use language for a variety of purposes. This is true for students in mainstream classes as well as those in ESL and foreign language classes. As Halliday (1984) has pointed out, students can learn language as they learn through language.

Who Is This Book For?

The idea for writing the first edition of this book came to us as we taught a course called Language Acquisition and Cross-Cultural Communication. The teachers in our graduate program needed a text that described different theories of language acquisition and also provided examples for putting theory into practice. In addition, as we worked with teachers in schools, we were reminded daily that teaching multilingual/multicultural learners involves much more than an understanding of theory, methods, and materials. We realized that this text needed to address social, political, and cultural factors that influence students' learning. That book and this new edition reflect our attempts to meet these goals.

Many of the examples in this text appeared in the first edition. Teachers found them useful and often told us how much they related to them. Some of the stories are new ones, vignettes we wanted to share because they helped us to better understand teaching and learning. All of the examples come from our own experiences and from the experiences of teachers we have worked with. It is our hope that teacher educators continue to find this book useful in courses dealing with learning theory, SLA, and social, political, and cultural factors that influence learning. These courses might be part of a preservice program for prospective teachers, part of a program for teachers wishing to continue their professional development, or part of a graduate program of study.

However, we do not intend that the audience for this book be restricted to people taking formal coursework or to designated ESL or bilingual teachers. We hope that mainstream teachers like John will also find this book useful. In fact, we wrote this book with several possible audiences in mind. One audience includes teachers, counselors, paraprofessionals, and others who work with second language students and who wish to continue their own professional development through independent reading. As student populations change and increasing numbers of English learners enter our schools, it is important for all the professionals working with these students to be knowledgeable about current theories of language acquisition and to be aware of the social and cultural factors that influence students' academic performance. We have presented explanations of theory and examples of successful classroom practice that should clarify many of these issues. We encourage educators who are not taking formal courses to meet with colleagues in pairs or small groups to reflect on the ideas presented here.

We have also written this book for school administrators. Administrators provide leadership in curriculum, and they support the efforts of classroom teachers. School demographics have changed radically. In many schools, language minority students have become the numerical majority. For administrators to carry out their role, they need to be aware of the psychological and social factors that influence the academic performance of second language students as well as their curriculum needs.

Finally, we have written this book for parents and for community members interested in school improvement. Parents and other community members play a key role in the academic success of language minority students (Valdés 1996). We discuss in some detail ways in which the social context of schooling influences the educational context. We also describe successful programs that involve parents and other community members. Second language students can succeed when home and school work together to provide them access to the best possible education. We hope that parents and other members of the general public will find the examples and explanations here helpful as they increase their own involvement in programs to improve schooling.

At the end of each chapter we have included a section called "Applications." These are not intended as end-of-chapter tests or exercises that must be completed for a grade. Instead, they are invitations to explore in more detail the concepts raised in the chapter. We hope that they will help readers apply the ideas to their own experiences. We believe that people learn by doing, and the applications ask readers to do something with what they have read or to read related material. We have asked our own students to try these activities, and they have reported that the applications enabled them to relate the concepts being studied more directly to their own teaching. Since we also believe that learning takes place in social interaction, we have suggested that the activities be completed in pairs or small groups. With our students, this sharing has led not only to the expansion of ideas but also to the building of a supportive community.

Our book, *ESL/EFL Teaching: Principles for Success* (1998a), focuses on the various methods that have been used to teach English as a second language. In that book we outline a series of principles that constitute our orientation toward teaching and learning. This orientation is holistic and learner-centered. We include a number of examples of classroom practice to illustrate these principles. In the present book, we examine the process of language acquisition. However, we retain the same basic orientation toward teaching and learning and again attempt to illustrate that orientation with specific classroom examples.

Terms to Describe Students

We wish to comment on the terminology we use to refer to the students we write about in this book. It is always difficult to choose a descriptive term for any group because the words used may, in fact, label or limit the people in that group (Wink 1993). For example, the frequently used label for non-English speakers, LEP, focuses attention on what students cannot do. All of us have limited (or no) proficiency in a number of languages.

In the past, we have referred to students in our schools who do not speak English as their first language as *second language learners* or *bilingual learners*. We use these terms to make the point that these students already have another language, and English is an additional language. However, we have become uncomfortable with these terms since we are aware that many English language learners are, in fact, adding a third, fourth, and even fifth language to their repertoire. Therefore, the terms *bilingual learners* and *second language learners* might also be seen as limiting.

The term we currently use is *English language learners* or simply *English learners*. Even native speakers of English are English language learners in a sense, but students for whom English is not the native language face the task of learning English. This term focuses on what these students are trying to do, what they have in common, so it is the term that we will use most frequently.

Organization of the Text

The basic question we explore in this book is, "How can teachers provide students who are between worlds access to second language acquisition and to the content-area knowledge they need for academic success?" To answer this question, we raise a series of smaller questions. In the first section of the book, "The World Inside the School," we consider questions from the school context. Then, in the second section, "The World Outside the School," we consider questions from the societal context. The final section, "Bringing the Worlds Together," suggests ways educators can bring the world of mainstream school society and the world of English language learners together through classroom-based research.

The first eight chapters focus on the school context. Chapter 1 poses the question, "Who are our English language learners, and what factors influence their academic performance?" In this chapter, we present a series of case studies of English learners to provide specific examples for the research and theory developed in later chapters. Chapter 2 asks, "What influences how teachers teach?" Here we consider how beliefs, theories, and practice influence teaching. We look in detail at the changes one teacher has experienced in moving from an eclectic to a principled approach. Chapter 3 raises the question, "How does learning take place in explorer classrooms?" In this chapter we explain what explorer classrooms are, and we develop a general theory of how students learn. In Chapter 4 we turn to second language issues and ask, "What do we acquire when we acquire a language?" This question is more complex than it appears, and the answer has important implications for teaching second language students. Chapter 5 then follows with the question, "What are the principal theories of second language acquisition?" In this chapter we review SLA theories and develop a view of second language acquisition that is consistent with the general view of learning presented in Chapter 3.

In Chapters 6, 7, and 8 we further develop the idea of teaching as exploration by presenting classroom examples of explorer teachers putting acquisition theory into practice. Chapter 6 asks, "How do explorer teachers celebrate learning and make it meaningful?" The question for Chapter 7 is, "How do explorer teachers respect learners and their ways of learning?" And Chapter 8 centers on the query, "How do explorer teachers celebrate students' first languages and cultures?"

In the next three chapters we turn to the societal context for education. In Chapter 9 we ask, "What influences do community, teacher, and student attitudes have on learning?" Chapter 10 investigates the question, "How can teachers help schools develop an intercultural orientation?" Chapter 11 discusses the important role of family, asking, "How can schools involve parents?"

In the last section of the book, we suggest ways to bring the worlds together. Our question is, "How can teachers improve their practice through classroom-based research?" We suggest that when teachers investigate factors that impact their students in both the school and the societal context, they can modify their practices and help students who are between worlds succeed in both their worlds.

In each of the three sections, we present current theory and provide examples of teachers working effectively with second language students. We hope that this information will be useful to teachers, counselors, paraprofessionals, administrators, parents, and others involved in the education of language minority students. We are aware that no easy answers to the questions we are raising exist, but we are convinced that all students benefit when educators working with them are aware of current research and effective classroom practice.

We began this introduction with a quote from John, who was "amazed" that all the students in one of his classes spoke English as a second language. Being amazed is a good first step in learning. By studying SLA theories, the sociocultural influences on bilingual learners, and the effective practices of teachers working with diverse populations, John will gain the knowledge he needs to better provide for all his students who are between worlds.

1

Who Are Our English Language Learners, and What Factors Influence Their Academic Performance?

We begin this book with case studies of several English language learners. Teachers who wish to understand the complex interaction of factors that affect the performance of their students can benefit from reading these stories and from conducting case studies of their own. These studies help show how factors from both the world of the school and the world outside the school influence the academic performance of second language students. Case studies provide a good starting point for understanding the research, theory, and practice described in this book, and this knowledge can help educators respond in an informed way as they work with their English language learners.

Each case study is based on a real student in a real school setting. Some reflect our personal experiences with English language learners. We have lived and worked in several multilingual communities; our family is bilingual and now, through marriage, bicultural as well. The other case studies were conducted by teachers studying second language acquisition in the graduate education program at our university. To help the teachers discover the strengths of their immigrant students, we have them read about and discuss SLA and the importance of students' first languages and cultures. They also study the ways the community context affects schools. Then the teachers choose one second language learner to work with closely. We wrote of John's experience in making this choice in our Introduction. They read, write, and talk with their student. The teachers share with each other what they are learning from their experiences as they write up their case studies. Through their research on one student and their interactions with their peers, many of these teachers begin to change the way they view the language minority students in their classes and to adapt the way they teach.

The teachers in our classes agree that it is one thing to read about English language learners and discuss SLA theories in the setting of a college classroom; it is another to work with the students directly and apply what one has read. However, when our teachers take the time to study one student carefully, they gain a new perspective on all their English learners. As Desiree wrote,

> I am now a strong advocate for case studies. It is too bad that a case study is not mandatory for all teachers. A case study forces you to really get to know the children. I know that what I have learned will help to make me a much better teacher.

Katie, a teacher whose case study we describe below, explained even more specifically how her experience would influence her in the future:

1. I will expend more effort in getting to know my students personally.
2. I will provide individual time for each student as often as possible.
3. I will never again assume that "what I hear" is "what they know."
4. I will arrange my classroom/curriculum around whole, real, purposeful, meaning-filled experiences.
5. I will find, value, and exploit each student's contributions and talents.

While we realize that no two students are alike and that no two students have the same needs, there are commonalities among learners that help us approach our teaching in a more informed way. We include here the case studies of eight students at different grade levels and with different educational, cultural, and linguistic backgrounds. After each, we list several of the factors that may have influenced that student's success or failure. It is important to be aware of the different forces involved and consider them as we work to provide our students who are between worlds access to second language acquisition and content-area knowledge. Our students need both for academic success.

We ask readers to compare the students in the case studies below to English learners with whom they have worked and to think about the differences and similarities in the factors that may have influenced them.

Eugenia

Five-year-old Eugenia attends a bilingual kindergarten in a small rural community in the Central Valley of California. She was born in the United States in the apartment of a family friend, because her mother, an illegal alien, was afraid to go to a hospital. Shortly after Eugenia's birth, her parents became legal residents under the amnesty laws for migrant laborers who had worked in the United States over a period of years. In the past her parents did seasonal field labor, moving often and leaving the children with relatives in Mexico at times, but after both parents got jobs in a canning factory, the family settled down.

Though neither of Eugenia's parents speaks English, and neither has had much formal education, both parents believe that her education is very important. They see school as the hope for their children's future. At first they were concerned about the fact that Eugenia's teacher used Spanish for some instruction. One of their high school sons had had negative experiences with bilingual education and had recently dropped out of school. However, Cándida, Eugenia's energetic Puerto Rican teacher, was able to explain to her parents why she teaches in Spanish and how building a strong first language base would help Eugenia in English in the future. Cándida convinced Eugenia's parents to sign the waiver form to allow Eugenia to receive primary language instruction. Because Cándida speaks Spanish and has shown an interest in them and their child, Eugenia's parents now come to the school frequently to ask for advice or offer to help.

Eugenia has thrived in Cándida's classroom. Cándida provides many opportunities for her kindergarten students to begin to read and write. For example, the classroom playhouse doubles as a "store," and includes paper, pencils, and lots of cans and boxes so that the children can "take orders" and "prepare meals." The class spends time every day reading predictable books, singing and reciting poetry in both Spanish and English. Because the class creates language experience charts and class books and does lots of brainstorming, Eugenia is comfortable with writing and experiments with writing in both Spanish and English for different purposes.

Eugenia has had a very positive year in kindergarten. Cándida believes that Eugenia will succeed in school. "She is lucky enough to have a supportive and caring home environment," Cándida explains, "which will help her weather academic difficulties or disappointments and tolerate and defeat racism and expectations of failure. She has strong self-esteem."

Perhaps Cándida is optimistic because she is seeing these Hispanic children at the very start of their school experience, and she has such a strong belief in them. In her own words, Cándida describes why she feels she can work well with her students:

> I believe that being a Latina from the South Bronx helps me understand my kids not only linguistically, but also philosophically. I know the challenges that face these children, but I also know that if someone cares, their chances for success are great.

Analysis

At this point Eugenia is doing well. Cándida is giving Eugenia a positive start, and she has supportive parents who are eager for her to succeed and are willing to help her in any way they can. Her teacher, a Hispanic herself, is sensitive to the needs of both Eugenia and her parents. In addition, her teacher is giving Eugenia the kind of curriculum she needs, including first language support, a print-rich classroom environment, opportunities for social interaction, and experiences with meaningful literacy activities.

However, other influences may affect Eugenia in the future. Eugenia's parents are laborers without education or English skills. They will not be able to help her with her academic studies as she moves into the upper grades. Though they are now in the United States legally, the uncertainty and transience of the past and their socioeconomic status may keep them from being as confident as they need to be in dealing with schools. An older brother has already encountered problems and dropped out of school while the parents watched helplessly.

As Cándida herself points out, many Hispanic children face challenges of racism. Eugenia's teacher is optimistic, but her background as a New York City Puerto Rican is different from that of her students, whose families come from rural Mexico. We have hope for Eugenia, but we must look at both the positive and negative influences that might affect her in the coming years.

Mony

Unlike Eugenia, who lived most of her early years in the United States before attending school, Mony arrived here as a refugee from Cambodia just as she was entering kindergarten. The school she attended was a large, inner-city elementary school of over one thousand students from many different linguistic and cultural backgrounds. Since most of the students were Spanish speakers from Mexico or Hmong speakers from Laos, Mony had only a few other Khmer speakers from Cambodia to rely on. Her parents, also overwhelmed by their new surroundings, were of little help, as they spoke no English and were concerned about finding work and maintaining a household for Mony and her siblings in a new country.

Mony's kindergarten teacher recommended that she be placed the next year in Katie's prefirst class, a transition year before being placed in first grade. Katie's classroom had twenty-eight students, and many were English language learners from Mexico, Laos, Vietnam, Cambodia, and Korea. Katie was intrigued by Mony, who "seemed 'deeper,' more serious than students who, though 'silent' in English, converse freely with their L1 [first language] peers." Mony followed directions and participated silently in most activities. Her artwork was so impressive that Katie, a veteran teacher of ten years, commented that Mony was "the most advanced six-year-old artist I'd ever seen." Mony avoided eye contact with most people and preferred the company of the one other Cambodian child in the room. In fact, if her peers paid too much attention to her, Mony would stick her tongue out at them, trying to make sure Katie didn't see her do it.

Though Katie could coax Mony to come close to her for cuddling during quiet times and comforted her when she had crying periods, she could not convince Mony to converse with peers in Khmer or discuss her fears and concerns in her first language. Just as Katie felt she might be beginning to connect with her, Mony was transferred to another school. Katie wrote a note to administrators at the transfer school. "I worried that [Mony's] darting tongue and serious look might get her into unfair trouble, that her lack of oral language would be confused with lack of intelligence, and I wanted someone to know of her treasured artistic ability," she explains. She received one brief follow-up call.

Since Katie teaches at a year-round school and went on vacation shortly after Mony left, she chose to do her case study on Mony in her new school setting. She decided to visit Mony in her new classroom, talk and read with her, and continue an interactive journal she had begun with Mony when she had been in Katie's class. Katie visited Mony ten times and kept anecdotal records of their time reading, writing, and talking. In this smaller classroom environment, Mony seemed almost like a different student. Katie's reflections reveal how much her visits taught her.

> I was amazed at Mony's proficiency in English and shocked at what I'd wrongly perceived it to be when she was in my class. It sounds so simple, but if we as teachers put more effort into *who* we're teaching, more of the *what* would take care of itself. When we concentrate on programs, or strict timelines, we lose sight of the important human element.

Having looked closely at one student helped Katie see that human element anew.

Analysis

Mony is a refugee child who arrived in the United States with no preparation for the dramatic changes she encountered. Busy teachers who have many other things to be concerned about often do not realize just how traumatic the changes are for refugee children who leave behind war-torn countries or homelands ravaged by natural disasters.

Mony found little support at the large school she attended. Her response was to watch silently and try to absorb what was going on around her. As we will see later, many English learners have a silent period as they absorb the language, and Mony was no exception. Her silence and seeming defiance were wrongly perceived by her kindergarten teacher as lack of ability, and even Katie, who recognized her skill in art, underestimated her proficiency in English. She was surprised at Mony's rapid progress when she visited her new school.

Many immigrant children get lost in our school system. Yet, if we can find ways to get to know them as individuals, show an interest in them, and meet their specific needs, we give them greater chances for future school success.

Salvador

Salvador entered Ann's multiage second- and third-grade bilingual classroom as a third grader. His previous teachers had warned Ann how difficult he was and had pretty much written him off as unreachable. He had been in a bilingual kindergarten and first grade and then had been transitioned to an English-only second grade because it was reasoned that he was not learning to read and write in Spanish. When he failed in English, he was put into Ann's class, which was designed for struggling students.

Ann soon discovered that Salvador was disruptive in class and refused to try to read or write in Spanish or English. He would often cry and throw tantrums and start arguments with classmates both in class and on the playground. Ann spoke with Salvador's mother, who was also at a loss about what to do with him. His behavior at home was similar to his behavior at school. His mother's response was to give him what he wanted, to placate him. She had a high school education in Mexico, was attending English classes, and hoped to get a job soon. She could help Salvador at home, but he would not often let her. Ann learned that his father was frequently absent from the home, since he worked in other parts of the state or returned to Mexico. She also came to discover that Salvador's worst outbursts occurred when his father returned home, even though Salvador was always very excited about his father's homecomings.

Ann's classroom offered many opportunities for students to do shared and pair reading in Spanish and English. She organized her curriculum around themes and encouraged her students to write in journals, create books, and summarize content readings by making charts and graphs. She suspected that much of Salvador's behavior stemmed from his lack of confidence in his own reading and writing. She gave Salvador responsibilities, such as having him take roll, or track for the class when they read a poem or big book. Ann celebrated any and all of Salvador's positive responses, but was frustrated by his frequent disruptive behavior. By the end of the year, Salvador had improved somewhat in his ability to take part in the classroom routines, but Ann and his mother decided that he was not ready to go to fourth grade, where the academic content was demanding and the curriculum was entirely in English. Salvador was still struggling to read and write in Spanish.

The next year, Salvador's teacher was Francisco, who also found Salvador to be difficult. Francisco helped Salvador to see that anger was a response that was hurtful not only to his classmates but to Salvador himself. His teacher's gentle insistence on positive behavior and cooperation were calming for Salvador. Francisco also played soccer with the students during recess, and Salvador loved soccer.

Since Francisco had a similar routine to the one Ann had used, Salvador was more ready to read and write and participate in group projects. By midyear, Francisco began to see real progress. Salvador actually completed a book on his own, following the pattern of a class book about farm animals and their sounds. This seemed to be a breakthrough for Salvador. He wrote and read more confidently in Spanish and began to read and write in English.

Salvador's year with Francisco was important. He continued to get literacy support in his first language, with routines similar to the year before. In addition, Francisco was a Latino male who insisted on good behavior and maintained high expectations. By the end of the year, Salvador was beginning to show significant academic gains. Both Ann and Francisco have watched Salvador's progress in fourth and fifth grade. While he is not the strongest student, he is progressing well and his former behavior problems have all but disappeared. When Francisco visited the school recently, Salvador greeted him and told him how well he was behaving and how much better he was doing in school.

Analysis

Salvador is an example of a student who had many complicated forces influencing him. Though his mother wanted to help, she seemed at a loss, and her husband was seldom home. The school had no specific proof, but there was a suspicion of violence in the home when the father was in residence. This seemed to affect Salvador and his behavior directly.

Salvador's first years of schooling were inconsistent. Teachers soon labeled him and did not appear to know much about him. He was placed in an all-English classroom when he was not yet literate in his first language. Before coming to Ann's class, Salvador's teachers considered him a discipline problem and didn't perceive him as a capable student. Ann gave him responsibilities and held high expectations for him. Her classroom provided a consistent routine of reading and writing in Spanish, and Salvador was expected to participate in all activities with the class. Although he still misbehaved frequently, Ann laid a foundation for his eventual success. Francisco built on that foundation, and Salvador is doing much better now.

Even though Salvador has made great progress, his home situation is unstable. He will soon enter his teen years, always a difficult time. He will also have to make the transition to middle school. These outside forces will make success more difficult, but he has developed better self-discipline and his academic skills are steadily improving, so if he continues to get good teachers, he has some chance for success.

Sharma

Rhoda, a fifth-grade teacher in an elementary school in a rural farming community, describes her first impression of her Punjabi student, Sharma, and Sharma's mother.

> She walked into my classroom and smiled at me with warm, giving brown eyes. Her dark brown hair was neatly braided, and she politely introduced me to her mother and her baby sister. The woman's traditional Indian silk was embroidered in rich primary colors setting off her beautiful olive skin. In accented English she asked for a few moments of my time. She asked that I arrange for the school's Punjabi aide to spend time with her daughter so that she would not fall behind the rest of the class. I was intrigued by this caring mother and wanted to know more about her soft-spoken daughter.

As Rhoda gathered information for her case study, she learned a great deal about Sharma.

Sharma and her family had moved back and forth between India and the United States several times since her birth in California. The family's middle-class life in India was comfortable, but Sharma's parents were concerned that the primitive rural school near their home in India would not provide their daughter with the future they wanted for her. They tried twice to succeed economically in the United States and once even left their children with relatives in India while they looked for work in the States. Finally, both parents found jobs in the community where Rhoda taught. The father worked for local farmers and the mother was employed at a local packing plant.

Sharma's parents speak English, but they use Punjabi with Sharma and her two younger sisters, who were also born in California. Sharma and her sisters dress in Western clothing for school and make an effort to fit into the activities in which the other students participate. The parents have allowed their children to give up some of their traditions, because they think that adopting Western ways is necessary for school success. They believe in hard work and have high academic expectations for their children. On weekends the girls go to the local Sikh temple to develop their first language abilities and to learn about their religion. They also participate in Punjabi holidays and traditions.

Sharma has attended the same rural school from kindergarten through fifth grade. Though the school has a bilingual program for Spanish speakers, only limited primary language support is available for Punjabi students. Sharma is an active member of her fifth-grade classroom community. She especially seeks out friends among Caucasians in her class. Her social English is animated and full of the same idioms used by her peers. She tends to avoid contact with other newer and less proficient Punjabi students, although she is willing to be helpful with information about India or to support the newcomers when asked.

Sharma is categorized as proficient in English by the test the school administers to its second language students. However, Rhoda has noticed that the language of some content-area texts is a challenge for Sharma, and Sharma, on her own, looks for resource books, pictures, and charts to help make sense of some of the more difficult content.

Rhoda hopes that Sharma will continue to study her native language so that she will develop that resource as she progresses in English. Rhoda summarizes her concerns about Sharma's future as follows:

> Although Sharma has had some advantages other language minority students have not had, she still has a problem with not being able to work to her potential because of lagging academic language development. As she continues to be exposed to comprehensible input, and continues to develop academic language, concepts will become less cognitively demanding. Because Sharma does not have a strong background in reading and writing Punjabi, it would appear that her primary language needs continued support. Teachers should continue to appreciate new Punjabi students for who they are and model this acceptance to their classroom communi-

ties. They should allow them to speak out of their personal experience so that students like Sharma can understand that "traditional" Punjabis have as much value as their Americanized counterparts.

Analysis

Many factors have influenced and will continue to influence Sharma's progress in school. Her parents are both educated and speak English well when compared with other immigrants. On the other hand, their socioeconomic status is not high. The family has experienced financial stress in the past and for this reason has had to move often. They presently live in a small farming community with little sensitivity to the needs of immigrants, especially those from a culture so different from the mainstream American culture. Teachers at the school have little understanding of the Punjabi way of life and customs.

The family maintains their home language and culture; yet her parents want Sharma and her siblings to succeed academically in a society that is very different from their own. Their expectations for their children are very high, almost demanding. Sharma must do well in a competitive school system but also maintain, to some extent, traditional Punjabi customs. This creates a struggle for Sharma, who even avoids social contact with Punjabi students who have recently arrived.

Sharma seems to be thriving despite these difficulties. Though no teachers speak Punjabi, a Punjabi-speaking aide works with those students who need first language support. Sharma's parents are quick to seek assistance from the school when they think their daughter needs it. Sharma herself interacts freely with her Anglo peers and seems well adjusted socially. Presently, she is able to function well in both the Punjabi social context and the school context. It remains to be seen if she will continue to be able to do this successfully.

Tou

Kathy, a junior high school English teacher, chose Tou, a Hmong student, for a case study because he is typical of other junior high school students she has. In describing her choice she explained that Tou "typifies many of my rather academically apathetic, immature boy students." The population at Kathy's school is approximately 75 percent Hispanic, 10 percent Asian, 8 percent African American, and 7 percent Caucasian. Like many of Kathy's students, Tou tested well below the fiftieth percentile on reading and struggled academically. Tou's academic achievement is typical of long-term LEP students. These are students who come to our schools as second language learners, never become literate in their first language, develop native-like conversational English, but do not develop the academic English needed for school success despite several years of schooling in English.

Kathy described why she chose Tou for her case study:

Tou is not generally well liked. His small stature and immaturity certainly contribute to this unpopularity. I have witnessed several instances of racial slurs aimed at Tou and the isolation that has ensued. The normal adolescent self-doubt and low self-esteem combined with the hostility he encounters daily seem a certain formula for failure.

Tou, now fourteen, is the youngest of seven children in a refugee Hmong family. He was born in a refugee camp in Thailand but spent only a few months there. After his birth, his family lived briefly in Hawaii and then moved to the midsized city in California where he now lives with his father and two of his older brothers, who are married with children. His mother is living with a daughter and her family in another city several hours away. Separation of parents is difficult for any child, but because Hmong place great value on family unity, Tou is deeply affected as his family stands out as an exception.

The family came to the United States with the hope of finding not only freedom but a better life. Economic and emotional problems, however, have kept them from achieving their goals. Tou's father, who was a farmer in Laos, does not speak English, is not literate in Hmong, and does not have any job skills appropriate to his inner-city neighborhood.

Tou has attended seventh and eighth grades in Kathy's inner-city school. Most of the students at the school are from low-income families living in run-down apartment complexes. Many of the parents are unemployed laborers or refugees on welfare. Although Tou was an extremely reluctant participant in most class activities in seventh grade, Kathy was able to engage him during a unit on folktales. He read independently and, with a partner, wrote a story about a young child getting a puppy of his own. He ended the first semester with Kathy "on a definite upbeat." He seemed to be proud of the work he was doing and was given an award for effort and improvement at the end-of-semester assembly.

However, the school is on a year-round schedule and after an eight-week semester break, Tou's positive attitude seemed to disappear. He began a pattern of frequent absences, and his behavior changed. Kathy describes the change as follows:

> He often would come to school toward the middle of the week and then start his weekend early—kind of a two-day school week, five-day weekend model! When he was there, his antisocial behavior was more obvious, and students began to ask me not to seat them close to Tou.

This behavior eventually led to an emotional conference in which Tou's father, with the help of a Hmong-speaking aide, told of his hopes and dreams, of what America meant to him, and of his aspirations for his children. He told how one older brother had dropped out of high school because of involvement in gang activity and how worried he was that Tou was following the same failed path.

After that conference, Kathy saw that there was a change in Tou's behavior, though not a transformation. "Truthfully, it was old-fashioned parental hovering, teacher monitoring, and weekly progress reports sent home requiring Dad's signature that kept Tou in school the last two months of school." His teachers and father did manage to get him through seventh grade, and he was promoted to eighth, an event Kathy explained as "not lifelong success, exactly, but an achievement nonetheless."

In eighth grade Kathy and the other teachers at her school worked in teams to give students more stability. While Tou's work in eighth grade was satisfactory, and while he functioned well within the safe, familiar environment of the team classrooms, outside of class for any length of time, he would get into fights with students of other ethnic groups. There was strong suspicion that he was part of a Hmong gang.

Later that year, Tou was given a "social transfer" to a different junior high school in the district. It is unclear whether he was transferred because school officials were concerned about the trouble he was getting into or if the transfer was requested by his father in the hope that a change of schools would give Tou a new start. Eventually, Tou was transferred back to Kathy's school, where he was placed in Opportunity, a class that is like a continuation school in which students are given one last chance to succeed. Kathy summarized her concerns for Tou and students like him at the end of her case study.

> This experience made me sadly aware that my students are all individuals with diverse and complicated needs and that I can never hope to solve them all. Just my one-on-one interviews with Tou and my special efforts to talk at least briefly with him every day pointed up that all my students need that attention. I feel stretched to the limit.

Analysis

As Kathy points out, Tou's situation is a complex one. Many negative factors are at work, and they appear to be outweighing the efforts his father and his teachers have made to help him. Tou is the youngest in a large family that is caught in a struggle to survive in a new and challenging culture, a culture that has little in common with their own. The home situation for Tou is not a happy one. His parents are separated, a situation that is unusual in traditional Hmong culture (Bliatout et al. 1988), and is a source of embarrassment now. He lives with his father, who does not speak English and cannot find work. Older siblings either did not get schooling or had trouble in school. One brother has a history of gang membership. Tou does not see many examples of academic achievement in his family.

In his large inner-city junior high school, Tou is like many students with social and economic problems who become involved in gangs. He is not well liked even among Hmong students. Though he doesn't fight other Hmong students, he does get into frequent fights before and after school with students from other ethnic minority groups. In the classroom, he is a loner and does not work well with others. He frequently cuts classes.

The teachers in Tou's school made an effort to meet their students' needs by forming teams. However, for Tou, these efforts appear to have come too late. Tou has entered Opportunity, the school-within-a-school that provides a last chance. One fears that this change will not be enough for him. In fact, Kathy told us that the caring teacher for that Opportunity class works very hard with students, but that it is well known that he spends more time at his students' funerals than any other type of event. Students in Opportunity have lost hope and many commit suicide or are killed during family violence or in gang warfare. The outlook for Tou is discouraging.

José Luis, Guillermo, and Patricia

We first met these three teenagers in 1984, less than a week after they arrived in Tucson, Arizona, from El Salvador. A few days before they flew to Tucson, they had watched as their father, an important military official, was assassinated in front of their home in San Salvador. The three had narrowly escaped being arrested and perhaps even murdered themselves. In fact, sixteen-year-old Guillermo had two bullet wounds in his leg when he arrived in the United States. Their stepmother in El Salvador distanced herself from the three teens for her own safety and that of a two-year-old daughter, who was their stepsister. José Luis, Guillermo, and Patricia, alone in a country that had suddenly become hostile, sought asylum with their aunt, a fellow doctoral student and friend of ours at the university. Through that connection, we often had the opportunity to spend time with these remarkable teens over the next six years. We maintain contact to the present.

Although they had studied English at private bilingual schools in San Salvador, their comprehension of English and ability to communicate in English was extremely limited when they first arrived. Their aunt, a dedicated academic, was anxious to get them into school and working toward school success. All three were enrolled in a local high school almost immediately and admonished by their aunt that they must do well in all their subjects. She warned them that there was no time to be wasted, and that she would not tolerate irresponsibility.

The aunt, who had an older, ailing husband, found them an apartment near her and supported the three financially the best she could. They also received some sporadic financial help from aging grandparents in El Salvador. Therefore, the teenagers were soon almost entirely on their own, trying to cope with a new culture and language. Each handled the situation in a different way.

The oldest at seventeen, José Luis felt responsible for the other two. He also felt somehow at fault for not having saved his father, and wrestled with that guilt. He studied day and night, smiling little, and taking almost no time for relaxation. English was a struggle for him, and he spent hours with a dictionary, translating his textbooks and studying for tests. Classes in algebra, calculus, and physics were less linguistically demanding, so he soon concentrated on them as a possible specialization. He graduated from high school with a President's Award for excellent academic scholarship just two years after arriving.

Guillermo responded in a totally different way to his new surroundings. He was the most outgoing of the three. He worked hard to make friends and joined high school clubs almost immediately. He talked to anyone who made an effort to understand him and soon became involved in school government. His grades were not extremely high, but he studied enough to earn a B-minus average and qualify to attend the university.

Patricia depended more on our family for emotional and personal support at first. At thirteen, she was the youngest of the three and the only female. Her aunt wanted her to be responsible for the cooking and cleaning of the apartment the three siblings shared, but those responsibilities and the adjustment to the new language and culture were often too much for her. Her brothers seemed to understand, but they also insisted that she be part of the threesome. She studied and made friends, but in some ways was the most affected by the move and the loss of her father. English probably came faster to Patricia than to her brothers. She spent more time with our family, and our two daughters helped introduce her to customs and fads in the United States.

The three teens and their aunt became involved in our church shortly after their escape from El Salvador. The church family was especially important when they applied for asylum in the United States. At that time, refugees from El Salvador had to prove their lives were endangered to be granted asylum. Even though they had newspaper articles about the assassination of their father, it was difficult to establish that the three children were in danger. When the hearing for their asylum was held, church members took time off from work to attend. That show of support impressed the judge and probably was instrumental in his filing a positive report with the federal government.

All three children eventually attended the university in Tucson and graduated. José Luis completed a master's degree in engineering and is presently working for the City of Los Angeles. Guillermo studied engineering and international economics as an undergraduate and is completing a master's degree in architecture at the University of Southern California. Patricia finished a degree in chemistry, worked for a pharmaceutical firm in Arizona, and then transferred to Los Angeles where she lives with her two brothers. They are financially secure and enjoying their lives as young professionals.

After almost ten years in this country, the three went back to El Salvador for a visit. It was the first time that they felt they could do so safely. The trip was very traumatic for all three, and they struggled with fears of being harmed. The visit turned out to be a good one, however, and they were able to reconnect with friends and family. They now consider the United States home. They probably will not return to El Salvador to live, despite intentions to do so when they first arrived.

Analysis

Certainly the three teenagers faced overwhelming obstacles when they came to the United States. Their only relative here was an aunt who had never had children and who had her own personal responsibilities including the care of a sick husband, graduate studies, and teaching. The three young people had to learn to live on their own almost from the beginning. Money was tight and had to be budgeted, something the three had never had to do before.

The trauma of their father's assassination was difficult to cope with, and the three rehashed the scene and what might have been many times. They were immediately enrolled in a public school where they had to deal with the academic work in English, and establish their own identities apart from the other Hispanics in attendance. They were not Mexicans, and their background was very different from almost all the other students.

That background was probably what helped them the most. They were from a prominent family in El Salvador. Their relatives, including their aunt, knew high government officials, including former presidents. They had pride in their past and a strong sense of their worth. They had attended good private schools in San Salvador and had traveled to the United States and Europe. Although they did not speak and understand English well, they had studied English grammar and did have a strong background in Spanish language and literature as well as in academic-content areas such as math and science.

Once they arrived in Tucson, they found different kinds of support. Their aunt provided the money for the basics of living, and they received some funds from family in El Salvador. Eventually, with the encouragement of their aunt and others, they earned academic scholarships. They did not have to depend on welfare. They also had emotional and social support from people in the community. Our family often did things with them on weekends, delighting in introducing them to American culture and advising them about schooling and finances. The church provided another important support. They had weekly and sometimes biweekly contact with Americans with whom they had the chance to use English for real purposes. Their past experiences in El Salvador, their aunt's academic expectations, their social interactions with an American family, and the support of a church community placed José Luis, Guillermo, and Patricia in contexts that influenced them positively.

Francisco

Francisco came to the United States from El Salvador at age fourteen. He was raised by his grandmother in the countryside of El Salvador several miles from the nearest village. His mother, Concepción, left him and his brother and sister when their father deserted her. Concepción was desperately poor and had been told by distant relatives that there was hope for work and a better life in the United States. After a desperate border crossing, Francisco's mother made her way to relatives in the Central Valley of California, where she struggled to survive. Concepción's distant relatives took half her salary to transport her to work in the fields and give her shelter. She ate day-old tortillas and beans for weeks to save a small amount of money to send to her children and mother in El Salvador.

After a time, a foreman saw how Concepción was being taken advantage of and intervened to protect her. She eventually married this man from Mexico and between the two of them, they saved enough to buy a home and pay lawyers to arrange for their own legal residency and that of Concepción's three children back in El Salvador.

When Francisco arrived in the United States at age fourteen, he was immediately enrolled in a large, inner-city high school of three thousand students. Up to this point, his life had been that of a country boy on a small farm. He was lucky to have attended a nearby village school, so he was literate in Spanish, but he was certainly not prepared for secondary school in a country in which all his instruction would be in English.

Francisco remembers little of his first years in high school. He was placed in ESL classes where he was given worksheets to fill out and dialogues to memorize. He took vocational classes but few academic courses. He remembers praying every time he entered a classroom that he would not be called upon. He was afraid he would not understand the questions and that he would not have the English words to answer even if he did understand.

For Francisco, the bright spot in his life in the United States was the school soccer team. In El Salvador he and his friends had spent hours playing soccer, and here in this large high school, he was recruited by the assistant soccer coach. Francisco played well, and when he graduated from high school, the coach, an elementary school teacher affiliated with a small local university, arranged for Francisco to attend the university on a soccer scholarship.

Francisco was not prepared for the academic work of the university. He had only been in the United States for four years, and his high school classes had not provided the background he needed for the rigorous coursework he encountered at the university. Though he was encouraged by his mother, and he studied for hours, his freshman year was an academic disaster. He considered dropping out, but the soccer coach visited his home, talked to his mother, and encouraged him not to give up.

During his sophomore and junior years, Francisco continued to study very hard and little by little improved his grades. He did well in Spanish courses and decided to study education to become a bilingual teacher. He also became friends with, and eventually began to date, the daughter of two professors at the university. She was bilingual in Spanish and English, and she and her family helped Francisco with advice and academic work.

Francisco graduated with a B average and did well in his fifth-year teacher-education program at the university. He is the same teacher we described in the Salvador case study above. And, if the reader has not already guessed, he is now our son-in-law. We know his story and his family well, and see Francisco and his family as an example of immigrants who struggled against incredible odds to achieve the American Dream.

Analysis

Francisco came to the United States with little idea of what was waiting for him. His own country had been ravaged by war. His mother sacrificed a great deal to bring him to this country. Concepción had high expectations for Francisco, but little to no understanding of the challenges he faced. She had no education herself, did not speak much English, and could not help her children with their schooling. She saw her role as that of providing food, shelter, and love, and assumed that her children would respond by getting an education. After all, she had suffered separation from them so that they could have a better future.

Francisco was literate in Spanish when he arrived in this country. However, he had been taught in a rural school with few facilities. He had to learn English, catch up on the content-area studies he had not had exposure to in El Salvador, and adjust to a completely different lifestyle and culture. He had the support and love of his mother and a close-knit extended family who had moved to the area over the years, but his only support to enter the mainstream was through his soccer coach. When he did meet our daughter and our family became involved in his life, he was introduced for the first time to many mainstream customs, attitudes, and values. It is still amazing to us and to Francisco that there are so many differences between the cultural practices of different enthic groups within the United States.

Chham and Navy

Chet Chham, his aging parents, his wife, and their two children arrived in the United States in the late spring of 1975, shortly after the fall of Phnom Penh. They were sent by a Catholic relief agency to a coastal town in northern California. Chham and his wife were part of a large group of Vietnamese and Cambodian refugees who attended Yvonne's daytime ESL class the following September. These refugees were in the first wave to arrive in the area after the Vietnam War, and their stories were incredible. Since then, stories from these and other refugees from Southeast Asia have been widely reported (Criddle and Man 1987; Bliatout et al. 1988; Ouk et al. 1988).

Chham and his wife, Navy, had been among Cambodia's educated elite. Over five thousand people attended their wedding in Phnom Penh in a ceremony that lasted three days. Navy's father was the minister of education, and Chham's father was a high military official. When Phnom Penh fell to the Khmer Rouge, Chham, a military officer, knew he and his family would be killed if they remained, so he arranged their departure for the United States. In a matter of a few days, they became refugees dependent on relief agencies in a country whose language, religion, and culture were foreign.

Chham and Navy were lucky. They found employment quickly. He took a job in a lumber mill and she found work as a hotel maid. His parents were too old to work, but they were able to take care of the two elementary-aged children when they were not in school. Whenever their work schedule allowed it, both Chham and Navy attended ESL classes. They were fluent in Khmer and French, but their English was too limited for them to attend the local junior college.

They faced many challenges and changes. These included their new jobs, relying

16

in part on government aid, having to learn English, and adapting to a new culture. In addition, they were attending school with other refugees from different cultural and social backgrounds. Students in the ESL classes included farm laborers from Mexico, Portuguese fishermen from the Azores, refugees from Central America, wives of college students from the Middle East, exchange students from Japan, restaurant owners from Korea, as well as other Southeast Asian refugees. Perhaps the students that made school adjustment the most difficult were the ones from closest to home. In the same classroom there was a Vietnamese army general, Vietnamese peasants, and Cambodian peasants. Historically, these groups of people have either had no social contact or been enemies. In the ESL class, they sat next to one another as they struggled together to learn English.

Chham and Navy never showed any negative reactions to the situation at school. In fact, they were always cheerful contributors to class discussion, school programs, and collective celebrations, including meals. They seldom looked back, but instead planned ahead. Chham knew he needed to go on to junior college, and he and his wife explored different possible majors. Navy soon found herself pregnant with a third child, so she and her mother began taking in sewing. They specialized in sewing dresses for Cambodian celebrations such as weddings.

When news of the genocide in his country began to leak out (Criddle and Mam 1999; Ouk et al. 1988), Chham found living in the United States more painful. He once told Yvonne about a close friend who had decided to return to Cambodia to try to find his wife and children. This emotional story was a tragic one because Chham had little hope of ever seeing his friend again. This, of course, brought home to him the tragedy of his many lost friends and family members, not to mention the loss of his country. News of the genocide marked the beginning of the social and political organization of Cambodian families in the area and throughout California. Periodic meetings were held, and Chham was one of the leaders. He and his contemporaries realized that if their culture was to be maintained, it would have to be done outside Cambodia.

Throughout all the adjustments and the taking on of new responsibilities, Chham and Navy continued to attend adult ESL classes faithfully. They studied when they could and brought questions and problems to class. A major concern was for their children's schooling. They became informed about the public school system and were careful to communicate as best they could with the schools. They knew their children needed English and American culture, but they did not want them to forget their own heritage. They made sure that holidays and important festivals were celebrated in a traditional way, and they worked to teach their children their first language at home. Still, they worried as their children became more and more Americanized in what seemed to them a short time. When a teenage niece wanted to pick her own Cambodian husband instead of marrying the one the family had chosen for her, a major Cambodian community meeting was held. The customs were changing too quickly, and it was hard for everyone to adapt.

We eventually moved and lost touch with the family. Almost twenty years have gone by. Recently, however, we read a newspaper account of a Cambodian gathering in a town not far from Chham and Navy's city. We were both concerned to read that two former Cambodian military men got into an argument about how the war some twenty years before had been fought. In a fit of anger one man shot the other. The victim's name was Chet Chham. It may not be the same person we knew, since the name is a common one, but those military men had undoubtedly had experiences similar to those of Yvonne's former student. The experience of living through the war, escaping to freedom in the United States, and surviving the trauma of adjustment, only to be killed in an argument over the past, is an irony difficult to contemplate.

Analysis

Like the teenagers from El Salvador, Chham and Navy came to the United States with a strong sense of who they were. Their families were prominent members of Cambodian society, and Chham and Navy had expectations of raising their children as they had been raised. Both attended private schools in Cambodia and had also studied in France. Chham was at the height of his military career when the war changed their lives completely.

Overnight, Chham, his parents, Navy, and their children left almost everything behind to flee to the United States. In many ways, they were fortunate. They flew into California almost directly. They quickly found jobs and a place to live. They had a strong educational background and expected to attend school to learn the English language and to become familiar with American culture.

However, many difficulties surfaced. Though they never complained, the change from having five thousand people attend their wedding to working as a laborer in a lumber mill and a maid in a hotel must have been very difficult for the couple. Chham's parents were completely lost in the West, and refused to leave their small house or have anything to do with the new—and, to them, hostile—world outside their home. The children attended public schools and seemed to do well, but Chham and Navy feared that they were losing their first language and their culture.

The news of the genocide of Cambodians was a terrible blow. Suddenly, Cambodians in the United States had to band together or lose a national identity. This often caused conflict with younger Cambodians who wanted to live like Americans and forget the past. Chham had to help settle several conflicts that involved arranged marriages.

Meanwhile, the ESL classes provided still another challenge. The adult students came from many different backgrounds. While Yvonne tried to highlight the positive aspects of the diversity in her class, it was not easy for people from different social and economic classes as well as from different political perspectives to study together. The students responded well, but their differences created an added tension they had to deal with daily.

In addition, it was difficult for Chham and Navy to meet basic needs. When

18

Navy became pregnant, there was not only another child to care for but also the necessity for her to find different work. The job at the lumber mill became less steady. In addition, Chham had trouble finding a course of study he could complete in a short time at the local junior college.

We have lost contact with Chham and his family, so we don't know their present circumstances. We hope the story in the newspaper was not about our friend. We have known many other refugees who came to the United States as adults and, while some have adjusted and are living fairly well, the past still haunts many. Questions of what might have been are left unanswered.

Factors Leading to Student Success or Failure

Our focus in this and the following seven chapters is on the world of the school. However, we recognize that the school context exists within the broader societal context. The teacher's view of language, learning, teaching, and curriculum, all make a difference, but factors from the societal context outside the school play an important role as well. The way that students interact with one another and with teachers, the attitudes, expectations, and goals people have, as well as the attitudes and values of the community, all shape the outcomes for students living between worlds.

Teachers may not have control of all the forces, in or out of school, that affect student learning. Nevertheless, it is important for teachers to be aware of these factors. By studying the particular contexts that affect their students, teachers begin to take on new attitudes and to try new teaching strategies to build on the strengths they see in their students. We recognize that whether a particular student succeeds or fails may have little to do with curriculum itself. Success or failure may be more related to what goes on outside the classroom. As Sue and Padilla (1986) comment:

> There is no question that English proficiency is essential to educational success, occupational achievement, and socio-economic mobility, but these occur in a sociocultural context. Understanding this context can help to explain educational attainments of ethnic minority students and to provide alternatives that can lead to improved educational outcomes for these students. (35)

An understanding of the various elements that influence student school performance can help teachers in several ways. First, it can keep teachers from blaming themselves, the curriculum, or student ability if students are not doing well. Second, when teachers understand the role of external factors, they can begin to work for changes that would benefit their students in areas beyond the classroom. Finally, teachers can resist acceptance of negative stereotypes about minorities, and they can help their students develop positive attitudes toward diversity. They can do this by discussing with students the various factors that contribute to their academic success or failure, including the negative attitudes others may hold toward them because they are members of minority groups. They can then enlist the support of students, parents, and community members in creating positive environments for learning.

Cortés' Contextual Interaction Model

We base our analysis of the factors that affect student success on Cortés' Contextual Interaction Model (1986). Schools are charged with educating all students. If some students or groups of students fail consistently, an explanation must be found. Cortés warns against single-cause explanations, asserting, "This model . . . seeks to incorporate a multiplicity of factors that may influence educational achievement" (23). According to Cortés, any one factor—such as intelligence, language proficiency, or socioeconomic status—cannot be expected to account for varying degrees of success among different groups. The stories above show this clearly.

Cortés points out that we often attribute success or failure to single causes because we confuse cause and correlation. Just because two things occur together, we cannot conclude that one causes the other. For example, students who speak English as another language may do poorly in school, but speaking a second language does not necessarily cause school failure. Finally, Cortés notes the "tendency to decontextualize explanations" (16). Often, specific factors such as race, language, or socioeconomic status may contribute to school success or failure, but looking at any one of these factors, or even some combination, out of context may lead to false conclusions. According to Cortés, the question we need to ask is, "under what conditions do students with similar sociocultural characteristics succeed educationally and under what conditions do they perform poorly in school? In other words, within what contexts—educational and societal—do students of similar backgrounds succeed and within what contexts do they do less well?" (17).

Cortés' Contextual Interaction Model provides a framework for answering this question. Figure 1–1 is an adaptation of his model that illustrates the ways that the societal context influences the school context. The societal context includes general community attitudes, often shaped by the mass media, families and their educational levels, the culture and ethnicity of the community members, teacher and student attitudes, and legal mandates that regulate education.

The societal context, the world outside school, influences the school context. That context includes the general orientation of the school toward its students, levels of staffing, curriculum and programs, teacher and student knowledge and skills, students' language proficiency, resources and materials that are available, and other factors, such as parent involvement.

The Contextual Interaction Model is dynamic. Societal and educational contexts constantly change as new families enter the community and the school. For example, when we visited the Midwest this spring, educators were talking about the impact large numbers of refugees from Somalia was having on their classrooms. These educators had adjusted for their immigrants from Mexico, but immigrants from another part of the world brought new challenges.

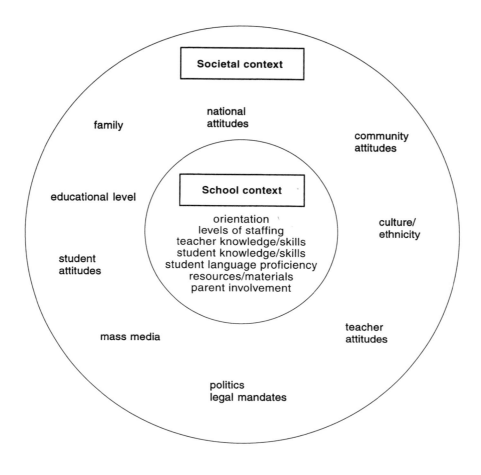

FIGURE 1–1   *Contextual Interaction Model*

The model is a two-way model. The school context is influenced by the larger social context, but the social context is also impacted by attitudes, knowledge, and skills of the students who leave schools and return to the community. We have seen this in the past as immigrants from Japan and Korea, and more recently Southeast Asia and Mexico, have graduated from college. Some have left their own immigrant roots and become part of the mainstream. These immigrants change the mainstream community, but their departure also challenges the immigrant communities. Parents and grandparents often feel abandoned. On the other hand, if educated immigrants return to their communities, they often present a challenge to traditional values.

The children of educated immigrants may feel conflicted because they are not sure of their own values or identities.

Students' success or failure results from complex interactions of dynamic contexts. Our case study stories above certainly show this. No one factor can explain success or failure, but change in any one area may alter the dynamics of the whole system in such a way that success is more likely. For example, Francisco's success was influenced by his mother's sacrifice, his soccer coach's assistance, and the insights he gained from his relationship with our family.

In the following chapters we will consider the different contexts in more detail, beginning with the school context. Throughout this book, we want readers to keep the stories of real-life second language learners, like the students we have described here, foremost in their minds. We will refer to these examples, as well as others, as we discuss the different factors that have influenced and continue to influence students who are between worlds. We hope that by drawing on research, theory, and successful practice, we can provide readers with a better understanding of the factors that contribute to academic success or failure for their second language learners.

Applications

1. Choose two of the case studies described in this chapter. Compare and contrast the factors that have influenced, are influencing, and may influence school success for each. Refer to Cortés' Contextual Interaction Model. Discuss your comparisons in pairs or a small group.

2. Choose one of the students discussed in the case studies that reminds you of a second language learner you know. Compare and contrast the factors that affect the schooling of both. Discuss your comparison in pairs or in a small group.

3. In small groups choose a case study described here, or the story of a second language learner you know. On butcher paper or an overhead, list the factors that seem to predict school success and those that seem to limit success in each case. Share your results with the large group, and make a composite list of positive and negative factors.

4. Choose a second language learner who seems to be especially successful in school or one that seems to be struggling. Interview that student and/or family members to try to determine what factors might be influencing school performance. Before the interview, compile a list of possible questions with others and discuss culturally appropriate ways of approaching the interview.

2

What Influences How Teachers Teach?

When we visit classes, we see teachers using a variety of techniques and methods to help their students learn English and academic content. This variation is not surprising. In fact, even within the same school and at the same grade level with a similar student population, teachers differ considerably in how they teach. Why is this?

We continue our exploration of factors in the world of the school by turning from looking at second language students to considering their teachers. The basic question we wish to explore here is, "What influences how teachers teach?" A number of factors seem to be at work, and these help to account for the variation in classroom practices we have observed (see Figure 2–1). For one thing, teachers have been students themselves, and often the way they teach reflects the way that they were taught. In addition, teachers have studied teaching methods, and what they learned in their education classes affects how they teach. Teachers, especially new teachers, are influenced by the other teachers at their school and by their administrators. Sometimes teachers use new techniques in their classrooms because they have heard about them in the teachers' lounge or during a staff development session. In some school settings, administrators require teachers to use certain methods. If teachers change schools or grade levels, there is new content to be covered. New colleagues with new ideas influence their practice. Another factor that plays a role in how teachers teach is the materials that are available (or required) for them to use.

Legal mandates have always generally influenced how teachers teach. Recently,

Influences	Results
past experiences	teach as we were taught
educational experiences	teach as we were taught to teach
colleagues/ administrators	teach as others teach or as we are required to teach
changes in teaching situation	adjust teaching to new school or level or new students
materials	teach using available or required materials
politics	teach as those outside of education mandate
students	teach in response (or reaction) to the students

FIGURE 2–1 *Influences on How Teachers Teach*

though, politicians have discovered that education is a particularly important issue for voters. In some states, legislation has limited the use of students' native languages for instruction. Various groups have set standards for students and have passed laws that specify the use of particular teaching practices to meet those standards. Many states have recently required all students, including English learners, to take tests to show that they have met state standards. As a result, many teachers spend considerable time in test preparation.

An essential influence on how teachers teach, and one that should receive careful consideration, is the students themselves. For example, the increase in English learners has prompted many teachers to try new ways of teaching. A teacher's practice, then, changes over time in response to new experiences, new studies, new materials, new types of students, new legal mandates, and a new emphasis on testing.

We begin to answer the question, "What influences how teachers teach?" with Yvonne's story. She has moved through different stages of understanding about how language is learned and how language and content might best be taught. Her experiences provide a context for the ensuing discussion of the factors involved in developing a principled orientation toward teaching. We hope that Yvonne's story will help our readers reflect on their own beliefs and practices. Greater awareness of why we teach the way we do can help us adopt a principled orientation and make the changes necessary for providing the best education for all our students.

An Eclectic Teacher Becomes Principled

Yvonne studied several different languages in high school and college. Her four years of high school Latin were taught through a grammar translation method in which students memorized grammar rules and vocabulary and carefully translated great works such as *The Odyssey* and *The Iliad* from Latin to English. The study of Latin was considered a good scholarly exercise that would provide a base for English vocabulary development, but there was never any consideration that knowledge of the Latin language might be useful outside the Latin class.

As a high school junior, Yvonne, who at the time had no intention of ever becoming a teacher, decided to study Spanish. Students in her Spanish class studied less grammar and vocabulary than in the Latin class. Instead, they memorized dialogues that they practiced and recited. The most memorable and enjoyable activities in the Spanish class were learning and performing the Mexican hat dance and singing songs in Spanish. Yvonne continued her study of Spanish at the junior college. The advanced class was tedious, with grammar tests and long hours spent repeating drills in the language laboratory.

It wasn't until she went to the university as a junior majoring in Spanish that it dawned on Yvonne that there was more to language learning than memorizing rules and taking tests. Her Spanish grammar class was going well, but she was put into a Spanish literature class with an instructor who lectured only in Spanish. For the first three weeks of class, she took limited and inadequate notes, because the language seemed to fly by her unintelligibly. She knew something had to be done, so she made plans to go to Mexico that summer.

The Mexican summer experience was a turning point in her Spanish proficiency. Yvonne's train trip to Guadalajara gave her the opportunity to put the language she had learned to real use. She was amazed when her carefully formed sentences were understood, and somewhat shaken when rapid answers came shooting back. She and three fellow students stayed with a family while she studied in Guadalajara, and because she had the strongest Spanish language background of the three, she soon found herself in the role of language negotiator. Her success with the family, a brief romantic interlude, and exciting weekend travel excursions convinced Yvonne that she had found her niche. Her interest in the Spanish language and the Latino culture led naturally to her decision to become a Spanish teacher.

Back in the United States, Yvonne enrolled in a cutting edge teacher-education program. In just one year, students in this program got both a teaching credential and a master's degree in education. Teacher training included videotaped micro-teaching sessions that allowed student teachers to view their performance and critique their lessons. Methodology classes presented the latest techniques of leading different kinds of audio-lingual drills. These techniques were based on a behaviorist view of learning. In fact, one of her education-methods professors was considered an international language-teaching expert. Yvonne accepted the idea that learning, and especially language learning, consisted of forming habits. All her own language instruction had assumed that kind of a model. In her classes, students had memorized dialogues, and teachers had corrected errors quickly. Yvonne and her classmates had repeated their lines as their cheerleading teachers led them rapidly through carefully selected language-pattern exercises. Yvonne's teacher-education classes prepared her to teach as she had been taught.

She received her credential and landed a job in an inner-city high school. Despite all her preparation, her first teaching position was a real eye-opener. She was teaching five classes a day of Spanish 1. Her Audiolingual Method (ALM) Spanish 1 book included lesson after lesson of dialogues and drills. Her students hated what they called the "boring repetition" and "stupid dialogues." Yvonne was devastated. She wanted her students to love speaking Spanish as much as she did. She remembered her positive experiences in Mexico but had forgotten how bored she had been when forced through similar drills.

Faced with 150 resisting and restless high school students each day, Yvonne began to look closely at the lines from the dialogues that the students were repeating. Instinctively, without really knowing what she was doing, she began to change the dialogues to make them more relevant. "A mí no me gustan las albóndigas" (I don't like meatballs) became, "A mí no me gustan las hamburguesas con cebolla" (I don't like hamburgers with onion), and the students were encouraged to expand the talk to include other things they did not like. She even gave them choice in the dialogues they practiced. Yvonne wanted her students to realize that Spanish is a language that real people use for real purposes. She invited some friends visiting from Mexico to her class. The students prepared and asked questions they wanted to know about teenagers in Mexico. That class period was one of the best of the year.

The classroom context for learning was improving. However, contexts interact, and what goes on outside the classroom has a great impact on curriculum. Yvonne soon found herself in trouble on two very different fronts. In the first place, the department chair discovered that Yvonne was giving students vocabulary lists with words that were not part of the department curriculum and was encouraging students to create their own dialogues. The problem, of course, was that the students were not always saying things correctly and were undoubtedly learning some incorrect Spanish. The department chair, a strong advocate of ALM, did not want students to develop bad language habits. In the second place, as she attempted to use more authentic Spanish with her students, Yvonne realized that she had not learned enough "real" Spanish to truly help her students say everything they wanted to say.

Yvonne decided to find an opportunity to improve her Spanish proficiency. She and her adventurous husband, a high school English teacher, decided that they should live abroad, so they both took teaching jobs at an American school in Colombia, South America. Yvonne found herself with absolutely no background for her teaching job. Educated as a high school Spanish teacher, she was assigned to teach fifth grade in South America using curriculum from the United States. Some of her students spoke English as a foreign language and would never visit the United

States. Others were native speakers of English whose parents expected them to attend college in the United States.

Like many teachers faced with a difficult assignment for which she was not prepared, Yvonne relied heavily at first on the textbooks the school provided. Basal readers from the United States as well as social studies and science textbooks were the center of her curriculum. Again, however, she found herself responding to her students. Many of the basal reading stories were boring or completely unrelated to the students' interests and needs. The social studies and science texts were almost impossible for the students to read and understand. Though other materials were not easy to find, Yvonne centered much of what she and the students did around projects, stories, and discussions. Since most of the teachers in the school were experiencing the same problems, they shared ideas about what was working in their classrooms.

The teaching couple returned to the United States after a year, more fluent in Spanish. Yvonne's husband found a job teaching high school in a small city, but there were no high school Spanish jobs. When a local welfare agency in their new town called to ask if she would volunteer to teach English to Spanish-speaking adults, Yvonne decided to try it. Her first class of students included two Mexican women with no previous schooling and a college-educated couple from Bolivia. With no materials, not even paper or pencils, and diverse students, Yvonne, in desperation, asked the students what English they wanted and needed to learn. Starting with any materials she could get, including props, maps, pamphlets, and resource guides, Yvonne soon found herself teaching thirty to forty adults daily on a variety of topics including nutrition, shopping, community services, child care, and geography.

Yvonne's class became a part of the public school's adult education program, and Yvonne began teaming with another teacher who also loved teaching adult ESL. The two collaborated daily, making up skits, writing songs, organizing around themes, and creating a community with students who came from Mexico, Central America, South America, Northern and Eastern Europe, the Middle East, Japan, Korea, and Southeast Asia.

Though Yvonne had come a long way from having students memorize dialogues and do drills, she was still uncomfortable about what she should be doing to teach language. She and her team teacher, a former high school English teacher, often would pull out traditional grammar sheets and do a part of their daily lesson with some of those exercises "to be sure the students understood the structure of the language." When those lessons seemed to go nowhere, especially with adults who had little previous schooling, the grammar books were dropped in favor of books with stories and discussion questions. However, the readings were seldom related to student needs and experiences, so the two teachers kept returning to skits, songs, and projects created around relevant themes.

Yvonne and her partner had an additional experience that stretched them in new directions and strengthened their conviction that language learning was more than memorizing grammatical rules and repeating pattern drills. The two were asked to teach as adjunct instructors in an intensive English program at the local university. A large group of Japanese college students had arrived, and although these students had extensive background in English grammar and vocabulary, they understood and spoke little English. Initially, the Japanese students resisted classroom activities that were not carefully organized around grammar exercises, but Yvonne and her partner worked hard to get the students to take the risk to speak English in class and in the community. Several of the Japanese students came to appreciate the emphasis on using English for real purposes and began to attend the adult ESL classes as well as the university classes.

After she had taught the Japanese students for two years and the adults for nine, Yvonne and her husband decided that they would like to teach abroad again, taking their children along. They moved to Mexico City, where new learning and teaching experiences awaited them. They first taught professional adults English in a large language institute. The institute was moving away from using a textbook based on audiolingual methodology to a new series using the Notional-Functional Approach, so both Yvonne and her husband learned about teaching language communicatively around functions such as apologizing, giving directions, and making introductions, and around notions such as time or space.

Since their teaching schedule did not fit the school schedule for their young children, Yvonne left her job with adults and began teaching fifth grade at the bilingual school her daughters attended. The school was typical of most private schools in Mexico City. The student body for the kindergarten through sixth grade had about five thousand students. The playground was a huge expanse of cement with no trees or play equipment of any kind. Classrooms had one chalkboard in the front of the room, with a raised platform for the teacher's desk. There was one bulletin board, decorated monthly by the teacher and checked by the supervising administrator. Desks were bolted in rows filling up the entire room.

The school where Yvonne taught had classes of only forty students. This school was popular because of the small class size. Other schools had sixty or more in a classroom. Yvonne soon learned that most parents in Mexico City, if they could scrape together any money, sent their children to a private school such as this because public schools had larger classes and fewer materials.

At this bilingual school, one half of the day was taught in Spanish and one half in English. The English curriculum was centered around basal readers and textbooks from the United States, as it had been in Colombia, and the Spanish curriculum around Mexican government texts. The school required teachers to follow the textbook-based curriculum carefully. All assignments involved copying and memorizing. Students' needs were viewed only in terms of passing the textbook or government tests that were administered by the school monthly. Discipline was strict. Students stood up to answer questions and were not to speak otherwise.

Fortunately, the administration of this school discovered that Yvonne had a master's degree in education, a very high degree among Mexican teachers at schools like this. Many elementary teachers in Mexico have little training beyond high school.

After teaching a month of the regimented fifth-grade curriculum, Yvonne found herself the administrator in charge of the English curriculum for twenty-three teachers. She began to reflect on how many times she had found herself in positions she was unprepared for and yet how similar her conclusions were each time. Again, she wondered how meaningful the curriculum was for the students. If the Mexican students were studying at a bilingual school so that they could learn to read, write, and speak English, were the United States textbooks appropriate? Should they be reading in basal readers about blond, blue-eyed Americans going to an American birthday party or going ice-skating in snowy weather? Would they really learn English when their teachers rarely allowed them to speak English, or any language, in class, and when the teachers rarely spoke to them in either English or Spanish?

Yvonne encouraged the teachers to center their curriculum around themes of possible interest to children of various ages. She collected stories and information related to celebrations, science topics, and biographies of famous people that seemed to lend themselves to language use and content learning. She encouraged teachers to involve students in drama and music using English songs and plays. She helped teachers write plays for their students and tried to encourage conversation activities. However, all of this was done on a limited basis, as the school requirements were stringent and any activities beyond preparing students for tests were considered frills.

After two years of teaching in Mexico City, Yvonne and her husband moved back to the United States, where her husband began graduate study and she took a position teaching senior composition and freshman English at a private high school. The composition class was organized around a packet of materials that students were to follow carefully, completing assignments at their own pace with no class discussion. The freshman English class curriculum included short stories, a library unit, the play *Romeo and Juliet*, and study of a grammar book written in England. Again, Yvonne looked at her students, this time all native speakers of English, and wondered about teaching to their interests and needs. In this situation, unlike the Mexico and the high school Spanish experiences, the English department chairperson was flexible and sympathetic to deviations from the set curriculum. Before the year was over, Yvonne had students in the composition class meeting in groups, having whole-class discussions, writing joint compositions, and sharing their writing. She largely ignored the grammar book for the freshmen, had them write and edit their own compositions, and encouraged discussion of their reading. Before teaching *Romeo and Juliet*, Yvonne planned with another freshman English teacher to have their students view the movie *Westside Story*, which provided them with valuable background for the Shakespeare play.

However, Yvonne did not feel that her previous experiences were best utilized by teaching English to high school students, so the following year, she went back to graduate school and worked as a graduate teaching assistant in the Spanish department. Her graduate work included both a second master's degree, this time in English as a Second Language, and doctoral work in education. In her ESL program she studied SLA theory and second language teaching methods. Many of the writers advocated a communicative approach to teaching language. She was especially impressed by the work of Krashen (1982), who differentiated between acquisition and learning, a distinction that made sense to Yvonne because of her own language learning and teaching experiences.

While her ESL classes were interesting, it was her doctoral studies that really challenged Yvonne to think seriously about learning and teaching and the relationship between the two. She began studying about language learning with a focus on the development of second language literacy. As she read the work of Ferreiro and Teberosky, K. and Y. Goodman, Halliday, Graves, Kolers, Heath, Lindfors, Piaget, Smith, and Vygotsky, Yvonne began to make connections among her language learning and teaching experiences and the theories she was studying. She realized two things: First, what she was learning about made sense because of what she had experienced in her own language learning and her many teaching jobs. Second, much classroom practice was not consistent with current theory.

As she studied, Yvonne made her beginning college Spanish classes her laboratory. With her first-year Spanish classes, she talked about how children learn language, how language is acquired naturally in a risk-free environment, and how language must have meaning and purpose for learners. Students wrote in Spanish daily in their journals, and she responded in writing. Students read current articles of interest to them, working in groups to interpret the Spanish. Students learned Spanish in the course of investigating themes such as friendship, professions, and dating customs. One of the most successful projects was a pen pal exchange between students in different college classes. Yvonne realized that students would devote more energy to writing a nongraded assignment, a letter to a peer, than to writing a theme in Spanish for the instructor to grade.

After graduation, Yvonne and her husband found positions at a small college. Yvonne now works with teachers of second language learners. Each day her beliefs that teaching must be geared to student needs and that learning occurs when students are interested in the topic they are studying are confirmed. Yvonne has learned many lessons through her experiences, but perhaps the most important of these is one she came to late in her teaching career: that theory informs practice, and reflection on practice can shape a teacher's working theory. Yvonne, like most teachers, began with an eclectic view. She used whatever seemed to work. By reflecting on her practice in the light of theory, Yvonne was able to move away from eclecticism and develop a principled approach to her teaching.

Orientations Toward Teaching

When we talk about becoming principled, we are really talking about implementing practices consistent with our beliefs about language, learning, teaching, and curriculum. These beliefs are what we refer to as our "orientation." A principled orientation is one in which the beliefs are based on theory tested in practice.

Without being fully aware of it, Yvonne began her career as a Spanish high school teacher with a certain set of beliefs. She believed that language learning involved habit formation and that practice and memorization would result in language learning. She used the audio-lingual method, which was consistent with this orientation. In fact, her department chairperson insisted that she use only ALM materials from a textbook. Yvonne was asked not to allow her students to create their own dialogues because they might "develop bad language habits." The techniques Yvonne used included memorization of dialogues and practice of language structures in controlled drills. However, she also used techniques that were not consistent with her method, such as allowing the students to create their own interview questions and encouraging uncontrolled discussion on topics not included in the textbooks.

Yvonne found herself repeatedly struggling to follow the curriculum and materials she was given while trying to meet students' needs. She was uncomfortable drilling students and teaching isolated grammar, because she did not see how these activities were helping her students learn language. On the other hand, such techniques seemed to be accepted ways to teach language. Other teachers talked confidently about doing "what works," and that seemed to be good advice. Yvonne tried several techniques but didn't totally trust her own instincts. After she had had a variety of teaching experiences and also had begun to read theory, Yvonne was able to develop a more consistent and principled orientation to teaching.

It is not always possible to determine a teacher's orientation simply by observing her techniques. For example, a teacher who structures the class around themes using literature and process writing may teach a minilesson on capital letters. That same lesson might also be taught by a teacher using a traditional grammar approach to language teaching. The technique, the lesson on capital letters, could be observed in classrooms of teachers with two quite different orientations. The first teacher teaches the minilesson because she has seen that students do not use capitals correctly in their writing, while the second teacher teaches capitals on a particular day because that is the point in the curriculum where capitals are to be taught.

Our beliefs about language, about how people learn, and about how we should teach, all form our orientation. While our ideas are not fixed, and while they change as we continue to learn and study, they guide the methods and techniques we use. At any given time, we strive for consistency at the three levels—orientation, methods, and techniques. At the level of our basic beliefs, eclecticism reflects a lack of well-thought-through principles. However, at the level of technique, a principled teacher may be eclectic.

Many language teachers work in schools that have adopted a method and the materials that go with it. It is important to understand, however, that methods are based on certain beliefs about language, teaching, and learning. Take the audio-lingual method, for example. A teacher who adopts this method gets a long-term plan, usually in the form of a textbook. The book includes a set of techniques. Students memorize dialogues, the teacher leads pattern-practice drills, and so on. The book is based on beliefs about learning taken from behavioral psychology (language is habit learned through repetition) and structural linguistics (language patterns are more important than individual vocabulary items; patterns can be learned inductively).

When a teacher follows a method, then, the techniques and the basic beliefs are thrown in at no extra charge. It's a package deal, much like the basal reading programs. And as with the basals, the teacher may end up playing the role of technician, delivering instruction that someone else (or a team of "experts") has devised. If we start by adopting a method, we leave the answer to the question "How can we provide our students with access to second language acquisition?" in someone else's hands.

Since teachers are professionals rather than technicians, they reflect on their practice as they refine their beliefs about teaching. They make their own decisions. They know that in order to teach language effectively, they must understand both language and learning. They move away from eclecticism and develop a principled orientation to language, learning, teaching, and curriculum.

Theories of Learning: Images of the Learner

A teacher's orientation affects the way that he or she views students. Lindfors (1982) suggests three ways that teachers may look at learners: as plants, builders, or explorers. When we ask, "What influences how teachers teach?" we often find the answer in the images of learners and views of learning that teachers hold. Figure 2–2 summarizes information about Lindfors's images of the learner.

Learner as Plant

The first image sees the student as analogous to a plant. In this view, the teacher provides students with all they need in order to "grow." This traditional image is reflected in the word *kindergarten* (garden of children) and in the often used description of a student as a "late bloomer." The assumption is that if the teacher

Image	Role of Learner	View of Learning	Influence on Learning
Plant	Passive	Behaviorist	Environments acts on learner.
Builder	Active	Cognitive	Learner acts on environment.
Explorer	Active	Transactional	Environment acts on learner, and learner acts on environment.

FIGURE 2–2 *Images of the Learner*

provides the needed information, the student will bloom with new knowledge. As Lindfors observes, the limitation of the plant image is that "we are not simply well adapted for getting watered . . . we are well adapted for actively making sense of language as we interact meaningfully with others in a language-filled world" (146).

The plant image is associated with behaviorist psychology. Behaviorism is based on the belief that learning is the result of the environment acting on the learner (Harste et al. 1984). Learners are seen as passive, waiting for teachers or materials to give them what they need to learn. Behaviorists see learning as a process of stimulus and response (Skinner 1957). The audio-lingual method that Yvonne used was based on this theory. Her job was to provide lots of stimuli in the form of oral language drills. The students were expected to respond, often without much focus on the meaning of what they were saying. The goal was the formation of good language habits. The students may have been actively responding, but they were not really engaged in high levels of cognitive activity.

Learner as Builder

Lindfors proposes a second image, that of the builder. "In the builder image, the child acts on his or her environment . . . constructing his or her own meanings, interpretations, understandings, and expressions from abundant and diverse encounters with people and objects" (146). The builder image is based on cognitive psychology. A cognitive view assumes an active learner who constructs knowledge by acting on the environment. Cognitive theories are based in part on the work of Piaget (1955), who spent a great deal of time observing young children at play as they developed concepts. His descriptions of assimilation and accommodation and "decentering" have contributed to our understanding of how people learn.

Piaget explains the process of concept development as one of assimilation and accommodation. He maintains that learners change new experiences to make them fit in with their present concepts (assimilation), and adapt their concepts as they add new experiences (accommodation).

For example, Yvonne had a certain view of teaching when she took her first job. It was based on her own experience as a learner and on the teachers she had observed. As she taught and studied, she came into contact with other teachers and with other ideas about teaching. She assimilated these new ideas to fit her schemas, her current notions of teaching. However, as the new ideas came in, they changed her view. She accommodated her view of teaching as the result of additional study and experience. Assimilation and accommodation are ongoing processes that help shape our understandings. As a result, the way Yvonne views teaching and learning now is much different from when she began her career.

Piaget also pointed out the importance of decentering, or looking at experiences from a variety of perspectives. He noted that young children are egocentric. They are limited to a single point of view. As they mature and have more experiences, they can take on additional points of view and gain new understandings. In this process, they develop the ability to abstract out of their experience certain characteristics of objects or experiences and form categories. For example, a child might develop the concept of "bicycle" as a vehicle with two wheels (as opposed to a three-wheeled tricycle). As children get older and have experience with more kinds of bikes, they may categorize them differently (three speed versus ten speed; mountain bike versus street bike). As children see new kinds of bikes, their concept of "bicycle" changes. Similarly, as these children grow up, their parents may develop new ways of categorizing bikes (as, for example, more or less expensive).

When people learn additional languages, they can also move away from a single point of view. They can decenter and take on new ways of understanding language. Knowing two languages allows a person to step outside the framework imposed by a language and see it differently by comparing it with other languages. This helps explain why many English speakers first learn English grammar when studying a foreign language. It is only at the point of stepping outside English and seeing it from a different perspective that they are able to effectively expand their understanding.

Even though there is a strong theory base to support a constructivist view of learning, when teachers hold the image of students as builders, certain concerns arise. Lindfors points out two problems with the builder image. First, the learner is seen as doing all the work. This means that the teacher is limited to a support role, a complete reversal from the plant image, in which the teacher's role was the active one. Instead, Lindfors suggests that neither the teacher nor the learner has exclusive responsibility in the learning process.

A second problem with the builder image is that it implies that the meanings the learner constructs are permanent. Once a student has built a certain concept, it is solid and impervious to change. For example, from this perspective, once a student has read a book, he or she develops a concept of the story that will never change. Yet, we all have gone back to reread a book and constructed a very different meaning from it. The problem with the builder view is that it contradicts the belief that as we learn concepts or language, we revise our understandings accordingly.

Learner as Explorer

Lindfors's explorer image represents a third possibility, that both inner and outer forces are equally important in the learning process. We use Dewey and Bentley's (1949) term *transaction* to describe this view of learning. Instead of seeing students as plants who passively wait to be fed information, teachers can view students as explorers who actively try to make sense of the world. Instead of conceiving of students as builders who take what they learn and construct fixed knowledge, teachers can look at students as explorers who continually revise their understandings as they live through and reflect on new experiences.

An example might help make the idea of transaction a bit clearer. In one course that our graduate students take, Cultural Diversity and Education, they read various novels about ethnic groups in California. *Rain of Gold* (Villaseñor 1991) is a particularly popular one. However, different students read it differently. For example, when

Francisco read this book, he connected the experiences of the characters—who leave Mexico and their lives there and suffer many hardships to come to live in the United States—with his own Salvadoran family's experiences. He never before had thought of his own immigrant experiences as important enough to be portrayed as "literature." Francisco now shares his stories with his students and encourages them to tell their family stories. Toni, a Mexican who experienced discrimination in California schools as she grew up, read the book with interest, also comparing the characters to her own family members. She came away from the experience of reading the book with a new sense of pride in who she was and where she had come from. She intends to share that pride in who she is with her own Hispanic students. Judy, an Anglo from an affluent family in a small farming community, was amazed to read about the background of the book's characters. She had never before thought of the field laborers as people with dignity, pride, and an important history. Judy now views the Mexican American students in her classroom as well as those in the Latino community in general with a new respect. Reading *Rain of Gold* changed Francisco, Toni, and Judy as they transacted with the text. All three now view themselves, their teaching, and their students differently because of their experience reading the book.

The explorer image is "at one and the same time active, healthy, interactive, and dynamic" (148). Lindfors cautions that the difficulty with creating explorer classrooms is that schools and teachers usually view students as performers instead of explorers. "The goal has traditionally been that children will demonstrate what they know and can do, rather than that they will explore in order to know and do better as they go along" (148). In explorer classrooms students ask questions, they initiate investigations, they are involved in diverse experiences, they constantly interact, and they engage in meaningful activity.

Conclusion

Yvonne's story shows how teachers change in response to new experiences and how their view of their students also changes in this process. Yvonne first followed a method that caused her to view her students as plants. Her audio-lingual lessons provided the nurturing her students required in the form of drills and dialogues. She soon moved to a different view. With her adult ESL students, for example, she began to see her role as one of providing interesting materials and activities through which they could construct knowledge. She was still in control, but the students played a much more active role in their learning. They were builders, not plants. Now Yvonne sees her teacher-students (and herself) as explorers, and, with them, she investigates different aspects of teaching and learning second languages. She may be the expedition leader, but she does not pretend to have all the answers as she and her students pursue topics of inquiry together.

These three images of the learner, then, correspond to different views of learning. Both our role as teachers and our relationship to our students can change depending on the image we hold. If we see students as plants, our job is to transmit knowledge to them. If we see students as builders, we provide the raw materials they use to construct knowledge. But if we see students as explorers, we recognize that they can pose problems and raise questions, and that during our joint investigations, we can construct knowledge together (Wells and Chang-Wells 1992).

Applications

1. Think about a language class you have taken or taught. (If you cannot identify a second language class, a first language reading, writing, literature, or language arts class is fine.) Try to identify the orientation of the teacher and some of the techniques used to teach that class. Discuss this in pairs or groups.

2. Look back over Yvonne's story. Do any of her experiences make you think of something similar that you have experienced with teaching or learning? Discuss this with a partner or in a small group.

3. Review the images of the learner discussed above. Categorize the following common classroom activities as consistent with the plant, builder, or explorer images. Be ready to defend your choices.

spelling tests	pop quiz
look up definitions	do a science experiment
write sentences with vocab. words	discuss meaning of a story
interactive dialogue journal	do a literature study
memorize a dialogue	read aloud for accuracy
recite a dialogue (memorized)	organize in centers
repeat a dialogue	write and act out a play
lecture	illustrate a story
web main ideas	student interviews
repeat after the teacher	shared reading
answer comprehension questions	brainstorm
do a Venn diagram	practice penmanship
write a book report	take a matching test
quickwrite	write a response to readings
guided reading	

4. Interview a teacher who has had at least ten years of teaching experience. (Use yourself if you have taught for several years.) What has influenced that teacher's curriculum decisions? What are your conclusions about how that teacher views learners? Does he or she generally view learners as plants, builders, or explorers? Brainstorm possible interview questions with a group.

5. Explore the resources available for ESL teachers by visiting at least three of the websites listed in the appendix. Come prepared to describe what you found at each site.

3

How Does Learning Take Place in Explorer Classrooms?

When teachers view themselves and their students as explorers, they create classroom experiences where learning takes place as the class reads, writes, and talks while investigating topics of interest. In these classes, students learn both content and language as they answer questions that interest them. We continue our investigation of the world of the school by presenting a model that helps to account for the learning that takes place in explorer classrooms.

The model we will present holds that learning, and especially language learning, must always be regarded as a social process. As Faltis and Hudelson (1998) point out, "learning and language acquisition overlap to a great extent in the sense that both are social, contextual, and goal-oriented. That is, individuals learn both content and language as they engage with others in a variety of settings and to accomplish specific purposes" (85). While it is generally accepted that children go through a process of creative construction as they form and test hypotheses about academic content subjects and language, the learning they do is always social. According to Hudelson and Faltis, "learning does not happen exclusively inside the heads of learners; it results from social interactions with others that enable learners to participate by drawing on past and present experiences and relating them to the specific context at hand in some meaningful way" (87). This social view of learning applies to all learning, including learning a first or second language.

A Model of Learning

One general model of learning, consistent with the explorer image, has been developed by Cochrane et al. (1984). These authors identify six steps involved in learning:

1. Demonstration
2. Intent
3. Self-concepting
4. Learning by doing
5. Feedback
6. Integration

Demonstration

According to Cochrane et al., learning begins with a demonstration. For people to learn something, they must first observe someone else doing it. A demonstration could be as simple as hearing someone speaking another language. A demonstration may or may not be intentional, because the person providing it may not even be aware that he or she is demonstrating something. In this respect, demonstrations differ from modeling, which is a more conscious act that many teachers use as a technique.

Teachers need to be aware that the demonstrations they provide may lead students to incorrect hypotheses. For example, teachers sometimes present the progressive tense by speaking aloud as they perform certain actions. "I am walking to the board. I am writing my name. I am turning toward the class." Despite the teacher's good intentions, one group of second language students we observed concluded that English speakers use progressive tense when they want to think aloud about what they are doing. As this example shows, it is important to embed language use in authentic contexts.

The relationship of the learner to the demonstrator is also important. If the person providing the demonstration is significant to the learner, the learner is more apt to pay attention to the demonstration. For example, if older brothers or sisters speak and interact in another language, they provide important demonstrations for younger siblings, giving the younger children the desire to speak and understand the second language as well.

Intent

We are constantly surrounded by demonstrations, but we only attend to some of them. For example, many teenagers see their parents cleaning or cooking, but they pay very little attention to these activities. In order for learning to take place, according to Cochrane et al., learners must form the intent to learn. In other words, as the result of the demonstration, <u>learners must decide that they would like to do what someone has demonstrated</u>. It is not enough for teenagers to see their parents cleaning the house. Unless the teens form the intent to clean the house, they will not learn how. Many parents of teenagers are amazed when they discover that their children have no idea about how to do simple chores that they have seen their parents do countless times.

Self-Concepting

The next step in learning is self-concepting. For the intent to become reality, learners must be able to conceive of themselves as actually doing something. Yvonne helped her high school Spanish students see themselves as Spanish speakers when she invited her Mexican friends to visit her. She and her students prepared questions for the visitors ahead of time. As the Mexican visitors answered the questions, they provided important demonstrations—real people using language for real reasons. Yvonne's students asked questions because they were interested in finding out the answers, and in the process they began to see themselves as people who actually could communicate in Spanish.

Many teachers we have worked with tell us, "I'm not a good language learner" or, "I just can't learn languages." Though we would say that their language learning experiences were probably not very good, the sad but important point here is that they do not see themselves learning and using another language.

Learning can be short-circuited at any stage. If no one provides a demonstration, we won't form the intent to learn. If we decide that the risks of trying are too high or that the rewards for success are too low, we can't imagine ourselves ever doing the activity. This is why many teachers strive to create a classroom where students can take risks. In the English language classroom, students receive demonstrations from English speakers, but whether or not students are willing to try to speak English in class depends on the risk involved and the benefits the students believe are attached to learning English.

Learning by Doing

Cochrane et al. also emphasize the fact that people learn by doing. As the authors point out, people learn to read by reading, and they learn to write by writing. Second language students learn English or any other language by using that language. However, it is important to make a distinction here between learning by doing something meaningful or just practicing a teacher-imposed activity. When we practice, we are usually preparing to do something for someone else that will be tested in the future. On the other hand, when we do something meaningful, we do it because we ourselves are interested in it.

When Yvonne had her college Spanish students write pen pal letters to another class, she created a situation in which students learned through doing as they used language for real purposes. In her adult ESL classes, Yvonne's students read in English to find shopping bargains or to plan trips to visit relatives in other cities. In each case, students learned language when they used language to meet their real-life needs.

Feedback

In the process of doing, our learning continues in response to the feedback we receive. The feedback in situations out of school comes quite naturally. If we try to use a new language as we buy an item in a store, we get feedback from the clerk, who either understands what we are asking for or has no idea of what we want. In schools, feedback may come in several different forms, and the form of the feedback may affect the course of the learning.

If an ESL teacher responds to students' questions by correcting the grammar, students may learn to concentrate on producing grammatically correct sentences. If the teacher criticizes the students' pronunciation as they try to use a new language, the students may think more about correct pronunciation than the meaning of what they are saying. On the other hand, a teacher who responds to the message a student is trying to convey provides feedback that keeps the student focused on making meaning in the new language.

For example, Ann, a college student who had a great deal of experience speaking Spanish, including two periods of her life when she lived in Mexico, complained about an incident in her advanced Spanish conversation class. Her Spanish professor kept interrupting her and correcting a grammar point during a discussion. She explained, "When he interrupted me for the third time, I refused to say another word. The frustrating thing was that I really was interested in the topic and wanted to say something." The feedback Ann received kept her from learning. So it is important that we, as teachers, find ways to provide feedback that will encourage learning.

Maureen recently described a simple activity in which she helped her adult ESL students improve their pronunciation by providing them with feedback. However, this feedback did not have the same effect as the feedback Ann received in her Spanish class. Maureen had noticed that her students were not hesitant to talk, but that they had difficulty understanding one another's English. Maureen asked the students to tape some of their discussions. Then she asked individual students to listen to themselves as they talked. She reported that many of her students were very surprised at how they sounded. They realized that their pronunciation was difficult to understand. The feedback provided by the tape helped them make changes in the way they talked.

Maureen found a way to provide the kind of feedback that helped her students in their acquisition of oral English. Feedback, then, should encourage learners to revise their hypotheses about what they know, move forward, and increase their understanding. Negative feedback discourages learners and learning. Positive feedback leads to the acquisition of new knowledge and greater language proficiency.

Integration

Integration is the final step in the learning process. It involves adding new knowledge and skills to what we already know. This occurs in a process similar to assimilation and accommodation, which we discussed in Chapter 2. Learners assimilate new information by shaping it to fit what they already know. Accommodation involves changing what we know in light of the new knowledge. In the same way, integration is a continual process of connecting new understandings to what we have already learned. Once we have integrated new knowledge, we use it comfortably; it becomes part of us and can be accessed as we become more knowledgeable or more skilled.

Real-Life Learning

All the steps come into play in everyday learning. For example, when we decided to spend our summers in Maine in a rustic cabin on a small island on a lake, we had no idea how much new knowledge we would need to live in this new setting. One of the kinds of knowledge we needed concerned driving and taking care of a boat. Both of us had driven a motor boat before, but we hadn't owned or cared for one. Our first summer was sort of a nightmare. We had trouble starting the boat, landing it at our dock, putting on the boat cover, tying the boat securely to the dock on a windy day, and refueling it. However, we saw others demonstrate the handling of boats with ease, and we could imagine ourselves (self-concepting) driving the boat just as others were doing. We practiced often, as we needed the boat to get off the island, and so we learned by doing. We were encouraged with each successful outing, which provided us the feedback we needed. We had made it home again in one piece! Now, in our fourth summer of writing in our Maine getaway, we are both quite comfortable with the boat. We have integrated knowledge about how to handle and care for our boat including understanding about proper lines (*not* clothesline) for securing it, differences in steering when the wind blows different ways, and how to use bumpers to protect the boat from damage when it beats on the dock in storms. That learning about boats has not stopped, however. Neighbors continually suggest new gadgets, new ways of doing things. This new information is integrated into what we already knew about the boat, so that now, we feel almost like experts.

After reading about the Cochrane et al. model of learning, Michelle, a graduate student and a bilingual teacher, related the model to her own acquisition of Spanish:

> My first year of teaching, 90 percent of my students were non-English-speaking. As a very young child, I had been raised speaking Spanish, but I had not spoken much Spanish since I had started kindergarten. Though I understood Spanish quite well and my parents spoke it at home, I could not speak it. When I began teaching, I definitely had the need to learn to speak Spanish immediately. The demonstrations came from my home (a Spanish-speaking family), as well as from school (Spanish-speaking students). The intent was quite obvious; I needed a way to communicate with my students, and so I wanted to be able to speak Spanish. I also went through

self-concepting. I imagined myself speaking Spanish to my young students. I learned by doing. I communicated with my students in meaningful situations. They provided instant feedback; either they understood me, or they giggled when I said something wrong. Finally, I integrated this newly practiced skill with my already known ideas of the Spanish language. I understood the language, and as I practiced and integrated my new skill, I could respond more understandably and confidently.

Guillermo, one of the case study students described in Chapter 1, provides another good example of the learning model steps. Before coming to the United States, he had many demonstrations of success from the influential people around him who had traveled extensively and spoke at least two languages. These demonstrations helped him form the intent to speak English. Once he arrived in the United States, he saw that his aunt was finishing a Ph.D. program at a large university. This demonstration showed him that it was possible to succeed in this country through education. He began to see himself as an educated English speaker. He formed this self-concept even though he knew the risks involved in trying to succeed academically in a new language.

From the first day of school, he learned by doing. He made friends with English-speaking American peers, and he soon joined clubs. He never hesitated to talk to his teachers or other English-speaking adults or to ask questions. Most of the feedback he received kept him focused on making meaning in his new language. He learned English as he studied academic content. He continually integrated the new knowledge of English and academic subjects that he learned.

Though he did not receive straight A's in academic work, he became an accepted part of the English-speaking community while he was still learning English in high school. Once in college he not only did well in his coursework, he was so outgoing and active in student affairs that he received one of only two invitations to work in Washington, D.C., with a state senator during the summer. Over time, his interests have shifted, but he continues to see education as the key to success. He has learned Italian and traveled to Europe several times, again following the demonstrations of adults he knew in his childhood. Currently, Guillermo is completing an M.A. degree in architecture. His story clearly shows the steps of the learning model in action.

Joining the Club

Smith (1988) uses the metaphor of joining a club to describe the process people go through as they learn something new. We might see the club as the context in which the learning process can most easily occur. Guillermo literally joined school clubs, but he also joined the English-speakers' club. Learning occurs in clubs for the following reasons:

1. It is meaningful. (We ignore things that are meaningless.)
2. It is useful. (We ignore things that don't serve our purposes.)
3. It is continual and effortless. (We stay in the club once we are learning and are not aware of the roles we play as club members.)

4. It is incidental. (We do not focus on what we are learning but on what we are doing as we accomplish our purposes.)
5. It is collaborative. (We draw on the expertise of other club members to help us accomplish our purposes.)
6. It is vicarious. (We learn from others without effort if they are the kind of people we admire and we want to do what they do.)
7. It is risk-free. (We are accepted into a club. Clubs are safe places for learning.)

In explorer classrooms, teachers and students form clubs as they pose and answer questions about topics of interest. Language learners in these classrooms use their new language as they engage in meaningful inquiry. Their focus is not on the language but on using the language to accomplish their purposes.

We often say that the best way to learn a new language is to live in the country where that language is spoken. Certainly, going to France to learn French could be seen as joining the French-speakers' club. In France, French is meaningful and useful. Learning is continuous, incidental, and vicarious. Of course, whether or not the learning is risk-free depends on how other club members (native French speakers) respond. In fact, the key to learning is acceptance into the club, and just going to a country may not result in club membership at all. Some Americans live abroad, but they spend all their time with other Americans, forming their own community within the foreign country, and as a result they don't learn the language spoken there. We have to want to join a club, and club members must be accepting for learning to take place.

Taking a French class could also be a step toward joining the French-speakers' club. The same factors would affect learning in a classroom. The difference between going to France and taking a French class is that the class includes an officially designated teacher. Smith describes the teacher's responsibility as twofold: making sure that clubs exist and that no student is excluded from them. In the case of literacy clubs, Smith says, "In simple terms, this means lots of collaborative and meaningful reading and writing activities, the kinds of things that are often characterized as extras, reward or even 'frills'" (15). In a French class, this would mean that the students are hearing and using French for purposes that are meaningful and interesting to them in a risk-free environment.

Clubs are places where learning takes place during social interaction. Smith takes a transactional view of learning. Learning is an ongoing and dynamic process of exploration. Smith's metaphor for learning as joining a club challenges traditional views of teachers transmitting information or of students gathering information and building knowledge. Instead, club members acquire knowledge as they interact with one another.

Vygotsky's Social View of Learning

In this chapter we have been considering how learning takes place in explorer classrooms. The model of learning developed by Cochrane and colleagues helps outline the steps learners go through. Smith's metaphor of learning as joining a club suggests that learning is a social process. This social view of learning has been most fully developed by Vygotsky (1981). The ideas he developed—the Zone of Proximal Development and the distinction between spontaneous and scientific concepts—contribute to a fuller understanding of how learning occurs. Goodman and Goodman (1990) amplify Vygotsky's idea of proximal development zones by focusing on the individual learner.

Zone of Proximal Development   levels of mastery

For learning to take place, instruction must occur in a student's Zone of Proximal Development, which Vygotsky (1978) defines as "the distance between the actual developmental level as determined by independent problem solving and the level of potential development as determined through problem solving under adult guidance or in collaboration with more capable peers" (86). According to Vygotsky, learning results when we talk with someone else, an adult or a more capable peer, in the process of trying to solve a problem.

Vygotsky's idea is that for any kind of learning, the learner has a certain zone in which the next learning can take place. For example, a student might use the "-ing" forms of verbs to express progressive tense, as in "I studying English." The next area of learning for this student might be to add the auxiliary verb *am* to produce a more conventional sentence: "I am studying English." With the help of a teacher or a more proficient English speaker, a student might begin to use auxiliary verbs in this and other sentences. A student who already uses this tense correctly would not benefit from the instruction at all, and neither would a student who is just beginning to study English and uses only simple present tense. The Zone of Proximal Development refers to the area that is just beyond what the student can currently do. Good teachers try to aim instruction at this zone.

what the students are able to master currently

Another way to think about the Zone of Proximal Development is to consider two students who both score 60 percent on a math test. This score would represent their independent level. A teacher might work with both students and then retest them. One student's score might rise to 70 percent while the other student might get an 80 on the second test. This would suggest that the two students had different Zones of Proximal Development. One was ready to take a big leap with a little help while the other could make only a modest gain.

Mike provides us with an excellent example of how he works in his students' Zones of Proximal Development during literature studies in his fourth-grade classroom. Mike works in an inner-city school, and many of his students are English language learners. He believes that literature studies are important for his students' learning. It is clear that Mike has found ways to support his students' growth:

> I continue to explore this exciting concept of literature study, students self-select books and then meet in book groups to determine how many pages to read each day to complete the reading within a time frame I decide. The students are then invited to read, as a group, with a partner(s), or by themselves.

As students read, I float about, keeping anecdotal records of things students might be doing to make meaning from their texts. I have also joined in with groups as they have read, or even read with a group to provide some support and demonstrations of ways to approach reading and talk about it. Students are also encouraged to have a shared reading arrangement where they periodically stop and just do a "quick talk" with a partner about what they think is going on in their reading or to ask for clarification. This is to support the meaning making process.

I do wander in and out of groups and will ask them what they are finding, and then offer some direction as to things that I would like for them to be on the lookout for in the text. I base my comments on the kind of interests I see the readers having. I also will have readers give regular response (though not always written) on their reading. I want to get a look at how they are transacting with text.

*reading
should be
of interest
+experience)*

It is important to note that Mike is not the only one in the classroom helping students move within their Zones of Proximal Development. The way literature studies are organized in Mike's classroom, peers help each other understand and learn too.

Personal Invention and Social Convention

Central to the concept of the Zone of Proximal Development is the view of learning as a process of internalizing social experience. Vygotsky emphasized the role of social forces working on the individual. Goodman and Goodman (1990), however, argue that "language [and other aspects of learning] is as much personal invention as social convention" (231). The Goodmans present a view of learning that recognizes both the effects of social forces and the efforts of the individual learner: "Human learners are not passively manipulated by their social experiences; they are actively seeking sense in the world" (231). Social interaction is crucial. Individuals present their personal inventions to a group, which provides feedback that the learner can use to shape the inventions in order that they conform, to some degree, with social conventions.

We see this process occur when young children begin to write and invent spellings for the words they use. Over time, if children are exposed to lots of print, their spellings change, moving steadily toward conventional usage. The key is to achieve a balance between the two forces of invention and convention. The Goodmans compare invention and convention with the centripetal and centrifugal forces that keep a satellite rotating around the Earth. Both forces are needed to keep the satellite in orbit. In the same way, in classrooms, if students are allowed to write any way they wish, they may produce spellings no one can read. On the other hand, if teachers insist on correct spelling, some students may choose not to write at all.

Helen was able to help her student, Magdalena, move from invention to convention by engaging her in writer's workshop:

At the beginning of the year, Magdalena was not concerned if her work was readable or followed any of the conventions of standard English. She knew she was putting down her thoughts and ideas, and that was what I emphasized to her. I felt confident that her spelling and grammar would come along if she felt more comfortable in class, was allowed to write in a writer's workshop environment, and was exposed to more text. I decided to follow my instincts and only focus on one area with Magdalena. I wanted her to understand that writing is a process and that her misspellings were normal for a child who knew two languages. Recently, she started asking more questions about sentence structures and about the "right way" to spell. During a conference time with her group, she and I worked together to pick out the types of words she seemed to misspell or misuse most often. Then we problem solved the reasons why these words might cause her grief when writing. Most of the words we found were words she could spell correctly when she reread her writing.

Helen encouraged Magdalena to invent spellings to get her ideas down on paper. At first, Magdalena was not concerned with correct spellings. However, in the context of a writer's workshop Magdalena wanted her teacher and other students to be able to read what she had written, so she started to ask her teacher how to spell words. Helen helped Magdalena develop strategies that allowed this English learner to make her writing more conventional. If Helen had insisted on correct spelling from the beginning, Magdalena probably would not have developed the confidence to write. Helen took her cue from her student and helped her focus on spelling once Magdalena had produced writing she wanted others to read.

When English language learners try to communicate in their new language, they often invent structures or words based on what they know about the language. For example, many students learning Spanish use "Yo gusto" instead of the irregular, conventional form, "Me gusta" for "I like," since other verbs add *o* to form the first-person singular. When students use forms like "Yo gusto" (personal invention), they receive feedback and eventually respond by modifying their language to the conventional form "Me gusta" (social convention).

Yvonne's Venezuelan friends were amused when she used *coliflor*, the word for cauliflower, to refer to a hummingbird. Two conventional words are *colibrí* and *chupaflor*, and Yvonne seems to have combined these in her invention. In cases like this, when second language learners' inventions depart too far from social conventions, the feedback provided by native speakers helps learners seek a new way to express themselves. In the process, they learn a new language.

Spontaneous and Scientific Concepts

The Goodmans' theory of invention and convention claims that both personal and social forces influence the development of concepts. Their view fits well with Vygotsky's notion of the Zone of Proximal Development. Vygotsky says that we learn in social situations when others provide the help that shapes our inventions toward the social conventions of a particular society.

Vygotsky distinguishes between two kinds of concepts that people can form in this process. Spontaneous concepts are ideas we develop fairly directly from everyday experience. For example, we know what "car" means if we live in a society in which people drive cars. We develop the concept for "car" by riding in cars and seeing cars. The word *car* becomes a label we can use to talk about this concept. We develop spontaneous concepts without any special help. They are simply part of our daily lives.

Scientific concepts, on the other hand, are abstract ideas that societies use to organize and categorize experiences. The concept of "transportation," for example, is a scientific concept. We use this term to categorize a number of different means of conveyance, whether the mode be a car, a bus, a boat, or an airplane. Children do not learn scientific concepts from exposure to everyday events. Most often, they learn them in school. Different societies and different academic disciplines develop particular sets of terms that children learn as part of their school experience.

Vygotsky conducted a number of experiments to show how scientific concepts developed as a result of schooling. In one experiment he showed adults who had not received formal schooling pictures of objects such as a hammer, a saw, a log, and a hatchet, and asked which one didn't fit. These adults would say that all of them were needed. You need a hatchet to chop down a tree, a saw to cut it into logs, and a hammer to pound nails into the logs to build something. He presented the same pictures to a second group of adults from the same cultural and linguistic background. This group, which had received formal schooling, would pick out the log as different. In order to pick out the log, the adults had to categorize the objects using abstraction (three of these things are tools) rather than focus on the functional properties of the objects.

In the same way, presented with pictures of a bird, a rifle, a dagger, and a bullet, the first group argued that you needed all of them (the bullet goes into the rifle to shoot the bird, and you use the knife to cut it up), and the second group said the bird was different because the other three were weapons. Both groups had developed the same spontaneous concepts, but only those who had gone to school had developed the scientific concepts needed to categorize these objects.

The ideas of spontaneous and scientific concepts are important in two ways when we apply them to language learning. Krashen (1982) makes an important distinction between acquiring a language and learning one. We will discuss the scientific concepts "acquisition" and "learning" more fully in Chapter 5, but at this point we simply want to suggest that we acquire a language in the same way that we develop spontaneous concepts: in the course of daily living and without much conscious awareness of the process itself. On the other hand, if we study a language in school, we usually learn scientific concepts, such as "verb" or "present tense," that we can use to categorize aspects of the language. As Krashen points out, acquisition allows us to use language to communicate, while learning gives us abstract terms to talk about the language. Thus, there is a similarity between Vygotsky's ideas about spontaneous and scientific concepts and Krashen's ideas about acquisition and learning.

Similarly, Cummins (1981) makes a distinction between conversational language and academic language. This again is an important difference that we will discuss in more detail later. Here, we wish to suggest that conversational language is what we use to communicate spontaneous concepts and talk about daily events. On the other hand, academic language involves the use of terms to talk about abstract concepts that we usually learn in school. Cummins notes that for most students, it takes much longer to develop academic proficiency in a new language than to develop conversational proficiency. It appears that we acquire the language to express spontaneous concepts before we pick up the language for scientific concepts. However, students who have had schooling in their first language already have scientific concepts available to guide their thinking, and they simply need the terms to express those concepts in a new language.

The Role of the Teacher

How do teachers in explorer classrooms help English learners develop the academic concepts and language they need to succeed in school? The role of the teacher is one of *mediation*, to use Vygotsky's term. A teacher (or other adult or more capable peer) mediates experience by helping the learner make sense out of it. The teacher asks questions or points out certain aspects of a situation. Mike helped his students mediate their learning through literature as he provided demonstrations, helped them to form groups and ask questions, and encouraged "quick talks" when they had difficulty understanding the texts.

Mediation is different from intervention, which literally means "coming between." We may want the police to intervene to stop a fight, but a teacher shouldn't intervene between a student and the student's learning. Teachers who mediate learning provide a "way" or medium that helps students gain new understandings. What students can first do with the help of a teacher who mediates, they can later do alone. The questions and suggestions of the teacher are a kind of learning tool that students can use. First students need the teacher to help, and later students can solve the same kind of problem on their own.

Good instruction supports learning for as long as the learner needs it and then allows the student to work independently. Many of us have had the experience of help that didn't last long enough. We go to the hardware store, and the technician explains very clearly how to install the equipment we are buying. Then, once we get home, we can't recall how to put the pieces together. We needed more mediation, more instruction within our Zone of Proximal Development.

Cazden (1992) describes three ways a teacher can mediate learning: by providing scaffolding, by modeling, or through direct instruction. Figure 3–1 gives an overview of these three types of adult assistance.

Scaffolding

Vygotsky argued that learning takes place when an adult or more capable peer asks questions, points out aspects of a problem, or makes suggestions, working in a learner's Zone of Proximal Development. Bruner (1985) referred to this kind of help

Type of Mediation	What the Teacher Does	What the Students Do
Scaffold	Provides assistance to help students solve problems by asking questions, probing, pointing out aspects of a problem or answering questions	Use information provided to try to solve problems and accomplish tasks
Model	Shows through actions or materials how students should do something	Follow the model provided to produce something similar
Direct Instruction	Tells students how or what to do or gives students information to learn and then apply	Follow directions, practice, or memorize information and then display the knowledge

FIGURE 3–1 *Types of Adult Assistance*

as verbal scaffolds. A scaffold is an appropriate metaphor for this kind of assistance. A scaffold supports a building during its construction and then is taken down once the building is completed. Cazden (1992) defines a scaffold as "a temporary framework for construction in progress" (103). A teacher, for example, might ask a student who has written a composition to expand on a certain point, to provide more information to support an argument. The teacher's questions provide the scaffold that allows the writer to move beyond what he or she produced by working alone. A native speaker might ask a nonnative speaker to rephrase or clarify a request, and in the process the nonnative speaker might start to develop the conventional forms needed for communication in the new language.

Marjorie, a fourth-grade teacher whose classroom has many second language learners, uses buddy partners and cooperative techniques with her students. She has found that when she uses other students as "teachers," all students are able to progress. In a response to some reading in a graduate ESL methods course, Marjorie explained how students can provide a scaffold for one another:

It's been interesting to watch the interaction this last week as my class has been reading the book *The Real Thief,* by Stieg. One group of three girls has especially caught my eye. One of the girls is one of my top students academically, having been on the honor roll all year. The other two girls have been in the United States for about two years and their independent reading level would be considered preprimer. As a team, all three are able to read and enjoy the book, even though many of the words are difficult. As one of the "lower" students reads along, every fourth or fifth word, she stops and asks, in Hmong, "Ab tsi?" (What?). The "top" student explains and on they move.

Scaffolding also occurs when the teacher or a peer provides a structure with slots to be filled in by the student. Teachers will, for example, read predictable stories to children and then pause for the children to fill in words using the language pattern established. This approach is more controlled than the scaffolding Marjorie describes.

Another example of controlled scaffolding, called reciprocal teaching, has been developed by Palinscar (1986). During reading sessions, teachers ask a series of questions designed to help students make predictions, generate questions, give summaries, and clarify ideas. Teachers then instruct students in how to ask these same kinds of questions. Eventually, students take on the role of teacher and ask other students the questions. Reciprocal teaching involves students in teaching one another. The questions serve as scaffolds that help students understand what they are reading.

Scaffolds support learners by providing a structure they can rely on to build their competence. One role for a teacher is to provide scaffolds or to create situations where students can do this for each another. However, there is a danger that the intentions of the learner may be ignored. A scaffold should help learners do what they are trying to do. This is different from a kind of instruction that helps learners do what the teacher wants them to do.

Modeling   SHOWING

A second kind of adult assistance is provided by modeling. Modeling is something a teacher can do with an individual, a small group, or an entire class. It is an intentional action by the teacher. For example, if a teacher wants to help students understand directionality in reading, she might decide to model directionality by reading a big book and moving her finger under the print to indicate left-to-right movement. In doing this, the teacher models one aspect of reading.

An example of modeling comes from Sandra, a teacher of fourth-, fifth-, and sixth-grade newcomers who arrive with little previous schooling or with interrupted schooling. Most are migrant children with little background in English. As a prewriting activity, Sandra often writes on the overhead in front of the entire class, talking about conventions she uses in her writing, In an early writing lesson, Sandra's modeling is a prewriting activity in which she writes a description of her family on the overhead and offers a commentary such as the following:

> In the first sentence, I indent, and the first letter is a capital letter. "My family has five people." Notice that I put a period at the end of the sentence. "My husband's name is Alfredo." Notice that I have a capital letter at the beginning and for my husband's name.

As Sandra writes and talks, she models the kind of paragraph and the conventions she wants her students to write.

Sometimes materials can provide the model teachers need. When Sandra was working on a nutrition unit that had evolved naturally from a plant unit, she wanted to help her students answer the question, "Where does our food come from?" She read aloud a book, *Where Does Breakfast Come From?* (Flint 1998), which describes how products such as milk, cereal, pancakes, and bread come from the field or farm to the table. This book provided the model for Sandra's students. They worked in cooperative groups and drew posters of a food of their choice, describing how it progressed from the field to the table. Students chose favorite foods such as pizza, cookies, and pie. They interviewed teachers at the school to find out what ingredients they used for favorite pie and cookie recipes and presented their posters to the class. These final projects included not only where products like flour and pizza sauce come from (wheat, tomatoes, peppers, cheese) but also the recipes for how to make the favorite dish. Sandra would never have gotten such excellent participation without the model she provided.

Direct Instruction Guide/TELLS STUDENTS WHAT TO DO

Finally, teachers can support learning through direct instruction. As Cazden explains, in direct instruction, "the adult not only models a particular utterance but directs the child to say or tell or ask" (108). A parent might say "Bye-bye" and wave to a friend when leaving, and then tell the child, "Say bye-bye." Children's television host, Mr. Rogers, used direct instruction frequently: "Boys and girls, this is a crayon. Can you say 'crayon'?"

As Cazden says, "direct instruction seems to focus on two aspects of language development: appropriate social language use and correct vocabulary" (108). Direct instruction might occur in an ESL lesson in which students first practice introductions. The teacher has three students come to the front of the class to demonstrate the correct form:

MARY: Albert, this is Bill.
ALBERT: Nice to meet you.
BILL: Nice to meet you, too.

Then the teacher divides the students into groups of three to practice introductions, telling them to rotate the roles so that every student gets to play each part.

Direct instruction is perhaps most often associated with the teaching of reading. For example, many standards of reading instruction call for explicit, direct instruction of phonics. Reading programs often include materials that instruct teachers to present lessons in a step-by-step manner. For example, in a typical lesson, a teacher may direct students to produce each sound in a word and then blend the sounds to produce the complete word. Students then practice this skill with a series of words.

Direct instruction occurs in other settings as well. When a teacher is unhappy with the way her students leave their tables to line up, she takes the time to explain the order in which she wants groups to line up and who in each group should go first. Once she has explained the procedure to the students, she has the students go through the process until they are able to follow her instructions exactly.

Lecture is also a kind of direct instruction. As a high school social studies teacher talks about the key battles of the Civil War, his students take notes. They know they need to learn this information for a test that will be given later.

In language teaching, direct instruction is common when teachers explain grammar rules or have students repeat words or dialogues. For example, when Yvonne was teaching Spanish traditionally, she explained to students that in Spanish, descriptive adjectives follow the noun. Her students translated sentences from English to Spanish putting the adjectives after the nouns. When Yvonne was using the audio-lingual method to teach, she had students repeat after her the lines of a dialogue, and then they practiced the dialogues in pairs while she walked around and corrected their pronunciation.

Mediation in Explorer Classrooms

The three types of mediation—scaffolding, modeling, and direct instruction—all support learning, but there are important differences. Scaffolding is more indirect and supports students in what they are trying to do. Modeling and direct instruction are aimed at transmitting information or skills that the teacher feels are important. Both modeling and direct instruction usually require a specific final product from the student.

Direct instruction, modeling, and scaffolding may all have a place in an explorer classroom. These are all ways teachers can help mediate learning. However, a teacher who tries to establish an explorer classroom would deemphasize direct instruction and modeling and only use these techniques in response to observed student needs. For example, a teacher might give direct instruction during a minilesson on quotation marks if she has noticed that a group of her students are having difficulty with writing conversations. Or, she might consciously model the kinds of questions students could ask one another in peer writing conferences if students are having difficulty responding to one another's writing. Sandra's modeling supported her students so that they could accomplish tasks and build academic competence. In these cases, the teacher bases her instruction on her observations of her students and her knowledge of language, teaching, learning, and curriculum.

Conclusion: Learning as Exploration

Together, the theories presented here provide support for adopting a transactional view of learning and an explorer image of the learner. The theorists we have discussed all view learning as an active process of constructing meaning in collaboration with others. We have developed this general view of learning in some detail to provide a context for our discussion of the different theories of second language learning in the following chapters. We will evaluate those theories by considering how consistent they are with the view of learning that we have developed here, because we believe that learning a second language is only one instance of the more general process of learning.

Applications

1. Think of something you have learned to do. For example, have you learned to speak a second language, to play a musical instrument, or to build something? Relate the six steps of learning that Cochrane et al. propose to your own experience. Do your experiences fit what the theorists have suggested? Discuss this with a partner.

2. Think back to a learning experience where someone helped you to succeed. How does your experience fit in with Vygotsky's idea of a Zone of Proximal Development? Share your experience with others.

3. Learners are creative, but their learning is controlled by people and situations that surround them. In a small group, brainstorm some examples of how social conventions influence inventions. Share your ideas with the larger group and discuss the implications invention and social convention have for teaching.

4. Cazden describes scaffolding, modeling, and direct instruction. Think of examples of each that you have done or have seen done with second language learners. Share the examples in a small group.

4

What Do We Acquire When We Acquire a Language?

In our discussion of the world of the school, we reviewed different theories of how people learn in order to create a context for our discussion of how people learn languages, particularly how people learn second languages. Our contention is that language learning is a specific instance of a more general process, and that any theory of language learning we hold must be consistent with our beliefs about learning in general.

Before we discuss theories of second language acquisition, we wish to consider what it is that people acquire in developing a second language. We can only say *that* someone has acquired a language if we first agree on *what* that entails. What do we know when we know a language? Linguists such as Noam Chomsky have focused their work on this question.

> Chomsky seeks to attain two parallel, interrelated goals in the study of language—namely to develop (i) a Theory of Language and (ii) a Theory of Language Acquisition. The Theory of Language will concern itself with what are the defining characteristics of natural (i.e. human) languages and the Theory of Language Acquisition with the question of how children acquire their native language(s). Of the two, the task (i) of developing a Theory of Language is—in Chomsky's view—logically prior to task (ii) of developing a Theory of Language Acquisition, since only if we know what language is can we develop theories of how it is acquired. (Radford 1981, 1)

Chomsky's claim, then, is that we need to decide on what language is before we can consider how people acquire languages. For Chomsky and other linguists, what we acquire is a grammar. The term *grammar* has several different meanings, but for linguists a grammar is a set of rules people use to produce and comprehend a language. Speakers of a language are not usually consciously aware of the rules they use. They can put sentences together and they can understand what others say, but they can't usually tell you how they do it. What Chomsky and other linguists attempt to discover is the nature of these subconscious rules.

Competence and Performance

Chomsky makes an important distinction in his study of language between competence and performance. He claims that "a grammar of a language is a model of the linguistic competence of the fluent native speaker of the language" (quoted in Radford, 2). A speaker's competence is what a speaker can do under the best conditions. Our competence represents a kind of idealized best ability. As we all know, our performance seldom matches our competence. In most situations, we don't perform up to our full ability. We may be nervous, tired, bored, or simply careless.

Previous linguists studied language by analyzing what speakers said or wrote. They based their descriptions on actual performance. Chomsky, on the other hand, wanted to look at underlying ability, so he ignored many slips of the tongue and described language by considering what speakers know is "right" when they have a chance to think about it—a kind of edited speech or writing. Chomsky felt that only by considering speakers' underlying competence could he get at the rules they use to produce and understand a language.

The concept of competence is important for linguists studying a language. It is also important for teachers trying to determine how proficient a student is. We should remember that a student's actual performance may not fully show his or her underlying competence. For example, ten-year-old Francisco, educated in both Mexico and the United States, understands, speaks, reads, and writes English well despite having an accent. When he arrives at a new school, his teacher first tries to engage him in friendly conversation and then calls on him to answer questions. He responds haltingly because he is nervous and is unaccustomed to the informal classroom atmosphere. Based on his performance, his teacher assumes Francisco understands and speaks very little English. Actually, Francisco's competence in English is much greater than his performance would suggest.

Johnson (1995) points out that all of us develop both linguistic and interactional competence in our primary language. That is, we develop knowledge that allows us to use language to communicate following the unwritten social rules of a particular group. As students learn a new language, they must also learn how people who use that language interact in different social settings. Students' performance in classroom settings will reflect both their linguistic competence and their interactional competence in the new language and culture.

Teachers can help students to work up to their levels of competence in the classroom. As Johnson comments,

> Teachers must recognize that differences in second language students' linguistic and interactional competencies exist, and, more importantly, that these competencies are the result of a process of socialization and do not represent cognitive or social deficiencies. Second, teachers must create classroom events that allow for greater variability in both the academic task structures and the social participation structures, so as to maximize second language students' competencies. Teachers must also make their expectations and intentions clear, and in doing so, make explicit the implicit rules for participation in classroom events. (71)

Teachers also need to be aware that students' performance in certain contexts may not be a good predictor of their competence in other contexts. For example, some students appear to be very proficient in everyday conversational English. They can joke with friends and talk about current events of interest. However, these same students may have great difficulty with the academic language of content-area textbooks and tests. Competence, then, is tied to particular functions of language use. We do not have a general language competence. Instead, we have (or lack) competence in using language for certain purposes.

Leny, a Dutch woman teaching English in Venezuela, provides a good example of a language learner whose performance in a specific context did not reflect her competence. She was learning Spanish and had developed good basic skills, but in one setting, she appeared to lack competence:

> There are many occasions when my performance in a foreign language does not reflect my competence in that language. One of those occasions was at the hairdresser. The lady helping me did not seem to have the time or the interest to let me explain in my basic Spanish what I wanted, and on top of that, the whole shop was looking at me, the "gringa." I then tried to explain with gestures what I meant, with the result that I came out with a very different haircut than I wanted. This being the only decent hairdresser in town, I went back there a few times, but each time I wrote down beforehand what I wanted, although I was perfectly capable of saying it. But I knew that I just would draw a blank again as soon as I got into the shop.

Leny's story is instructive. The hairdresser did not really listen to her. Other customers began to stare at her. Even though she had developed some basic Spanish, she could not access it in that context. As language teachers, we need to remember that our reactions to students play an important role in their performance. For Leny, that one negative experience carried over to future visits. She was able to develop a strategy (writing things down) to overcome the problem, but many younger students never find ways to use the language they have already developed as they attempt to function in a new language.

[handwritten margin note: our reaction to our student performance can affect their output (performance)]

Competence and Correctness

They must read, so teachers can view, and correct language.

People acquire competence in one or more languages, but their ability to produce and comprehend the language or languages is not the same as their ability to use the conventional or standard forms of the languages. The competence we are describing is not the kind of conscious knowledge usually associated with school grammar lessons. It is not the ability to put commas in the right places or to use *different from* rather than *different than*. Those are matters of usage and are typically associated with standard written language.

The kinds of rules Chomsky and other linguists refer to when they speak of "grammar" are the rules that allow people to use language to communicate. It is our knowledge that something "sounds right" in the dialect we speak. Many native speakers have this kind of competence but lack the ability to produce standard writing. School success depends on mastering conventions of usage, but these are something learned in school or other formal settings, not something we normally acquire when we acquire a language. However, if our experience with a new language includes opportunities to read different kinds of texts, we can acquire a good command of formal written language. For that reason, it is important for teachers to engage students in reading rather than only focusing lessons on oral language.

Functions of Language and Kinds of Competence

One way to answer the question, "What do we acquire when we acquire a language?" is to say that we develop the language we need to do certain things. Smith (1983) points out that language can serve three functions: the referential function, which speakers use to get and give basic information; the expressive function, which speakers use to show their attitude toward what they are saying; and the integrative function, which speakers use to mark their social identity. These three functions of language match with the two basic types of competence that someone acquiring a language needs to develop: grammatical competence and communicative competence. In the following sections, we explain each of the three functions and then describe the two kinds of competence related to these functions.

Referential Function

THINGS IN THE WORLD

The most basic function of language is the referential function. We use language to refer to things in the world. This is the function that allows me to say, "My name is David" or, "I live in California." We need to be able to get and give basic information to survive, so the referential function is probably the first language function acquirers develop.

In traditional ESL classes, teachers usually begin with basic vocabulary—classroom objects, clothing, food, transportation—and basic sentence types—simple statements with "be" and simple statements with action verbs in the present tense. This approach is designed to give students the tools to talk about everyday things. In other words, these classes begin by supplying students with the words and structures they need to perform the referential function of language.

Expressive Function *How we feel* (Taking a stand)

Just getting and giving basic information is not enough for someone to function fully in a language. We also need to be able to show our attitude toward what we are saying. This is the expressive function of language. Part of what we acquire when we acquire a language is this ability to show how we feel about the topic under discussion.

Gee (1988), explaining the expressive function, notes that "when we speak, we do not just talk about the world . . . we take a particular perspective or viewpoint on the information we communicate" (204). We reveal our viewpoints, our attitude, by stressing certain words, by pausing, even by choosing from among synonyms those words that carry the emotional tone we wish to communicate. Synonyms may have roughly the same referential meaning, but they differ in the emotions they trigger. There's a big difference between "I dislike cats" and "I abhor (despise) (detest) cats." Speakers signal their attitudes by the choices they make among synonyms such as these. When we acquire a language, then, we acquire not only the ability to communicate certain ideas, but also ways to express our attitudes toward those ideas.

Integrative Function *Adaptation to our surroundings.*

We use language to get and give basic information, and we also use intonation and vocabulary that helps us show how we feel about what we are saying. However, there is also a third important function that language plays. When we acquire a language, we also acquire the integrative function, and this is what allows us to indicate our social status in relationship to the people we are speaking with. In other words, we learn to vary our language for social purposes.

Gee (1988) suggests that two forces motivate language use. These are "the desire for status in regard to whatever reference group(s) one admires and the desire for solidarity with those one views as peers" (212). Since languages give speakers options, different ways to say the same thing, second language learners must be aware of the social effects of choosing one way of saying something over another if they seek status and/or solidarity. Proficient language users are able to change from more to less formal registers depending on their audience and purpose for speaking. Language variation to mark social class can include changes in syntax, vocabulary, or pronunciation.

While we were in Venezuela, for example, we noticed that our maid spoke more rapidly and dropped many endings when talking to members of her family. At first we thought she was speaking more slowly and clearly to us because we were foreigners. However, when other Venezuelan professors came to our home, we realized that she spoke the same way to them as she did to us. What we discovered is that she changed her dialect when speaking to people she perceived to be of a higher social status.

All of us do this in our native language, often without being aware of it. Politicians are often especially good at shifting to a "down home" variety of the language when trying to gain votes. They speak quite differently back at the Capitol. A tension always exists between solidarity and status. In many contexts, we have to choose language that achieves a connection with others or language that elevates us above them. In classrooms, teachers should realize that asking students to speak or write a certain way has definite social consequences for the students. At times, solidarity with their peers may be more important than the academic achievement that could come from using a higher status variety of the language.

Part of what we acquire when we acquire a new language is this ability to choose language that reflects status or solidarity in appropriate ways. For example, when we taught at the university in Mérida, Venezuela, many of our interactions with other professors and with students took place in Spanish. We could communicate, but we did not always choose the right variety of language to achieve either status or solidarity. The relationship in Latin America between students and professors is different from the relationship we have with our graduate students in the United States. In Venezuela professors maintain a position of such high respect that students do not expect their professors to treat them like friends. We came to realize that in interactions with students, we needed to remain rather formal and even demanding if we wished to keep their respect as well as the respect of the other professors with whom we worked. This meant that the kind of language we used with students had to be different from the language we used with other professors.

Acquiring a language is complex. We need to know the words and how to put them together. Otherwise, we can't get and give basic information. But we also need to be aware that the particular words we choose and the way we combine and express them shows how we feel about what we are saying and also shows how we feel about the people with whom we are communicating. In order to use language to perform these three functions, we need two different kinds of competence: grammatical competence and sociolinguistic competence.

Grammatical Competence *knowledge on language*

Grammatical competence is knowledge of a language that allows us to get and give information about the world. It allows us to say, "Today is Monday" or, "The man chased the dog." Linguists such as Chomsky have described grammatical competence. Their research focuses on the areas of phonology, morphology, syntax, and semantics.

Phonology refers to the sound system of a language. Each language consists of a set of sounds (phonemes) that speakers use to indicate differences in meaning. English has about forty phonemes. Linguists often use minimal pairs to determine phonemes. If two words differ by just one sound, then that sound must make a difference in meaning in the language. For example, since *pet* and *bet* are separate words (they mean different things) and since the words differ only by the first sound (/p/ versus /b/), then those sounds must be phonemes in English.

Developing grammatical competence involves learning which sounds in a language make a difference in meaning, and being able to distinguish and produce their sounds. Phonology does get more complicated. Phonemes change in different contexts. For example, the /t/ sound in *cotton* is different from the /t/ sound in *letter*. These variations are called allophones, and competent speakers produce the right one in each word.

Sounds change in other ways as well. The plural ending in *cats* has an /s/ sound, and the plural in *dogs* has a /z/ sound. That's a rule that native speakers follow and that English learners must acquire. It's not a rule that someone can state (unless that person studies linguistics). It's a rule that a person with grammatical competence can use.

Morphology is our knowledge of the structure of words. It involves knowing how to put words together. English morphology is fairly simple compared with that of other languages. English relies more on the order of the words (the syntax) than on prefixes and suffixes.

In English we use certain kinds of word endings to show changes in tense or number. These are called inflectional suffixes. For example, we use "-ed" to show past tense and "-s" to show plural. Having grammatical competence involves being able to recognize and use these suffixes.

Both prefixes and suffixes can be added to base words in English to create new words. This is referred to as derivational morphology. For example, we can add "-er" to many verbs to create nouns. We add "-er" to *teach* to make *teacher*. We know that the meaning of *teacher* is related to the root word *teach*. Adding "-er" adds the meaning of "one who," so a *teacher* is one who teaches. In the same way, we can put the prefix "un-" in front of an adjective to create a word with the opposite meaning. Someone who is "unhappy" is "not" happy. Grammatical competence includes knowledge of derivational morphology, both the meanings of the new words, like *teacher*, and the knowledge of which prefixes and suffixes to use. We say "un-" before "happy" but "dis-" before "content."

Syntax is the area most linguists working in English have focused on, since English relies heavily on the order of words to convey meanings. We know that there is a big difference between "The man chased the dog" and "The dog chased the man." This difference in meaning depends on the order of the words.

Having grammatical competence involves knowing how to put words in the right sequence. It also includes knowing what words must go in a sentence. For example, if a sentence begins with "He put," we know that the sentence must include an object, "He put the pen," and a location, "He put the pen on the table." In this respect, syntax is tied to particular words, and for that reason, some linguists refer to the "lexico-syntax." When we acquire a language we acquire knowledge of how certain words go together.

Another aspect of syntax involves knowing that certain kinds of sentences are related to one another. For example, statements and questions are related. The statement "Today is Wednesday" is connected to the question "Is today Wednesday?"

Competent speakers of a language can form different kinds of questions related to statements in this way.

Semantics is a fourth aspect of grammatical competence. Semantics has to do with word meanings. If we know English, we know that *dog* refers to a particular kind of animal, and *cat* refers to a different kind of animal. Meanings can be complex. Both *dog* and *cat* can have secondary meanings. You can *dog* it at work, and someone can be *catty*.

Semantics also has to do with the knowledge of words that commonly go together. Words like *dog* and *cat* are usually associated with other words referring to animals. Words like *boat* might be connected with *water* or *lake*. We organize concepts into categories and use different terms to refer to more general or more specific ideas within the categories. *Cook* is a general term, and *bake* or *roast* are more specific. The three words are in the same semantic field. Grammatical competence involves a knowledge of how such fields are organized.

Semantics can also refer to how one word links to another. A word like *boy* refers to a person in the world. A word like *he* refers to some other word we have mentioned or referred to. Knowledge of semantics includes the ability to distinguish between content words like *boy* and grammatical function words like *he* and to understand the role each one plays in giving and getting information.

This is a very brief overview of some of the aspects of grammatical competence. We simply want to give you some idea of the kinds of knowledge speakers acquire as they acquire a language. In order to get and give basic information, speakers need phonological, morphological, syntactic, and semantic knowledge. That's what we all acquired as we picked up our native language, and it's what English learners need to develop as they acquire English. Grammatical competence allows us to talk about the world, but we need more than grammatical competence to function effectively in a new language. We also need communicative competence.

Communicative Competence   *Speaking*

A second kind of competence that language learners need to function in a new language and culture is communicative competence. As Hymes explains, "The ability to speak competently not only involves knowing the grammar of a language, but also knowing what to say to whom, when, and in what circumstances" (quoted in Scarcell and Oxford 1992, 68). Learning a language, then, involves more than developing grammatical competence. Learners must also develop the knowledge of how to use the language appropriately in different social situations. Hymes puts it very well when he says that we need to know *what* to say to *whom*, *when*, and *in what circumstances*. The norms for communicative competence vary from one linguistic and social group to another, and part of what we acquire when we acquire a language is the ability to function effectively in different social groups.

We became more aware of the importance of helping students develop communicative competence while living in Venezuela. Both of us speak Spanish well enough to communicate (we have grammatical competence), but at times we found ourselves lacking in communicative competence. For example, in Mérida there is a very popular bakery where many people go to get fresh breads, rolls, and pastries. At certain times of the day, the long counter of the bakery is crowded with people two or three rows deep. We found ourselves avoiding these busy times because we had trouble getting the attention of the clerks. The orderly rules for taking turns that applied in the United States didn't apply at the bakery.

On one occasion Yvonne waited helplessly for twenty minutes as people came, called out their orders to the clerks, and left with their purchases. Finally, a man noticed how long she had been standing there, and he called to the clerk to help the señora. Yvonne knew what words to use, she could understand the Spanish, but she simply could not call out her order aggressively as had all the Venezuelans who preceded her. She lacked the communicative competence needed to buy bread in that situation.

Communicative competence is the ability to say the right thing in a certain social situation. This is hard enough in one's first language, and developing communicative competence in a second language is even more difficult. A professor friend of ours from Venezuela came to study with us in California. We took trips with her along the coast and to Yosemite with the dean of our graduate school and his wife. Our Venezuelan friend was very impressed with the views and continually exclaimed, "Oh, my God! That's so beautiful!" In Spanish, "Dios mío" (My God) is a very common expression that carries little emotional impact so she thought nothing of the direct translation. However, coming from this sophisticated professor in that company, the words sounded completely inappropriate because in English the expression is much stronger. In other settings with other people, there would be nothing unusual about her words. One of the problems for second language learners, especially for adults, is that teachers will seldom explain sociolinguistic gaffes. However, students benefit when teachers help them develop both grammatical and communicative competence.

A second example from Spanish is the word *epa*. In Venezuela, that expression is used to get someone's attention. However, one must be careful not to use the word in certain social situations. It's fine, for example, for college students to use it to get a friend's attention around campus, but if a female in a nice restaurant used the expression to call a waiter, it would be considered very rude. Of course, there are hundreds of examples like this in every language, and as educators working with English language learners, we should be sensitive to our students when they know the words but use them inappropriately.

Even commonplace practices such as issuing and receiving invitations vary from one culture to another, so grammatical competence isn't all one needs to communicate effectively. After one month in Venezuela, we were feeling a bit hurt because we had not received any social invitations to homes, despite the fact that people were friendly at work. Several people had mentioned to us that we should stop by sometime, but we waited for a specific invitation. Luckily, we had a talk with a sociolinguist who was also new to Mérida. She also felt isolated so decided to explore with her students how *la visita* (the social visit) was done in this town. The students explained that it is the obligation of the newcomer to visit first and that what we considered a casual comment had really been a definite invitation. She also discovered that if we, in turn, wanted people to visit us, we would need to specifically say, "Come by sometime and see where we live." That way people would feel free to visit us as newcomers. We needed to look at invitations in a new way to understand the social environment in which we lived.

Widdowson (1978) points out, "The learning of a language, then, involves acquiring the ability to compose correct sentences. That is one aspect of the matter. But it also involves acquiring an understanding of which sentences, or parts of sentences, are appropriate in a particular context" (3). Widdowson refers to the knowledge of how to compose correct utterances as "usage," and understanding how to use those expressions correctly in various social contexts as "use." This distinction between usage and use is similar to the distinction between grammatical and communicative competence.

Johnson (1995) points out that one specific social context in which our students need to function is the classroom. Classrooms have very clear (if typically unstated) rules that govern topics for conversation and writing and roles for participants in communicative exchanges. What students need, according to Johnson, is classroom communicative competence, which she defines as "the knowledge and competencies that second language students need in order to participate in, learn from, and acquire a second language in the classroom" (160). Teachers can help students acquire a new language by making the rules for classroom interactions explicit. To help students acquire a language, we also need to help them learn how speakers of that language interact in different social settings.

Students also need to learn the rules for communication in settings beyond the classroom. Teachers can help prepare their students to communicate in these different settings. For example, when teaching adult ESL, Yvonne and her teaching partner, Jean, helped students develop language for the situations they would encounter every day. The teachers and students role-played buying groceries at the supermarket, going to the doctor, applying for jobs, and communicating in parent-teacher conferences. This role-playing created a social context for language use, and the students developed the communicative competence they needed to function in these different settings.

Communicative competence also involves learning how to enter a conversation or to end one. In our native language, we seem to know instinctively the rules for contributing to an ongoing discussion. However, English language learners often have trouble knowing when to add to a conversation. They may jump in at what seems to be an inappropriate time, or they may remain silent.

We have often entertained international students who have advanced levels of English. They do quite well in conversation during dinner at our house. But when it comes time to say good-bye, things often become awkward. Students do not want to seem impolite, so they stand at the door and prolong the departure, trying to find the right way to leave without offending the host. They have acquired a great deal of English, but they haven't fully developed this aspect of their communicative competence.

Both grammatical and communicative competence apply to writing as well as to speech. Students need to learn the correct forms for producing connected written language just as they need to learn how to produce connected spoken discourse. The rules for writing, like the rules for speech, vary from one context to another. The rules for writing e-mail messages differ from those for writing memos. And memos are very different from formal academic papers.

The rules for writing vary within a language, depending on the kind of writing, and they also differ across languages. Kaplan (1966) argues that formal writing in English follows a direct pattern with few deviations. Writers state their main points in the introduction and then present each point in sequence. In contrast, formal writing in Romance languages often includes a deviation away from the straight-line organizational style of English. A business letter in Spanish should include questions about one's health and family and should not move too quickly to the main point, since that would be perceived as abrupt and rude. Writers from the Mideast often use parallel structures. In fact, ESL writing instructors in English often complain that their students from the Mideast say everything twice. And writers from parts of Asia often adopt a very indirect style. Rather than just coming out and "saying it" as English requires, a Chinese student writing in English might seem to be approaching an idea from different angles without ever really saying directly what he means. Apparently, in Chinese it would be insulting to say things too directly because that would imply that readers couldn't figure things out for themselves.

Of course, Kaplan is making generalizations here, and within any language or culture group there is variety in writing, just as there is in English. A number of scholars have questioned Kaplan's findings (see Wong 1992). However, it is good for teachers to be aware that even when students seem to have developed high levels of both oral and written English, they may still use a style of speaking or writing that reflects the norms of their first language and are not appropriate for the language they are learning. These students have not yet developed full communicative competence in English.

Competence and Learner Strategies

In the process of developing grammatical and communicative competence, effective language learners also develop a number of strategies that allow them to comprehend and produce language even when they lack the words, the structures, or the knowledge of appropriate social use. Strategies help students process both written and oral language. As students read, for example, they may come to a word they don't know. Strategic readers use context to try to determine word meanings. They may read on to see if additional information might help them comprehend the text. They might go back and reread to pick up additional cues. These strategies are appropriate for both native English speakers and English language learners.

English learners also need strategies that enable them to participate in conversations. Part of what we acquire when we acquire a language is the ability to communicate even when we lack linguistic resources. Teachers can help English learners acquire English by making them aware of these strategies and encouraging their use. As long as English learners are active participants in conversational interactions, they will continue to acquire grammatical and communicative competence.

The most natural response when we don't know how to say something is to use nonverbal strategies. We play a kind of charades, hoping that our actions will lead the listener to produce the desired word. We indicate *big* by spreading our hands apart and *small* by holding them close together. Nonverbal cues can include facial expressions, gestures, or movements. Good second language teachers often use these same kinds of cues to help make the target language more comprehensible, and English learners will often mimic the gestures when they can't remember a word.

An English teacher in China reported that she always carried pen and paper with her so she could draw to express her meaning. She also found an effective strategy for ordering food: "In restaurants you could go around to other tables and point at the food you liked to order. We found out this was a good thing to do, as people took this as a compliment that you wanted to eat what they were eating."

A person acquiring a second language can also use different verbal strategies to express meanings. Most often, the strategies are used when the learner lacks a particular word. Figure 4–1 lists a number of these strategies.

One strategy language learners use is to make up a word to describe something in hopes that the person they are talking to will supply the target-language word. Wells and Chang-Wells (1992) recorded a conversation in which Marilda employs this strategy by coining the word *windfinder* for "weather vane." A teacher we work with reported that one of her students asked if she could use the "pencil fixer." The teacher realized her English learner needed to use the pencil sharpener.

Strategy

1. Coins a word
2. Uses a paraphrase
3. Uses a cognate
4. Uses literal translation
5. Overgeneralizes
6. Asks for the word
7. Uses an L1 structure
8. Avoids a word, structure, or topic
9. Engages in conversations and activities

FIGURE 4–1   *Communication Strategies*

To understand language

65

Language learners may also paraphrase, using a word or phrase that they hope is equivalent to the word they lack. Marilda, for example, could have referred to the weather vane as "the thing that helps us see which way the wind is blowing" rather than coining the term *windfinder*. While in Venezuela, Yvonne often found herself paraphrasing when talking to the maid about different kitchen objects and foods. When looking for the missing spatula, she asked for "the white thing that has rubber on the end to clean out the bowl," and when describing a fruit drink as opposed to pure juice, she asked for "the juice that you add water and sugar to."

When Chirsta, a student teacher, interviewed Moua for her case study, the Hmong student explained that his dad "puts in wind makers . . . cold wind makers" for a living. After a bit of probing, Christa figured out that Moua's father installs air conditioners. By using paraphrase, Moua was able to get his message across. Another teacher wrote about how her student used paraphrase. A small group of students was reading a book about what some children gave their mother for her birthday. The text did not name the gift, but the last page contained a colorful picture of a flower vase. One of the boys in the reading group asked, "What is that thing that you use to put flowers into?" This paraphrase allowed the teacher to help him find the word he wanted.

If a person is studying a language related to his or her native language, a good strategy is to use cognates. English and Spanish, for example, have many words in common derived from Latin roots. For example, the Spanish noun *parque* is a cognate for *park* in English. When an English speaker can't think of a Spanish word, he or she can often substitute the English equivalent. A variation on this strategy is to use a word from the speaker's native language but add a target-language ending. For example, an English speaker learning Spanish might claim that someone was "pushe-ando" her. She uses the English word that she knows, *push*, and adds the common Spanish ending equivalent to the English "-ing" form to express *pushing*. We know of one student who lost her wallet in Spain. Another American tried to help by asking some Spanish-speaking friends if they had seen Kim's *walleto*. She put an appropriate suffix on what she hoped was a Spanish word.

When students know more than two languages, they may extend their use of cognates by choosing a word from a second language to use when communicating in a third language. Belinda, who is a native English speaker, reports that she often used Italian words when she tried to communicate in Spanish.

Using cognates is a good strategy, but sometimes, a language learner assumes that words are cognates when they are not. ESL student teachers we worked with in Venezuela would ask, "Did you use a sweater when you went to the mountains?" They assumed that the Spanish word *usar* meaning "to wear" was the same as the English word *use*. Relying on cognates is a good strategy, but false cognates like this one can trip students up.

In the same way, students may think that idioms are equivalent across languages and translate the native language idiom directly into the target language. This can result in expressions that target-language speakers find humorous. For example, in

English a shady deal is said to be carried out "under the table," so an English speaker might translate that expression directly into Spanish. However, in Spanish the same idea is expressed as "under the water," and a translation of the English idiom would probably confuse a Spanish speaker.

A very common strategy that many second language learners use is to assume that the language they are learning is completely regular. They then overgeneralize a rule and apply it to a word that does not follow the pattern. This strategy is used by young children acquiring a first language as well as by second language learners. For example, English-speaking children at a certain stage will often use a past tense form like "goed" because they assume that all verbs form the past tense the same way. English learners use the same strategy. Moua used the word *becomed* as he talked with Christa. He also used *golds* for the plural of gold, overgeneralizing the rule for forming plurals.

A more direct strategy many students develop is to simply ask, "How do you say . . . ?" In fact, this is a handy phrase that most teachers give their students early in a language course. This strategy works very well in a language class in which the teacher is bilingual. It doesn't work as well in a setting in which the other people don't speak both languages. If a Spanish speaker asks, "How do you say *usar* in English?" I can only help if I can translate *usar* from Spanish to English. The other problem with using this strategy too much is that it interrupts the flow of conversation more than the other strategies we have described.

A strategy similar to using a cognate is to use a structure from the first language to express an idea in the target language. This strategy focuses on longer stretches of language rather than just words. For example, a Spanish speaker might say, "I have a book red," using the appropriate Spanish structure but with English words. This strategy works well when the two languages have the same syntax. Even in cases where the order of words is different, the listener can usually understand the sentence.

In addition to these specific strategies, learners can use more general strategies in the process of acquiring a second language. One strategy, avoidance, is not productive, while the other, engagement, is the mark of a successful acquirer.

When specific strategies fail, language learners may simply avoid using a word, structure, or topic. For example, they may avoid a topic because they don't feel competent to talk about it in the target language, or they may stop in the middle of an explanation or story because the linguistic demands are simply too great. Cohen and Olshtain (1993) describe examples of avoidance during an experiment in which second language speakers had to make requests in different social situations. For example, one student intended to form the sentence "I don't have any excuse," but stopped before the last word because, as he reported, he wasn't sure how to pronounce the *x* sound. In another case, a student wanted to explain her late arrival at a meeting by stating that the bus had not come, but she couldn't think of how to say that in English, so she changed her message to "I missed the bus." It is not always easy to tell if language learners are using avoidance. David recalls several times in

Venezuela when he thought about bringing up an idea in a conversation but then decided not to when he realized that he simply didn't have the vocabulary he needed to explain his ideas.

Avoidance is different from the other strategies we have described. All the others allow a language learner to participate in a conversation or complete a written assignment. Avoidance removes the learner from the communicative event. Teachers can help students develop productive strategies so that they don't avoid using the target language to communicate. However, teachers should be aware of students' level of language proficiency and plan activities in which the students can use their new language successfully. Further, teachers should not force beginning students to produce too much language too early, since students may become frustrated if they are asked to produce at levels beyond their current competence.

Rather than avoidance, successful language learners practice engagement. They find ways to interact with speakers of the target language. Belinda, for example, was able to enter into conversations in Arabic by relying heavily on a few all-purpose phrases, accompanied by appropriate intonation. She depended on the words for *yes*, *okay*, *thank God*, and *If God wills it*. These words and phrases allowed Belinda to participate in a conversation. It is this conversational interaction that results in acquisition. García (1999) reports on research by Wong-Filmore and Valadez, who found that children who were the best language learners used three general strategies:

1. They joined groups and acted as if they knew what was going on. Even when the children didn't fully understand what the group was doing, they joined in and were included in the conversations and activities.
2. They used a few words to give the impression that they could speak the language. Even with limited linguistic resources, the children were able to say enough to become part of a small group. They needed to produce some language to be accepted, and they found ways to do this.
3. They found friends who would assist them. The best language learners paired up with a more proficient speaker who could help them understand what was going on.

By using these three general strategies, good language learners were more fully involved in the activities of the class, and in the process, they acquired the language of instruction.

Conclusion

In this chapter we have considered what people acquire when they acquire a language. We began by distinguishing between competence and performance. Competence is our underlying ability—what we can do under the best circumstances. Performance is what we actually do. Teachers recognize that students' performance may not reflect their competence. If students are nervous or simply unfamiliar with classroom routines, they may not perform up to their competence.

Competence should not be confused with correctness. Native speakers of a language can produce and comprehend the language, but they may not know all the rules of formal written usage. When we say that someone acquires competence in English, we are not claiming that the person can punctuate sentences correctly. Instead, competence is the ability to understand native speakers of a language and to express ideas in the language.

We described three functions of language and two kinds of competence. When we acquire a language, we acquire the ability to get and give basic information (the referential function), show how we feel about what we are saying (the expressive function), and indicate how we feel about the people with whom we are communicating (the integrative function). To perform these three functions of language, we need both grammatical and communicative competence. Grammatical competence allows us to put together words and sentences to talk about the world. With grammatical competence, we can carry out the referential function of language. Communicative competence is the knowledge of how to use language in social situations. It is knowing when to say what to whom. We need communicative competence to carry out the expressive and integrative functions of language.

In the process of acquiring a language, learners develop strategies to compensate for their lack of linguistic and communicative competence. We described several strategies learners use, such as paraphrase and literal translation. These strategies help students communicate even when their competence is limited. One strategy that may impede language acquisition is avoidance. Students may not try to use the new language if they are asked to talk about certain topics before they have the vocabulary and structures they need to carry out this task successfully.

What do we acquire when we acquire a language? We acquire grammatical and communicative competence along with strategies that allow us to carry out the referential, expressive, and integrative functions of language. Now that we have addressed the question of what we acquire, we are ready to turn to the other important questions: "How do people acquire languages?" and "What can teachers do to help students acquire language?" These are the questions we explore in the following chapters.

Applications

1. Early in this chapter we talked about the difference between performance and competence, and gave a couple of examples. Can you think of some examples in your own learning or in the learning of students you work with where performance did not reflect competence? Discuss this with a small group.

2. Grammatical competence is not the same as grammatical correctness. Explain the difference to a classmate.

3. Communicative competence includes the ability to use language that is appropriate for the social situation. Have you been in any situations where you used a second language in ways that you later discovered were not appropriate? Share these with classmates.

4. Second language learners develop a number of strategies like paraphrase, translation, and avoidance. Think back on your own learning of a second language. Did you use any of these strategies? Have you noticed your students using them? List some examples to share.

5

What Are the Principal Theories of Second Language Acquisition?

We have looked generally at how learning takes place, and we have also considered what people acquire when they acquire a language. In this chapter we turn to the important question, "How do people acquire a second language?" To answer this question we will examine in detail the principal theories of second language acquisition. A knowledge of these theories enables teachers to make informed decisions about how best to teach second language learners.

Theories of SLA are based on research from different fields. We begin this chapter with a brief overview of the types of research that have informed current theories.

SLA Research: Psycholinguistic, Sociolinguistic, Neurolinguistic

Research in second language acquisition has been carried out from different perspectives. Researchers from the different areas ask different questions and use different methods to investigate how people learn a second language.

Psycholinguists look for insights into SLA from both linguistics and psychology. They examine the system of language the learner is developing. This system is referred to as the learner's interlanguage. An interlanguage is the version of English an English language learner speaks. It is different from the English of a native speaker, and yet it is a regular language with rules and a logic of its own.

The kind of english the student speaks!

Psycholinguists use evidence from errors to determine learners' strategies as their interlanguage develops. For example, if someone produces a form like "goed," the strategy is overgeneralization. The learner is applying the past tense rule to an irregular verb.

Seliger (1988) identifies three major questions psycholinguists ask about SLA:

1. How does the learner develop his or her second language system? What are thought to be the processes involved?
2. What role does previous knowledge, such as the first language, play in second language acquisition?
3. What psychological characteristics contribute to successful second language acquisition? Are there good learners and bad learners? (20)

Teachers can easily see that the answers to these questions have important implications for the teaching of English learners.

Neurolinguists are concerned with how language is represented in the brain. Advances in technology have increased our understanding of how the brain processes language. Neurolinguistic research is a relatively new field, and the findings of neurolinguists are only beginning to be applied to language teaching. These are some of the questions that neurolinguists are attempting to answer:

1. Where in the brain are first and second languages located?
2. What are the ways that languages with different characteristics are represented in the brain?
3. Is there a critical period for second language acquisition?

Sociolinguists consider the influences of social and cultural factors on language development. Beebe (1987) lists some of the major questions that sociolinguists attempt to answer:

1. Is interlanguage variation systematic or random and, if systematic, according to what social variables does it vary?
2. Does the learner's interlanguage change over time?
3. What is the role of sociolinguistic transfer in L2 development?
4. What is the nature of L2 communicative competence?
5. What is the "cause" of variation in interlanguage? (3–4)

All three areas of research, psycholinguistics, neurolinguistics, and sociolinguistics, have contributed to the development of current SLA theories.

Theoretical and Applied Research

Research in SLA can be either theoretical or applied. Examples of theoretical research would be a study of the natural order of acquisition of morphemes or a study of the relationship between intelligence and language aptitude. A theoretical researcher, for example, might develop a theory that the effects of reading in the second language will be reflected in students' second language writing. The researcher might then look at the writing of second language learners for evidence of the effects of reading. As Krashen (1985) observes, "Purely theoretical research does not have a direct impact on the second language classroom but adds to our knowledge of how second languages are acquired" (46).

In contrast, applied research, according to Krashen, "attempts to answer practical problems directly without recourse to theory" (47). An example of applied research would be a study that compares two methods of language teaching to see which method results in higher levels of language proficiency. For example, a researcher could have students read and write, setting up different ways of organizing these activities. Some students would read, discuss, and write. Others would read and then write with no discussion. By looking at the student writing from the two groups, the researcher could determine if the discussion improved the quality of the writing, thus giving teachers some specific ideas to help students in their second language writing. This sort of research could be done without reference to any particular theory of learning.

Krashen suggests that both theoretical and applied research form the basis for SLA theory. A theory of second language acquisition must fit the findings of theoretical research, but "a valid theory must also be consistent with the results of applied research" (47). In other words, both kinds of research are necessary in the formation of SLA theories. Further, "methodology in second language teaching is related to second language theory, not directly to research" (47).

Attempts to apply research directly have not been productive. In his own research into the acquisition of morphemes by second language students, Krashen found that certain morphemes were acquired earlier than others. For example, the third-person singular *s* of regular present verbs (as in "he runs") is a morpheme that takes longer for English learners to acquire than the plural *s* (as in *books*). Krashen maintains that research findings such as these cannot be directly applied to practice. As he himself says, "I made this error several years ago when I suggested that the natural order of acquisition become the new grammatical syllabus" (47). He realized that he could not use the research to design a grammar textbook. Instead, the research helped him develop a theory of SLA that downplays the direct teaching of grammar.

Krashen believes that SLA theory acts to mediate between research and practice. Teachers can benefit from the knowledge they gain in their daily practice. However, they must always consider theory as they reflect on their practice. As Krashen asserts, "Methodologists are missing a rich source of information . . . if they neglect theory," (48) and "without theory, there is no way to distinguish effective teaching procedures from ritual, no way to determine which aspects of a method are and are not helpful" (52). A knowledge of SLA theory, then, allows a teacher to reflect on and to refine day-to-day practice. With that view in mind, we describe two important theories of second language acquisition.

⟨K Schumann's Acculturation Model

One important theory of SLA comes from the theoretical, sociolinguistic research of Schumann (1978), who claims that acquiring a new language is part of a more general process of acculturation. For Schumann, language acquisition can best be understood by looking at what happens when people from one cultural group are transplanted into a new setting.

The Hmong people provide a good example of how acquiring a new language is part of a more general process of acculturation. The Hmong who came to the United States from Southeast Asia moved not only across a great physical distance but across time. Many of the Hmong people who moved to our area in the Central Valley of California chose to settle there because a Hmong leader told them that in Fresno there was lots of farming. In Laos, where they were part of a nomadic, agrarian society, they used only hand tools. They practiced slash-and-burn agriculture. Hmong farmers who moved to California had to learn new words and new concepts. In California, they were confronted with the idea of land ownership. In addition, the farming in a highly technological society like the United States was very different. Here, farmers used scientific research as well as a variety of machines and chemicals to help them produce their crops. As a result the Hmong newcomers have had to rethink the whole idea of farming. For the Hmong, acquiring English is just one aspect of adapting to a new culture.

In his model, Schumann focuses on sociocultural factors that act on the language learner. He bases his theory on studies of individuals acquiring a second language. He does not discuss any internal cognitive processing that might take place. Much of the theory can be understood by examining Schumann's analysis of one learner, Alberto.

Alberto, an adult from Costa Rica, acquired English without formal instruction. Alberto's English proficiency was much lower than might be expected, and it improved little over the ten months Schumann studied him. Even though he was intelligent and interacted regularly with native speakers of English, Alberto's own English remained limited. Schumann's analysis was that Alberto's social and psychological distance from speakers of the target language accounted for his lack of proficiency. As Brown (1980) explains, "Schumann's hypothesis is that the greater the social distance between two cultures, the greater the difficulty the learner will have in learning the second language, and conversely, the smaller the social distance (the greater the social solidarity between the two cultures), the better will be the language learning situation" (133).

According to Schumann, eight factors influence social distance:

1. *Social dominance.* Social dominance refers to the power relationships between two groups. Social distance is greatest when one group dominates the other. Social distance diminishes if the two groups have roughly equal power in society.

74

2. *Integration pattern*. Social distance is greatest when there is a pattern of limited integration between the two cultures, and it decreases when there is greater integration.

3. *Enclosure*. Social distance is increased when the learner group is self-sufficient and doesn't need to interact with members of the target culture in daily activities. Social distance decreases when enclosure is lower.

4. *Cohesiveness*. Social distance is increased when the learner group is tight-knit, and social distance is reduced when the learner group is less tied together.

5. *Size*. When the learner group is big, there is more apt to be social distance from the target culture. A small learner group is less distant.

6. *Cultural congruence*. Social distance is increased when the two groups are very different culturally, and the distance decreases when the two groups are more similar.

7. *Attitude*. Social distance is increased when the learner group has a negative attitude toward members of the target-language culture, and it is decreased when the attitude is positive.

8. *Intended length of residence*. Social distance is greatest when the learner only intends to stay in the country a short time. Social distance decreases when the learner intends to stay in the country for a long time.

In almost every case, Alberto fell into a category that predicted limited acquisition. For example, in the area of social dominance, Alberto, who worked in a factory, was in a subordinate social group to those English speakers with whom he was in contact. This social distance limited the integration pattern. Factory workers did not interact regularly with those who managed the factory. Alberto's group had what Schumann refers to as high enclosure. They had their own churches and publications, including newspapers, and this kept them apart from the mainstream culture. He was part of a fairly large, cohesive group of Latin American immigrants, and this limited his contact with English speakers as well. His culture differed from that of the target culture, and attitudes between the groups were either neutral or negative. In addition, Alberto intended to stay in the United States only a short time, so he had little interest in becoming proficient in English.

In addition to social distance, which describes relationships among social groups, Schumann identifies a second factor that can be used to predict the degree of language acquisition: psychological distance. In situations in which social distance neither strongly promotes nor inhibits language acquisition, psychological distance may play a crucial role. There are three main factors that determine the psychological distance a second language learner has from the target language and culture.

1. *Motivation*. Those with a high motivation to learn the language are more likely to learn the language than those with low motivation.

2. *Attitude*. Those with a positive attitude toward the language and culture are more likely to learn the language than those who hold a negative attitude.

3. *Culture shock*. When a newcomer experiences culture shock, it is more difficult to learn the new language.

An important component of psychological distance is a student's attitude toward members of the cultural group whose language he or she is learning. García (1999) reports on two studies that show the importance of attitude. In one, Gardner and Lambert found that the positive attitude of English-speaking Canadians toward French-speaking Canadians increased their motivation to learn French. In another, Ramírez found that Chinese, Japanese, and Chicano students who had a positive attitude toward English speakers developed high levels of English proficiency. Schumann's theory suggests that a positive attitude toward members of the target-language group decreases the psychological distance between the learner and the group whose language he or she is learning.

When Yvonne was doing her intern teaching, she was given two classes of high school sophomores in her Spanish 1 classes. Over two-thirds of the students were boys on the junior varsity football team. They had signed up for the intern teacher because they had failed Spanish 1 the year before with an older, strict, and very traditional teacher. Needless to say, Yvonne had students with low motivation (they preferred football to Spanish), and their attitudes toward learning Spanish were negative (they didn't really want to learn Spanish, and besides, last year's teacher proved to them that they couldn't learn it).

When we first moved to Colombia, David didn't speak any Spanish. We lived with a Colombian family who did not speak English. David found living in a new country very challenging, and it was difficult to be the only person who could not communicate. Everything was different from what he was used to and he soon found trying to learn a new language and adjust to the new culture overwhelming. For a period, he did not even try to learn Spanish. He was suffering from culture shock.

It might be helpful to look at several examples of language learners who reflect the kinds of social and psychological distance Schumann has identified. Amy, for example, a language learner with a positive attitude, was the subject of a case study carried out by Kim, a graduate student. Amy went to Costa Rica to work with a local church. She wanted to be of service in the country she visited, and she wanted to learn Spanish for use with Spanish-speaking friends in California. During her time in Costa Rica she was in contact with only one other American. She participated with church members and lived with a Costa Rican family. Several factors decreased the social and psychological distance for Amy. She was part of a very small group and her living and work situation resulted in constant integration with members of the target-language culture. Enclosure was low and social dominance was not a factor, since Amy was a volunteer worker. Although there were cultural differences, the two cultures were somewhat congruent. In addition, Amy had a very positive attitude toward Spanish speakers and high motivation to communicate. All of these factors help account for her gains in Spanish proficiency.

Moua, a sixth-grade Hmong student who has struggled in school, was the case study student of Chirsta, another graduate student. Several factors have contributed to Moua's school performance. One of these is the social distance he has experienced. He is part of a subordinate social group. The Hmong immigrants in California have generally worked in low-income jobs. He is part of a large, cohesive community. There are stores that specialize in Southeast Asian food, and there are Hmong radio and TV stations, so the enclosure is high. Moua is the second oldest of seven children, and there is a large extended family. Nearly all his friends are Hmong. As a result, there is little integration with members of the mainstream culture. Even in school, there are many other Hmong students. The Hmong culture is not at all congruent with mainstream U.S. culture. All these factors contribute to increased social distance. On the other hand, Moua has a positive attitude toward English speakers, and his family plans to remain in the United States permanently, so his motivation to learn is high.

Another good example of a student who experiences great social distance from the community of English speakers is Nafa, a Lahu girl. Janie had Nafa as a student, bonded with her, and became close to her family. Janie tells Nafa's story. The Lahu come from Laos, where they form a minority group that lives in the mountains. Nafa lives in a small farming community in California. Many other Lahu families have moved to this area. They represent a high enclosure group, a cohesive community with a pattern of limited integration with the mainstream culture. Like Moua, Nafa is part of a large family, and most of her social activities are with extended family members. Nafa's parents work in low-paying jobs, as do many of the other Lahu. As a result, the Lahu are in a socially subordinate position. All these factors contribute to social distance and inhibit language acquisition.

Song provides a rather extreme example of social distance. He is a Chinese speaker whose family moved from Hong Kong to Venezuela when he was a first grader. Song's family wanted him to learn English and sent him to an American international school. He entered first grade with very limited English and is still struggling with academic English in second grade. This may be, in part, because of his social distance from English speakers.

Song's family speaks Chinese at home. They live within a Chinese-speaking community and socialize with other Chinese families. There are several supermarkets, stores, and restaurants in the city that are Chinese-owned and operated, so the cohesive group has high enclosure and limited integration with the Spanish-speaking community. Song is driven to school by a Spanish-speaking driver and is often left at home with a Spanish-speaking maid. Song's mother does not speak English, and his parents are seldom home to help with homework.

In this setting, Song has little exposure to English or contact with English speakers outside school. Spanish is the language of the wider community, and access to English language and culture is very limited. This is often the case for students in

limited communication in practice L2

English as a foreign language settings. It is not surprising that even in very good American schools, students like Song struggle to learn English. There is considerable social and psychological distance between their primary culture and English.

Matt and Francesca, two members of an adult ESL class, represent both extremes of Schumann's hypothesis. Matt emigrated to the United States from Yugoslavia as a boy. His parents came to live in a coastal village in northern California. Matt became a fisherman like his father, married, and had a family. Though he maintained his native language, he was surrounded by English speakers and participated in social events in the fishing community. After he retired, his wife died and his children moved away. He was lonely, so he arranged to marry a woman from Yugoslavia who wanted to come to the United States.

When the couple began attending adult ESL classes, Matt was nearly eighty years old and his wife, Francesca, was seventy-two. They had been married for five years. Matt spoke perfect English, but he felt Francesca needed to learn some English so that she could function effectively in the community. Francesca was a strong and demanding woman who was constantly frustrated by her new country and culture. She experienced severe culture shock. She liked to cook and sew but did not like to do things outside of the home unless it was to attend church or visit the few other women in the community who could speak her language. The couple came to class almost daily, but Francesca resisted even listening most of the time, unless the class discussions centered around shopping, cooking, or gardening. Finally, the couple stopped coming to class. Matt felt he was too old to insist, and Francesca decided she didn't need to learn any more English, since she was able to do her shopping and meet her basic needs. Among other factors, such as their different ages when they came to the United States, Matt and Francesca represent two extremes in social distance. Matt felt close to the mainstream culture and developed a high level of English proficiency. Francesca experienced greater social and psychological distance, and one result was that her proficiency in English remained limited.

Schumann claims that for a learner to acquire full proficiency in a second language, he or she must be acculturated, because SLA is just one aspect of the larger process of acculturation. A learner who is socially distant from members of the target-language group might develop only limited grammatical and communicative competence in the target language.

It is important to note that acculturation is distinct from assimilation. A person can take on a new culture without giving up his or her primary culture. This is acculturation, and the result can be bilingualism and biculturalism. Some students are able to maintain their first language and culture and still learn English and succeed academically. Sharma, the Punjabi girl described in Chapter 1, for example, maintained her first language and many of her Indian customs and also adopted practices that allowed her to fit into mainstream American culture. Assimilation, on the other hand, involves losing one's primary culture and becoming "similar to" those of the target culture. Assimilation often results in loss of the native language and culture.

Schumann's theory has been attacked on several fronts. Larsen-Freeman and Long (1991) conclude their review of Schumann's theory by commenting that

> both group and individual social and psychological factors must surely have some role in a comprehensive theory of SLA, perhaps most obviously as variables conditioning the amount and type of target-language exposure the learner experiences. Equally clearly, on the other hand, it should come as no surprise if a mental process, (second language learning), is not successfully explicable by any theory which ignores linguistic and cognitive variables. (266)

Despite these limitations, Schumann's theory provides useful ideas about the effects of external factors on learning. Concepts such as social and psychological distance help us understand why certain people succeed or fail to learn a new language, but the help is limited because Schumann says so little about language and cognitive processing.

What are the implications of Schumann's theory for teachers? The acculturation model highlights the importance of social factors on acquisition. Teachers should create a classroom environment in which students can interact with and develop positive attitudes toward speakers of the target language. Acculturation does not require that students give up their primary language and culture. Models of education such as dual-language programs, where speakers of two languages learn in both, becoming bilingual and biliterate, fit well with Schumann's model. However, his theory has little to say about how teachers can plan instruction that would promote language acquisition. Perhaps for this reason, Schumann's model of SLA has not led to specific methods of second language teaching.

[handwritten margin note: acculturate - take on a new language without getting rid of 1st language]

Krashen's Monitor Model

A second important theory of second language acquisition is Krashen's monitor model. This theory is based on insights from psycholinguistics and neurolinguistics and draws on theoretical as well as applied research. While Schumann's acculturation model focuses on external social and cultural factors that affect language acquisition, Krashen's theory is based on internal psychological factors. It is considered a nativist theory. As Larsen-Freeman and Long state, "Nativist theories are those which purport to explain acquisition by positing an innate biological endowment that makes learning possible" (227).

Chomsky, Universal Grammar, and the Language Acquisition Device

Insights from the theoretical linguistic research of Noam Chomsky help form the basis for Krashen's theory. Starting in 1959 with the publication of *Syntactic Structures*, Chomsky has developed a linguistic theory that is widely accepted within the United States. Although this theory has been criticized for ignoring the social aspects of language development, it has revolutionized the field.

Chomsky - children are born with language
(Brain is wired)

Chomsky began with a basic question: How can we use a small number of rules to produce and comprehend an infinite number of utterances? The number of rules must be limited, because all native speakers of a language can acquire them in a fairly short time. The rules are subconscious. We cannot state how we put sentences together, but they are psychologically real—we are able to use them. Using these rules, speakers can generate a great number of sentences, most of which are not simply imitations but new expressions, never heard before.

Chomsky accounted for this ability by arguing that we need to look below the surface structure of spoken or written language. At that level, we may notice that two sentences that look quite different on the surface are simply two ways of expressing the same idea. For example, "The cat chased the mouse" and "The mouse was chased by the cat" are simply variations on a basic idea. At the same time, some sentences are ambiguous. One surface structure, such as "Visiting relatives can be boring," can have two underlying meanings (the people are boring or the act of visiting them is boring), or two "deep structures," in Chomsky's terms.

Chomsky developed a theory of linguistics that included a limited number of deep structures and a set of transformations. Speakers of a language learn the rules for producing the basic structures first, and then they learn how to generate the transformed sentences. For example, young children learning English generally produce active sentences such as "Bobbie broke the window" early on, and only later produce passives, such as "The window was broken by Bobbie."

Chomsky noted that young children acquire the basic rules of language without formal instruction and without extensive exposure to models of the language. Parents, for example, usually respond to the message, not to how children talk. Parents seldom try to correct the way young children pronounce words or put sentences together, and if they do try, it doesn't seem to have much effect. Parents know that fairly quickly children's language will become like the language of others in the speech community. If children can learn the rules of a language with such limited evidence and little correction, Chomsky reasoned, this must be because they are innately predisposed to do so. Other researchers have expanded on this notion. Pinker (1994) provides a particularly readable account. By only slightly exaggerating the point, he refers to the ability to acquire language as an instinct.

One important concept Chomsky has used to account for this ability to acquire language is universal grammar. Chomsky argues that all human languages have certain things in common. For example, all languages have pronouns. They all have ways to indicate number. All languages have something like a subject and a verb to show the actor and the action.

According to Chomsky, humans are born with an innate understanding of those aspects of language that are common to all languages. Children don't have to start from scratch to figure out how language works. Instead, their job is to learn the specific details of the language they are exposed to. To use an analogy, humans are hardwired for any human language, and what they need to do is to learn the software for the programs that people around them are running. Pinker points out that children's errors are usually overgeneralizations of rules. For example, children often use forms such as *goed*, trying to make irregular verbs follow the regular rule for past tense. On the other hand, there are some errors that children never make. For example, children learn to turn statements into questions, so "The boy is tall" becomes, "Is the boy tall." They make this question by moving *is* to the front of the sentence. Later, they learn to add relative clauses and produce sentences such as, "The boy who is next to me is tall." They can turn these sentences into questions as well: "Is the boy who is next to me tall?" However, studies of language acquisition record no instances of children creating questions like, "Is the boy who next to me is tall?" Children don't seem to consider this possibility even though it would seem logical to move the first *is* in the statement to the front rather than the second one to form the question. The fact that children don't make certain kinds of errors suggests that they are not considering all the possibilities language has to offer but are choosing among a limited set of options that are part of universal grammar.

To take one example, all languages have words that help show spatial relationships. In English, these words are prepositions. In a sentence like, "I put the keys on the table," the preposition *on* shows where the keys are in relation to the table. In English, words like *on* are called prepositions because they come before (*pre*) the word that tells the position. Other languages have postpositions, words that come after (*post*) to tell positions. In a language with postpositions, we would say something like "the table on" instead of "on the table." If humans are born with an innate knowledge that their language will have a word that tells position, their job is simply to find out whether the word will come before or after the word it refers to. There are just two possibilities, and by listening to their parents, children can decide which order to use, even with only a few examples.

All languages have pronouns, words that replace nouns or noun phrases. This makes communication more efficient. We can use a little word like *he* to replace a whole phrase such as "the man whose dog ran across my flowers yesterday." Pronouns are part of universal grammar. In some languages, the pronoun must always be present in the surface structure. In English we can't drop the *he* from the sentence (unless we use the noun phrase). But in other languages, the pronoun is indicated in other ways, such as the ending on the verb, so a speaker may drop the separate pronoun word. For example, in Spanish, "Yo hablo" and "Hablo" are alternative ways to express the same idea, "I talk." Spanish speakers can drop the *Yo* because the ending on the verb also indicates who is speaking. Since children are born with universal grammar, they know in a subconscious way that languages have pronouns. What they have to figure out is whether in the language they are acquiring the pronouns can be dropped or not. In Spanish they can, and in English they can't. That's a much easier job than figuring out what pronouns are and how they function. With just a few examples, a child can learn which way his or her language works.

Another concept that Chomsky has described is the Language Acquisition Device, or LAD. He argues that humans have a kind of mental organ or part of their brain that allows them to use the limited evidence they get from the language they hear to form rules. For example, children acquiring English quickly learn to produce the correct form of the plural. In *cats*, the plural *s* has an *s* sound, but in *dogs* the *s* sounds like a *z*. In a word like *bus*, the plural takes on an *iz* sound (remember that young children aren't relying on spelling here). In experiments, young children can give the correct plural form for a nonsense word. If one monster is a *wug* then two are *wugs* and the plural *s* is pronounced like a *z*. Children can't be imitating to produce this form, they must be using a kind of internal rule, and it is the LAD that helps them develop these rules quickly and without any overt correction. The LAD is a kind of biological development, and humans "grow" language in their minds almost in the same way as they "grow" an arm or a leg.

Chomsky's claims apply to children acquiring their first language. Krashen has developed a theory of second language acquisition that holds that concepts such as universal grammar and the LAD apply equally well to children or adults acquiring a second language. Krashen's (1982) theory of SLA, the Monitor Model, has had a great impact on classroom practice. Even though Krashen's ideas have been debated and sometimes discounted by other researchers, they have been widely accepted by practitioners because they are understandable and because teachers can see positive results when they apply Krashen's ideas in the classroom. Krashen's Monitor Model consists of five interrelated hypotheses. In the following sections, we explain the hypotheses and then provide real examples and an analysis of each.

The Acquisition-Learning Hypothesis

Krashen begins by making an important distinction between two ways of getting a new language. The first of these is acquisition. According to Krashen we acquire a new language subconsciously as we receive messages we understand. For example, if we are living in a foreign country and go to the store to buy food, we may acquire new vocabulary or syntactic structures in the process of trying to understand what the shopkeeper is saying. We are not focused on the language. Rather, we are using the language for real purposes, and acquisition occurs naturally as we attempt to conduct our business. Acquisition can also occur in classrooms in which teachers engage students in authentic communicative experiences. Krashen (1985) has shown that we can acquire language as we read. In fact, since people are able to read more rapidly than they speak, written language is a better source for acquisition than oral language.

Krashen contrasts acquisition with learning. Learning is a conscious process in which we focus on various aspects of the language itself. It is what generally occurs in classrooms when teachers divide language up into chunks, present one chunk at a time, and provide students with feedback to indicate how well they have mastered the various aspects of language that have been taught. A teacher might present a lesson on regular verbs in the present tense, for example, giving attention to the *s* that is added to third-person forms in sentences such as "He walks." It is this structure that students are expected to learn. Learning is associated with classroom instruction and is usually tested. It is less common in the world beyond the classroom.

A good example of the acquisition/learning distinction comes from the experiences of José Luis, Guillermo, and Patricia, who were profiled in Chapter 1. The teens studied English in El Salvador. This was a case of learning the rules and structures of the language. When they came to the United States, they did know some English, but it was very limited. In their new home in Tucson they were immersed in English and began to acquire the language as they used it daily.

Krashen argues that children acquire (they don't learn) their first language(s) as they use language to communicate and to make sense of the world. Krashen claims that both children and adults have the capacity to acquire language because they possess a Language Acquisition Device, first put forward by Chomsky. He claims that acquisition accounts for almost all of our language development and that learning plays a minimal role. Second language classrooms can be viewed as places for acquisition, but more often they are understood as arenas for learning.

When teaching second language learners, Yvonne was constantly struggling with the difference between acquisition and learning, though she had not studied Krashen's theory and did not even know about it until graduate school. She was worried that students needed to learn the grammar, because that is how she had been taught language. However, she saw that students were more involved and more successful when they talked and read about things that were related to their lives. Discussions of taxes, unemployment, nutrition, cultural conflicts, and television programs got students involved in using language, and they acquired language as they used it. Yet, the textbooks available for teaching all seemed to emphasize direct or indirect teaching of grammar and vocabulary. Yvonne had to depart from traditional approaches to change her classroom from a place for learning to a setting for acquisition.

Example of Acquisition/Learning—Fred

Fred Jones studied three years of German in high school and two more years in college. After college he joined the army and was sent to Germany. He found that he could read signs and some newspaper articles, but he had a great deal of trouble in trying to communicate with native Germans. After he was discharged, he went to work for a company that assigned him to head a branch located in in Mexico City. On arrival, he took a crash course in Spanish. At the same time, he had to try to communicate with his fellow workers, entertain important Mexican businessmen, and use Spanish for daily life transactions such as shopping. After only six months, Fred's spoken Spanish was much better than his German had ever been. What might account for this?

Analysis

Fred learned German in school, but this learned knowledge was not very helpful to him in Germany. On the other hand, he both learned and acquired Spanish in the course of his studies and his daily interactions in Mexico. As a result, his ability to understand and speak Spanish is much better than his German proficiency.

Acquisition/Learning—John

John studied four years of high school Spanish. Despite lots of drill and practice with dialogues and exercises with grammar, he could not really understand the Spanish of Hispanics in his community. In college he met María and fell in love. Her family, who felt that maintaining their native language was very important, spoke only Spanish at home. John found that within a short period of time, he was able to understand the conversations at family get-togethers and even contribute at times in Spanish. What had accounted for his rapid increase in Spanish proficiency?

Analysis

This is another contrast between acquisition and learning. John had learned some Spanish in school, but with María and her family he was in an ideal situation for acquisition in a natural setting. Family discussions were on topics of interest to John, or the conversations were rich in context. For example, María and her mother would discuss a recipe while cooking, or John and his in-laws would watch a sports event on the Spanish television station. The Spanish input from María's family was comprehensible. As a result, his proficiency improved rapidly.

The Natural Order Hypothesis   *applies to acquire language*

Krashen's second hypothesis is that language is acquired in a natural order. Some aspects of a language are picked up earlier than others. For example, the plural *s* morpheme added to a word like *girl* to form *girls* comes earlier than the third-person *s* added to the word *walk* in "He walks." Most parents are aware that phonemes like /p/ or /m/ are acquired earlier than others, like /r/. That's why English-speaking parents are called *papa* or *mama* by babies, not *rara*. In the area of syntax, statements generally precede questions. Children do not acquire the structure of questions early, so they often use statement structures such as "I go store, too?" or "You like teddy?" to pose questions. Krashen points out that all learners of a particular language, such as English, seem to acquire the language in the same order no matter what their first language may be.

Krashen bases this hypothesis on studies carried out by Dulay and Burt (1974). These researchers collected samples of speech from Chinese- and Spanish-speaking students learning English. They found that both groups acquired English morphemes in about the same order. They found, for example, that students acquired the plural *s* form fairly early, but the third-person *s* of "He walks" came much later. These early studies were subsequently confirmed by the work of a number of other researchers.

The natural order applies to language that is acquired, not language that is learned. In fact, students may be asked to learn aspects of language before they are ready to acquire them. The result may be good performance of the items on a test but inability to use the same items in a natural setting. In these cases, students' performance may exceed their competence.

In teaching Spanish, Yvonne found that the expression for *like* in Spanish was a late-acquired item. In Spanish, "I like" is *Me gusta* (It is pleasing to me). If the things I like are plural, I say *Me gustan* (They are pleasing to me). This structure caused no end of confusion for Yvonne's beginning students. She worked with them diligently, explaining how the structure worked and giving examples. Even those who did well on the department test that covered the structure, however, had not acquired the structure. When Yvonne asked her students to evaluate the course in their daily diary at the end of the semester, almost all the students incorrectly wrote "Yo gusto" for "I like." They knew that *yo* meant *I* and knew the verb *gustar* was "to like." So they simply conjugated the verb as a regular verb despite the emphasis on learning the expression *Me gusta*.

Most books used in language courses present grammar in a certain order, but since linguists have only a rudimentary understanding of the complete order of acquisition of phonemes, morphemes, syntax, and so on, no book can be written that can claim to mirror the natural order. Even if such a book were written, students would invariably be at different stages, and in a class of thirty students, no grammar lesson would be appropriate for everyone. Krashen, however, points out that if a teacher focuses on acquisition activities, rather than trying to get students to learn certain grammatical points, all students will acquire language in a natural order. The rate of acquisition of morphemes and structures will differ for different students, but the order will be the same.

Example of Natural Order—Mrs. Gomez

Mrs. Gomez is a bilingual second-grade teacher. She does lots of reading and writing with her students in Spanish. During ESL time, she believes that students need large doses of drill and practice to master English. She teaches her students how to use the *-ing* form of the verb with the auxiliary form of *be*. So the students practice, "We are going to the library"; "I am going to the cafeteria." What she cannot understand is that when her students ask her questions or tell her things in English informally, they consistently leave the *be* auxiliary out of the constructions: "Teacher, we going to the park." "Look teacher, I swinging high!" What might be the reason for this?

Analysis

Several different factors are at work here. Mrs. Gomez seems to feel that while first languages are acquired, second languages must be learned. As a result, she drills her students on parts of the language during ESL time. Mrs. Gomez doesn't recognize the difference between learning and acquisition, and may not be aware of the natural order of acquisition. Natural order studies show that verbs with *-ing* (*going*) come in early, but the auxiliary verb comes later, so students first say "I going" and later add the *am*. She drills her students on the progressive forms, but since they haven't acquired the complete forms yet, they don't use them correctly in natural situations.

The Monitor Hypothesis   *difference*

The monitor hypothesis helps explain the different functions that acquisition and learning play. Acquisition results in the vocabulary and syntax we can draw on to produce utterances in a new language. Without acquisition, we could not produce anything. Learning, on the other hand, provides us with rules we can use to monitor our output as we speak or write. The monitor is like an editor, checking what we produce. The monitor can operate when we have time, when we focus on grammatical form, and when we know the rules.

Yvonne applied her monitor during her oral exams for her doctorate. Her committee of five had asked her several questions in English about language acquisition and language learning that she had answered fairly comfortably. Then, one of her committee members asked a question in Spanish, a clear suggestion that Yvonne should also answer in Spanish. Her most vivid memory of the incident was how much she was checking to be sure her Spanish was correct, how much she was applying her monitor. In particular, she was careful to watch for the correct use of the subjunctive mood, verb endings, and adjective agreement, all aspects of Spanish that she had learned rather than acquired. In this situation, Yvonne was focusing on form. She did not want members of her doctoral committee to judge her Spanish as substandard. It seemed especially important in this setting to speak "proper" Spanish. Of course, what she actually said was secondary and to this day she cannot even remember what the question was.

The problem with using the monitor during speaking is that one must sacrifice meaning for accuracy. A person can't concentrate on the form and the meaning at the same time. On the other hand, the monitor is useful in the editing stage of writing. At that point, a writer has time to think about correct form, and the focus on form, rather than meaning, is appropriate. In contrast, at the rough draft stage, writers who slow down and think about correct form may forget what they were going to write. Monitoring is helpful if the monitor is not over- or underused, but even then, the monitor can only check the output.

The teens from El Salvador differed in their use of the monitor. Guillermo in particular focused on communication. He seldom monitored his output and was at times difficult to understand. Nevertheless, he was enthusiastic and personable and used a number of strategies (gestures, tone of voice, and so on) to be sure his listener understood. Guillermo underused his monitor even though he had studied English grammar and knew many of the rules.

His brother, José Luis, on the other hand, was quiet and shy. He did not like to speak English unless he could produce language that was grammatically correct. He too knew the rules, and he applied them carefully. His focus on form kept him from expressing his ideas freely. He overused the monitor.

Patricia seemed less self-conscious than José Luis. She generally concentrated on what she wanted to say rather than how she would say it. At the same time, she did check her output to be sure she was producing understandable English. She also knew the rules and seemed to have found an optimal use of the monitor.

Teachers can help students become optimal monitor users. It does help to know the rules, but it's essential to know when to apply them and when to concentrate more on the meaning of a message. Sometimes teachers hope that by correcting their students' errors, they will increase students' proficiency. However, Krashen (1985) claims that while error correction in learning situations allows students to modify their knowledge of learned rules, it has no effect on their acquired language. "According to the theory, the practice of error correction affects learning, not acquisition. When our errors are corrected, we rethink and adjust our conscious rules" (8). Since the monitor can only be accessed under certain conditions, error correction has limited value. Learning, according to Krashen, has no effect on basic language competence.

Example of the Monitor—Miss Smith

Miss Smith studied Spanish extensively in high school and college and spent a summer in Guadalajara, Mexico, where she lived with a Mexican family and spoke Spanish every day. After graduation, her company sent her to work in Spain. During her first meeting with local Spanish company representatives, she was conversing fluently in Spanish until she began to use an irregular verb in the subjunctive and couldn't remember the correct verb form. As she tried to decide what form to use, she paused and lost her train of thought. For the rest of the meeting her Spanish was halting and stilted. What could have accounted for her performance?

Analysis

Miss Smith has acquired a good deal of Spanish. However, in a formal setting she begins to overuse her monitor. She tries to remember and apply the rules for the subjunctive and carry on a conversation at the same time. As a result, her rate of speech slows down. She can't focus on what she is saying and how to say it at the same time. She is overusing her monitor to the point that she can no longer communicate effectively.

Example of the Monitor—Mary

When Mary was in the first and second grade, she lived in Mexico City and attended a bilingual school where she and her sister were the only *gringas*. While there, she learned to speak Spanish fluently. After returning to the United States, she attended a bilingual school. She also made friends with some children recently arrived from El Salvador. When Mary conversed with her Salvadoran friends, her Spanish was fluent, but when she had to take a Spanish course in high school several years later, she was frustrated at times by the rules of grammar and accents. What might be causing Mary's frustration?

Analysis

Mary has acquired Spanish, but the school puts an emphasis on rules that must be learned. Even though Mary can understand and speak Spanish, she has not studied the rules needed for formal written Spanish, so she does not have the rules to monitor her speech and writing.

Example of the Monitor—Yvonne

Yvonne studied Spanish in college, lived in Mexico and South America, and taught Spanish courses. After completing graduate studies, she got a position at a college as director of bilingual education. Because of her ability to speak Spanish and her interest in language arts, local school districts began to ask her to address parents in Spanish. Despite the fact that she feels comfortable speaking Spanish with Spanish-speaking friends, she gets nervous when addressing large groups in Spanish. Why might this be?

Analysis

Yvonne has learned Spanish and also been in a number of situations where she acquired Spanish. Normally, she can converse without overusing her monitor. However, when speaking in formal situations, she becomes nervous so she begins to overuse her monitor.

The Input Hypothesis

acquire language
acquire language 1 + 1
acquire language with understandable written or oral language

The key to Krashen's theory of language acquisition is the input hypothesis. He claims that people acquire language in only one way—when they receive oral or written messages they understand. Krashen asserts that these messages provide comprehensible input. In order for acquisition to take place, learners must receive input that is slightly beyond their current ability level. Krashen calls this i + 1 (input plus one). If the input contains no structures beyond current competence (i + 0), no acquisition takes place. There is nothing new to pick up. On the other hand, if the input is too far beyond a person's current competence (i + 10), it becomes incomprehensible noise, and again no acquisition can take place.

no language acquire i + 0

According to Krashen, comprehensible input is the source of all acquired language. Students do not have to produce language in order to acquire it. Only input leads to acquisition, and so output—speaking or writing—does not contribute to acquisition, although it may result in cognitive development. As Krashen (1990) notes, output can help people learn academic content, or, as he puts it, output can make you smarter.

language difficult to acquire i + 10

Since comprehensible input is the key to language acquisition, the teacher's job, quite simply, is to find ways to make academic content comprehensible. This is why the theory is so important for teachers. Most current language methods for teaching a second language are designed to help teachers develop techniques for turning academic content matter into comprehensible input (Freeman and Freeman 1998a).

Simplified Input   *(modifications)*

Studies by Hatch (1983) suggest that the kind of input that leads to language development is simplified input. According to these researchers, simplified input includes caregiver talk, teacher talk, and talk to nonnative speakers. Hatch identified some characteristics of simplified talk. The phonology includes fewer reduced vowels and contractions, and the rate of speech is slower, with longer pauses. The vocabulary is characterized by more high-frequency items, fewer idioms, and less slang. There are *no new language*

fewer pronouns, and speakers often use gestures and pictures. At the level of syntax, sentences are shorter, with more repetitions and restatements. Discourse includes more requests for clarification and fewer interruptions.

The problem with claiming that simplified input leads to acquisition is that simplified input may not contain new language structures or items. Krashen claims that we acquire language when we receive input that contains language slightly beyond our current level of competence. We could say that simplified input is necessary but not sufficient for acquisition.

During our year in Venezuela, one thing we noticed in early interactions with colleagues was that they often tried to provide us with simplified input. When speaking directly to us in a meeting, for example, they obviously slowed their speech. In fact, if someone in the meeting used slang, the meeting would usually stop and everyone would try to explain the expression to us. Our landlord spoke no English at all and was nervous about talking to us. In our first meeting, she used very slow speech and lots of gestures and pointing in an effort to make herself understood. She used all the techniques of an excellent language teacher even though she is a lawyer by profession.

Example of Input—Mr. Roberts

The students in Mr. Roberts's first-year Spanish class do well in his structured program, although they seem bored at times. Mr. Roberts is careful to introduce only one new structure at a time and drill that structure until the students have mastered it. Although the students are making satisfactory progress, the class seems to lack animation, so to liven things up Mr. Roberts decides to bring in a guest speaker to talk about dating customs among Mexican teenagers. Despite the fact that Mr. Roberts warned his guest to limit his vocabulary and grammatical structures, the speaker gets carried away with his subject and uses the full range of Spanish. Surprisingly, although the students don't understand everything, they seem to be following most of the lecture. In addition, for the first time all year, they seem interested. What is going on here?

Analysis

The speaker is using structures slightly beyond the students' current level of comprehension. The input is comprehensible because of the students' background knowledge, so it will contribute to their acquisition of Spanish. In addition, the students are interested in the topic and make an effort to understand it. For that reason, the input contributes to acquisition. (See also "The Affective Filter Hypothesis," below.)

Example of Input—José

José is in the fifth grade and doing very well this year, despite the fact that his fourth-grade teacher, Mrs. Lynch, recommended him for special education. Mrs. Lynch contended that José was in the lowest reading group, had done poorly on standardized tests, and could not do the worksheets assigned to him. José's parents asked that he be given another chance. In fifth grade his teacher had students do lots of reading and writing and work on projects in groups. The children did not use the basal readers or worksheets but did work with literature using drama, art, and music. In only two months, José's English has improved noticeably, and he is enthusiastically reading and writing in English. When Mrs. Lynch insisted that he be tested with the basal reader tests, José proved that he had jumped two grade levels despite the fact that he had not been working with worksheets or basal readers. What might be the reason for this dramatic progress?

Analysis

Mrs. Lynch emphasized the need for learning. Compared to native speakers of English, José did not do well with formal rules of the new language. José is now in a classroom where activities are designed to increase his acquisition and less emphasis is placed on the learning of formal rules. In addition, the kinds of activities his new teacher uses make the English input comprehensible for José. Because of this, José has acquired a great deal of English in a short time, and this acquired language has increased his overall proficiency, as shown on the reading tests.

The Affective Filter Hypothesis

The affective filter hypothesis explains the role of affective factors in the process of language acquisition. Even if a teacher provides comprehensible input, acquisition may not take place. Affective factors such as anxiety or boredom may serve as a filter that blocks input. When the filter is up, input can't reach those parts of the brain (the LAD) where acquisition occurs. Many language learners realize that the reason they have trouble is because they are nervous or embarrassed and simply "can't concentrate." Lack of desire to learn can also "clog" the affective filter.

Earlier we described Yvonne's high school Spanish class, which included twenty-three boys, all on the junior varsity football team, and three girls. Most of the students had signed up for the "new intern" teacher mainly because they had failed Spanish 1 the year before. Positive affective factors such as high interest or motivation can help keep the filter down, but those students had neither. Yvonne's major job was to try to lower the students' filter by getting them interested and convincing them that they wanted to learn Spanish.

Since Krashen's theory of language acquisition is based on input, in his discussion of the affective filter he only refers to language that is coming in, not to language the person is attempting to produce. In other words, the affective filter can prevent a person from getting more language. This hypothesis does not apply to a person's output, only to the ability to acquire language.

At times, students who have developed high levels of language proficiency may not perform up to their capacity. As we have explained, there are times when students are nervous, bored, or unmotivated, and their performance does not match their competence. This was the case for Leny, profiled in Chapter 4, who became nervous trying to speak Spanish in the beauty parlor. Students may also not perform well in a new language if they overuse their monitor. However, when Krashen refers to an affective filter, he is referring only to affective factors that block input.

Krashen's insistence on the importance of providing learners with comprehensible input in a risk-free environment sends an important message to teachers. As a result, Krashen's theory of SLA has had a strong influence on teaching methods. Krashen claims that older students can acquire a second language in the same way they acquired their first language, going through the same developmental stages, and that a classroom can be an optimal source of comprehensible input. In fact, the classroom may provide more comprehensible input than a trip to a foreign country where no attempt is made to ensure that input is comprehensible.

Traditional approaches to language teaching often require students to produce language before they have received enough comprehensible input. This became clear to us as we worked with student teachers in Venezuela. Because of their own experiences as students in English classes, the new teachers at first asked their students to say everything in complete sentences and even asked them to stand and recite what they were learning. Use of visuals was minimal, and chalkboards were filled with vocabulary lists and language structures. Although the topics of the lessons were personally interesting ones to the students—explaining likes and dislikes, or discussing similarities and differences among classmates—the insistence on output raised the students' affective filters. These beginning-level English students expended so much energy trying to pronounce words, learn vocabulary, get verb endings right, and put sentences together that little real language acquisition took place.

The student teachers began to use a variety of visuals and other strategies to ensure that the input they were providing was comprehensible. They allowed students to show comprehension through gestures and one-word answers. The emphasis in the classroom moved from control of vocabulary and structure to comprehension and interaction. What was most exciting was that the teachers saw how much more English the students were acquiring and how much more positive they were about the class. *making environment available to all / bring down affective filter.*

Example of Affective Filter—Peter

Peter accepts a teaching job in Colombia, South America, even though he doesn't speak any Spanish. Fortunately, his wife speaks good Spanish. Peter and his wife agree that she will translate for the two of them and also teach him the language when they get there. For the first few months of their stay, the couple lives with a Colombian family in which no one speaks any English. During meals Peter is frustrated because he can understand little and say nothing. He starts to resent being in his new culture. Besides, he is embarrassed by his inability to speak. After a few weeks he even refuses to try to speak Spanish and discontinues the lessons with his wife. Despite being immersed in Spanish, he doesn't seem to be learning anything. What might be the reason for this?

Filter high — hard to understand new language

Analysis

Although Peter is receiving comprehensible input, the input doesn't become intake that contributes to acquisition because Peter's affective filter is high. The filter blocks the input from activating the LAD. Factors such as culture shock and being dependent on his wife raised his filter.

Summary

As these scenarios show, Krashen's theory helps explain a number of common situations in which second language learners find themselves. The five interrelated hypotheses constitute Krashen's Monitor Model of SLA. Krashen (1985) sums up his theory by stating, "We acquire when we obtain comprehensible input in a low-anxiety situation, when we are presented with interesting messages, and when we understand these messages" (10).

Kristene, a graduate student and a bilingual teacher, wrote the following reflection on her own acquisition of Spanish as a second language after studying Krashen's theory.

> Perhaps my success in Spanish language classes (audio-lingual in junior high and grammar-translation in high school) came about because my first exposure to Spanish was through communicative practice in real situations as Krashen suggests. I lived in Spain at the age of ten for six months. My parents hired a tutor who spoke only Spanish. She took us to the beach, to town on the bus, shopping at *la plaza*, to church, to the movies, to the park, to buy bread at the bread shop. (I can still remember the fabulous aroma and taste of freshly baked Spanish bread some thirty years later!) The input was comprehensible!

Krashen would take this example from Kristene to support his theory. Kristene acquired Spanish in a natural order because she was in a setting in which the input was comprehensible and her affective filter was low. Later she learned some aspects of Spanish and she could use that learned knowledge to monitor her output. The result is that Kristene has developed a high level of proficiency in Spanish.

A Social Theory of Second Language Acquisition

Krashen uses the term *acquisition* to refer to an individual psychological process of developing a language. Since we use language for social interactions, it is important to also consider the social aspects of acquisition. Gee (1992) offers a definition of acquisition that expands on Krashen's by including a social component:

> Acquisition is a process of acquiring something subconsciously by exposure to models, a process of trial and error, and practice within social groups, without formal teaching. It happens in natural settings that are meaningful and functional in the sense that acquirers know that they need to acquire the thing they are exposed to in order to function and that they in fact want to so function. (113)

While Krashen focuses on the individual receiving comprehensible input, Gee speaks of people in social groups who acquire language through social interactions. The development of communicative competence comes from knowing the appropriate language for the social situation. This kind of competence develops naturally in social settings.

An example of this process comes from Yvonne's adult ESL class. Yvonne recalls one very respectful Hispanic man in her class. He worked in a lumber mill and learned a great deal of vocabulary from fellow workers. However, the teacher and several other students were a bit taken aback when he expressed his enthusiasm one day by exclaiming, "Goddamn right!" and his frustration by saying, "Shit!" These terms were acceptable at work, where they were even indications of camaraderie. In the work context, he had developed the integrative function discussed in Chapter 4. In the classroom, however, the expressions were not socially acceptable. The student in Yvonne's class had figured out how important it was to use certain expressions at work to be part of that social group. He had to learn, however, that the classroom was a different context, and he had to acquire the ways of speaking that were proper there.

Gee's view of language acquisition is consistent with the model of learning we presented in Chapter 3. In social groups, people receive demonstrations from others who use the target language. Because humans want to interact socially, they form the intent to speak the language. They see themselves as language learners and take the risk to communicate with others. They learn through doing. They receive feedback continually—either they understand and are understood or communication breaks down. The feedback is almost always directed at the meaning they are trying to convey, not at the grammatical form. They take the information from the feedback and integrate it with current knowledge as they acquire the new language.

Acquisition and Learning Approaches to Schooling

Acquisition and learning are two ways of getting knowledge and skills. School systems have used both approaches to instruct students. Some cultural groups value acquisition. They assume that children will learn by being around adults who are performing certain activities. They believe children learn best in apprenticeship situations. Phillips (1972) in her Warm Springs Reservation study found that the Native Americans she studied valued apprenticeship learning and performed poorly in classroom contexts that emphasized learning through direct instruction, competition, and individualized performance. However, most U.S. schools emphasize the latter approach. The recent movement toward standards and assessment is consistent with direct, explicit teaching. Learning is the expected result.

Schools often reward students' knowledge about subjects more than their ability to actually use the knowledge. Freire (1970) says that students in classes where teachers transmit knowledge (where students are treated like plants) only gain the ability to describe the content of the knowledge. "Mechanically memorizing the description of an object does not constitute knowing the object" (33). In other words, knowledge (learning) without experience (acquisition) puts us in a position where we possess only a hollow sort of understanding.

In some classrooms, reading is taught as a process of sounding out and pronouncing words. Some students can do this even if they don't understand the words at all. Other students do understand the words at a certain level, but they lack the experiences needed to fully comprehend what they are reading. Still others have rich background experiences that allow a different kind of knowledge to emerge from their reading. Freire (Freire and Macedo 1987) recalls his own introduction to reading: "My parents introduced me to reading the word at a certain moment in this rich experience of understanding my immediate world. Deciphering the word flowed naturally from reading my particular world; it was not something superimposed on it" (32). In Freire's terms, we must learn to read the world before we read the words.

While in Venezuela, Yvonne read children's literature in Spanish weekly with a second grader and a third grader. These children had been exposed to a system of teaching reading that emphasized "word calling." Students were rewarded for reading the words out loud without making an error. However, they had never been asked to talk about or encouraged to evaluate what they read and had seldom read anything of real interest to them. When the children first began reading the beautifully illustrated children's literature, they glanced briefly at the pictures and then dutifully read quickly and accurately. They were amazed when Yvonne encouraged them to talk about the stories, look at the pictures, and predict what might happen next. For these children, reading was reading the word only. The idea of reading their world in the words took some time for them to develop. It had never occurred to them that their world could have a connection to what they read.

Piaget (1955) also argues that learning should be based on students' real-life experiences. If students have only learning without the concrete experiences, their knowledge is of a kind that they can't really put to productive use. Unfortunately, this is what happens to many foreign language students. They study language (usually language structure and vocabulary) in a classroom but never use it for real purposes. Therefore, they quickly forget what little they once knew.

It appears that acquisition and learning lead to different kinds of abilities. As Gee (1992) puts it: "we are better at performing what we acquire, but we consciously know more about what we have learned" (114). In the case of second languages, acquisition allows us to speak and understand, read and write the language. Learning allows us to talk about (or pass exams on) the language. Many adults who have studied a foreign language in high school and/or college and received high grades never learned to speak or understand the language they studied. Their performance on grammar and vocabulary tests determined their grades.

The difference between the effects of acquisition (ability to use language) and learning (ability to talk about language) is most evident in the case of language learning. As Gee (1988) comments, "It appears that some substantive degree of inci-

[handwritten margin note: learning based on students' life experience]

94

dental learning [acquisition] must take place before intentional learning is very effi-cacious" (217). Otherwise, students learn about language, but they do not learn language. If acquisition precedes learning, and students can actually speak a language, it may be valuable for them to be able to talk, read, and write about what they can do and how they do it.

Our daughters, Mary and Ann, provide a real-life example of Gee's incidental (acquisition) and intentional learning. The two girls went to Mexico to live when they were in kindergarten, first, and second grades. While there, they attended a Spanish/English bilingual school where they were the only nonnative speakers of Spanish. Through social interaction with their peers and the study of content in Spanish, the two girls acquired enough Spanish (incidental learning) to pass Mexican government exams at the end of their two-year stay in Mexico.

When our family returned to the United States, both girls attended a Spanish/English bilingual school in Tucson, Arizona, and made friends with a family of El Salvadoran refugees. These experiences gave the girls enough Spanish input to continue their acquisition of Spanish in a natural setting (more incidental learning). However, when we moved to Fresno, California, their only exposure to Spanish was in structured Spanish (as a foreign language) class where worksheets and drills (intentional learning) drove Mary to drop Spanish altogether. Ann continued to study Spanish and soon joined a Spanish for Spanish speakers class, where there was more natural conversation and discussion in Spanish (incidental and intentional learning). In addition, Ann spent part of her senior year of high school as an exchange student, studying content subjects in a Mexican school (incidental learning).

In college, both girls studied Spanish. Mary was reluctant at first. However, she had acquired a great deal of Spanish because of her experiences outside school. She commented that she felt sorry for students "who don't already know Spanish." In fact, most students who go on to advanced language classes at a university have had some exposure to the language outside school settings. Ann took advanced grammar classes in college. Both girls are now proficient in Spanish. They acquired Spanish and they learned it as well. The two processes gave them different knowledge and skills.

It is important for teachers to reflect on this distinction between acquisition and learning. Learning can be valuable. It can help students analyze language. However, students need to acquire language if they are to use it for communicative or academic purposes.

Schumann and Krashen

Schumann's acculturation theory complements Krashen's monitor model. Schumann focuses on external, social factors that lead to language acquisition. Krashen's theory explicates the internal, psychological process that results in acquisition. Gee suggests that Krashen's theory has a social dimension as well.

Krashen (1982) comments that Schumann's acculturation hypothesis "is easily expressible in terms of comprehensible input and low filter level. Acculturation can be viewed as a means of gaining comprehensible input and lowering the filter" (45). Krashen also notes that his theory accounts for acquisition in a wider range of settings. "Moreover, the comprehensible input hypothesis accounts for second language acquisition in situations that acculturation does not attempt to deal with" (45). For example, with good teaching, a student can acquire a foreign language in a school setting without ever traveling to another country.

What About Output?

[handwritten annotation: Input — Knowledge intake. output — Production /in action (knowle...]

Krashen argues that acquisition occurs when learners receive comprehensible input, messages that they understand. Other researchers have given importance to output as well as input. Ellis (1990) refers to theories such as Krashen's as reception-based. Theories that include attention to output he classifies as production-based. According to Johnson (1995), "Reception-based theories contend that interaction contributes to second language acquisition via learners' reception and comprehension of the second language, whereas production-based theories credit this process to learners' attempts at actually producing the language" (82).

Long (1983) developed the interaction hypothesis, a theory of SLA that is reception-based. Long claims that learners make conversational adjustments as they interact with others and that these adjustments help make the input comprehensible. As Johnson (1995) points out, "Like Krashen, Long stresses the importance of comprehensible input but places more emphasis on the interaction that takes place in two-way communication and the adjustments that are made as a result of the negotiation of meaning" (83).

Swain (1985) also argues that language learners need the opportunity for output. She noted that students in French immersion classes did not reach native-like proficiency in French. These students were in classes where teachers did most of the talking. Peer interaction was limited, and when interaction occurred, students spoke only with others learning French rather than with native speakers of French. Based on her observations of these students, Swain proposed that second language acquisition depends on output as well as input. According to Scarcella (1990), Swain's comprehensible output hypothesis

> suggests that students need tasks which elicit . . . talk at the student's i + 1, that is, a level of second language proficiency which is just a bit beyond the current second language proficiency level. She claims that such output provides opportunities for meaningful context-embedded use for the second language which allows students to test out their hypotheses about the language and "move the learner from a purely semantic analysis of the language to a syntactic analysis of it." (70)

Swain's claim is that when we receive input that we understand, we focus on meaning—or the semantic level. However, in talking, we need to string sentences together, and that requires attention to syntax. Our syntactic analysis is probably not conscious, but producing output requires us to access parts of the language system different from that which we use to comprehend input.

One model of SLA that includes both input and output has been developed by Van Lier (1988) and is shown in Figure 5–1. Van Lier claims that certain conditions are necessary for certain outcomes. According to this model, if learners are receptive during exposure to a new language, their attention will be focused. If attention is focused, the language becomes input. If learners invest some mental energy in the input, they will begin to comprehend it. Language that is comprehended changes from input to intake. If learners practice with intake, they can retain the language and access it later. Language that can be accessed is considered uptake. Finally, with authentic use, learners can extend their language and use it creatively. It is the ability to use language creatively that is a measure of proficiency.

Van Lier's model traces the process of language acquisition from input to controlled output (practice) to authentic use in social interaction. This model is consistent with the model of learning presented in Chapter 3. For example, exposure is similar to a demonstration. If attention is focused, exposure becomes input. This parallels step two of the learning model, forming an intent. Investing mental energy turns input into intake, and this is similar to deciding to take the risk to learn. Intake becomes uptake if learners practice, and this is an instance of learning by doing. Uptake leads to proficiency during authentic use. In this stage, learners receive feedback and also integrate their new knowledge into their previous understanding.

Production-based theories of SLA such as Van Lier's and Swain's recognize the importance of input but add output as an important component. Krashen's argument

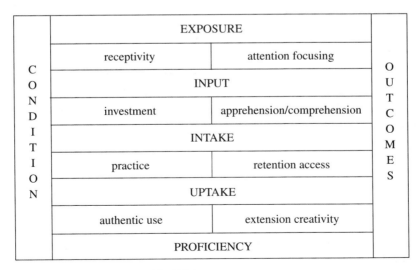

FIGURE 5–1 *Van Lier's Model of SLA*

is that output can't help us acquire new vocabulary or grammatical structures. One can't learn a new word simply by talking. At the same time, we learn language for communicative purposes, and no language teacher would feel successful if students never uttered a word of the new language. In fact, in most classes we have observed, students are asked to produce language too soon. If teachers require students to produce language before they have received sufficient comprehensible input, the students' affective filters may go up. They concentrate on production and block out the input they need to build the new language.

This phenomenon is very common. David remembers that in his beginning German class, each student was required to answer one of the questions from the book. The teacher went through the questions methodically. David (like others in the class) would count ahead to find his question and mentally practice it until his moment came. The problem, of course, was that David ignored all the German input that was available from the teacher and the other students because he was so focused on producing the correct answer. Not surprisingly, David failed to acquire any German.

The German teacher didn't provide much comprehensible input. He could have used more visuals and realia to make the German understandable. He could also have lowered the affective filters of the students by providing other ways for them to show they understood. For example, students could have responded with actions or gestures. They could have answered yes-or-no questions. Or they could have answered questions that required them to give a classmate's name (Who is wearing the blue shirt?). In an acquisition-oriented class teachers do expect students to show they comprehend the input, but they do this without requiring students to produce language beyond their current level of proficiency.

What About Grammar?

In our discussion of theories of second language acquisition, we have not addressed one issue that is central for many language teachers: grammar. Grammar is certainly an important component of most language classes. The reasons for this seem clear: Most people who become language teachers like grammar and know quite a bit about grammar. Besides, they probably received large doses of grammar in their own formal language education. In addition, a person teaching a language has to teach something, and the grammar of the language is a natural candidate. These are all reasons that language teachers teach grammar, but are they good reasons?

We want to make it clear that when we use the term *grammar* we are referring to language structure, not current usage. Structure can include many things. In early lessons, students learn forms of the verb *to be*. In later lessons, they might learn more complicated aspects of a language. For example, in English, some verbs take infinitives, some take gerunds, and some take both. We can say, "I like to swim" or "I like swimming." We can also say, "I want to swim." But we can't say, "I want swimming." Usage, on the other hand, might refer to the difference between *different from* and *different than*, or whether to put the comma inside the quotation marks or outside. Usage is best taught in the context of student writing. At the editing stage, students need to produce conventional English.

We also acknowledge that there are situations in which it is necessary to teach grammar. If students are to be tested on their knowledge of grammar, and if the teacher can't change the testing system, then the teacher should pay attention to grammar. Otherwise, the students may feel that the teacher is not meeting their needs, even though some research suggests that direct teaching of grammar isn't the best way to improve scores on grammar tests (Elley 1989). Student attitudes are important. Many teachers of adults have commented that their students know more about English grammar than the teachers do. At the very least, teachers need to know the grammar to preserve their credibility. But knowing something and deciding to teach it are two different things. We come back, then, to the basic question, "Does teaching grammar result in greater language proficiency?"

The issue of whether teaching grammar results in higher levels of proficiency is complex. Whether or not a group of students becomes more proficient depends on many factors. If I teach grammar and you do not and then a test shows my students do better than yours, can I claim that teaching grammar was the key? Even if the two groups of students were judged to be about equal when they began, I still couldn't claim that my grammar teaching was what caused my students to do better. When I teach language, I don't teach grammar exclusively, and maybe the other things I do teach help my students even more than the grammar lessons. Maybe my students are more highly motivated. Maybe they are better test takers. And what about the test? If the test is based on the grammar I taught, then my students should do better. In short, many factors could influence the results.

Given this complexity, some researchers have asked a different question: What kind of grammar instruction works best? Ellis (1998), for example, looked at four ways of presenting what he refers to as form-focused instruction. One way is to structure the input. "This option asks learners to process input that has been specially contrived to induce comprehension of the target structure" (44). Learners are not required to produce the structure, but they are exposed to large amounts of the structure and asked to attend to it. For example, students often say things like, "I am boring" when they mean, "I am bored," so structured input might focus on the difference between these two grammatical forms. For example, the teacher might give a series of sentences such as "The book is boring, so I am bored."

A second possibility is explicit instruction. Such instruction can be direct (the teacher teaches the rule and the students must practice it) or indirect. In indirect explicit instruction, students look at some sample of language and try to figure out the rule. That is, explicit instruction can be deductive or inductive. Explicit instruction is designed to raise students' consciousness of the grammatical form.

A third approach to grammar teaching is what Ellis calls production practice. This approach involves students in practicing certain grammatical forms. For example, a student might do a worksheet in which the task is to put the words *in*, *on*, or *at* into the appropriate blanks in a sentence.

Finally, teachers can teach grammar by providing negative feedback. When a student makes an error, the teacher can correct it, usually by providing the correct form. If the student says, "I have been here since two days," the teacher might respond, "Oh, so you have been here *for* two days. What have you been doing?"

As Ellis points out, most language teaching includes a combination of these methods, so it is difficult to know which one works best. Even if one method could be shown to be superior, the more basic question of whether teaching grammar is the best way to improve proficiency remains unanswered.

Terrell (1991), who collaborated with Krashen to develop a method of teaching compatible with Krashen's theory of SLA, has also written about the role of grammar instruction in a communicative teaching approach. Terrell's review of the research leads him to conclude that

> [i]n summary, research to date has not found EGI [explicit grammar instruction] to be the most important factor in second language acquisition. It may work by speeding up the entire acquisition process and it may help learners to avoid certain learning production . . . However, it is likely that no simple answer exists to the question of the effects of EGI on adult second language acquisition. Rather it is more probable that instruction about forms or structures of the target language is beneficial to learners at a particular point in their acquisition of the target language. (55)

What Terrell suggests, then, is that for adults some attention to grammatical forms can be helpful at certain points in their process of acquisition. This is consistent with Krashen's idea that learned rules can help students monitor their output.

Terrell goes on, like Ellis, to consider how to teach grammar. He begins by noting, "I use the term 'explicit grammar instruction' somewhat loosely to mean the use of instructional strategies to draw the students' attention to or focus on form and/or structure" (53). He then suggests three ways the explicit grammar instruction may aid acquisition:

1. *As an advance organizer to aid in comprehending and segmenting the input.* The Spanish teacher might tell students that in Spanish, adjectives have gender markings that agree with the gender of the noun. If the word for *book* is masculine, the adjective used to describe the book will end in *o*.

2. *As a meaning-form focuser that aids the learner in establishing a meaning-form relationship for morphologically complex forms.* In languages like Spanish, endings on verbs indicate the person doing the action. However, students may not notice these endings. The teacher might explain, for example, that verbs ending in *o* indicate that the person doing the action is "I," and then give the students lots of input with the *o* ending and ask them to notice the endings.

3. *By providing forms for monitoring which will be available for acquisition in the output*. The idea here is that if students monitor their output carefully, they may acquire more language. Terrell proposes that the learners' own output can become input as they monitor and think about what they say. When Yvonne was teaching English-speaking university students about the use of the subjunctive in Spanish, she talked to her students about her own acquisition of the Spanish subjunctive. She pointed out how she, after many years of acquiring Spanish, still often monitors herself when she uses a verb or impersonal expression that takes the subjunctive. She consciously (but very rapidly) thinks to herself, "Since the expression is *es necessario que* (it is necessary that), I need to put the verb that follows in the subjunctive." Yvonne then invites her students to try to do this when they are using Spanish and explains that they will not always notice if they are focused on the meaning of what they are saying, but that, with time, they will begin to do this.

Terrell feels that the benefits of explicit grammar instruction are limited. He does offer suggestions for providing instruction, but his real emphasis is on making input comprehensible.

Other writers have suggested ways of teaching grammar. For example, Adair-Hauck, Donato, and Cumo (1994) present a model of instruction called PACE. In this model, grammar is always first presented (P) in a meaningful context. For example, the teacher might read a story that contains many examples of the structure. Next comes attention (A). In this step the teacher highlights the grammar point. The third step is to co-construct an explanation (C). The teacher and students work together to figure out the grammar rule (when do I use *in* and when do I use *on?*). Finally, there is an extension activity (E) in which the students make creative use of the grammar structure in some meaningful way. Certainly, PACE is a better model than most grammar teaching, but it focuses on how to teach grammar and avoids the more crucial question of whether to teach it at all.

In Krashen's theory (1982), knowledge of grammar rules serves only one function, helping learners monitor their output. However, Krashen does offer one suggestion for teaching grammar. Students can study language as an academic content area. In the process of studying this content area, students would acquire language. Krashen points out, though, that "teachers and students are deceiving themselves. They believe that it is the subject matter itself, the study of grammar, that is responsible for the students' progress in second language acquisition, but in reality their progress is coming from the medium, not the message. Any subject matter that held their interest would do just as well, so far as second language acquisition is concerned, as long as it required extensive use of the target language" (120). The idea of teaching grammar as academic content fits well with the approach we advocate. Explorer teachers always teach language through content.

If strong evidence existed for teaching grammar, it would be widely published. Most language teachers would like to believe that teaching grammar promotes language acquisition. But there is little evidence to support this position. Most research articles focus more on *how* to teach grammar than on *whether* to teach it.

Teachers who choose to teach grammar should be aware that time spent on grammar instruction is time taken away from other activities. That is why Terrell, for example, relegates most grammar instruction to homework. He wants to use class time to provide as much comprehensible input as possible, since comprehensible input seems to be the key to acquisition.

Elley (1991) reports on one study that compared explicit teaching of grammar with providing input. The second language students in this study were divided into two groups. One group studied grammatical structures, such as comparatives (e.g., "My brother is taller than I am"). The other group listened to and read books that contained the target structures naturally. That is, the books were not specifically written to contain the structures. At the end of the experiment, both groups were given a test of grammar. For example, they were asked to complete sentences with comparatives ("My brother is taller _____"). The group that read and were read to did better than those who had directly practiced the structure. The 280 ESL students who read each day or were read to scored about 40 percent right on this test. The control group (143 students) who studied the grammar scored about 27 percent right. This study supports an acquisition approach to teaching second language students and suggests that receiving comprehensible input results in gains in all aspects of language proficiency.

Language Acquisition in Explorer Classrooms

As we have discussed, explorer classrooms are places where learners are not entirely dependent on teachers. Instead, learners and teachers explore big questions together. How does this work in the case of a second language? After all, if the teacher speaks the target language and the students don't, then the students must be dependent on the teacher.

The solution is to teach language through academic content. When teachers combine language and content teaching, the focus is not on the language itself. If the focus is on the language, learners may have little to contribute (at least at first) and may not be able to move beyond dependency. When the focus is on the content area, all students can contribute, even if their English proficiency is limited. As students and teachers inquire together, attempting to answer big questions by using content-area knowledge, students learn a new language almost incidentally. They gain access to second language acquisition. The teacher is sensitive to the constraints put on learners by their level of proficiency in the new language, and the teacher takes opportunities (teachable moments) to point out things about the new language as they arise naturally.

The view of SLA that we hold, then, is similar to Krashen's (1982), in that we believe that language is essentially acquired rather than learned. Like Gee (1988), we believe that acquisition is a social process, and that social interaction is important. In explorer classrooms, students between worlds gain access to second language acquisition and learn language through content-area study. In the next three chapters, we examine how teachers and students can work and learn together in explorer classrooms.

Applications

1. Whether we are learning a language or something else, we all have experienced the difference between learning and acquisition. Share a personal example.

2. Schumann's Acculturation Model suggests that the social and psychological distance a second language learner has from speakers of the target language affects language learning. Think of two second language learners you know who represent different social and psychological distances. Use the questions provided below to determine the factors that influence the two learners. Share with a partner.

Social Distance

1. *Social dominance.* Whose social group is more dominant?
2. *Integration pattern.* How much do learners integrate, or do they do most things apart from the mainstream?
3. *Enclosure.* To what extent does learner's group have their own resources for interaction, such as church, publications, clubs?
4. *Size.* How large is the group?
5. *Cohesiveness.* How much does the group "stick together"?
6. *Cultural congruence.* How are the cultural patterns and customs of the home culture and the target culture alike or different?
7. *Attitude.* What attitudes do the home and target cultural groups have toward one another?
8. *Intended length of residence.* How long does the learner intend to stay in the new country?

Psychological Distance

1. *Motivation.* Does the learner want to learn the new language?
2. *Attitude.* How does the learner feel toward the target-culture group?
3. *Culture shock.* Is the learner suffering culture shock?

3. Tape-record a young child who is acquiring his or her native language. Pick out examples where the child has overgeneralized language rules, such as adding *-ed* to *go* to form the past tense. Write down the examples and bring them to your group for discussion.

4. Share a second language learning experience that you (or someone you know) had when you applied your monitor (your learning) to your output.

5. Krashen claims that input alone results in language acquisition. Swain disagrees, citing examples of the importance of "comprehensible output." Do you agree with Krashen or Swain? Can you find any evidence to support your position? Discuss with a group.

6. What is your opinion of the direct teaching of grammar? Are there situations in which you think teaching grammar helps students develop a new language? Write down your opinions and share them with the group.

6

How Do Explorer Teachers Celebrate Learning and Make It Meaningful?

Dear Patty Trask

I am very happy to come to study in your class, I hope you can improve my English better than the last classes. Since I have come to study in your class, I have had chance to talk to my classmates. You put everyone into group, you let us talk, you have a very good experience and gesture about teaching, you know what students want to do, you stimulate students, it makes the students to pay attention to what you say or teach.

Some of my teachers don't care about students, They just keep teaching and teaching They don't let the students talk to each other, They don't let the students join in group to share ideas, it makes the students boring, sleepy and lazy.

Patty Trask, since I come to your class, you make me think of some of my vocabularies which I learned in the Refugee Camps, Thailand. I had studied a lot of vocabularies in the campos but now I forget them. I use some words once in a blue moon Then I never use again. I think when I was in Thailand, I was better in English than today, I don't know why? Do you know?

Thank you for accepting me to be your students, I will never forget what you have done for me forever. I have had a lot of teachers who taught me English, Lao, Thai, Braille, Sign Language and Hmong, but there are a few teachers who are friendly and care about students like you. I have a little bit experience about teaching, I know that most students like the friendly teachers, and the teachers who are for them, only.

Patty Trask, I know that I am still very poor in speaking, writing English but I am happy that I have you and my friendly classmates to help me improve it. I hope to speak better English in the future. Ok, I would like to stop writing like this.

Thank you for taking time to read this letter, may be it is difficult for you to read because my handwriting is not so good.

Thanks in advance

meaningful

Kou Chang

*Please forgive me if you see the words and sentences that aren't correct in spelling and grammar!

We open this chapter with this letter from Kou Chang, because it tells us in a student's words what explorer teachers do. Patty Trask teaches adult ESL students in a large, inner-city school district. Her student, Kou, wrote this letter spontaneously. It was not a classroom assignment. If we read the letter carefully, we learn important things about Kou and about his teacher and how she applies the explorer principles we introduce in this chapter.

It is clear that Patty and her students celebrate learning. Kou explains that he is "very happy to come to study" and that Patty has a "very good experience and gesture about teaching." One understands from Kou's letter that students enjoy learning from Patty. As Kou puts it, "you stimulate students."

It is also clear that Patty focuses on her students and makes the learning meaningful. Kou tells us that "some of my teachers don't care about students. They just keep teaching and teaching . . . but there are a few teachers who are friendly and care about the students like you." The learning must be meaningful, because Patty's approach "makes the students to pay attention to what you say or teach."

By organizing her classroom so that students can collaborate and by encouraging students to use different modes of learning, Patty implements two other explorer principles. Kou tells us that other teachers "don't let the students join in group to share ideas, it makes the students boring, sleepy and lazy." He emphasizes how helpful collaboration and talking about writing is by telling Patty later in his letter, "I know that I am still very poor in speaking, writing English but I am happy that I have you and my friendly classmates to help me improve it."

Kou is progressing well in English because of Patty's teaching, which Kou tells Patty is superior to that of other teachers he has had in his "little bit experience about teaching." Kou, in fact, is a prime example of the final explorer principle. Kou is multilingual. He communicates in Lao, Thai, Braille, American Sign Language, and Hmong. The previous languages he has learned contribute to his being such an articulate English language learner. Since literacy in other languages supports the acquisition of English, explorer teachers like Patty "support the development of their students' first languages and cultures."

Figure 6–1 lists the explorer principles that we believe should guide teachers working with multilingual students. These principles are based on the theory and research that we have discussed in the previous chapters. Research and theory inform practice; at the same time, practice informs research and theory. In this and subsequent chapters we will discuss each of the principles in more detail and give examples from a variety of contexts. As Wink (2000) acknowledges, "Each of us has her

---

Explorer Learning Principles

Celebrate Learning and Diversity
In explorer classrooms teachers and students celebrate learning together. They view the diversity within their classroom as a rich resource they can build on.

Focus on the Learner
In explorer classrooms teachers focus on their learners to gain important insights into the real needs of their students. They connect their background experiences and students' strengths to concepts they need to develop.

Make Curriculum Meaningful to the Students
In explorer classrooms teachers find activities that are meaningful to help their students use English for both social and academic purposes.

Organize for Collaboration
In explorer classrooms teachers provide students with opportunities to develop both communicative and academic competence as they interact with each other using language for real purposes.

Encourage Learning Through Different Modes
In explorer classrooms teachers encourage the development of both concepts and language while using several modalities. Students are encouraged to use a variety of ways to learn and share their knowledge.

Respect Learners
In explorer classrooms teachers respect their students for who they are and what they bring to the classroom. When teachers view students positively, they plan meaningful instruction that enables all learners to reach their potential.

Celebrate Students' First Languages and Cultures
In explorer classrooms, teachers support the development of their students' first languages and cultures even when the teachers do not speak those languages or come from those cultures.

FIGURE 6–1 *Explorer Principles*

own real world. It informs us; it enlightens us; it amuses us; it challenges us" (5). As you read this book and reflect on the research, theory, and examples given here, we hope that you will look at your real classroom world and implement the principles in ways that will help your students.

Celebrate Learning and Diversity

During a discussion about effective curriculum for English language learners, Miriam, a graduate student and a Spanish/English bilingual math and adult ESL teacher, brought up a very important aspect of all learning: celebration. Teachers in explorer classes at all grade levels celebrate the learning they and their students share. Rather than seeing the diversity in their classrooms as a burden, they welcome diversity, and this spirit of celebration is the first thing that strikes a visitor to their classes. Kou's letter gives us a sense of the value placed on both learning and learners in Patty's classroom. All students, especially immigrant students, must feel comfortable with and excited about learning.

Unfortunately, many immigrant students do not see school in their new country as a celebration. Francisco, whom we described in Chapter 1, was a frightened fourteen-year-old who, when he entered high school, prayed that the teacher wouldn't call on him. Elena, now a student teacher at our university, recalls her first learning experiences in this country as a twelve-year-old immigrant:

> I learned English by repeating words after a recorder and using flash cards. As a student I did not learn what the rest of the students learned: science, social studies, math, and other subjects. My teachers focused on teaching me English. I do not think teachers knew what to do with second language learners.

Elena and Francisco did not experience learning as a celebration. Instead, they felt different and alienated.

Susanne, a graduate student who teaches a third-grade class in a school where most of the students are Hispanic and speak English as their second language, recently discovered a way to help her students celebrate their diversity. Susanne read the research and theory related to second language acquisition and realized that at her school, the mandated curriculum, especially the reading curriculum, was not supportive of the English learners. Students were being treated as plants. The teachers depended on the adopted reading materials, which required explicit, direct teaching. Susanne feared that this behaviorist approach to teaching reading skills in a prescribed order would not promote language acquisition or reading for English language learners.

Susanne was determined that in her classroom her students would become competent readers through engagement with books. Her graduate classes had made her more aware of the need for her students to see themselves in the books they read. At a state bilingual education conference, she bought many books and nearly all had a Latino theme, because she knew her classroom library had few books related to her

Add to library book that include students' backgrounds

students' backgrounds. Though she expected her students to connect with the books, she had no idea how much culturally relevant books would excite them. She described what happened as she introduced the first book to her students:

> This afternoon I picked up *In My Family: En mi familia* by Carmen Lomas Garza. Time being limited, my purpose was simply to show the new books I had bought which were available in both English and Spanish and to encourage them to investigate and enjoy the Spanish text. The fever began as a slow burn as we discussed the wonderful cover illustration depicting an outdoor dance floor, people of all ages dancing, a musical ensemble, and simple light bulbs strung from posts. I asked my students what they thought of the cover and where they thought the dance was taking place. A roar went up. "MEXICO!"
>
> I decided to read a bit to see what sort of connections my students would make with the first short vignette described in the book, "The Horned Toads: *Los chameleons.*" The room erupted in wild conversations during the reading. Students were unable to contain their excitement; they had stories to tell and, all decorum aside, they were going to tell them! They shared with their neighbors, friends, and, of course, me. They knew about horned toads, desert environments, and fire ants that "really sting." By the next vignette, "Cleaning Nopalitos: *Limpiando nopalitos,*" there was no way to calm the wonderfully noisy groundswell of storytelling and sharing. I was entering *their* culture, a culture and tradition they were passionate to share.
>
> This sort of book begs interviews with parents, grandparents. It screams out for stories to be told, written, illustrated, published. I have been ignited; my students and I will read together, build together, and celebrate together.

Susanne found a way to celebrate their rich cultural diversity with her students. The spirit of excitement and celebration in her classroom resulted from her realization that she needed to find texts that connected to her students and their experiences.

Focus on the Learner

Parents and teachers like Susanne know that young (and older) children pay attention if discussion is focused on them, their needs, and their interests. A crying baby is distracted when a parent plays a favorite game, waves a familiar toy, or simply directs the conversation to the child: "Oh! Is that Tommy crying? Look, he's stopped! You're a good boy, aren't you! You just wanted some attention, didn't you?" Noisy and cranky ten-year-olds can turn into engrossed and eager children when a new game (or an old favorite) is pulled out, especially if adults join in.

However, not all classrooms reflect this basic understanding of the importance of focusing on the learner. In many traditional classrooms, the teacher or the content take center stage. With English language learners, the temptation is even greater to create a teacher-centered classroom. Because the teacher has the English proficiency the students need, it seems natural that the teacher should model the language and

Pay attention when the lesson is focused on them.

direct the lessons. However, teachers can't directly transmit knowledge of the English language any more than any other knowledge.

Lindfors (1987) provides an example of the pitfalls of a teacher-centered orientation with an excerpt from a textbook written for second language elementary school students. (The speakers in the following dialogue are given as T for teacher, C for class, and P for individual pupil.)

T: Class, ask [Juan/María], "How do you feel?"
C: How do you feel?
P: I feel [fine/good/well].
T: Class, ask [him/her], "Are you happy?"
C: Are you happy?
P: Yes, I am.
T: Ask [him/her], "Do you need to lie down?"
C: Do you need to lie down?
P: No, I don't need to lie down. (438)

This lesson at first glance seems to focus on the learner. Students are asking each other how they feel and whether they need to rest. A closer look, though, makes it clear that this is a teacher-directed lesson. Some students are told what to ask, and their classmate has only limited choices in answering. The student can be "fine," "well," or "good," but not sick. In fact, the sequence of sentences makes little sense. If the student is happy, why should classmates ask if he or she wants to lie down? Even though students may be actively involved in the lesson, it doesn't focus on them, their needs, or their interests.

Henrietta described a lesson she taught that stands in sharp contrast to the traditional lesson described above. She wrote about discovering the power of focusing on the learner when she was tutoring some college-aged international students:

I always wondered, "How do I find out what is of interest to the students?" Last week I had a wonderful experience with two of the adult ESL students I am working with for my practicum. I met with an Armenian student in a small room that had a world map on the wall. To start our meeting, I casually walked over to the map and asked her about the location of her home country and if she could tell me something about it. This initial question triggered an hour of her telling me about her country, the economic situation, the Moslem/Christian conflict, her family, her journey to America, and many details about her personal life. . . . I asked her if she would be willing to write an essay about her country, her story, and some of the struggles she went through. She is now working on that essay.

The other student I met with comes from Thailand. I do not remember how we got to talk about his job, but suddenly I found him talking about what mattered to him. He is a pastor of the Khmu people here in Fresno. He shared about his concern with the church and the young Christians in Thailand. His eyes glowed with excitement. Again, I asked him if he would be willing to share his story in an essay. This was exciting. This would give me the opportunity to learn more about him, about his concerns and interests, and about his literacy. It really happened—students had talked to me about what mattered to them!

The second explorer principle, to focus on the learner, allows a teacher to discover students' strengths and build on them as Henrietta did. In addition, in explorer classrooms teachers focus on their students to identify their needs. Susanne realized the controlled reading curriculum mandated by her school district was not meeting her students' needs, so she supplemented the mandated textbook with culturally relevant books that encouraged her students to engage in reading. Choosing relevant books and materials is one important consideration in teaching English learners. Another is developing curriculum that starts with students and allows them to draw on their backgrounds and strengths. Even students with limited English proficiency can communicate information about themselves, and in the process of authentic language use, they develop English. In the following sections we explore the idea of culturally relevant texts and organizing curriculum that draws on students' strengths and background knowledge.

Culturally Relevant Texts

Culturally relevant texts can engage diverse students in reading. However, finding culturally relevant texts for English learners is not simple. For example, many teachers collect folktales from different countries and read the ones that come from the country of their students' origin. While folktales can be relevant, especially to very recent immigrants who have either heard or read them, for students who have lived in this country for some time or for second-generation students, folktales may have little or no significance. In addition, folktales often are set in the past or in a make-believe setting that can actually be confusing to English learners.

Even when the characters in a story have the same ethnicity as the students reading the text, a book may not be culturally relevant. Goodman (1982) found that students from Hawaii were able to retell a modern-day story from a basal reader that contained no Hawaiian characters better than they could retell a Hawaiian folktale. Goodman provided a list of considerations in the selection of texts which included social, cultural, and economic backgrounds of the students, the setting of the stories, including the time period, the age and sex of the characters, and the language variations represented.

A. Freeman (2000) explored the topic of culturally relevant texts with Hispanic middle and high school students in an Arizona border community. Drawing on the Goodman list, she developed a rubric to use with the students, asking them to help identify what kinds of texts were relevant to them (see Figure 6–2). She also interviewed the students, did miscue analyses with different texts, and observed them in

Cultural Relevance Rubric
Ann Freeman 2000

1) Are the characters in the story like you and your family?

   Just like us .... Not at all

       4   3   2   1

2) Have you lived in or visited places like those in the story?

   Yes .... No

       4   3   2   1

3) Could this story take place this year?

   Yes .... No

       4   3   2   1

4) How close do you think the main characters are to you in age?

   Very close .... Not close at all

       4   3   2   1

5) Are there main characters in the story who are:
               boys (for boys) or girls (for girls)?

   Yes .... No

       4   3   2   1

6) Do the characters talk like you and your family do?

   Yes .... No

       4   3   2   1

7) How often do you read stories like these?

   Often .... Never

       4   3   2   1

8) Have you ever had an experience like one described in this story?

   Yes .... No

       4   3   2   1

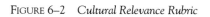

FIGURE 6–2   *Cultural Relevance Rubric*

classrooms noting the reading they were assigned. Freeman, like Susanne, chose a book written by Garza (1990) for her own miscue research with the students. She had students read the excerpt "Birthday Party," about a six-year-old celebrating her birthday with a piñata, from *Family Pictures: Cuadros de familia.*

Freeman found that the students' personal lives influenced how they interacted with texts. Marina told Freeman in an interview how her older brother had read to her as a child. When she was in fourth grade, he was murdered in a teenage love triangle incident. Marina was devastated and her school work and interest in reading suffered for several years. Her teachers, unaware of her personal life, labeled her as a slow learner and put her in special education classes.

When reading the birthday party vignette, Marina miscued when the text said, "My father is pulling the rope that makes the piñata go up and down." She read, "brother" instead of "father," perhaps identifying the central character pulling the rope with her older brother. In fact, listening to her own taped reading three times, she did not notice the miscue she had made. When she answered the questions in the cultural relevance rubric, Marina identified with the reading, changing the age of the character in the text to connect more closely to her own, saying that "the girl turned sixteen, and I'm fifteen" (Freeman 2000, 25).

As Freeman concludes, "While studies have shown that culturally relevant texts help support the reading development of English language learners, there has been limited discussion about how to determine the cultural relevance to individual students. Getting to know students on a personal level can help educators a great deal" (28–29). Using the cultural relevance rubric can help teachers find texts that connect with their students. By asking students the questions on the rubric, teachers can get to know something about their students' personal lives. However, English learners need to do more than read relevant literature in order to compete academically, they also need to develop content-area knowledge. Students learning English can learn language through content when the curriculum is organized around relevant themes.

Organizing Around Relevant Themes

Explorer teachers focus on the learner by organizing curriculum around relevant themes. Whitmore and Crowel (1994) and Kucer et al. (1995) provide concrete ideas for using themes with linguistically diverse students. Freeman and Freeman (1998a) suggest that organizing around themes based on big questions can be especially suitable for students in multilingual and multiethnic classes when the big questions connect to students' lives. One benefit of organizing curriculum around themes is that English learners can more easily develop academic language. The terms are repeated naturally during theme study. Rhoda, who wrote about the Punjabi student Sharma in Chapter 1, commented on the importance of theme study for developing vocabulary:

An element I've focused on has been helping language minority students develop academic language/ vocabulary. . . . I have often found that there is so much academic language in content areas that meaning often is lost in a maze of technical words. It struck me that the real backbone of meaningful academic language development has to come through integrated study. When students are given more than one slant on a topic, they have a greater chance to form deeper meaning and come away with a firmer grasp of a concept. It maintains students' dignity and self-esteem without forcing them to do meaningless vocabulary drills that have no context base and make them feel they are in the low/inept group.

Organizing around themes contrasts with traditional practices in which the day is divided into time periods, and math, science, social studies, reading, and language arts are taught separately without any connections being made among the subjects. Below we give an example of how one teacher integrated the content areas and focused on her bilingual students through a relevant theme.

From the Field to the Table

Sandra, a bilingual Spanish/English teacher originally from Argentina, teaches fourth, fifth, and sixth graders in a rural farming community. Her students, who are almost all newcomers to this country, speak Spanish or Mixteco or Triqui, languages of indigenous groups of southern Mexico. Most of Sandra's students arrive with little or no previous schooling. Few are literate in their first language and most lack confidence in themselves as learners.

Since many of the children are from migrant families, their schooling, once they start studying in the United States, is often interrupted. Work often takes families to northern states from May to early October, and family obligations take them back to Mexico in November and December. Sandra's challenge, then, is to provide these students with the literacy skills and academic concepts they have missed so that they can succeed in junior high and high school classes.

Sandra's classroom is a learning community. Her expectations for her students are high and she does not allow them to make excuses for not doing their work or not participating in activities. Students in Sandra's classroom understand how their classroom is set up, and what routines to expect as they engage in learning. Since her students have had little previous schooling and suffer from various degrees of culture shock, Sandra has found that having classroom routines helps them adjust to school and concentrate on learning to read, write, and problem solve. Her students must not only develop literacy in their first language but also prepare themselves to survive academically in English. Therefore, the daily routine includes many opportunities for students to develop literacy in their first and second language while learning language through academic content (Freeman and Freeman 2000).

Sandra also organizes around themes because this approach is especially important for her students. As she writes:

I believe that organizing around themes is important for my older emergent readers to grow academically. I know that these students do not come to school knowing what many mainstream students do, but they do bring with them world knowledge that can be the starting point of theme study.

Because Sandra's migrant students have a strong background in agriculture, she decided to use what they bring to school and include their knowledge in the curriculum. Her "From the Field to the Table" unit has two clear purposes. First, it helps her draw on students' prior knowledge and personal experiences. The unit focuses on them, since it relates directly to their lives. Second, this topic presents concepts her students may have missed in previous years of limited schooling.

The unit is part of a broader theme that is developed in a time frame of ten to twelve weeks. The entire theme includes seeds, plants, nutrition, and health. Each topic flows into the next, giving the students the opportunity to develop academic English vocabulary while they are gaining the concepts in Spanish. Sandra begins with the topic of seeds, which naturally moves into plants, and because plants are the main source of our daily diet, she follows with the topic of food and nutrition. She brings the cycle to completion by helping her students see that good health depends on the plants and crops their families help provide.

In fact, the contributions of the students' families are included from the beginning of the unit. To start, Sandra writes a note asking parents to send seeds and tell how they are planted. She has been impressed and touched when her students arrive with tiny packets of seeds wrapped and labeled. She later asks parents to share with their children traditional recipes. The idea of this activity is to later prepare some of those recipes in the classroom, analyzing the nutritional value of their ingredients and discussing how those products travel from the field to the table.

The response Sandra gets and the quality of information that the parents and students bring to different activities is exciting. The students are proud of their knowledge and that of their parents. The information they bring contributes expertise that the teacher does not have.

One morning at recess, a Mixteco girl who usually does not participate much told Sandra,

Teacher, yo sé hacer tortillas. Yo hago tortillas todos los días cuando llego de la escuela para mí y para todos mis hermanitos porque mi mamá está trabajando y viene tarde y muy cansada. Yo aprendí hacer tortillas desde que era muy chiquita viendo a mi mamá. A veces me levanto a las cuatro de la mañana para ayudarle a mi mamá antes de que se vaya a trabajar. Es bien fácil. Yo le enseño si quiere.

Teacher, I know how to make tortillas. I make tortillas for me and my brothers and sisters when I come back from school every day because my Mom is working and she comes back very tired late at night. I learned to make tortillas when I was little by looking at my Mom. Sometimes I wake up at four o'clock in the morning to help my Mom before she goes to work. It is very easy. If you want I can teach you.

This incident prompted Sandra to start her "From the Field to the Table" unit that year with tortillas. All the students decided that they wanted to teach Sandra, who is from Argentina, about tortillas, a typical food from their culture and the primary source of nutrition for many Mexicans. They wanted to show her how to make tortillas. Students were eager to take on the role of teacher and share their knowledge.

The class first read *The Tortilla Factory* (Paulsen 1995) in both English and Spanish. This book describes how corn seeds are planted, grown, harvested, and made into tortillas, which nourish the workers who then plant more corn. The class decided that they would demonstrate all the steps from the corn to the tortilla as a real-life "from the field to the table" example. They discussed the ingredients they needed for the project, where those ingredients came from, the different varieties of tortillas they cooked, and the different foods they ate with tortillas.

The Triqui and Mixteco students, who usually were ashamed of their culture and language limitations, became the experts. Students decided how they were going to demonstrate the steps. The students who were not demonstrating were assigned to take notes on the whole process. After the class had discussed the process and the materials needed for the activity, Sandra bought the ingredients, and the students brought the necessary utensils from home. The utensils were all handmade. Each utensil brought by the students was labeled, to help the recorders with unknown words. They included the *petate*, a basket that women hang on their back from their shoulders or head to collect the corn as it is picked; the *metate*, a stone used to grind the kernels with water for the corn flour; the *molcajete*, a stone bowl used to mash the ingredients to make the hot sauce for the tortillas; and the *comal*, a circular metal grill used to cook tortillas over an open fire. In the classroom, the *comal* was placed over an electric burner.

Once all the utensils and ingredients were placed on the tables, the students went straight to work. At the first table, they explained how the corn is gathered and how the people in their community arrange and keep it for later use. One of the students in this group showed the class different techniques for removing the kernels from the cob. After the corn was removed from the cob, another student soaked the grains and ground them in the *metate* by hand. Both students explained to their peers that this process is done on a weekly basis by their mothers at home or by the students themselves.

After this step was completed, students moved to the next table, where another group of students was preparing both a green chili and red chili sauce to eat later on with the homemade tortillas being prepared by their classmates. The students put the chilies and tomatoes over the *comal* to cook the skin and peel the tomatoes easily. Once the vegetables were ready, they put then into the *molcajete* and mashed the chilies and tomatoes together. They added salt, water, and a little bit of fresh garlic. They tasted the sauce, and when it was done, the students moved to the next station.

At the third table, the student who told Sandra she cooks for her family daily was in charge of making the dough for the tortillas. She showed mastery in preparing it, and she directed her helpers, showing them how to prepare each tortilla by hand or by using a *máquina*, a hand press for flattening tortillas. In a short period of time everybody at this table was working together to get the tortillas ready to be cooked.

The entire class was engaged. The students observing and taking notes were respectful of those working, and they were attentive to the process. Everybody was an active participant, and the cooks shined, proud to be the experts in front of their peers and the teacher.

When the tortillas were ready, the students at the fourth table started cooking them, flipping them over by hand as their mothers do every day. They taught Sandra how to turn the tortillas. Sandra admitted that her students quickly took over the job when they saw how inept she was. As soon as the tortillas were ready students started to prepare tacos of cheese, lettuce, tomatoes, and refried beans. Everybody feasted on the student-made tortillas.

In the following days, students worked at writing science books about making tortillas. Since students in Sandra's class have younger siblings in other classes in the same school, word about the tortilla project spread through the school. Teachers in the lower grades who were creating a recipe book invited Sandra's students to give their presentation to second graders. The second-grade teachers were amazed to see how confident and skilled these English learners were during their presentation. Sandra's students were proud of themselves because they could share with the little ones what they knew.

By drawing on her students' cultural knowledge, Sandra found a way to help them succeed in school. They expanded their literacy, their content knowledge, and their English. After studying tortillas, the students chose other foods, and for each they traced the steps involved in bringing the food from the field to the table. When teachers focus on their students and draw on their background knowledge and personal experiences in this way, they increase their opportunities for academic success.

Make Curriculum Meaningful to the Students

Sandra's students were involved in a theme that focused on their strengths and built on their background knowledge. Because the unit connected to their everyday lives, it was also meaningful. The third explorer principle, making curriculum meaningful for students, is important, because it is very difficult for students to learn when content is not meaningful. Research has shown that children learn their first language because it serves a purpose for them (Smith 1983; Halliday 1984). Babies' first words are ones that identify primary caregivers—*mama, dada, bapa*—or immediate needs—*wawa, agua* (Spanish for water). These needs are similar in different cultures. For Hmong children, for example, common early words are *mov* (food/rice) and *mis* (milk). As children grow older, they continue to learn the language that is necessary for them to get what they need, language that is meaningful to them. In classes for English language learners, it is equally important for language to be meaningful. In Stephen Cary's book, *Working with Second Language Learners: Answers to Teachers' Top Ten Questions* (2000), the author includes clear examples of how to make learning meaningful for English language learners as he answers questions commonly asked about working with second language students.

Pat, an experienced teacher who has taken classes in both reading and language development, has had the opportunity to visit many different classrooms with second language learners. Too often she has seen classrooms where reading instruction was not meaningful. In her responses for a graduate class, she wrote about two separate incidents that disturbed her. In the first classroom, students were working on a very controlled phonics program. Pat described the scene as follows:

> I saw twenty-nine second graders respond to flash cards by reciting the sounds, key words, and the rule it exemplified. Two Hmong girls, three very limited-English-speaking Hispanics, ten ESL Hispanics, and fourteen almost "at-risk" children knew the rules forward and backward, but could not apply them when they were given any text to read. The frustration level of this class was very high, and this instruction is not empowering them to become creative or resourceful.

The teacher undoubtedly had good intentions. She may have thought that giving these students real literature to read was too overwhelming, especially because many of the children were English language learners. It may have seemed logical to the teacher to start with the sounds of English and build up to complete stories. However, the students did not understand how the isolated practice of sounds, words, and rules was related to making meaning out of texts. Even though the students appeared to be actively involved in the lesson, this activity was not helping them become more proficient readers. The students were not getting meaning from the stories.

In another classroom that Pat observed, the teacher was using basal readers with traditional ability groups. Pat described the scene in one reading group that she had been asked to lead:

> The students read in a round-robin fashion. The students aggressively monitored each other, allowing no slips to pass unreported. One girl read very well, and I proceeded to ask what she thought would happen next. When she did not respond, another child in the group said, "She doesn't know. She only understands Spanish." She had apparently become quite adept at word calling, but since discussion does not seem to be encouraged, she had no idea what she was reading.

In this classroom, students corrected each other when words were misread. Reading was presented as identifying and correctly pronouncing words. Students, such as the girl Pat describes, focused on this external aspect of reading and failed to comprehend the story. It did not seem to matter if the students had absolutely no idea what they were reading, as long as they could "word call" correctly. This "reading" activity did not empower these students. There was such a strong emphasis on oral performance that students did not realize that reading is supposed to be meaningful.

Rusty, who was teaching in a summer school program for English learners, provides a sharp contrast to the classrooms Pat visited. He relates how he encouraged Jessica, a struggling reader and writer, by making assignments meaningful to her:

> In this ELD [English language development] summer school program, it has been neat to see the self-confidence grow in all the kids that I have the privilege of having in my classroom. As I look at the past four weeks, we have worked harder on the belief of "yes, I can," than on anything else.
>
> Jessica came up to me early in the first week and whispered that she couldn't write yet (during writer's workshop) because she hadn't learned how to read (and she was going into third grade). I convinced her that she either could or would before the week was out. We have done a lot of singing/chanting, choral reading, buddy-up reading, and individual reading. I also wrote specific poems using each of the kid's names, which we have done choral reading with, and it was remarkable what that has done for them—kind of like seeing their name in lights!
>
> During the last hour we have some aides come into our classroom and work with us. The students decided that they wanted to read their own poem to the aides. Jessica spent each afternoon with her barely bilingual grandmother, one of the aides, who helped her each day. I thought Jessica was going to burst with pride when she finished reading and everybody in the class clapped for her. And of course, now she is "writing" too! Sometimes she forgets what she wrote when we do author's chair, but she goes for it with gusto anyway. It is amazing what believing in yourself can do.

By making instruction meaningful, Rusty created a classroom and curriculum where Jessica and the other students were bound to succeed.

The Explorer Team

The Explorer Team, a group of four content-area teachers at King's Canyon Middle School, a large, inner-city school for seventh and eighth graders, has worked hard to engage their diverse students in activities that have meaning and purpose for them. Kathy, the teacher of the Hmong student Tou profiled in Chapter 1, is the language arts teacher. Kathy works with Pat, the history teacher, Cheryl, the math teacher, and Mike, the science teacher, to provide assignments that will involve their 140 students in relevant academic work. These four teachers collaborate to ensure that all their students have access to second language acquisition and academic content. The teachers develop themes and projects as they work with one group of students over a two-year period, through seventh and eighth grades.

The teachers want students to connect with each other and to work to make the school a true community. One of the first projects for the eighth graders is to make a survival kit for the incoming seventh graders. Figure 6–3 shows the cover of the survival kit Ramón created.

As the kit's cover shows, incoming students face many problems at King's Canyon. The population of approximately 75 percent Hispanic, 10 percent Asian, 8 percent African American, and 7 percent non-Hispanic white students live in neighborhoods where violence, drugs, and poverty are a way of life. Many of the students have moved several times within the inner-city school system. Some, like Tou, are refugees of war or poverty in other countries. Others have never traveled outside the city.

In his kit, Ramón provides incoming seventh graders with an overview of the school schedule and a color-keyed map (see Figure 6–4).

FIGURE 6–3   *Ramón's Survival Kit*

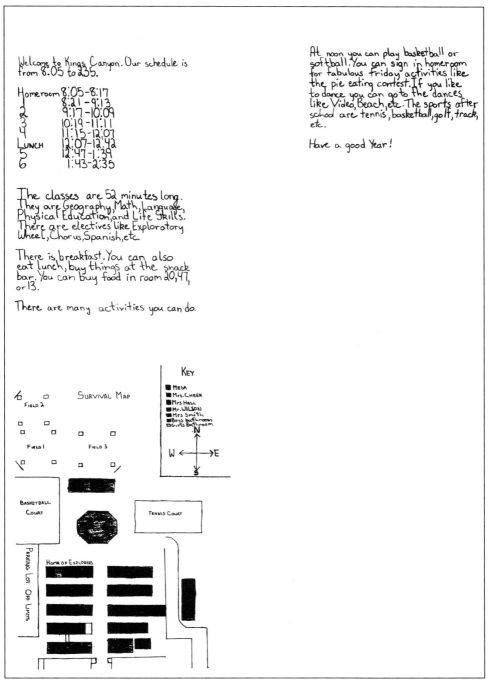

Welcome to Kings Canyon. Our schedule is from 8:05 to 2:35.

Homeroom 8:05-8:17
1   8:21-9:13
2   9:17-10:09
3   10:19-11:11
4   11:15-12:07
Lunch   12:07-12:42
5   12:47-1:39
6   1:43-2:35

The classes are 52 minutes long. They are Geography, Math, Language, Physical Education, and Life Skills. There are electives like Exploratory Wheel, Chorus, Spanish, etc.

There is breakfast. You can also eat lunch, buy things at the snack bar. You can buy food in room 20,47, or 13.

There are many activities you can do.

At noon you can play basketball or softball. You can sign in homeroom for fabulous friday activities like the pie eating contest. If you like to dance you can go to the dances like Video, Beach, etc. The sports after school are tennis, basketball, golf, track, etc.

Have a good Year!

KEY
■ MESA
■ Mrs. CHEEK
■ Mrs HALL
■ Mr. WILSON
■ Mrs. Smith
■ Boys Bathroom
■ Girls Bathroom

SURVIVAL MAP

FIELD 2

FIELD 1   FIELD 3

N
W ←→ E
S

BASKETBALL COURT

TENNIS COURT

PARKING LOT OFF LIMITS

HOME OF EXPLORERS

FIGURE 6–4   *School Schedule and Map*

Figure 6–5 shows the results of surveys Ramón conducted with King's Canyon students about their favorite lunches and popular brands of shoes. Ramón graphed the results as part of his math class and added the graphs to his kit.

Ramón created his survival kit with pride and care because the assignment had meaning and purpose for him. Students like Ramón enjoyed being the experts and preparing their survival kits. In the process, they read, wrote, and solved math problems.

After this initial activity, the Explorer Team teachers involved their students in a relevant theme that applied to all the content areas. They chose a theme that would be meaningful to their students and would continue to build community: "One World/One Family." Kathy explained why the teachers chose this theme:

> Adolescence is an emotionally vulnerable time. Middle school students are beginning to see themselves as individuals separate from a family unit but unsure about where they really belong. We strive for them to see themselves as part of one human family with cultural, language, and ethnic diversity as positive and beneficial to the well-being and fulfillment of all people.

During the theme, students discussed how they felt about differences among people. To explore attitudes toward difference, Kathy's language arts students read *The*

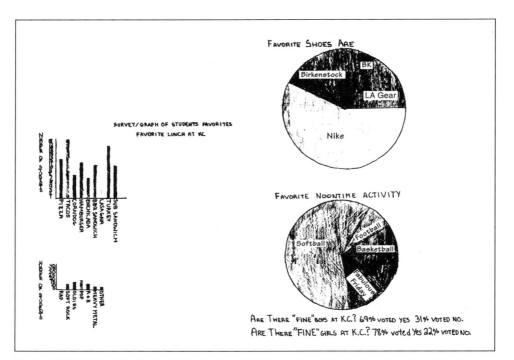

FIGURE 6–5 *Survey Results*

Acorn People by Ron Jones (1976). This book tells the true story of the author's work as a counselor at a summer camp for severely handicapped children. The teens in Kathy's class were initially repulsed by the handicaps of the children, especially "Spider," who has stumps for arms and legs, and "Arid," who must carry his waste in a plastic bag because he has no bladder. But soon the students began to realize that these children with physical deformities are people with feelings like every other kid.

In the process of reading, discussing, and writing about the book, Kathy's students carried out activities and discussed topics that were relevant to their own lives. In pairs, they made labels that represented different characters in the book. They guessed which characters the labels of other pairs referred to. The pairs explained why they chose the symbols they invented to represent the characters: A carrot represented the "vegetable" label given the severely disabled kids in the book who were considered worthless and incapable of human feelings; a lightbulb represented Martin, who, though blind, had brightness and ideas about the world and life; a crown represented Arid, who is crowned king at the dance in the story and is, in fact, as noble as a king. This activity led to a general discussion of how people get labeled and how labels can have positive or negative connotations.

Kathy asked her students to write in their literature logs about a time that they had experienced something similar to what happened to the characters in the book. Many of the students wrote about how they had been misjudged and labeled by others. These journal entries served as the beginnings of individual autobiographical projects, papers that are required by the district curriculum guides.

The final project for *The Acorn People* was to design and present a graphic that represented the setting, plot, character, and theme of the book. Students worked on this project in pairs. One pair created the graphic shown in Figure 6–6. The setting appears in the foreground on the right. The acorn necklace in the upper left was their choice as the key element in the plot. For character, the pair drew a dolphin to represent Spider, the boy with no arms or legs who, once in the water, was able to do anything. They titled their work, "Never Quit, Try Try Again," which was their choice of theme.

At the end of the unit, students reflected in writing on what they had learned. Several explained that they had discovered that all people are the same inside, and you should not judge people by the way they look. Other students told Kathy that reading about how these boys overcame their disabilities to live and enjoy life the best way they could gave them hope to keep trying and never give up on the goals they set for themselves. Certainly, this theme was meaningful and purposeful for Kathy's students.

Career Day

Another meaningful activity that the Explorer Team planned for their middle school students was Career Day. During the last month of school before graduation, sixteen community speakers were invited to the school to speak to the Explorer Team students. All 140 eighth graders prepared for the day by reading about a variety of

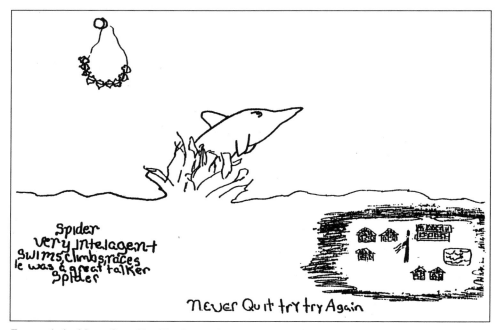

Spider
very intelagent
swims climbs races
le was a great talker
spider

never Quit try try Again

FIGURE 6–6 *Never Quit, Try, Try Again*

careers in the language arts class, by studying the economic aspects of careers, including reading graphs and charts in math class, and reviewing different career options in science class. The history teacher worked on a computer with all 140 students to access a database about the career interests each had. When Career Day arrived, the students had all thought about, read about, and talked about possible career options.

The speakers for Career Day represented the diversity of the students of the Explorer Team. A Hispanic described how he had given up a $60,000-a-year job to earn $40,000 as a high school counselor. When the kids asked him why, he said, "Because you kids are dropping out! That's why!" He then repeated his message in Spanish for emphasis. The students got the message. A retired African American principal told the kids, "I know it's hard. But it's not as hard for you to get to college as it was for me forty years ago!" A Hispanic female professor of sociology echoed his message, telling the students about how she grew up in a migrant family. She described moving from school to school and how she had had to work in the fields after school and then do homework after that. A Hmong woman who had recently been the commencement speaker at her college graduation explained how she had made it through high school and college essentially on her own. In her culture it was extremely unusual for a Hmong—especially a Hmong woman—to go to college. The Explorer Team students listened intently to the speakers, took notes eagerly, and wrote summaries of what they had learned. Several of the students chose a goal during Career Day, including a Hmong boy who had listened to a policeman explain how important he believed his job was to the community.

As a follow-up to Career Day, all 140 students were hosted by a local junior college for a tour and a free lunch. The guides for the many small groups were all junior college students who at one time had dropped out of school and were now studying again. Part of the time the guides spent with the Kings Canyon students involved sharing the struggles they had endured and the decisions they had made to return to college. The guides wanted to impress upon the junior high students how important school was for their futures. By looking at the faces of the middle school students as they listened to the college students, one could see that they were finding this experience both meaningful and purposeful.

Conclusion

We close this chapter with the story of the eighth-grade graduation for Ramón and his other Explorer Team members. The graduation was a true celebration, not only for the students but for Pat, Cheryl, Mike, and Kathy, the teachers who had worked so hard with them over a two-year period. Although they comprised less than a third of all the graduates at the school, the students from the Explorer Team received 90 percent of all the awards given out at the ceremony, including academic, athletic, and citizenship awards. When the Spanish teacher described the all-around outstanding student in Spanish, it was an Explorer Team student; when the computer instructor named the top student in computers, it was an Explorer Team student. The highest honor in wood shop went to an Explorer Team student. When the home economics teacher announced the all-around outstanding student, it was an Explorer Team student. And when the principal and vice principal gave out the outstanding citizenship awards, they went to Explorer Team students.

At the end of the ceremony everyone—teachers, administrators, parents, and the students themselves—marveled together. The celebration, like so many special occasions, was both happy and sad. Tears flowed as proud students and teachers hugged one another and promised to stay in touch. Something very special had happened with this group. They had bonded as they learned. They had formed a group that cared about one another. The students had begun as a diverse group of inner-city average-to-below-average students from many different backgrounds. Few thought much about their futures and, if they did, they did not consider college. When they graduated, they were students with expectations, students with determination, students with hope, and especially, students with a future. All of them now felt that they had access to further education.

Explorer teachers give all students a greater chance to succeed. What happened at Kings Canyon Middle School with the Explorer Team can happen anywhere when teachers celebrate learning and diversity, focus on their learners, and make the curriculum meaningful and purposeful. In the following chapter, we explore three more explorer principles that help lead all students, and especially English language learners, toward academic success.

Applications

1. In small groups, discuss how organizing teaching around themes helps second language learners. Share ideas about themes that could be used with your students.

2. Bring to class a list of books and other support materials that could be used to develop a theme with your students. Share and discuss.

3. Pick out three literature books that you think are culturally relevant texts for your students, referring to the cultural relevance rubric in Figure 6–2. Be prepared to describe to others why you think the books are culturally relevant.

4. Read a book to your students, then have them respond to the questions on the cultural relevance rubric. Did you discover anything new about your students from doing this activity?

5. Francisco and Elena had school experiences that kept them from celebrating learning and diversity. Have you experienced or observed students who have been kept from celebrating learning and diversity? Describe the experience.

6. Think about an experience in your own learning that you found meaningful. Describe it and try to identify why it was so meaningful to you.

7

How Do Explorer Teachers Respect Learners and Their Ways of Learning?

I was born and lived in India until I was ten years old. I am Zoroastrian, a minority in India. As a community we value education and most of the professional workforce pre-Independence was made up of Zoroastrians. I went to a very good, private girls' convent school. Most of the teachers used the transmission model of teaching. . . .

At sixteen I moved to Canada. I did well in high school and walked into university three months shy of seventeen. Was I in for a shock! My professors wanted me to voice my opinions, reflect, interact. I wasn't prepared for this. Why couldn't they just tell me what to learn, so that I could just give them what they wanted later on in the exams? That first year was tough to say the least, but I loved it. I enjoyed the cooperative groups, sharing ideas, learning how others perceived the same information, the different opinions. It was exhilarating. I loved the dialogue best of all. I learned more in my first year of university than I had in my entire school life, and it was not all content. I realized that here I would learn about the power of knowledge. The knowledge being where to find information, how to find it, and what to do with it. My perspective on what was important about education changed.

We open this chapter with Khushnuma's reflections on her educational experiences. After finishing her studies, she taught in Canada and Thailand. She recently completed an MA degree in TESOL, studying in Spain. Khushnuma is now a teacher at the American School of Bombay in India. She has adopted an approach to teaching that allows her students to experience the excitement she felt at the university. She organizes her curriculum around themes and provides lots of hands-on interactive activities, with students working in cooperative groups. She is excited to see that her ESL students as well as her native English speakers thrive in this environment.

Explorer teachers show respect for their students by organizing their curriculum in ways that draw on students' backgrounds and strengths. In Chapter 6, we discussed the first three explorer principles (see Figure 6–1). We gave examples of teachers celebrating learning and diversity, focusing on the learner, and making the curriculum meaningful to the students. In this chapter we will look at the next three principles. We will describe how teachers like Khushnuma organize for collaboration, encourage learning through different modes, and respect learners.

Organize for Collaboration

Social interaction is especially important for students learning a second language. Drawing on the research on cooperative learning and second language learning, Johnson (1995) explains that student-student interaction provides important experiences for second language acquisition.

> [S]tudent-student interaction in second language classrooms can create opportunities for students to participate in less structured and more spontaneous language use, negotiate meaning, self-select when to participate, control the topic of discussion, and most important, draw on their own prior knowledge and interactional competencies to actively communicate with others. (116)

English learners need to learn to use language that is appropriate to a variety of situations in order to develop communicative competence, and cooperative learning provides those situations. However, students learn more than how to communicate in a new language: they solve academic problems by working together, they acquire vocabulary by listening to one another; and as Van Lier (1988) has pointed out, they become more proficient language learners as they use the language they know for authentic purposes.

McGroarty (1993) explains that group work benefits English language learners in three ways: via input, interaction, and contextualization of knowledge. During whole-class instruction, it is difficult for teachers to provide comprehensible input at the appropriate level for each student. On the other hand, when students work in small groups, they are more apt to receive input that is only slightly beyond their current level of competence. Further, in whole-class instruction, learners get little opportunity to interact in the language. In small groups, interaction is much greater. All students have more opportunities to participate. They ask more real questions. And they produce "comprehensible output" (Swain 1985). Finally, group tasks allow students to develop academic language and content knowledge together as they solve problems.

Students acquire language and content knowledge as they negotiate meaning. According to McGroarty, "While there are many types of cooperative activities useful in a variety of subject areas, those requiring some negotiation among students who must solve a problem or come to a consensus are optimal for second language development" (37).

Explorer teachers with second language learners work to organize for social interaction (Enright and McCloskey 1985; Enright 1988; Holt 1993). They know that language develops in contexts of functional use. For that reason they create situations in which all their students use language for a variety of purposes and with a variety of people. Research on cooperative learning highlights the importance of heterogeneous grouping (Kagan 1986), and explorer teachers with second language students capitalize on the diversity their students provide. In their classrooms, diversity provides an enriched social context for learning together.

Teachers need to think carefully about how to group students. Some arrangements are highly structured, with each student assigned a role. A better approach, from our perspective, is to organize groups around student interests. Gayleen, a first-grade teacher in a multilingual inner-city classroom, expressed her beliefs about necessary conditions for positive social interaction:

> While I agree with the principles of cooperative learning, I find myself questioning the sometimes highly structured practice. I think too often our field takes a good idea and structures it to a degree where some things are lost. I am referring to the idea of having a recorder, time keeper, et cetera, which in my experience can make it artificial. Interaction can occur within an environment where everyone is a teacher and learner, or where the roles are interchangeable.

Gayleen's points are important. When collaborative groups work well, students take on roles naturally and these roles reflect their interests and strengths. For social interaction to be meaningful, all participants must have a real investment in what they are doing.

Students learn together in explorer classrooms doing many different kinds of things. They may read with a buddy or a cross-age tutor. Then, they discuss what they have read during a literature study. They confer with classmates and the teacher about their writing and then share the finished product by reading it to the class. They write letters for pen pals in other classes or other schools. They form teams to investigate topics and answer questions, and in this process of inquiry, they explore all the different content areas. Together, they decide on ways that they can take the information they have gathered and actually apply it to their lives. They consider how they can use what they have learned to solve real-world problems. In these classes, students collaborate because the social group structures serve real purposes.

A number of factors can promote collaboration. Both the physical setup of the classroom and the kinds of activities that are planned can inhibit or facilitate social interaction. Figure 7–1 contrasts factors that restrict social interaction with those that facilitate interaction.

Classroom Characteristics and Social Interaction

Restricts Social Interaction	Facilitates Social Interaction
Straight rows	Desks together in groups or tables and chairs
Students do not move from seats	Students move freely around the room
Materials are controlled only by the teacher	Students have ownership of the room and use and care for materials
Teacher works with reading groups while others work individually on worksheets	Students do shared reading, literature studies, and writers workshop
Work is completed by individuals for individual grades	Students work together on group projects for group grades
Silence is the golden rule	Students ar encouraged to talk together to share ideas

---

FIGURE 7–1   *Classroom Social Interaction*

Teachers promote interaction by grouping desks or tables together. If students can move around the room, opportunities for interaction increase. Of course, students have to learn when it is appropriate to talk to classmates and when it is not appropriate. Allowing students to be in charge of materials and to take responsibility for the room provides more opportunities for students to talk together. Class structures such as readers and writers workshop and theme investigations naturally involve students in pair and small-group discussions.

Grading is always an issue in group work. Some students resist working in groups because they worry that other students will not do their share. Teachers can organize projects so that each student has a specific responsibility, and can then give both individual and group grades. It often helps to have students reflect in writing on their contribution to the project. Some teachers have students who work in groups evaluate one another as well. The key, though, is to arrange the classroom to encourage students to talk together.

Building Intercultural Friendships: Collaboration Project

In classes where students work individually, student diversity may be regarded as a problem. After all, management is easier when all the students can be given the same worksheet with the expectation that all can successfully work on it by themselves

and all will finish in about the same amount of time. When students work collaboratively, diversity is an asset to be celebrated, since the varied experiences, knowledge,
and interests students in each group bring to the task at hand add to the potential for
learning. This interchange is particularly important for students who are developing
English proficiency, because as students talk, they learn both language and content
and at the same time learn to value themselves and others as learners.

An innovative project entitled "Building Intercultural Friendships Through
Story Development and Socialization" exemplifies how second language learners
and native English speakers came to value each other and learn from one another
(DeBruin-Parecki and Timion 1999). The project was developed in northern
Iowa as the result of a conversation between two middle school teachers and a
university professor. They were discussing the student diversity in area schools
and the need for integrating recent immigrant refugees into the mainstream.
Many local schools found themselves flooded with children whose native language was not English. The schools had few resources to serve the new students.
Often the English language learners had few opportunities to interact with native
English speakers, and the native English speakers had little understanding of the
new students.

The two teachers and the professor formed a team consisting of an ESL teacher
working primarily with Bosnian and Hispanic students, a language arts/social studies
teacher whose students were primarily natives of Iowa, and a professor whose interests were family literacy and multicultural education. The ESL class was located in
an old school with few resources, and the language arts class was a university laboratory school with abundant resources. The project goals were to

- Provide opportunities for social interaction between cultures
- Design and implement literacy activities that included reading, writing, listening, viewing, speaking, and art to promote friendship and understanding
  between cultural groups
- Measure students' changing attitudes about diverse cultures over time
- Involve the families of students in the development of intercultural friendships through their participation in planned writing exchanges and social
  gatherings

To begin the project, each class made a video to introduce themselves. This
involved scriptwriting. The immigrant students used their primary languages as
well as English in the videos. Then, students met one another at a pool party during which each immigrant student was matched with a native English speaker.
The project team organized games so that the students would get to know one
another.

The students wrote stories in their individual classrooms. Then they used computers to write collaborative stories in English, Bosnian, and Spanish. They were
asked to write about a holiday or family tradition special to their country or family.

Many of the Bosnian students chose to write about their recent war experiences. After the students wrote, the parents read the stories and responded to them. The students edited their work and published a multilingual text.

The refugee stories were indeed moving. In one story, "Anything for His Family," a Bosnian middle school student wrote in English and Bosnian about the period his family was forced to leave Bosnia to go to live in a Croatian refugee camp, "even if we were Bosnians, born in Bosnia." He told how the family had only "very old potatoes from last year and beans full of bugs, grass, and everything else" to eat. He ended by explaining, "I still remember those days when I was hungry." The accompanying bilingual parent response in Bosnian and English was also moving: "I'm glad that he put his feelings on the paper and other people can see and know what we went through."

In another story, a student told about the "hard days" when "people and children were scared of the army because they came to kill and hurt people. I lived through seven months of war with my family. It was hard." The parent response summed up the refugee experience well: "The story is true. All that happened in our city, like suffering, death, agony, and hunger for little children. I wish that it would never happen again to anybody."

This project is an example of collaboration that involved students in authentic sharing and learning. When the native English speakers read the stories, they saw the new immigrants to Iowa differently. Intercultural friendships were built. In the process, immigrant students acquired more English through communicating orally and in writing. The culmination of the project was a Family Literacy Fest, where families met and shared food and their stories. This project had a number of positive results. Students developed more positive attitudes toward members of other cultural groups. Students and parents from each group began to communicate more meaningfully with members of the other group. (For additional examples from the Building Intercultural Friendships Project publication, visit the Web site http://www.its-ps.uni.edu:200/learning/friends/friends.htm.)

Useful Collaborative Activities

Another effective way to get students to collaborate is through having them teach one another. Many teachers have found that buddy reading or cross-age tutoring can work well. Typically, students from an upper-grade class meet with younger students on a regular basis to read together or to work on different projects in social studies, math, or science. Often, teachers match students with the same primary language. Although the tutoring or reading is usually in English, students can help one another by using their shared first language. Successful programs require advanced planning, training for the tutors and tutees, and careful matching of partners. Samway et al. (1995) provide many practical suggestions for buddy reading programs with English language learners.

Yolanda, a sixth-grade Spanish/English teacher, found that cross-age tutoring had many positive effects for her bilingual students:

Cross-age tutoring has worked well for me. I have buddied up with a second-grade bilingual class. We match our students, and they keep the same child all year long (Spanish readers with Spanish readers). They meet once a week for thirty minutes. My sixth graders have learned so much from this experience. Once in a while I would worry about the noise level, but as I would walk around or sit and watch, I knew that language was blossoming, self-esteem was rising, and relationships were building.

When students study a new language, they expect to be able to communicate in it. Rigg and Allen (1989) comment, "Learning a language means learning to do the things you want to do with people who speak that language" (ix). When students share their ideas and their knowledge in social settings such as cross-age tutoring, students, both those who speak English as a first language and those learning English, increase their language proficiency.

Explorer classrooms buzz with a kind of controlled noise. Denise, a third-grade teacher with many English language learners, has begun to encourage more social interaction in her classroom. She reflects on her experiences as follows:

We as teachers try everything to get second language students to talk, then structure our classes to discourage everyone from talking! I now allow my students choice, and they can "pass" in oral activities. I have begun to do show-and-tell again in my classroom, only now everyone shares with a partner first, to be able to think of vocabulary and try the English out first. Then a few share with the whole group. Instead of saying, "Do your own work," I now say, "Ask someone in your group for help." I am hoping that bit by bit I will be able to tailor my classroom activities to benefit all my students.

Yolanda, Denise, and the teachers in the Building Intercultural Friendships Project are creating collaborative classrooms. Teachers like these build on the synergy that results from authentic social interaction among students who come from diverse backgrounds and have a variety of interests. These teachers help their students value one another as they learn from one another.

A final example makes the important point that social interaction actually improves students' academic work. Darrin, a high school teacher who was discouraged by the lack of interest his Hispanic students had shown in class activities, came back to graduate school to tool himself for a different type of teaching job. After he read about the importance of social interaction, he decided to encourage it in his classroom. The results were positive:

Today I had students pair up and talk about the Fourth of July weekend, about what they usually do on the Fourth, and a Fourth of July weekend they'll never forget. I went around to every single student and asked what he or she had done. I learned the Spanish word for *fireworks*, heard a hilarious story about a student who got run over by a boy on a bike, and found out that one student and her family had spent

*Collaborations —
allow student to
use the language.*

*2nd language student
write/read before they speak.*

the night on the floor because their house was shot up the night before. I felt un-easy taking a half hour of class, but when it was time to write, I couldn't believe the volume of stories that seemed to gush out of the students. Each student had two other students read and sign his paper. I've realized that, for my students' language acquisition and my own sanity, I must begin to initiate and foster social interaction in the classroom.

Darrin's lesson succeeded, and his students produced much better writing than ever before. Collaboration encourages English language learners to use language, raises their self-esteem, and helps them succeed academically.

Encourage Learning Through Different Modes

Some traditional teachers, especially those working with students who are considered at-risk, feel that students' oral language must be fully developed before the introduction of literacy. In the same way, traditional methods of teaching ESL follow a sequence of listening, speaking, reading, and writing. Many ESL materials provide separate lessons or even separate books for each modality. Often, for college-age students in intensive English programs, there are even separate classes for each of the four areas.

The idea that oral language should precede the development of literacy for bilingual students comes from the observation that children acquiring their first language first listen, then speak, and only later do they read and write. While it is true that babies develop oral language first, what they are really doing is developing the kind of language that most immediately meets their needs. Written language allows people to communicate across time and space, but a two-year-old communicates about the here and now, so reading and writing do not serve a meaningful function. Though research shows that young children notice environmental print and make hypotheses about written language (Goodman et al. 1979; Ferreiro and Teberosky 1982), they do not usually read or write before they speak.

In contrast, school-age students are already old enough to use all modes of language. All students need to use written language in school to succeed academically. If second language students have to wait until their oral English is well developed before beginning to read and write, they fall behind their native English-speaking classmates in academic-content areas. For this reason, explorer teachers encourage students to use a variety of ways to learn and express their understandings of both language and content.

Second language acquisition researchers have shown that students learning a second language often read or write their new language before they speak (Hudelson 1984 and 1986; Rigg and Enright 1986; Lindfors 1989; Rigg and Allen 1989; Fitzgerald 1993). In fact, many adults who study English as a foreign language learn to write and read it but never speak it! In some cases, their only communication with English speakers is through writing. Some students may learn to write first because they recognize the importance schools place on written language. In some ways, written language is easier to process than oral language, because oral language passes by quickly, but written language is available for reexamination. The speaker sets the pace for oral language, but the reader or writer sets the pace for written language. Many second language students do better on written assignments than on oral exercises because they can (and are willing to) take more time to process the written language.

One argument for developing all four modes simultaneously is that each supports the others. For example, what students hear can be the basis for what they later write or talk about. What students read can later be the basis for what they understand and talk or write about. Certainly, it is easier to understand something we are learning if we can read about it, talk about it, and write about it.

In fact, this idea of developing language and concepts by using both oral and written language together can and should be extended to include other ways of knowing. Many teachers try to include experiences for their students that go beyond the traditional four modes of learning. They recognize that learning can be demonstrated through other modes including art, music, and movement (Gardner 1984). In fact, teachers try to encourage their students to move between different semiotic systems to show what they are learning. For example, students might draw pictures, act out a scene, or do a dance to summarize a story they have read. In these ways, students show their understanding of what they read through a sign system other than words, through a different mode. In the same way, a student might read a word problem in math, solve the problem, and then represent the results with a graph. Again, the student is using different sign systems to process and represent meaning.

Denise, the third-grade teacher mentioned earlier who is now using collaborative learning, developed a unit that exemplifies the importance of focusing on the learner and building on their strengths while using different modalities. Denise's class includes many Southeast Asian refugee children. She felt strongly that, in studying the Pilgrims, her students should not learn only about the traditional American Thanksgiving Pilgrims and Indians. She decided to center her curriculum around the question, "What or who is a pilgrim?" She began with a literature book identified by the district for her grade level, *Molly's Pilgrim* (Cohen 1983). This book tells the story of a Russian refugee girl who teaches others in her class that recent immigrants are today's pilgrims. Denise believed that it was important for all the students in her class to consider what a pilgrim was and the ways they themselves were pilgrims. The class then read and discussed *Sara Morton's Day: A Day in the Life of a Pilgrim* (Waters 1989) to get an idea of the typical daily life of a Pilgrim in colonial times. The class also read and discussed a book about two immigrant children sailing to America, *Watch the Stars Come Out* (Levinson 1985).

Next, Denise read *How Many Days to America?* (Bunting 1988). She knew that most of her Hmong and Laotian students, like the family in that book, were in the United States because they had had to flee their own countries. The students and teacher discussed the difference between immigrants and refugees. They used two modalities by talking and then drawing a Venn diagram. The students decided that some immigrants come to a new country because they want a better way of life.

Others come because their lives are being threatened. As a homework assignment, the children interviewed their families, asking three questions: "Where did our ancestors come from?" "Where did they settle?" and "When did they come to the United States and why?" Conducting the oral interview and then writing it involved students in using two different modalities.

Denise was well aware that many of her Hmong students' parents were sensitive about this type of interview. Public sentiment is sometimes negative toward Hmong refugees because of a lack of understanding about why they came to the United States. Many people do not realize that the lives of most of the Hmong were in danger once the United States troops left Southeast Asia at the end of the Vietnam War. Because of the terrible memories of the war and the persecutions they have suffered, many Hmong parents will not discuss their past with their children. However, older siblings who know what happened typically believe that it is important for the younger generation to understand their history. Denise found that these brothers and sisters or older cousins were usually glad to answer the interview questions. After conducting the interviews, the children then shared in small groups in class what they learned about their past, rather than having to report to a large group. After the reading, the discussions, and the interviews, the whole class watched the video of *Molly's Pilgrim*, and in this way, Denise was able to include viewing in the unit.

As a final part of the unit, the students used another modality to complete an art project. Just as Molly's mother made and dressed a pilgrim doll in *Molly's Pilgrim*, Denise invited her students to make and dress a paper doll in traditional clothing. Denise explained how she organized this activity:

> Many mothers sew, and the children bring in fabulous pieces of fabric from Thailand and other countries. I put out all the scraps, give students a template of a doll run off on tag board, and with scissors and glue they make a pilgrim.

After the students made their dolls, Denise asked them to write a story. The children typed their stories on a word processor. Figure 7–2 shows two dolls and the stories students wrote about these dolls. The students' pilgrims and stories were put on a bulletin board, which, Denise said, "truly reflected the diverse cultures in my classroom."

In this unit, the students and teacher read together, talked together, wrote together, and watched the video, which was comprehensible to them after all their reading and discussion. In addition, the students designed a doll costume that reflected their own cultural background. Throughout the unit, Denise's students used a variety of modalities. Denise explained how exciting this unit was for her and for her students:

> I wanted to move away from the basal reader, so I decided to try to extend a piece of quality literature that was relevant to my students. I had no idea this would be so successful. The bulletin board display attracted a lot of attention, and this was a positive learning experience not only for my students but for many others at the school.

The Pilgrims

The pilgrim came from Laos to Fresno.And his name is
John he really come for freedom he come to American over
there.They have lots of people kill lots of people. So he come
they Country to are Country. He wear short and t-surt and pants
he like to play restling.

My Doll

My doll came from Thailand because she came to have
freedom. She came to have her own church and have her own place
to live and get freedom. The soldiers were killing them. She did
not want to be hurt so she came to have freedom in America.

FIGURE 7–2   *Pilgrim Dolls*

Moving beyond the traditional ways of teaching helps English language learners develop both language and academic concepts. Teri, a new teacher who is taking graduate classes because she wanted to be more effective with her English language learners, found that using visuals and encouraging movement not only is enjoyable for middle-grade students, it also helps them understand concepts and learn their new language. She wrote about how she involved her students in part of a lesson on the food chain:

> While standing in a semicircle, each student was given a color-coded card with the name and picture of a carnivore (red), an omnivore (blue), a herbivore (green), or a plant (yellow). The students were instructed, one group at a time, to link the strings attached to their cards to one or more cards of animals or plants that the object depicted on their card could eat. Cards were eliminated as they were "eaten." The remaining cards were those at the top of the food chain. Much discussion occurred as students worked together to find their place in the food chain and all students were highly motivated.

Teri and Denise have found that their students succeed in English and learn academic content as they explore concepts through different sign systems including listening, speaking, reading, writing, viewing, art, and movement.

Respect Learners

The multilingual/multicultural students who come to the United States bring with them a rich diversity and a wealth of experiences. Unfortunately, these students, their languages, their families, and their cultures are often not understood by others in schools. It is important that we work with immigrant students and their families as well as native English-speaking students, teachers, and administrators so that a mutual respect can develop. The Building Intercultural Friendships project described above is one example of how getting to know one another can bridge the gaps that exist. Doing case studies like those described in Chapter 1 is another way to learn about and come to respect immigrant students.

Valdés's (1996) research on ten Mexican immigrant families provides important lessons for educators. Valdés showed that what appears to be a lack of interest in education by Mexican parents is much more complex. Many Mexican parents lack an understanding of how the school system works. At the same time, many school officials lack an understanding of the families' perspectives and values. The title of her book begins with Con respeto (With respect), because Valdés wants the families she studied to know that she wrote her book in the hopes of promoting understanding among educators as she respectfully wrote their stories. She also used respeto in the title because in the Mexican culture, respeto has a meaning that goes beyond the English translation, "respect":

> Respeto in its broadest sense is a set of attitudes toward individuals and/or the roles that they occupy. It is believed that certain roles demand or require particular types

of behavior. *Respeto*, while important among strangers, is especially significant among members of the family. (130)

In summary, Valdés explains that *respeto* involves not only how people present themselves to others but also a "knowledge of the boundaries of roles and role relationships as well as the responsibilities individuals have in each relationship" (132).

Perhaps a key lesson from Valdés's work is how much we as educators need to understand about interactions with immigrant students and their parents. If respect is so complex and important to the Mexican immigrant families who have been studied, we can assume that this concept is complex when applied to other cultures as well. This became clear to us as we were teaching graduate students from Japan. Younger graduate students were hesitant to answer in class if older students, whom they must respect because of their age and experience, might also answer, or worse yet, did not know the answers. Most mainstream American students do not consider these factors when they answer a question.

Another example comes from an experience we had while giving out diplomas to MA graduates in a ceremony in Mallorca, Spain. The students came from many different countries and traditions. In Spain it is normal for men and women to kiss each other on both cheeks in greeting or celebration. As we presented the diplomas, we ceremoniously kissed each graduate until a Muslim woman from Pakistan approached. Her desperate shake of the head reminded David that it was not appropriate to kiss her. In fact, she would not normally have shaken David's hand, since there are various proscriptions against women touching males in her religion, but in this setting, she varied from her religious norms. Later, when we saw the woman on the street, we talked but did not touch one another.

Yvonne has worked with female Hmong graduate students over several years. These women, who are teaching as well as studying, are struggling to live between worlds. Their husbands and extended families, often with less formal education, have made demands on them that make it difficult for them to do advanced study, to work, and still carry out their home resposibilities. However, Yvonne has come to understand that she must show she respects their struggle without intervening. She understands that these women must meet the expectations of their own cultural traditions as they study and work within the mainstream culture.

To show respect, it is important that we understand our students and their customs, that we help them understand us, and that we strive to learn to live and work together. A very important part of showing our students respect is to assure them that they have worth and can succeed.

Labels — *with testing*

Unfortunately, in many of our schools, the first response to English language learners is far from a respectful one. The first thing schools do with our newcomers is test them for English proficiency. Many of these students are labeled limited English proficient (LEP) or non English proficient (NEP) (Wink 1993). In addition, a disproportionate number of second language students are referred for special services (Cummins 1984). Once students are labeled, teachers may respond more to the label than to the student. Labels like LEP suggest that the student is limited in some way, and instruction may be planned with that deficiency in mind. In fact, in one school district, the LEP students are further divided into "high" and "low" LEPs, as if one label were not enough.

Cummins (1996) discusses how labels can reflect negative connotations. He explains why he changed the word *minority* in the revision of his book *Empowering Minority Students*, because

> [t]o an increasing number of educators and communities, the term has assumed pejorative connotations and is also seen as inaccurate in view of the demographic realities and projections. So-called "minority" students (e.g. Latino/Latina, African American, Asian American, Native American, and other groups) currently constitute the "majority" school population in California and the nation's largest cities. (iv)

Wink (2000) describes an incident that clearly shows how the misnomer *minority*, as used to refer to English learners, brings with it negative impressions:

> Recently, a teacher was complaining that her students "weren't intelligent" and "couldn't learn." However, she was particularly annoyed because "most are minorities." Wait. Most are minorities? Then wouldn't they be majorities? . . . More and more, my sense is that when schools complain that they have so many "minorities," the hidden message is that the "minorities" have less value than the "majorities."

The graduate students in our program see this kind of attitude too often in the schools where they teach. Maryann, a Spanish/English bilingual teacher, expressed her frustration at seeing second language learners at her school automatically labeled as having learning disabilities:

> I could never get over the amount of students being referred to special ed at our school when I first started teaching. It wasn't even suggested that they go to the ESL classes offered as a pullout program. Immediately, teachers would assume that their class had learning problems. One teacher even went as far as to say (on a very serious note, mind you), that about 75 percent of his class must have some sort of learning disability and "Why didn't the school have some sort of program to work with these students?" I hardly need to tell you that 75 percent to 85 percent of our school's population is ESL.

It is important for teachers to realize that students who are labeled often begin to see themselves as limited. They develop low expectations, and those low expectations may confirm some teachers' beliefs that the students are deficient. In this way, a cycle of failure is established. It is critical that we, as educators, find ways to respect our students and value their strengths so that the cycle of failure can be broken.

Project VOICE

Project VOICE is a grant project that is attempting to break that cycle of failure. In the Fresno community where we live and teach, one-third of the students are English language learners. The school district reports that over one hundred different languages are spoken in the homes. Surrounding school districts also have large numbers of English learners, though they may not have the variety of languages. With this multilingual population in our area, local schools have sought teachers who can best meet the needs of the diverse school population. In particular, they have looked for teachers who represent the culture and language groups of their students.

A few years ago, the local county bilingual director came to our university with a state bilingual advocate and special projects director to ask us to work with them on a project to increase the number of bilingual teachers in our area. They asked us to work with local school districts on a grant to help support bilingual Hmong and Spanish-speaking paraprofessionals to become teachers. The grant was written in cooperation with several school districts, two junior colleges, and three county offices of education. The program is run by dedicated bilinguals including a director, a coordinator, an administrator, and a university student. When we launched this grant, we did not realize how much the paraprofessionals were going to teach us about respect, labels, and the schooling of bilingual children. We also have learned that supporting the paraprofessionals through their teaching credential is an important and challenging job.

We interviewed over forty candidates in the first year and each paraprofessional had an incredible story to tell. Most had come to this country speaking no English. They struggled in school academically and endured mistreatment and misunderstanding. Several had children of their own in school. All had a commitment to helping students like themselves have a positive school experience. All saw English learners as having strong potential. They all believed that teachers who understand the language and culture of their students can make a difference.

These paraprofessionals were nervous about the challenges of a university education but determined to try. In his first seminar in practice teaching, Gerardo wrote about his struggles and goals:

> My family has had a big part in my decision to become a teacher. I come from a family with very little educational background. However, education was very important to my parents. For them, education was seen as a way to escape from the harsh working conditions of farm labor. Working in the blistering sun or in the bitter cold were also a very good motivator that made me want to continue going to school. From these experiences I learned to respect the work of the poor and my values were shaped around this work ethic.

My educational experience did not have many bright spots. . . . Many times I felt as if I did not belong. There were those teachers who were cold and uncaring who made me feel as though I did not belong. Those teachers who told me that I should take auto shop instead of algebra because I worked well with my hands, those teachers who lost their patience with me because I couldn't understand them. . . . There were also those who challenged me, who believed in me, who made me feel I was important. I wanted to be like them. I wanted to help struggling students. These teachers were heroes to me. . . . I was taught that no matter how much adversity there is, we must do our best. I feel this is a very important attribute that a teacher must have in order to be successful.

Gerardo's story is one of many. As we listened to the stories and got to know the students, we were convinced that these paraprofessionals should be teachers. However, the candidates also needed the academic and moral support that they had not received in their previous schooling. The project staff worked to provide literacy workshops, mentoring, and especially encouragement. Monthly seminars and a summer literacy workshop have featured elements of critical pedagogy (Wink 2000), and we all have come to understand how important the title for the program, Project VOICE, is. The project has given the future teachers a "voice." It has helped them see they have the background and knowledge that gives them the voice they need to help others. In a yearly evaluation, one student wrote, "Project VOICE has been an awesome tool for me. I have learned to voice my opinions and I no longer think that my voice is unheard."

These Latino and Hmong paraprofessionals sometimes have needed to learn to respect themselves. Students wrote about their lack of faith in themselves and their potential. One wrote in the evaluation, "I am planning to continue with Project VOICE, but I have thought about dropping out because I see myself as a disappointment to the program, but Project VOICE has uplifted my spirits." Another explained, "Without Project VOICE, I would have dropped out of school by now. I have developed a voice and grown spiritually, emotionally, and mentally. Thank you very much."

Perhaps the experience that participants find the most powerful is a two-week, all-day intensive literacy experience called "The Learning Edge," to give these future teachers an "edge" in their studies at the university. During this workshop, the Project VOICE students read and discuss relevant literature, learn reading and writing strategies, and share their own learning experiences as Latinos and Hmong in public schools. Experienced classroom teachers help to lead the seminar along with the seminar developer and director, Bobbi Jentes Mason. Some excerpts from the evaluations of The Learning Edge show that this part of Project VOICE helps these students respect themselves as learners and future teachers:

Learning Edge has been an excellent experience for me. The most important thing that I learned was to believe in myself, not to mention my improvement in writing. I have a voice now, through writing.

Learning Edge has given me more confidence and my voice is louder now. I am proud of my identity and want to become a teacher like those who lead Project VOICE. I see my voice emerging in my reading, writing, and learning as a result of my Learning Edge experiences and my support team. I have felt that, through group learning, my voice has been heard.

As a result of Learning Edge, I have experienced my voice emerging through reading, writing, and learning.

The project has now seen its first graduates and first teachers. The new teachers have respect for all their students and see the diversity in their classrooms as an opportunity for teaching both language and academic content.

When educators hold this view, immigrant students are seen as valuable, important, contributing members of every classroom community. In the last section of this chapter we show how teachers demonstrate all the explorer principles we have discussed thus far, including celebrating learning and diversity, focusing on the learner, making curriculum meaningful to students, organizing for collaboration, encouraging learning through different modes, and respecting learners.

Culture and Family History

Several explorer teachers we have known have centered units on their students' culture and family history. These topics are naturally meaningful to all students. Student authors in Wayland's middle school ESL class, for example, are encouraged to share their experiences and culture through a book the class publishes collaboratively each year. The book is bound by a local library bindery and sold to students, parents, and community members. Students choose their own theme for the book and write about things that are important to them. Topics have included herbal folk remedies, cooking and art traditions, and challenging personal experiences.

In the 1990 book *New Americans*, Chao Vang showed the changes that his family had experienced across three generations (see Figure 7–3). He illustrated and labeled items that represented his culture, his parents' culture, and his grandparents' culture, showing differences in homes, schools, food, games, and celebrations. In the process of researching his topic, drawing and labeling his pictures, and discussing the project with his teacher and his classmates, Chao developed both his academic English proficiency and important social studies concepts.

Obviously, Chao invested a great deal of time and energy in his contribution for the book because it was personally meaningful to him. Chao's English was limited, but he was able to demonstrate his understanding of important concepts through art, and this allowed him to have a part in an important collaborative classroom project. In explorer classrooms like Wayland's, student diversity becomes a celebrated resource for learning.

FIGURE 7–3   *Chao Vang's Generation Chart*

In another middle school classroom, Shelly developed a long-term unit for her seventh- and eighth-grade social studies ESL students whose first languages included Spanish, Hmong, and Khmer. Since the seventh-grade social studies curriculum at her school begins with a unit on how people research the past, Shelly decided to make the curriculum meaningful to the students by having them research their own past and then helping them connect their past to the present. Under the broad theme of "Culture: A Pattern of Civilization," Shelly and her students explored the question, "What's my part in my family and my culture?"

To begin the unit the students and teacher chose several questions to explore:

Where do I come from?
What is my culture?
How does culture fit into society?
What are the cultural aspects of my family?
What is my role in my family and culture?
Why is culture important?

Shelly's rationale statement showed that she understood the importance of respecting her students and making learning meaningful for them:

> By creating a unit that validates the student's culture and personal views, the student will learn to appreciate his/her own culture as well as other cultures. If the student can appreciate other cultures, then the social studies material will have meaning and the students will enjoy studying it.

A description of one activity Shelly did with her students, "Making a Timeline," shows how Shelly encouraged the use of different modalities to promote academic development. In her written evaluation of the timeline activity, Shelly explained how engagement in that activity helped her students develop important concepts.

> This assignment took the place of having the students simply look at timelines in a text. The students were excited, since the subject was their life. This supports the idea that if the subject matter is relevant, a student will be interested and motivated to complete an assignment. My students practiced thinking about order of events as they prepared their timelines. It is important for the students to be able to order events in time. Students need to order events when they are reading, thinking about plots, or predicting events. They also need to order their thoughts before writing.

When her students did not know dates, Shelly suggested that they ask their families. Family involvement was so successful, she has decided to include families in the timeline the next time she does the activity. Shelly also found that the

Mutual respect in the classroom

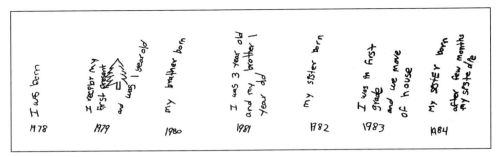

FIGURE 7–4   *Juan's Timeline*

timelines served as a nonthreatening way for some students to share things about their past, including tragic deaths in the family. Juan, a Mexican student, recorded the birth and death of a sister, his separation from his parents when they came to the United States to work, and his arrival in this country (see Figure 7–4).

After the students had completed their timelines, they displayed them around the room and shared what they considered to be significant events. They also created a large whole-class timeline with dates of historical events they were studying. Students helped fill in that timeline and enjoyed adding to it each time they studied a new event. Shelly explained how the personal timelines helped the students understand history better: "They have been able to compare their short lives with centuries of events, to put history in perspective, and to develop the concept that all things are connected through time."

By drawing on the diversity of experiences in the lives of their students, explorer teachers like Wayland and Shelly create rich learning environments in their classrooms. They create classroom communities in which all their students develop academic content and both academic and social language as they engage in activities that are meaningful to them. When explorer teachers have respect for their students, they organize their classroom in ways that show that respect and also help students respect one another. They also involve them in curriculum that helps students become bilingual and biliterate. In the next chapter we will further explore the importance of supporting our students' first languages and cultures as we discuss the final explorer principle.

Applications

1. Consider a unit you are planning to teach this year. How can you employ the explorer principles? List some ways you could begin the unit by building on the experiences and interests of the students. Share your list with others.

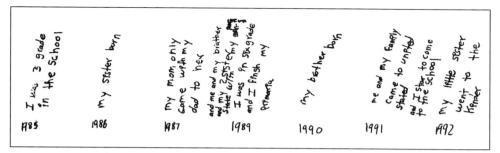

FIGURE 7–4 *Juan's Timeline (continued)*

2. Different cultures show respect in different ways. Think of some experiences you have had with cultures other than your own that have taught you about different views of respect. Discuss them with others.

3. Figure 7–1 lists characteristics of classrooms that either inhibit or promote social interaction. Use that chart as a checklist and evaluate your own classroom. Then list some changes you could make that would promote interaction.

4. Explorer teachers recognize the importance of helping students develop both oral and written language. In addition, students and teachers can use other modalities to promote or show evidence of learning. In a small group, brainstorm the modalities (besides or in addition to oral and written language) that you have used to present ideas and those that you have suggested your students use to show their understanding.

5. Bob Wortman, an administrator in Tucson, Arizona, has developed a checklist of factors that show evidence of a positive language learning environment. We have reproduced his questions here. Use this chart to evaluate your classroom and then list some things that you could change to make the environment for learning even more positive.

Evidence of a Positive Language Learning Environment

1. What is present in the room that encourages/invites/promotes/facilitates oral language development?

2. What is present in the room that encourages/invites/promotes/facilitates reading?

3. What is present in the room that encourages/invites/promotes/facilitates writing?

4. What utensils/resources are easily accessible to students for literacy activities?

5. What is present in the room that illustrates the relationships among talking, writing, and reading?

6. What is present in the room that reflects/promotes languages or dialects other than standard English that may be spoken by all or some of the students?

7. What is present in the room that fosters understanding of and respect for the cultural diversity of your community?

8

How Do Explorer Teachers Celebrate Students' First Languages and Cultures?

Lian, a graduate student from mainland China, read a children's story in Chinese to the other graduate students in Yvonne's bilingual methods course. After she finished, she told the class with an obvious show of emotion, "I just want to tell you all that it must be very important for children to have their first language spoken in school. I am a graduate student, and you don't know how much it means to me to have been asked to read this book to you in my native language, in Chinese!" Lian's experience helped the other teachers in the class understand how important first language support is in building self-esteem for students who live between worlds.

Lian's reading was just one way that these teachers, most of whom are monolingual English speakers, were sensitized to their own English language learners. Many of the teachers in this class experienced for themselves what learning in a second language is like, because the course content, including the rationale, theory, and research support for bilingual education, was taught bilingually in Spanish and English. For teachers who speak little or no Spanish, being presented content in a language other than English provided a new perspective. After only one class meeting, Paulette wrote the following:

> I noticed I felt kinder after last Tuesday's class toward my migrant and ESL pullout students. As you lectured in Spanish, it surprised me to find how short my attention

span was. And when I was no longer willing to listen or make an effort to interpret, how easy it was to talk or think of something else. It was good to see you cope with all of us good-naturedly and patiently. There are many similarities between my seven- and eight-year-olds and your thirty-plus-year-olds!

The teachers' final self-evaluations for the graduate class have been revealing:

I have learned what it feels like to be in a classroom where the teacher speaks in a language other than mine.

Having a class that was conducted in part in a language that I didn't know was refreshing, but I got more than that out of it because I sensitized myself to the needs of my students.

These responses show that the teachers not only learned theory, but also internalized their understanding of the need for first language support for their students.

In this chapter we discuss the final explorer principle (see Figure 6–1), which calls on teachers to celebrate their students' first languages and cultures. Even when the need to support and develop the native language is understood, there may be many barriers that keep teachers from doing what is best. In the first place, there are many different languages spoken in classrooms and few teachers who speak those languages. Materials in different languages are often difficult, if not impossible, to find. In addition, the general public opposes the use of any language other than English in the classroom.

The best way to develop students' first languages is through bilingual programs. Below, we briefly review the rationale and research base for such programs. We recognize, however, that many teachers who do not teach in bilingual programs still want to support their students' primary languages and cultures. In the second part of this chapter, we describe a number of ways that teachers have found to offer first language support even when the teachers do not speak their students' first languages.

Theoretical and Research Base for Bilingual Education

Teachers working with English language learners recognize the importance of helping them develop competence in English. It seems logical that the best way to develop English proficiency is to immerse learners in an environment where they hear, speak, read, and write English all day. Although the idea that "more English leads to more English" is logical, it is contrary to research that shows that the most effective way for second language students to develop both academic concepts and English language proficiency is through the development of their first language (August and Hakuta 1997; Collier 1995; Cummins 1996; Krashen 1996; Krashen et al. 1998; Crawford 1999).

The general public and some educators have opposed bilingual education and called for English-only instruction despite research showing that bilingual education works. Greene (1998) reviewed over seventy-five studies designed to evaluate the effectiveness of bilingual education. What he found was that many of the studies often cited to support English-only instruction were seriously flawed. Some cited studies were even unavailable; others were not appropriately controlled, or measured the effectiveness of bilingual support after an unreasonably short period of time. There were some studies used in support of English-only that were not even evaluations of bilingual programs. Greene, who is not a bilingual educator but carried out this study for the Thomas Rivera Policy Institute, evaluated the studies that were well conceived and came to the following conclusion:

> With this technique known as meta-analysis to summarize the scholarly research, I find that children with limited English proficiency who are taught using at least some of their native language, perform significantly better on standardized tests than similar children who are taught only in English. In other words, an unbiased reading of the scholarly research suggests that bilingual education helps children who are learning English. (1)

Krashen (1996) uses research results as a base and then helps us understand why the results support first language instruction. He argues that we acquire language when we receive comprehensible input, messages that we understand. For second language students, use of the primary language can help make input comprehensible. To learn a second language, students need to have an understanding of what they hear or read. If students enter our schools speaking languages other than English, and if English is the only language of instruction, then the students may simply not understand enough English to acquire the language or to learn any subjects taught in the language.

Skutnabb-Kangas (1983) expands on this point by asking what happens when "the child sits in a submersion classroom (where many of the students have L2, the language of instruction, as their mother tongue), listening to the teacher explaining something that the child is then supposed to use for problem solving." In this situation, "the child gets less information than a child listening to her mother tongue" (116). If a child fails to understand even a few words, he or she may lose the meaning of an explanation.

An example will clarify this point. Picture a kindergarten class where most of the students speak English but five students speak only Spanish. The teacher, Ms. Smith, is a monolingual English speaker. Early in the year, Ms. Smith wants to review colors and shapes with her students. Because she wants to make the input comprehensible, she gathers some realia for the lesson. She has a green square block, a yellow block the shape of a triangle, an orange ball, a long blue scarf, and a white egg. Ms. Smith tells the children that they are going to review their colors. She holds up the green block, and the teacher and students say the color, "green," together. Next, she points to the yellow block, and the students call out the color, "yellow." They go through this routine with each of the objects, and then the teacher points to other color objects in the room, such as the children's clothing. Eventually the non-English speakers begin to figure out what the teacher and students are doing. "Oh, we're talking about color! I get it. The ball is orange, my shirt is orange, and the pumpkin is orange."

At about the time those students have figured out that they should focus on color, Ms. Smith says, "Now let's talk about shapes." She holds up the green block and says, "This is a square!" The English learners, however, are saying to themselves, "I thought it was green!" She holds up the egg and says, "This is an oval." The English learner is thinking, "No, that's white!" Ms. Smith explains that the yellow block is a triangle, the blue scarf is a long rectangle, and the ball is round. The native English speakers are with the teacher all the way, but the English learners are struggling to make sense of what is happening.

The children learning English are expending a great deal of energy trying to understand what the teacher is teaching, but during part of the lesson, they are confused. Just when they figure out that they are looking at color, the teacher switches to shapes. While the lesson provides the native English speakers a good review of colors and shapes, the non-English speakers are acquiring very little English and are not learning the important academic concepts the teacher is presenting.

In this example, the students would have learned a great deal more English if there had been a preview of the lesson in Spanish. If an aide, a bilingual peer, or another teacher could have explained to the children in Spanish that the teacher would be teaching colors and shapes and then reviewed the colors and shapes briefly in Spanish, the Spanish speakers would have been much more engaged and would have been able to acquire more English vocabulary during the lesson in English.

One excellent strategy for working with second language learners, then, is preview, view, review. If the teacher, a bilingual peer, a bilingual cross-age tutor, a bilingual aide, or a parent can simply tell the English learners in their native language what the upcoming lesson is about, the students are provided with a preview. During the view, the teacher conducts the lesson using strategies to make the input comprehensible. With the help of the preview, the students can follow the English better and acquire both English and academic content. Finally, it is good to have a short time of review during which students can use their native language. For example, students who speak the same first language could meet in groups to review the main ideas of the lesson and then report back in English. Figure 8–1 outlines the preview, view, review technique.

The preview, view, review technique provides a structured way to alternate English and native-language instruction. Simply translating everything into a student's first language is not productive, because the student will tune out English, the language that is harder to understand. There is no research support for concurrent translation. Using preview, view, review can help teachers avoid concurrent translation and can also motivate students to stay engaged in the lesson. Listening to a second language is more tiring than listening to one's native language. Second language learners may appear to have shorter attention spans than native speakers, but in real-

152

Preview/ View/ Review

Preview
first language

The teacher or a bilingual helper gives an overview of the lesson or activity in the students' first language (this could be giving an oral summary, reading a book, showing a film, asking a key question, etc.)

View
second or target language [English]

The teacher teaches the lesson or directs the activity in the students' second language

Review
first language

The teacher or the students summarize key ideas and raise questions about the lesson in their first language

---

FIGURE 8–1 *Preview/View/Review*

ity, those students may be suffering from the fatigue of trying to make sense out of their new language. Often teachers complain that their English learners misbehave and don't pay attention. An observer in Yvonne's bilingual methods class might have concluded that her graduate student, Paulette, had a short attention span and was being rude when talking to her neighbor, but as Paulette wrote, it is very tiring to try to listen to something you don't understand. Knowing that there is a specific time in the lesson when their first language will be used helps English learners attend to the main part of the lesson, the "view," in English.

Krashen (1996) explains that providing primary language instruction to English learners gives them two things: knowledge and literacy. When students develop literacy and content-area knowledge in their first language, they can transfer their ability to read and their academic skills to their second language. On the other hand, if they have to learn new information and learn how to read through English, they often do not accomplish either.

Maryann, the teacher we talked about in the last chapter, discovered that one of her students who was perceived to have a learning problem had not yet developed literacy in any language when he entered her fifth-grade classroom. She explains:

At the beginning of the year one student came to my class with the report (from the previous teacher) of not having the patience to learn anything, that he didn't even try, and that perhaps he should be referred to special ed. He came to the school from Mexico in the third grade, and I teach fifth grade. After a few weeks in my class, it was quite obvious that this young man was brilliant. He was eager to learn, but he just didn't know how to read and this was very humiliating to him. No one ever took the time to teach him to read in Spanish, and he had learned English too fast, so he couldn't stay in our ESL program. Whenever we did written assignments, he left the room mentally and started disrupting others. I began giving assignments orally in Spanish and English and giving this student some extra positive attention. This has changed his attitude. He has begun to read in Spanish and accepts help from his classmates willingly.

Maryann realized that what her student needed was literacy, so she taught him to read through his primary language. It is easier for students to develop literacy in the language they speak and understand best. That ability to read then transfers to reading in a second language.

Differences in primary language schooling help account for differences in students' school performance in English. Consider José and Felipe, who arrived in Mrs. Enns third-grade classroom in September. Both boys had just come from Mexico and did not speak any English. In April of that year, Mrs. Enns wanted to refer Felipe to be tested for learning disabilities, as he was doing poorly in her class. José, on the hand, was doing very well. When the bilingual specialist conferred with Mrs. Enns, they looked at the previous schooling of the two boys. Felipe had lived in a rural area and had had interrupted schooling. He never learned to read or write in Spanish and missed most of the content instruction of the early grades. José, on the other hand, came from Monterey, a large city, and had attended school since preschool. His report card from Mexico showed that he had received 8's, 9's, and 10's, high grades in the Mexico system. The difference in the boys' academic performance in English can be accounted for by the difference in their primary language schooling.

In another case, Francisca arrived in Mr. Churchill's class from Mexico City to attend sixth grade in a school that is 85 percent Hispanic. After eight months, Francisca was doing better academically than many of her Mexican-ancestry classmates who had attended school in the Central Valley all their lives. Mr. Churchill thought Francisca was more motivated and tried harder. However, when he began to study bilingual education, he investigated Francisca's past educational history. He discovered that Francisca had studied in Mexico City and was a top student in Spanish in all subject areas there. Mr. Churchill could see that her schooling in Mexico had provided the literacy and content-area knowledge she needed to succeed in English. She already knew how to read and she knew the concepts in Spanish, so her literacy and academic knowledge transferred to her second language. In contrast, many of her classmates who had come to school speaking Spanish had never had instruction in their primary language to build the kind of knowledge base that Francisca had.

CUP and SUP

The ability to transfer knowledge and skills from one language to another can be explained by what Cummins (1981) calls a common underlying proficiency (CUP). What we learn in one language is available in a second language because concepts are not stored by language. Instead, we build a proficiency that underlies any language. If we understand the water cycle or the concepts of reflection and refraction, for example, it doesn't matter what language we learned the concepts in or what language we use to demonstrate our comprehension of the concepts. The concepts form part of our underlying academic proficiency. If we are learning a new language, we do need the vocabulary for talking about the concepts, but we already have the concepts themselves.

Students also build up an underlying language proficiency. This is why it is so important for students to fully develop their first languages. If students stop using their first languages when they enter school and begin using English, it may be more difficult for them to develop their general linguistic proficiency. On the other hand, in classes that encourage use of first languages as well as English, all students can continue to develop their common underlying proficiency in both language and academic content.

Thomas and Collier (1997) analyzed data for over seven hundred thousand language minority students in different types of support programs from districts in various regions of the United States. They looked at English learners' standardized test scores on reading in English from kindergarten through high school. They concluded that students who had received strong cognitive and academic development through their first language at least through grade five or six did better on tests in English through the high school years than students who received more limited first language instruction.

Cummins (1981) contrasts the idea of a common underlying proficiency with that of a separate underlying proficiency (SUP). Those who hold to the SUP theory must believe that what we learn in one language goes to one part of our brain and cannot be accessed when we are learning and speaking another language. This must be what opponents of bilingual education believe when they say that students learning in their first language are wasting time. They should only be learning in English. Research by Cummins and others finds support for a common, rather than a separate, proficiency, and if that is the case, then concepts learned in one language can transfer to another. By supporting the use of primary languages, teachers facilitate the development of all students' common underlying linguistic and academic proficiencies.

One rainy night Yvonne was able to bring home the idea of a common underlying proficiency clearly to teachers in the graduate bilingual methodology class. She showed the class a large poster of different cloud formations with Spanish labels. Pointing to the poster, using gestures, and drawing attention to the rain and clouds outside the classroom, Yvonne explained the different types of formations in Spanish. Afterward, teachers discussed what made the discussion comprehensible.

[handwritten margin note: Must use primary language to develop 1st and 2nd language]

A major point several made was that they had taught about those same cloud formations in science in English. Therefore, their background knowledge helped them make sense of the instruction in Spanish.

Cummins's idea of a common underlying proficiency helps to explain why students like Francisca and José with previous education in their own country often do better academically than students who have been in English-speaking schools longer but never received any schooling in their native language. Students who have had instruction from the beginning in a language they can understand develop concepts, negotiate meaning, and learn to read and write. When they begin studying in an English-speaking country, they transfer those abilities to the new setting. On the other hand, second language learners with no schooling in their first language may have difficulty making sense of English instruction, because they lack the background knowledge that the students who were educated in their own countries had already received. By providing primary language instruction, bilingual programs help build academic knowledge and language skills that English learners need.

Conversational and Academic Language

Another important concept related to bilingual education is the difference between academic and conversational language. Cummins (1996), Collier (1989), and Hakuta et al. (2000) have shown that it takes from four to nine years for English language learners to achieve on a par with native English speakers on standardized tests in English. This finding has important implications for student placement and curriculum planning. A disproportionate number of second language students are placed in special education or, at the very least, labeled and tracked into lower-level classes because the distinction between the acquisition of conversational language and academic language is not well understood.

It takes approximately two years for a new immigrant to acquire conversational language. Conversational language is the language we use to carry out activities that are rich in context, such as shopping, asking for and giving directions, or playing games. So, for example, if we were to move to Lithuania to live, it would take us about two years to carry out daily living tasks using the new language. We would be able to go to stores, ask for basic necessities, exchange common greetings, use the bus system, and engage in conversations about topics we already know about after about two years in the country. We would not, however, be ready to attend college classes, or take notes or tests or write essays at that point. That would take considerably longer.

This contrast is important for teachers and counselors to understand, because English learners may appear to speak English, often without an accent, but may not do well in academic school tasks that have little context, such as reading texts without pictures, taking tests, or writing essays. This leads to the assumption that the student is lazy, when in fact the student simply needs more time to acquire academic English.

In Chapter 5 we discussed Song, the Chinese-speaking student who was placed in an American school when he arrived in Venezuela in the first grade. We described the social distance from English that Song experienced because his family in Venezuela associated with the Chinese community, and he spent other time conversing in Spanish with maids and the chauffeur. Over time, Song did acquire conversational English, but Mary, Song's second-grade teacher, realized that Song was struggling with the academic language of school:

> By the time Song entered my classroom, his English had improved to the point where he could communicate effectively, but it was still quite low. He was very strong in math and spelling where the answers were seen to be precise, but seemed lost with the more cognitively demanding areas like writing, reading, social studies, and science. He often would seem to completely tune out during class discussions and activities, and he would frequently have absolutely no idea what we were talking about when I would call on him. His seeming lack of focus during class began to affect his relationships with his classmates. The other students thought he was lazy and began to resist having to work with him.

Mary recognized that Song had the conversational language that Cummins identified, but had not yet acquired enough academic English to compete with peers in challenging content-area activities. He could do math computations, which were less language dependent, and he could memorize spelling words he did not have to really understand or do anything with, but he had difficulty when he was required to write or read more difficult texts. This caused his peers to devalue him as a learner.

Belinda, who teaches in Vancouver, Canada, shared the following example to show that teachers do not always recognize the distinction between academic and conversational language proficiency.

> A number of years ago, one of the classes I was responsible for was an "incentive" class. These students apply and/or are recommended to an enriched program based on test scores and classroom performance. I was teaching their grade-eight humanities class, and was struck by the very poor writing standard of a number of the students. I could immediately identify these students as Chinese speakers, and upon checking their names, confirmed my suspicions. When I discussed the situation with the person in charge, she admitted that she had been very confused by these students' writing, which in places was nearly incomprehensible, and yet they spoke with no Chinese accent whatsoever, and behaved like Canadian-born Chinese, or, in other words, like native speakers. They had been admitted primarily on the basis of math scores. I have since encountered many instances where a student's communicative effectiveness, that is, his ability to function very well orally in familiar, everyday topics, masked his very weak performance in literacy skills.

Bilingual programs can help students develop literacy and academic knowledge in their first language while they are learning English. Some bilingual programs last only two or three years. That is about the time it takes students to acquire conversational proficiency in English. More effective programs last six or seven years; research shows that it takes that long for students to develop academic language proficiency.

Strategies to Support Primary Languages

When students in bilingual classes develop their native language, they gain both literacy and academic concepts. In many schools, though, bilingual education is not feasible because a school may lack bilingual teachers, or classes may include students with a variety of primary languages. Even in these circumstances, teachers can find ways to use their bilingual students' first languages and promote academic success. Several researchers and teachers (Auerbach 1993; Brisk and Bou-Zeineddine 1993; Brisk and Harrington 2000; Freeman and Freeman 1993) have reported ways in which teachers have successfully supported students' first languages when the teachers themselves did not speak those languages. These creative approaches include the following:

1. Ensure that environmental print reflects students' first languages.
2. Supply school and classroom libraries with books, magazines, and other resources in languages in addition to English.
3. Have bilingual students read and write with aides, parents, and other students who speak their first language.
4. Encourage bilingual students to publish books and share their stories in languages other than English.
5. Allow bilingual students to respond in their primary languages to demonstrate comprehension of content taught in English.
6. Use videotapes produced professionally or by the students to support academic learning and raise self-esteem.

Below we provide examples of how teachers have implemented each of these strategies.

Environmental Print

One of the first things many teachers do is to enrich the print environment in their classrooms. Research supports the importance of environmental print in children's development of literacy (Goodman et al. 1979; Ferreiro and Teberosky 1982; Freeman and Whitesell 1985). In her first-grade classroom, Kristene drew upon the importance of environmental print by having a *Podemos Leer*/We Can Read bulletin board right by the door of the classroom so that everyone could see it. Students brought in products they used with their families, such as Cheerios boxes, Sprite cans, Mi Rancho tortilla bags, and VIVA paper towel wrappers to put up on the board. The colorful, familiar product labels in Spanish and English provided the rich context Kristene's students needed to move into reading. Kristene found that this real-world bilingual bulletin board often was the center of lively discussion in Spanish and English for her first graders as they formed hypotheses and began to distinguish the letters and words on the labels.

Kathy, a kindergarten teacher who has students from Mexico, Laos, and Cambodia, has made it a point to have the number and color words on her bulletin board written in English, Spanish, Hmong, and Khmer, the language spoken by her Cambodian students. She enlisted the aid of district bilingual tutors and parents to help her with this project. In the process of collecting this information, she discovered that Khmer numerals are different from the Arabic numerals we use, so she put both the numerals and the number words up in Khmer (see Figure 8–2). The day after Kathy put up these words and numbers, a Cambodian girl walked up to her, tugged on her skirt for attention, and pointed to the Khmer writing saying, "Teacher, that's me!" Students do notice when teachers make the effort to use environmental print in their students' first languages.

Lonna, who works with older students, had both students and bilingual aides write proverbs in their first languages and then translate them into English. These were then typed or printed neatly on colored construction paper, laminated, and cut

FIGURE 8–2   *Kathy's Color and Number Words*

to make bilingual bookmarks for students and classroom visitors. On one side of each bookmark the proverb is written in the native language, and on the other it is translated into English. Figure 8–3 shows the messages on both sides of two bookmarks, one in Laotian and English and one in Hmong and English.

Sam, a bilingual resource teacher in a farming community with a high Hispanic population, encouraged teachers to have students write signs to announce school events in Spanish as well as English. Sam was working with a group of Spanish-speaking children who were planning a sing-along. The group wanted to invite the principal, so Sam suggested that they make a sign. The principal was delighted with the large butcher paper sign the first graders wrote in Spanish. Despite a few invented spellings, the message was clear: "QueRemos envitrLa a cantar con nosotros el miércoles al Las 1:30 P.M., en el cuarto de La musica" (We want to invite you to sing with us on Wednesday at 1:30 P.M. in the music room). The first graders showed a sophisticated understanding of writing conventions by adding the accent over *miércoles* correctly and by experimenting with comma usage. The principal put the sign up in her office so that visitors could see it. She also made a point of coming to the sing-along.

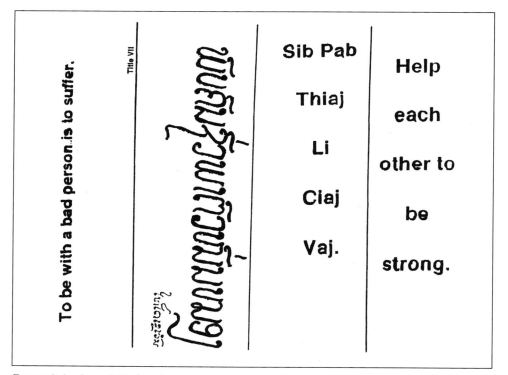

FIGURE 8–3   *Lonna's Bookmarks*

Resources in Languages Other Than English

Environmental print in students' primary languages sends a strong message that the school values diversity in language, literacy, and culture. For students to develop into proficient readers, however, they also need books, magazines, and other resources in their primary languages. Teachers who make the extra effort to support literacy in languages other than English have seen the difference this makes (Hudelson 1987; Freeman and Freeman 1997; Krashen et al. 1998).

Often, schools have limited print resources in languages other than English. The challenge is to distribute the books equitably. In a school with a high Latino population but only a limited number of books in Spanish, the principal bought library book carts with wheels for each classroom. He filled the carts with a variety of children's literature, including books in Spanish, and put one cart in each class. The carts were then moved periodically to different classrooms. In this way, every classroom had an interesting new supply of books every few weeks.

When Kay, a bilingual resource teacher, found that there were not enough books in Spanish for her school, she applied to the local reading association for a mini-grant for books in Spanish. Her school now has a very exciting selection of literature books in Spanish for teachers to share. Sharon, another teacher at Kay's school, wrote a grant proposal to provide the school with quality children's encyclopedias and dictionaries in Spanish so that Spanish-speaking children could engage in the same type of research as their English-speaking peers. Teachers like Kay and Sharon have made an extra effort to support their bilingual students, because they know that this effort pays off in student success.

Materials in other languages can also be used very specifically to support the class curriculum. For example, Melissa teaches fourth grade in a school with a high Latino population. The district encourages instruction in Spanish and has given teachers at each grade level money to buy Spanish books. The teachers in the fourth grade pooled their allotted money and bought books in Spanish that provided resources for the various themes they were studying, including studies of the ancient world. Melissa, who does not speak Spanish, has found that her English language learners, even those who appear to be very proficient in their conversational English, first go to books in Spanish when they select materials for research on the thematic units. As the students learn more about the content, they switch between books in Spanish and English.

Sue, another monolingual teacher in the same school district, was concerned that many of her Hispanic students seldom took part in literature study discussions. Even though she could not read Spanish well, she decided to encourage the quietest of her bilingual students to organize a literature study group using a chapter book in Spanish. They had watched as others had engaged in literature studies in English, so they knew what a literature study was and were able to lead themselves through the book. Sue immediately noticed the difference in the way these third graders responded. Although they had been quiet and reluctant to participate in literature study groups when the books and discussion were in English, they were animated in their response to books in Spanish. They summarized in English for Sue what they were discussing and learning. When the literature studies had been all in English, these students had not entirely understood the texts and/or they had not felt confident enough to participate. Because of this positive experience, Sue has already begun the search for a wider selection of interesting chapter books in Spanish for the next literature study.

Publishers have responded to the increased number of English learners in schools by producing many more books in languages other than English. Spanish speakers make up the majority of second language students in the United States, and literature and content-area books in Spanish are generally available through many publishers (Freeman and Freeman 1997, 1998b). A variety of texts is also available in several Asian languages. However, for other languages, such as Hmong or Bosnian, fewer resources are available. Teachers can support students by becoming knowledgeable about the resources that become available for the language groups at their schools. The key is for someone to take the time and effort to scout out the possibilities and order the texts that students at their school need.

Help from Aides, Parents, and Other Students

Once primary-language books and magazines are available, students need help in using these materials. If teachers do not read and write all the languages of their students, they can find others who will work with them. These "others" may include bilingual aides, parents, and other bilingual students.

Bilingual paraprofessionals can help in a number of ways. For example, they can read to and with students in the students' primary languages. If students engage in literature studies using primary-language literature, aides can meet with groups to join in their discussions. They can also respond to students' writing. During writer's workshop, they can confer with students writing in other languages. Aides can also assist in content-area instruction by providing previews in the first language for concepts the class will investigate in English. After students have conducted content-area study, aides can review the concepts in students' first languages.

In some classes, unfortunately, the bilingual aides are assigned the job of teaching English to the second language students. We say that this is unfortunate because these aides are hired for their proficiency in another language, not their proficiency in English. In many cases, they may be the only adults in the classroom who can provide primary-language support. For that reason, teachers should make use of their expertise. For example, aides can preview in the students' first language a story that the teacher plans to read later in English.

Bilingual parents are also excellent resources for primary-language support. Several teachers we have worked with have invited parents of their bilingual students to participate in classroom events by reading to the whole class in their first language, by teaching the class songs in the first language, and by leading context-rich activities such as crafts and cooking in the first language. The teachers have found that all the students have enjoyed these activities even if they have not understood everything. These bilingual experiences have led English-speaking students to ask interesting questions and encouraged class discussions about the positive benefits of bilingualism. In addition, the bilingual parents and their children feel a sense of pride in their heritage language and culture.

Older students can also provide first language support. Kay, the bilingual resource specialist mentioned earlier, established a cross-age tutoring program at her school to support Spanish speakers. She organized the program so that students in grades seven through high school read and wrote with elementary students during an elective period. Kay matched these "Teachers of Tomorrow" with younger students who had the same first language. Kay insisted that her tutors read and write only in Spanish or Punjabi, the two second languages represented in the school district. She told them, "English is all around. You are the experts for the younger kids who need primary-language instruction." Not only did the younger students benefit from the academic support provided by their tutors, they were also exposed to positive role models.

Kay prepared the older students well for working with the younger students. She provided demonstrations of how to support reading and writing and how to encourage the younger students to talk about what they were learning. The "Teachers of Tomorrow" actually made their own plans for their time with their younger charges. During two classes each week, they discussed with Kay and others how their teaching time had gone. An exciting result for the older students was their changing perception of themselves and their future. With Kay's enthusiastic support, several have begun to investigate college programs to prepare themselves to become teachers.

Bilingual peers can also provide first language support. Rhoda, a fifth-grade teacher who speaks very little Spanish, has found that having one bilingual student help another benefits both students. Orlando, a fluent English speaker, had been reluctant to use his first language, Spanish, since he had been transferred out of the bilingual program in first grade. He did not want anyone to think he could not speak English. However, when Javier came to the fourth-grade classroom from Mexico, he needed help in Spanish. At first Javier struggled along without any first language support, but Rhoda was not satisfied with his work. She decided to ask Orlando to help her by reading with Javier and editing his pieces in writer's workshop. She explained to Orlando that she could not read Spanish, and Javier needed someone who could work with him. Soon the boys were reading books together and having animated discussions. During writing time, Javier's writing changed dramatically from two- to three-line statements to full-page stories in Spanish, because he now had a real audience for what he wrote.

Orlando, in turn, took a new pride and interest in his native language. During a minilesson on English capitalization rules, Orlando pulled out a book in Spanish that he had been reading with Javier and explained to the whole class, "In Spanish, it's different! You don't capitalize days of the week or the months." Both Orlando and Javier benefited from working together in their first language.

Student-Authored Literature

While it is important to have professionally published books and magazines in students' primary languages, students are often equally interested in reading stories or articles that their classmates write. Many teachers have students publish quite professional-looking books in English for their classroom libraries. As technology improves in schools, new ways of producing books become available. A good resource for teachers is Condon and McGuffee's guide to publishing digital books, *Real E-publishing, Really Publishing!* (Condon and McGuffee 2001). In addition, schools often publish newspapers or newsletters. Second language learners should not be left out of these important experiences. Instead, they should be encouraged to write and publish in their first languages to enrich the resources in the classroom.

An example of a student publication with a wide audience comes from Ripperdan, a small K–8 school in central California. About 85 percent of the students are Hispanic, many of them from families of migrant workers. Pam, who taught seventh- and eighth-grade language arts at Ripperdan, shared an all-school project, which is an example of how schools can publish student work. For several years the entire school was involved in process writing, an area of the curriculum strongly supported by the school administration. As a culminating project, the teachers and the principal worked together to collect poetry for an anthology. All the students in the school were invited to participate. Nobody's piece was rejected. Since the students all had writing folders, they picked their favorite poem to submit for the book. Since students were encouraged to write in both Spanish and English, several students chose poems in Spanish.

The bilingual anthology the school published included pictures of the students. The dedication page was printed in both Spanish and English to show how the school values all the community members. Figure 8–4 shows one page of poems in Spanish that students wrote to their mothers.

When the book was completed, an ice-cream social was held. Parents and other relatives were invited. The student authors read their poetry in Spanish and English. Each family received a copy of the book. The poetry anthology was even put on sale at a local children's book store. The students were excited and pleased that people actually bought their book.

Some student writing has had an even wider audience. Jefferson School is a fourth-, fifth-, and sixth-grade school in the farming community of Hanford, California. Each month, one grade level is responsible for publishing the school newsletter, *The Jefferson Connection*. Except for a one-column message written by the principal, the entire paper is planned, written, laid out, and illustrated by the students. Each

Mi Mamá

La primavera
Me gusta ver con el sol -
Brillando.
Pero mas me gusta
Mirar mi mamá -
Sonriendo.

Catalina Hernandez
Cuatro grado

Madre

Madre. cuando yo sea
Grande te voy a comprar
Un carro para que te
Deleites manejando.

Te dare muchisimas
Joyas y te comprare
Un vestuario.
Una mansión te obsequiaré.

Los mares navegarás
En el barco que tendrás.
Mascotas y regalos
Mil, en las navidades.
   ¡Abundaran!

Kenia Rivera
Tercer Grado

Cuando Sea Grande

Madre, cuando sea grande
Te compraré un carro,
O un tren, o tal vez un
   ¡Avion!

O quizas te compre una mansión.
O simplemente flores de colores.
   ¡Muchos colores!

Rocio Zuniga
Tercer grado

FIGURE 8–4 *Ripperdan Poetry*

classroom has a computer, and students learn to use different software programs to produce a professional-looking paper. Articles feature people and events related to the school. Each newsletter begins with the following affirmation:

> At Jefferson School we are committed to developing productive citizens by providing equal opportunity for each child to attain his/her maximum potential, academically, socially, emotionally, and physically. We strongly believe that this goal can only be accomplished by the combined efforts of a united staff, students, parents, and community.

In an effort to ensure equal opportunity for all students to write and for all parents to read, some pages of each newsletter, called "Comunicación Escolar al Hogar" (School Communication to the Home), are written in Spanish. Figure 8–5 shows one such page.

All of the classes in the school have a daily writer's workshop. When their grade level is responsible for the paper, classes brainstorm possible topics for informational articles, editorials, creative writing pieces, and even comics. Since the school is a magnet school for both gifted and newcomer students, the two groups work together on many projects. Often, the students in the gifted program help English language learners as they edit their pieces in English. The native Spanish speakers, in turn, teach the non-Spanish speakers some Spanish as they help them translate what they have written for pages in Spanish. Although the Spanish translation is not always perfect, all the students feel very proud of their publication. Participation is high, as 250 to 300 students, including non-English-speaking students, see their writing in print each year.

Individual teachers can also promote student writing in their primary languages. Lisa is a fifth-grade teacher at an inner-city multilingual school. As she studied the importance of first language support, she decided to take a survey of her students' interest in reading in their primary language. Of the six Spanish speakers in her class, three knew how to read in Spanish and the other three wanted to learn. She describes an important finding from the surveys:

> It was no surprise to see that the one student who received four years of bilingual education was way ahead of her peers. It was very beneficial for me to give this survey to her. Prior to giving this survey, I didn't realize how literate she was in Spanish. Now she helps me edit and revise one of my Spanish speaker's stories.

The surveys led Lisa to find ways to help her students develop first language literacy. Lisa was saddened to read what one student wrote—"I forgot how to read Spanish because some words are hard for me"—and touched to read the words of another who wrote, "I like to read in Spanish because it is my language." Lisa, who had some Spanish proficiency but had not used it before with her students, began to read books

The Jefferson Connection

Hanford Elementary
School District

Comunicación Escolar al Hogar

Hanford,
California

JEFFERSON CONNECTION   MARCH 1992   PAGE 8

Las Misiones

Nuestra clase esta estudiando de las misiones. Nosotros les vamos a mandar una carta para que nos den información. Les pedimos para que nos manden una foto de las misiones para saber como se miran. La información debería ayudarnos con nuestro reporte. Estamos escribiendo para recibir una idea de como se peliaban en las misiones. Nosotros pensamos que todos deben estudiar de las misiones.

Enrique Bello
Mario Puga
Salón 62

EL NIÑO PERDIDO

Un dia un niño dijo hace mucho frio. dijo. "no tengo casa." Despues hailo periodicos y discos. Ahi se durmio y cuando. despertó se encontro una casa. Alli estaba una señora y le pregunto. "Ya despertastes." El niño dijo. "¿Quien es usted?" La señora dijo. "soy tú mama." El niño dijo. "ya me acorde." y vivio feliz con su mama en su casa.

Rogelio Arnaga

DECIR NO A LAS DROGAS

Les anuncio este mensaje para que sepan que a las personas que toman drogas se pueden enfermar de los pulmones. Porque sus pulmones se ponen negros y los dientes amarillos. Si alguien dice que si te da un poco de droga mejor di. si a la vida y no a las drogas. y por favor sigue estas reglas que te dice el papel.

¿Qué es una familia?

Es cuando agarro regalos todos los dias porque me quiere mi familia.
Es compartir mi carta de reporte con mi familia.
Es cuando nos compran ropa.
Es las mamas que nos quieren.
Es la que nos hace de comer.
Es la que nos da dinero.
¡Eso es una familia!

Enrique Bello

Say No To Drugs

I tell you this message so you could know the persons that take drugs. They get sick from their lungs. Their lungs get black and their teeth turn yellow. If somebody says take drugs say no and walk away. Say yes to life and please follow these rules. for your own happiness.

Blanca De Lira
Room 12

EL DÍA DEL AMOR

Durante el día del amor toda mi familia y yo hicimos una fiesta porque era el día de San Valentin. Mi mama hizo came de pollo y otras cosas. Lo último que comimos era un pastel de fresas. Mi papá nos dio dinero a todos. Ese día era el primer dia que celebramos juntos aqui en Hanford.

FIGURE 8–5   *Jefferson Newsletter*

in Spanish that were on the same topic as the themes being studied and to sing songs. The results were exciting to her: "It was rewarding to see the enthusiasm, because this was the chance for the Spanish speakers to be the experts."

Lisa also began to collect more Spanish books for her classroom and encouraged her students to write books in Spanish. However, she worried about her Southeast Asian students who had had no first language instruction and were, in fact, losing their primary language. She asked these students if they had books in their languages. One Hmong student brought a book that the Hmong students shared. Lisa was pleased with the result:

> One of the students brought a Hmong reader from Laos. One of my students wrote, "I enjoyed doing this because it teaches me more Hmong. It is like you are in Hmong. Yes, I want to read more Hmong book because you could learned Hmong story." Another student wrote, "I loved to read in Hmong. My dad speak Hmong and English, and Lao."

Lisa decided to ask her Hmong and Cambodian students if they would like to make books in their primary languages for the first graders at the school. In this way, the students learned to write a little of their language and the younger children read the books in their primary language. Lisa's students wrote books about simple topics such as colors and days of the week, but the experience was important for them. One of the Khmer-speaking students from Cambodia wrote about the project (see Figure 8–6).

Even though Lisa doesn't speak the first languages of all her students, she has found creative ways to encourage students to read and write in their first languages.

Some teachers have used published books as a basis for student-created texts. Elaine had her bilingual tutors who spoke Lao, Hmong, and Khmer translate the words of popular, limited-text books from English into their native languages. Elaine had them type the translations on the computer, putting just a few lines on each page and leaving large blank spaces. The students "read" the translated books by comparing the text of their native language with the English texts. Then they illustrated the books. These native-language versions of the popular English books were then laminated and put into the classroom library. Elaine now has several student-illustrated books in Lao, Hmong, and Khmer for her students to look at and use.

A final suggestion for providing first language materials in the classroom is the use of teacher-made books. Doua, a Hmong bilingual resource teacher for a large inner-city district, has tried to collect materials and produce materials in Hmong. One creative way to do this is to make culturally relevant books using photographs. Doua took colorful pictures of Hmong young people dressing in traditional costumes for the Hmong New Year. She arranged the pictures in sequence and then wrote a description of what was happening in each picture in Hmong. She named the parts of the Hmong costumes and described how the costumes are assembled. This book is

I felt happy because I kind of learned to write and read in Khmer. The Cambodian words was hard to write but I know my name in Cambodian so my name wasn't That hard at all! Thsis how I write my name in Khmer: ᤁᤄ

FIGURE 8–6   *Khmer Student Writing*

important because it not only helps Hmong students learn to read in Hmong, it also helps Hmong students maintain their cultural traditions.

Primary-Language Response

Often, English language learners sit silently in classrooms where the content is taught only in English. It is easy for teachers who do not speak their students' first languages to assume that their multilingual learners are not understanding or learning anything. It is important to give students some way of demonstrating that they have understood the course content and that they have learned something from what has gone on in class.

Jane, a monolingual teacher who served as the language arts mentor in a school district where 98 percent of the students are Hispanic, worked with fifth graders on a unit on Martin Luther King, Jr. The students saw a film about Dr. King, they read a book about his life, and they read and talked about his "I Have a Dream" speech. Four students did not participate much in the class activities because they had just arrived from Mexico and spoke little or no English. At the end of the unit, Jane asked her students to write a summary of what they had learned. She encouraged the students who were not confident enough to write in English to summarize their learning in Spanish. Lucinda, who had been completely silent during the unit, showed in her summary (Figure 8–7) that though she spoke little English, she had understood a great deal.

Lucinda's summary shows not only that she understood what was happening during the study of Dr. King, but that she had some background in schooling in Spanish. Though her Spanish is not completely conventional, she writes clearly and uses fairly sophisticated vocabulary and structures.

Another summary shows us a very different kind of second language learner. Roberto had had very limited previous schooling in Mexico, where he had lived in a remote village. Like Lucinda, he remained silent during the class activities centered on Martin Luther King, Jr. However, when asked to summarize, he hesitated

---

Martin Luther King Jr

Martin. luther King Jr nacio el dia 25de
Enero del 29. el era negro y defendio a los
de su raza porque en ese tiempo abia
mucha descriminacion en los autobuces los
negros tenian que sentarce atras de los
autobuses porque enfrente era solo para los
blancos. el los defendio asta que los
mataron el queria que todos tuvieran
livertad. murio el 4 de abril del 68.

Martin Luther King Jr was born on the 25th of January in [19]29. He was a black man and defended those of his race because in that time there was much discrimination on the buses the black people had to sit down in the back of the buses because in front was only for the white people he defended them until they killed him he wanted everyone to have freedom He died the fourth of April of [19]68.

FIGURE 8–7   *Lucinda's Writing*

and indicated to Jane that he really didn't write well. Jane encouraged Roberto to do the best he could. His writing (see Figure 8–8) revealed his limited previous schooling, but it also showed Jane that he had, in fact, understood and learned from the unit.

Too often students who come to school with little educational background are left out of the academic studies in which other students participate. It is important to include all students, even those who do not read and write fluently in their first languages. In fact, when students are not literate in their first languages, they can be encouraged to draw to show what they have understood of the content that has been taught.

Janet taught middle school science. She was unsure of what to do with the new

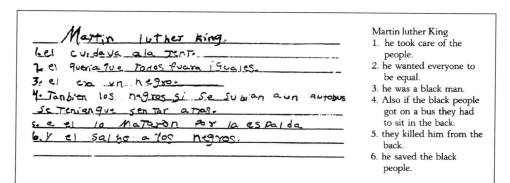

Martin luther King

1. he took care of the people.
2. he wanted everyone to be equal.
3. he was a black man.
4. Also if the black people got on a bus they had to sit in the back.
5. they killed him from the back.
6. he saved the black people.

FIGURE 8–8   *Roberto's Writing*

students who came into her class from Mexico. They spoke no English, but they were eager to participate in whatever way they could. Because the class was studying the parts and functions of the body, Janet was able to use different methods to enrich the context for all her students, but especially for those non-English speakers. She showed a film that discussed and illustrated parts of the body and their functions. She also had a model of a body that students could disassemble. In groups, students discussed the body parts and functions. They were allowed to use their first language as they did this. After the group discussion, Janet answered questions using lots of gestures and drawing on the board.

As a culminating activity, all the students drew bodies on large pieces of paper, showing the organs inside. They then labeled the parts and explained the functions as they understood them. Janet's Spanish-speaking students pleased and surprised her with their depth of understanding as they labeled the bodies they drew and described the functions. Figure 8–9 shows one student's work. Janet also spent class time sharing the vocabulary of the body in Spanish, so that her English-speaking students could learn some Spanish.

Videotapes

Teachers of English language learners can use both print and nonprint resources to involve their students in literacy activities. Increasingly, professional videotapes are available in students' primary languages.

Mary, a Spanish/English bilingual first-grade teacher, discovered some bilingual videos about history, science, social studies, art, and folklore. One day in class, she showed the Spanish version of a video called *The Glass Blowers of Tonolá* to her students. When the narrator explained where this factory was located, Feliciana exclaimed, "That's the town where my dad was born!" After the video, the students brainstormed in Spanish and English what they had seen. The following day the students enjoyed watching the video with English narration and then did their daily journal writing. Mary wrote about Jorge's response.

> We wrote in our journals after watching *The Glass Blowers*. Jorge asked me which encyclopedia would tell about glass blowing. I helped him find the entry for "glass," and he drew a picture like one he had seen in the video in his journal. It was exciting to see how he had been moved to seek something in our room to stay in touch with this new information.

Perhaps even more important than the content the students learned is that they knew this video took place in their native country. The video begins with a shot of the Mexican flag blowing in the wind. As Mary began the video, Felipe, a boy who seldom spoke up in class, showed that he immediately connected with the video by proudly announcing, "México, eso es mi país" (Mexico, that is my country).

In an effort to give some needed first language support in languages other than

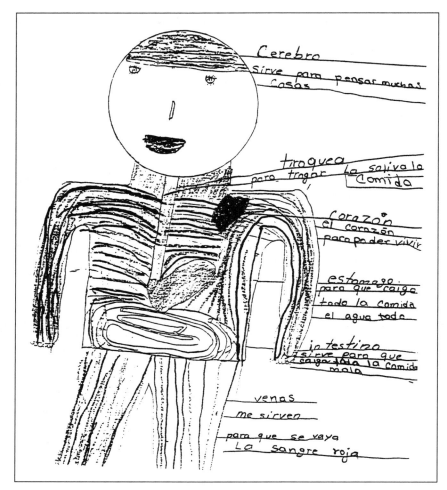

FIGURE 8–9 *Body Parts*

Spanish, school districts have produced videos in various languages. One school district has produced five videos in Hmong centered on five big book stories, including *The Little Red Hen* and *The Three Billy Goats Gruff*. The latter video begins at the zoo with a close-up look at goats. The film then moves to different kinds of bridges with a discussion of what one normally sees under them. Each tape ends with a reading of the story in Hmong as the illustrated pages of the big book are shown. These videos and the reading in Hmong help prepare Hmong-speaking students to participate when the teacher later reads the book in English.

Eva, who has had a large number of Hmong-speaking students in her classroom, used the *Three Billy Goats Gruff* video and was very excited about how her first graders responded. In a journal entry she wrote for a graduate class, she described the experience in some detail:

> The day we viewed it, I began by reading the story in English to my entire class. One of my children, Yee, who has very little English, had trouble paying attention while I read. She played with paper scraps on the floor, tried to braid a classmate's hair, et cetera. Then I put on the video. This time Yee watched attentively. She grinned from ear to ear as she listened to the story. You could see that the English-only students were getting a little bored with the video, but generally they were trying to follow along.
>
> At the end of the video, I asked the class how it felt to not be able to understand. They acknowledged that it was hard. I told them that was how Yee must often feel. We decided that maybe now if we read it again in English, Yee might find it easier to pay attention. The students decided that it might be fun to change the "Clip, Clop, Clip, Clop" to the "Tee, Tah, Tee, Tah" that we heard on the video. It worked! Yee not only paid attention to this second reading, but read along with us. You couldn't help but see how happy it made her.

Elaine drew upon Eva's experience and extended it. She decided to use *The Little Red Hen* with her fourth-grade class of Hmong, Spanish, Laotian, and Cambodian students. She first read the story to the whole class in English, and the class discussed it in English. Next, she introduced the Hmong video:

> I told the students that we were going to watch a video in a language that only some of us could speak and asked them how we could understand. They immediately said that we could ask the people who spoke that language, or we could look at the pictures. I turned on the video and the fun started!
>
> My students are encouraged to speak their own language in the classroom, but I have never seen so much enthusiasm to speak someone else's language. All of the students were leaning on the Hmong students to explain what was being said, and the Hmong students just glowed in happiness. My Hmong students became the experts that the other students relied on.

Elaine was very excited about how well all of her students responded to the experience of watching the Hmong video. She asked her students to write about how they felt watching the video in Hmong, a language that had not been used for school instruction before. Juan, a native Spanish speaker, explained how he felt and how he solved his problem. Being a second language learner himself, he knew that his classmates could be a helpful resource (see Figure 8–10).

Hmong students seldom have the opportunity for instruction in their first language because there are almost no Hmong-speaking teachers and not enough aides to meet their needs. The response to the video from Mai, a Hmong girl in

Whene I was listening and spaecing
Hmong I Was all confused. So I sat
betwiing Zong, Long to tell me
what ther saing so they did it was
funney.

FIGURE 8–10 *Juan's Video Response*

Elaine's class, showed Elaine why it is so very important to use students' first languages when there is the opportunity (see Figure 8–11).

As Mai points out in her journal response, "I am a Hmong person and I am going to speak Hmong almost my whole life." In fact, we hope she will never lose her first language and that teachers understand how important it is for second language learners not only to learn English but also to maintain their first languages.

In many cases, professionally made videos are not available. However, students and teachers can work together to create their own resources. Paulina, a Spanish/English bilingual second-grade teacher, used a student-made video for a Halloween celebration. She and her students love *It Didn't Frighten Me* (Goss and Harste 1985), which is also available in Spanish as *No me asustó a mí.* In this pre-

When I was listening and speaking
Hmong I was very coftable becaube
I am a Hmong person and I
am going to speak Hmong almost
my whole life. Well may alittle
of english too because you have
to read if you're in a bisness.
Thats all, gotta go.

FIGURE 8–11 *Mai's Video Response*

dictable, patterned book, a young boy talks about all the different creatures he sees outside his window after his mother turns out the light at night. These creatures, including an orange alligator, a pink dinosaur, a blue bear, and a spotted snake, do not frighten him.

Paulina and her students decided that they could reenact the story, choosing their own characters and adding their own adjectives. They made a picture-frame stage for the children to stand in. Each child chose a creature or character and dressed up like that character. In addition, they made themselves name cards with descriptive adjectives. Children chose costumes and labels to fit the descriptions, such as "a big, black witch" and "a great green Ninja turtle." Then the entire class recited the book's pattern in both Spanish and English, filling in the names of the creatures in the frame. Other classes were invited to watch this bilingual presentation as part of the Halloween celebration. The presentation was videotaped for parents to see on Back to School Night. Paulina and the parents especially noticed how proud the children felt as they played their parts and later watched themselves on video. This video is now available for Paulina to use with future classes.

Encouraging students to make videos in their first languages not only gives students a sense of pride, it can also help monolingual English-speaking teachers view their students in new ways. Linda, a pullout ESL teacher, discovered how important it is, both for the students and for their teachers, to allow students to use their first languages. Several of her second language learners came from a fourth-grade classroom whose members were reading *Stone Soup*. When the whole class decided to dramatize the story in English and videotape the results for an open house, Linda's students produced a second version in Spanish. She wrote about her experience of watching her ESL students perform the play in Spanish:

> It was so exciting to see the video of the Spanish-speaking play. The students were confident, they spoke fluently, and their performance was superb. They were not the same students that I hear trying to speak and read haltingly in English. As I watched those students, I couldn't help but wonder how many of our very own second language learners have been labeled as learning disabled or even handicapped, or at the best, have succeeded only to an academic level of mediocrity when in their own language they would have been at the top of the class!

Professionally made videos provide important background support that allows English learners to better understand academic content. Perhaps even more important, however, are videos made by the students themselves in their primary languages. These videos help students value their first languages and value themselves.

Promoting Bilingualism and Pride in Culture

Teachers like Eva, Elaine, Mary, Paulina, and Linda have found how well students respond to the extra efforts that they make to support their students' first languages. In particular, Linda discovered that her ESL students were capable of much more than she had expected. That lesson is an extremely important one.

In fact, as teachers, we sometimes forget to emphasize the value of bilingualism in our students. Helen, a middle school language arts instructor, teaches in a rural school in which all the English learners speak Spanish as their primary language. Helen explains how she supported these students' first language in an inquiry project she implemented.

> What would happen in my seventh-grade language arts classes if I started to use conversational Spanish on a daily basis? Would my English language learners react differently to my class? Would the use of primary language cause their grades to go up and their oral participation to increase? When I started studying bilingual education, these questions began tumbling around in my mind. . . . I began to make a point of using Spanish each day with the entire class. I started with simple things, like teaching the whole class how to say the date in Spanish, teaching the class how to count, and teaching them greetings and conversational phrases.
>
> Some days I would start the class off by talking only in Spanish, which would force my non-Spanish speaking students to ask my bilingual students to translate for them. Every time I spoke with my Spanish speakers, I would use Spanish as well as English in our dialogues.
>
> At first, I received lots of shy looks and giggles from my English language learners, and my non-Spanish speakers would either try to figure out what I was saying or blurt out that they did not speak Spanish. I was not discouraged by their early reactions.

Helen was persistent, and at the end of the first month she began to see some results from her efforts.

> Two extremely shy Hispanic girls who struggled academically began to openly use Spanish during class work time. They also started helping to translate into English what I said to the whole class in Spanish, something they were too shy to do at first. For the first time during literature studies, the two girls joined a group of native English speakers instead of choosing to sit by themselves. They chose kind, nonjudgmental peers who were willing to speak in both Spanish and English.

Helen noticed that her Hispanic students also began to share more and volunteer more as a result of her use of Spanish. Perhaps the most important change was the difference in their grades. Many of her Spanish speakers' grades moved an entire grade higher. Helen summarizes what she believes happened.

> When I started using Spanish during their class, I was indirectly giving them permission to use their primary language. I think I was telling them to feel proud regarding their ability to speak more than one language. . . . Next year, I plan to start the school year using both Spanish and English. I also want to emphasize the need for knowing both of these languages in our country.

Kim teaches an adult ESL class in New Jersey. Her students come from all over the world. She makes a special effort to get these adult students, who know a great deal about the world, to share about their cultures and backgrounds as they practice English. She shared some techniques she uses to accomplish this goal:

> Not only do we focus on customs of their country, but we enter into controversial (hot) topics that relate to world affairs. They give their opinion based on their cultural background. We incorporate other skills as well by first asking the students to research in the form of using the Internet, watching the nightly news, reading the newspaper or a magazine article, or interviewing people in the community. The students come to class fired up to present. It is important to note that these same students, in the grammar and writing class, seldom participate and often miss class.
>
> Another related idea is to ask students to prepare and present a leisure activity. This may be replicating simple childhood games, reenacting holiday traditions, or teaching how a special food is prepared. They are encouraged to research and share the significance of the tradition.
>
> With beginners, I may have them tell about the holidays of their country. As they discuss in small groups, I record what they say. I once noticed that a Turkish man and Japanese teenager who had been virtually silent suddenly were fighting for airtime! After the recording, I typed up the stories for the rest of the class to read.

A final example of how teachers can help others value bilingualism and biculturalism comes from Roxie, who teaches in a school with very few bilingual children. One year, she had a Portuguese-speaking child, Melissa, in her first-grade classroom. Roxie made sure that Melissa got help from the classroom aide and that Melissa's older brothers often read with her at home. Melissa's parents showed great interest in her work and were always ready to do whatever was needed to help their daughter succeed. Though Melissa struggled with English, she also participated and made good progress, so it was decided that she could go on to second grade.

The following year, Roxie was sitting in the teacher's lounge one day when she was surprised to hear one of her fellow teachers, who had never had Melissa in a class, comment, "Melissa is behind her classmates because she doesn't speak English at home." Roxie felt that it was important to respond to the teacher's comment. She told her, "I do not feel that Melissa is behind her classmates, because if you look at the whole picture, she is the only one in her class who speaks two languages fluently, and she's only seven years old. I think that's an accomplishment." Later Roxie felt especially good to see Melissa on the playground and have her announce proudly that on her last report card, she had received four A's.

The teachers whose classroom activities we have described provide us with examples of how bilingual students' first languages and cultures can be supported. As the number of second language students continues to increase, our challenge is to continue to search out materials and experiment with methods that allow bilingual students to become fully proficient in both their languages, so that they do not have to choose between worlds but can live successfully in both.

We have spent several chapters exploring the world of the school and developing ideas about language, learning, teaching, and curriculum, because those are the areas over which teachers have the most immediate control. However, we recognize that students' school success or failure often depends as much on what goes on outside the classroom as inside it. Many of the students we presented in the case studies in Chapter 1 were exposed to excellent teachers. It was factors in the societal context beyond the school that affected these students more than what happened in their classrooms. In the next section of this book, we step back to look at the broader social context and the factors in that context that affect the school performance of students between worlds.

Applications

1. Think of an English language learner that you know. Does that student speak, read, and write his/her first language fluently? How do you know? How might the students' first language proficiency be affecting the learning of a second language? Discuss this in a group.

2. Do any of the six strategies to support primary languages remind you of something you have done or seen done with second language students? Discuss this with a small group. Can you think of additional strategies?

3. Take one of the strategies that you would like to try with English language learners. Use the strategy, or your variation of the strategy, and come back and share your experience with others.

4. In Yvonne's class, students observed signs in their towns in languages other than English. They took pictures of the signs or wrote down what the signs said and where they were located. Then they discussed their findings with other teachers. Try this in your community. Are there signs in languages other than English? What kinds of things are advertised and where are the signs located? Share your results with others.

5. Yvonne's teachers also collected menus, newspapers, and other resources in languages other than English. Try this in your community. What non-English print resources are available that could be brought in to your class?

9

What Influences Do Community, Teacher, and Student Attitudes Have on Learning?

Lea, a young Latina teacher, was born in Mexico to an Irish-ancestry father and a Mexican mother. Because of her light coloring, she often finds herself in the middle of conversations with Anglos who, believing she is "one of us," make negative comments about minorities. She has both observed and experienced how teachers' attitudes can affect students' school success. She wrote about her feelings in response to readings she had done about bilingual education.

For some reason, in our culture, any language besides English is seen as inferior. Often, children whose native language is not English experience feelings of inferiority when they are in the American school system. Add to that their cultural history in the United States and their socioeconomic status, and you have a prescription for failure. To simply say students are failing because of "language deficiencies" takes away the focus from the real deficiencies in the U.S. educational system. Also, it leaves no explanation for African American and Native American students' difficulties in school; therefore, they are seen as inherently retarded. I don't want to make learning English seem "irrelevant" to school success, but often people focus on that one issue. When Chinese American students succeed in school and Mexican American students don't, the blame automatically is placed upon those students and their parents. One woman with whom I work asked, "Do they [Mexicans] really want to succeed in school?" No. . . . Mexican students *love to fail*. No one, of course, would ever say that about an Anglo or Asian student.

The attitudes that Lea encountered are not uncommon and are partly based on the fact that immigrant students do struggle in school. Hispanic students are of special concern because of their high dropout rate. In fact, in 1995 the Hispanic Dropout Project (HDP) was established to study this problem, because "nearly one in three (30 percent) of the nation's Hispanic students between the ages of 16 and 24 leave school without either a high school diploma or an alternative certificate such as a GED" (DiCerbo 2000, 2). The HDP listed several attitudinal barriers that keep schools from solving the Hispanic dropout problem and concluded that it was critical to "[d]epoliticize education for Hispanic Youth separating it from debates about language policy or immigration" (2).

In previous chapters we looked at ways that explorer teachers approach curriculum to help their English learners. In this chapter we consider how issues beyond strategies and curricular approaches influence student achievement as we look at how community, teacher, and student attitudes affect teaching and learning. To frame our discussion, we present various perspectives on why different ethnic groups fail in school in the hope that this discussion will help readers evaluate their own attitudes toward the multilingual populations in their schools and communities. We then consider community and teacher attitudes more specifically and conclude by looking at how students' own attitudes affect their success or failure in school.

Perspectives on Failure

As they analyze the perspectives held by our society toward minority groups, Sue and Padilla (1986) and Díaz, Moll, and Mehan (1986) point out that there are many explanations for minority group failure which simplify complex issues. For example, explanations tend to be context free. That is, the explanation is applied to all immigrant students who fail, without considering any specifics about the individual students, including their background and experiences in and out of school. Context-free explanations, then, are applied to a group of students and assumed to fit all situations and all students. These explanations are also usually single-cause explanations. In other words, they put forward a sole reason for behavior or results and do not consider alternatives. Below we discuss the three most common single-cause, context-free explanations of school failure for immigrant students: genetic inferiority, cultural deficit, and cultural mismatch. These perspectives are summarized in Figure 9–1. We then propose that the Contextual Interactional Model (Cortés 1986), which asks educators to look at the complexity of school success and failure in specific settings, is a better way to account for student progress.

Genetic Inferiority

A context-free interpretation that has been widely accepted historically is genetic inferiority. The argument has been that certain minority groups do better than others because of genetic factors. Oftentimes the groups labeled as inferior have been the

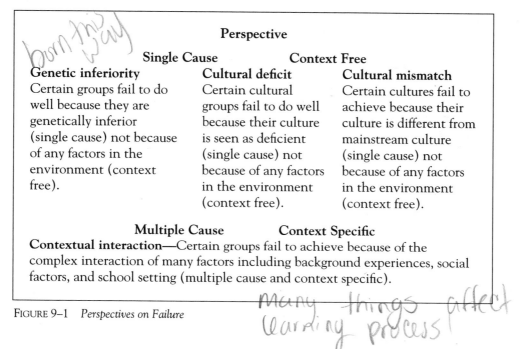

FIGURE 9–1 *Perspectives on Failure*

newest immigrants to arrive; so, for example, at one time the Irish received this label, at another time the Polish immigrants, and more recently the Hispanics. Unfortunately, this view has not entirely disappeared. A local Hmong leader in our community who publishes a Hmong/English newspaper described the kinds of calls the paper sometimes receives:

> Some of the people who called me at my office were terrifying, telling me that American people don't need the Hmong; Hmong people came to America to collect American tax dollars; Hmong people are lazy, just like the Hispanic and African-American people. Hmong people just want to produce babies after babies and they don't want to work. (Yang 1992, B9)

Such responses reflect a genetic inferiority perspective, which blames the minority group for any failure to succeed. It precludes any possibility for change, since hereditary factors are permanent. No consideration is given to Hmong individuals, such as the newspaper publisher introduced above, who is obviously succeeding, nor to the factors that challenge the Hmong in our society.

Cultural Deficit

Cultural deficit explanations differ from genetic inferiority ones because here the focus is on cultural factors rather than hereditary factors. Comments such as "What did you expect? José is from mañana land?" or "You can't trust those people—in their culture, it's okay to cheat" are examples of cultural deficit attitudes. As with the genetic inferiority perspective, the cultural deficit view is another single-cause explanation of failure. Student failure is understood to result from a deficient culture, and no other factors are seen as relevant. This view also assumes that the mainstream culture has no deficiencies.

Not long ago, we learned that a university supervisor wrote an evaluation of a student teacher in which he commended her for working "hard to challenge and reward her pupils, especially those with learning or cultural handicaps." The supervisor's positive comments about the student teacher revealed that he held a cultural deficit view of her students, who were mainly second language students. This is a stance that labels certain cultures as flawed and students who come from those cultures as handicapped. The comment on the evaluation sent a subtle, negative message to the student teacher about those students and what her expectations for them should be. It also might have kept the student teacher from examining other factors that might be affecting her students' school performance.

A possible response to a cultural deficit interpretation of minority-group school performance would be to attempt to change what are regarded as deficient cultural conditions or practices. Parent or family intervention programs are an example. However, there are caveats that should be considered. Valdés (1996) studied ten Mexican migrant families in depth. She discusses the culture of the families she studied and the concerns she has for intervention programs based on a cultural deficit view:

> It is true that the families were not producing successful schoolchildren. It is true that there were many things they did not know about American schools and American teachers. It is also true that they were poor and they were struggling to survive.
>
> What is not true is that the parents in the study were bad parents, or that they did not know how to parent well, or that they did it poorly. (200)

In her study, Valdés identified many important values that the families passed on to their children, values that should not be lost. She is worried about programs that attempt to "cure" the "problems" that "deprived" students have in order to make them more like the mainstream population. A context-free interpretation would assume that "fixing" the parents so that they reflect the mainstream culture is the solution. Valdés would call for a more context-specific approach in which the schools and parents would work together to draw on the strengths within the culture and validate the strengths children bring to school in order to lead them toward academic success. In Chapter 11, we describe parent programs that value students' culture and build on the strengths that learners and their families bring to the learning situation. However, other factors besides the culture of the home contribute to school success or failure for language minority students.

Cultural Mismatch

Recently, rather than speaking of a cultural deficit, researchers have presented the idea of a cultural mismatch. The word *mismatch* may refer to differences in the language of home and school or differences in how cultures typically interact. While the term *cultural mismatch* is more positive than *cultural deficit*, the underlying assumptions are usually the same. According to this view, something must be done to change the culture so that it can be more like the mainstream, which is perceived as clearly superior. As with the previous two perspectives, this viewpoint may be used as a single-cause explanation to account for failure and is often applied in a context-free manner. In other words, other factors in the situation need not be considered to solve the "problem."

If teachers or other school personnel take the view that a cultural mismatch is the cause of a student's poor academic performance, they may send the message that something is wrong with the student's culture and stress the importance of the student's adopting school norms at the expense of his or her native language and culture. Loretta, a Hispanic high school teacher, has struggled with how she had to give up so much of her culture to get where she is now. In response to reading about how the denial of the first language at school confuses students about their identity, she wrote the following:

> In the book, we read about the idea of "language mismatch," where the language at home is different from the language of the school. I understood this concept as what we, my family, called Spanglish. I feel that I fall under this category. My spoken and written English is not as good as I would like it to be, and my Spanish is even poorer. As a Mexican American, I used to feel alienated from both groups of kids. I really did not fit in with the Anglo Americans because we did things differently at our home (for example, we ate with a tortilla instead of using a fork). Also, I did not fit in with the Mexican American students who spoke Spanish and were more traditional in their customs than my family. As a student, I was not proud of my culture because I felt I did not belong to any group. As an adult, I feel I was deprived of my language and of being proud of my culture. Presently, my goal is to become proficient in Spanish.

The most obvious kind of mismatch occurs when students enter school speaking a language other than English. Teachers generally recognize that English learners need to develop a new language to function in school. What is frequently overlooked is that these students may also need to learn new ways to use language. As Heath (1986) says, "Not only is there the general expectation that all children will learn to speak English but also the assumption that they have internalized *before* they start school the norms of language used in academic life" (148).

Schools require children to use language in certain ways. If children's patterns of language use at home are different in significant ways from the uses at school, children may experience difficulties. Heath (1983) has written extensively about differences between uses of language, or ways with words, between homes and schools. She points out that "[f]or all children, academic success depends less on the specific language they know than on the ways of using language they know" (144). When children don't know the ways of using language that the school expects, they may fail. However, this does not necessarily imply that home language use must change. Heath also argues that "[t]he school can promote academic and vocational success for all children, regardless of their first language background, by providing the greatest possible range of oral and written language uses" (144).

In other words, schools can be places where students expand their repertoire of language use. Too often, classroom discourse is limited to asking students questions, getting short answers, and affirming or rejecting those answers. Instead of a limited kind of discourse in schools, it would be beneficial to encompass the different ways with words that children bring to school rather than retaining a narrow range of uses that excludes much of the language of the home and the community.

School success depends to a great extent on a student's ability to use language in ways the school values. Heath suggests that schools can better serve all students by bringing to conscious attention the different functions of language that students are expected to be able to use. For example, teachers can point out the different uses of language required by different school subjects. A science report has a form different from an English essay. Teachers can also ask students to observe language use in the school and contrast it with use in different institutions outside school. In the course of their investigations, students can record and transcribe conversations, analyze them, and write reports. This sociolinguistic study would make all students more aware of how language is used in different social contexts. Students can also examine how certain kinds of jokes, rhymes, and language games are specific to each culture. They can collect proverbs and try to find out if different cultures have similar sayings.

Through these linguistic studies, students would begin to understand how different kinds of language are used in different contexts to accomplish a variety of functions. As Heath says, "A major benefit of teachers' and children's attention to the wide variety of language uses outside the classroom is increased language awareness on the part of all" (180). As students and teachers become more aware of the narrow range of language functions available in school, they can incorporate more of the community language uses in school activities. The result is a greater match between uses of language in home and school, and this benefits all students.

Rather than viewing cultural differences as mismatches, schools can embrace the diversity that enriches the school experience for all students. Yolanda, a fifth-grade bilingual teacher in a school serving rural students of Hispanic background, provided a positive response to diversity. She was concerned that several of her bilingual students seemed ashamed of their culture; they did not want to engage in any activities in Spanish and often said, "Why are we doing this in Spanish? Let's just do it in English." To help her students take pride in their culture and language, she wrote the poem that appears in Figure 9–2.

I'm a Mexian-American
which I proudly exclaim!
I come from two worlds
Mexico and America.

At home, I can speak
Spanish, "¡Si, como no!"
     or
English, if I please
That's bilingualism.

In my two worlds,
I can chose to eat
tortillas with chorizo
     or
eat white bread with ham.

I can listen to lively mariachi music
     or
listen to some jams.

In my two worlds
I can be a beautiful bronze brown
     or
anything in between!

I can have a name like Enrique or
     Guadalupe
which for the rest
can really be a test.

In my two worlds
I can find teachers,
lawyers, mechanics
and farmworkers.

I can hear many say,
"Get out of the two worlds
and come into one!"

BUT . . .

My worlds are so beautiful
I prefer and love to see
life through BOTH for
as long as I can
cause I'm proud to be who I am!

     By Yolanda Shahbazian
     Dedicated to Room 19
     April 1989

FIGURE 9–2 *Yolanda's Poem*

Yolanda applied a context-specific solution because she knew her students and what they would respond to. She stressed that the difference between the two cultures did not constitute a deficit on the part of Spanish speakers. Further, she did not see the difference as a mismatch. Instead, she encouraged students to develop their potential in both languages and cultures.

The Contextual Interaction Model

We return to the case studies from Chapter 1 to make the point that the Contextual Interaction Model (Cortés 1986) provides a more satisfactory analysis than does a context-free, single-cause explanation of students' school performance. The students described in Chapter 1 came from different cultural, social, economic, and educational backgrounds. In addition, those students were put into different school settings upon arriving. Some of the students were extremely successful and some were struggling academically. Once we know students' settings and their backgrounds, it is more difficult to label them or devise simple solutions for helping them.

Our adaptation of Cortés's model (Figure 1–1) shows that the societal context—the world outside school—influences the school context. The societal context includes many factors, including the families who send their children to the school, their cultural and ethnic heritage, their attitudes and perceptions of schools and education, and the educational level of the parents. In addition, the societal context includes general social attitudes of community members, many of which are shaped by the mass media and politics and by national attitudes. Often the political issues result in legal mandates for schools. Teacher attitudes and student attitudes are also part of the societal context. These are forces that teachers and students bring with them to schools. All these societal factors have a strong impact on schools. They create the contexts in which teachers work. In the following sections we first look at how community attitudes and politics influence schools. Then we consider how teacher attitudes and student attitudes help shape education for English language learners.

The Societal Context: National and Community Attitudes

The community in which immigrants live, work, and go to school helps form the societal context. The attitudes and perceptions of community members shape school programs and policies. In a community such as Fresno, which has a large immigrant school-age population, negative attitudes toward immigrants have clear educational consequences. For example, the influx of immigrants caused overcrowding in schools, but until recently, citizens have voted down school bonds to provide money to build new schools. In surrounding districts, school bonds continue to be rejected. Many people who vote against the bonds state plainly that they have no intention of paying for the education of the immigrants in our schools. These openly hostile remarks are a reflection of a climate that is anti-immigrant.

The anti-immigrant climate in Fresno has been shaped, at least in part, by state and national events. To take one example, former governor of California Pete Wilson led an active campaign to reduce services to undocumented immigrants and their children. Through a private, noncampaign-related organization of supporters, the Governor Wilson Forum, Wilson sent a full-page open letter to President Clinton in *The New York Times*, *USA Today*, and the *Washington Post* calling for wholesale reform and urging congressional repeal of federal laws requiring states to pay for education, incarceration, and health services for illegal immigrants. In addition, he proposed that the children of illegal immigrants born in this country not be given citizenship, a proposal that would call for a change in the Fourteenth Amendment of the U.S. Constitution.

Wilson's letter, presented as it was at the national level, helped create an atmosphere in which others at the community level felt free to express negative attitudes toward immigrants. Only a few days after Wilson's letter to Clinton was published, a letter to the editor appeared in our local paper which stated the following:

This city has seen an unprecedented boom in both legal and illegal immigration in recent years, and now we have high crime rates, housing developments, and neighborhoods being turned into squalid, rat-infested havens of crime and crowded with wrecked cars. In general, cities and towns . . . are rapidly decaying because of uneducated and uncaring residents from other countries who are not used to running water or basic sanitary conditions.

Adverse feelings of the general public toward services for immigrant children, and illegals in particular, were so strong in that period that David East, one of our graduate students, wrote a letter in defense of the group, pleading for support and understanding (see Figure 9–3).

These attitudes were prevalent in California in general, leading to passage of Proposition 187 in 1994. The proposition was "designed to crack down on 'illegal aliens' by excluding them from most government services, barring their children from public schools, and directing officials to report anyone suspected of being undocumented" (Crawford 1999, 237).

Though the proposition has not been enforced because of challenges to its constitutionality, it caused a great deal of harm. When the bill passed, many university students put on black armbands as a sign of protest. The day its passage was announced, one Hispanic student approached Yvonne in tears saying that, though she was a legal immigrant, the proposition put fears into her about what would happen next. David East's sentiment that "California could be following Hitler's footsteps in 'dealing' with the 'problem' of immigration" fit what the university student said: "It makes me feel as though being Hispanic is like being Jewish during the beginning of Nazi Germany." Indeed, many immigrant parents reported that rumors about the proposition seriously affected their children. Many young students were afraid to go

---

LETTERS TO THE EDITOR

Immigrants, schools

The "burden on schools" that Valerie Reeves spoke of in her April 11 letter is not the burden of educating immigrant children, but of producing caring, productive citizens who think beyond the racial borders so firmly entrenched in America's psyche.

The children of illegal taxpaying immigrants are poor and brown of skin. Their culture is different from that of the average white, middle-class American. Whenever publicity blesses this group, it is usually of a negative nature. It seems only natural to turn against this group, particularly when the state is in a financial crisis. It appears that California could be following Hitler's footsteps in "dealing" with the "problem" of immigration.

As an educator who works primarily with immigrant children, I know that almost all of them stay in this country for the rest of their lives. If we choose to hide our heads in the sand and deny an education to these children, their future and our future will be no better, only worse.

To deny these children an education because of immigration status seems cruel and mean-spirited. These children have no control over their parents' decisions. They do, however, hold the keys to their future through the power of education.

I became a teacher because I felt children deserved a fair chance at life. I wonder why Ms. Reeves became a teacher.

J. David East
Squaw Valley

FIGURE 9–3   *David's Letter*

to school for fear that they might be taken away or that their parents would be deported in their absence.

Immigrant students entering school, whether they are in the United States legally or illegally, are affected by laws like these, which reflect community attitudes. These attitudes form an important part of the societal context within which educators function. Public sentiment against immigrants is felt by administrators, teachers, and students alike. Programs like bilingual education, which are perceived as being intended for illegal immigrants, are criticized at the very least and often eliminated because of misunderstanding and the desire of those in power to maintain the status quo in the face of a growing non-English-speaking population.

Community Attitudes and School Programs: Bilingual Education

Negative attitudes about immigrants have been reflected in opposition to bilingual education. Yvonne has received threatening letters and angry phone calls because she has the title of Director of Bilingual Education at our university. The letters and phone calls have made it clear that bilingual education is un-American and mainly exists to educate unwanted illegal immigrants. As David East points out in his letter, educating all students, legal or not, is really in our best interest for the future. However, that is not the way many people in communities with large second language populations feel.

Cheryl, a bilingual fifth-grade teacher, writes about her experiences in the same small farming community where David East worked, before she became a teacher and before she was bilingual:

> In 1973 I was a young housewife with two small children, and our family needed extra income. The district had a bilingual program that had a parent involvement component. I was hired as a community aide for this follow-through program, to be a liaison between the school and the community.
>
> I was the only non-Hispanic community aide in a community that was composed of approximately 80 percent Hispanics. I was assigned the "north side" of town because most of these community members were fluent in English. In fact, most were Anglo property owners who saw the follow-through program as a threat to the community. I couldn't understand it then, and I have a difficult time understanding now how educating and empowering your community is considered a negative thing.
>
> The community (the ones with the power) fought this program with a hateful vengeance. The school board fired administrators who implemented and favored the program. They even fired the district superintendent. They also made it unbearable for many young, idealistic teachers who came to the district with ideas of making exciting changes in the system. Most of them left by 1974. The board finally refused enormous amounts of federal dollars and phased things back to "the way they were."

Cheryl's story shows the link between community attitudes and school practices. In her district, bilingual programs were abandoned because of community sentiment, not because of any educational deficiencies.

The controversy surrounding bilingual education provides a good example of how national and community attitudes impact school policies and practices. In Chapter 8 we reviewed the research and theoretical base for bilingual education. This base is sufficiently strong to warrant implementation of bilingual programs. However, bilingual education has come to symbolize both the waves of immigration and the social and economic problems that communities perceive as resulting from that immigration. Bilingual education is widely misunderstood, but it creates an emotional reaction from the general public.

Bilingual Education or English-Only?

At the national level, the opposition to bilingual education has taken the form of a movement known as English Only and is strongly supported by groups like U.S. English. Crawford (1992) explains that the movement for Official English legislation, begun by Senator S. I. Hayakawa in 1981, had a thrust "not only *for* English but *against* bilingualism" (1). Opponents of bilingual education claim that there are overwhelming numbers of immigrants and explain that teaching in languages other than English will (1) cause division and dissension, and (2) keep immigrants from learning English. In addition, they make it clear that speaking English is American and speaking other languages is un-American (Holmes 1993). Linda Chavez has been a prominent spokesperson first for U.S. English and later for the Center for Equal Opportunity. When she was president of U.S. English in 1987, she made clear the position of many bilingual education opponents:

> Unless we become serious about protecting our heritage as a unilingual society—bound by a common language—we may lose a precious resource that has helped us forge a national character and identity from so many diverse elements. (Crawford 1999, 67)

Chavez resigned from U.S. English in 1988 when a memo from the organization's chairman, John Tanton, was published. Tanton "warned of a Hispanic political takeover in the United States unless something was done about immigration and high birthrates" (68). Tanton critiqued Hispanics for "taking bribes, being Roman Catholic (which was a threat to separation of church and state), exhibiting low 'educability' and high dropout rates, failure to use birth control, having limited concern for the environment, and dividing the country by speaking Spanish" (68).

What was and still is disturbing about this kind of response is that bilingual education arouses "passions about issues of political power and social status that are far removed from the classroom"(Crawford 1999, 13). The press seems to encourage these tensions. And the effects are felt in the classrooms as well as in the community.

English-Only: The Influence of the Press and Disinformation

Crawford's own interest in bilingual education began when he was an investigative reporter newly assigned to education. The then Secretary of Education,

William Bennett, had recently delivered a speech calling the Bilingual Education Act a "failed path, a bankrupt course," and a waste of taxpayers' money (Bennett 1985). When the education community reacted, Bennett's office claimed that they were receiving hundreds of letters and those letters were five-to-one in favor of Bennett's view.

Crawford (1992) read the letters and what he found disturbed him:

> [M]ost of the "supporting" letters had less to do with schooling for non-English-speaking students than with illegal aliens on welfare, communities being "overrun" by Asians and Hispanics, "macho-oriented" foreigners trying to impose their culture on Americans, and—a special concern—the out-of-control birthrates of linguistic minorities.

Crawford explained that many of the letters ended with calls for Official English, such as "WHOSE AMERICA IS THIS? ONE FLAG. ONE LANGUAGE" (4).

His discovery that opposition to bilingual education was based on issues not related to pedagogy led Crawford to investigate issues related to bilingual education more thoroughly. He has reported on research that shows how first language support leads to academic success and how this research is buried under negative publicity. This publicity, fueled by organizations like English Only and the Center for Equal Opportunity, creates a negative attitude toward bilinguals and toward bilingual education. In fact, proponents of bilingual education have labeled the information put out by these organizations *disinformation*, a method of diverting people from facts.

> The term "disinformation" refers to the systematic spreading of false information in order to confuse and disorient the opposition. Although the term is usually associated with the activities of groups such as the CIA and former KGB (and more recently tobacco companies), the phenomenon of disinformation is no less evident in debates on domestic political issues such as the education of bilingual students. (Cummins 1996, 195)

Perhaps there is no clearer example of the power of disinformation than the English Only campaign in California, which led to the passage of the English for the Children initiative, Proposition 227.

Proposition 227

More immigrants have settled in California than in any other state. A popular perception has developed that immigrants are lazy, take unearned welfare money, don't try to learn English, join gangs, and are generally the source of many of the problems that exist in the state. During the 1980s and 1990s negative attitudes toward immigrants surfaced in public arenas. For example, there was an increase in conservative talk shows. The topic was often immigrants who "wouldn't speak English in stores or on the streets" and "were taking welfare benefits without earning them."

Newspaper headlines connected low test scores to the English language learners, and school bonds failed because many residents attributed the increase in student population to the presence of immigrant children. Even local newspaper columnists, usually more liberal in their views, expressed concerns about teaching children in their native language.

Crawford (1999) noted that many journalists nationwide highlighted political controversies surrounding bilingual education, repeating and reinforcing stereotypes of bilingual education as

- a self-perpetuating bureaucracy designed primarily to provide jobs for Hispanics
- a "politicized" curriculum that puts a higher priority on ethnic pride than academic achievement
- a pedagogy that keeps children from assimilating in the mainstream
- an obstacle to English acquisition (227)

The last two points on Crawford's list were key for Unz, the leader in the fight for the passage of California's Proposition 227, the English for the Children initiative. Unz, a software millionaire and politician, took on the campaign, and in fact, continues it now in other states across the country. Unz attacked the efficiency of bilingual programs, claiming to be an advocate for bilingual children. He drew support from Jaime Escalante, the teacher whose experiences were dramatized in the movie *Stand and Deliver*, and Hispanic teacher Matta Tuchman. The proposition was complex. As Crawford explained, it was

crafted to meet conflicting political and policy goals. Unz sought to outlaw a program that many parents wanted without appearing to restrict parental choice; to tie the hands of school boards that favored bilingual education without seeming to usurp their authority; and to eliminate protections for LEP students while shielding the law from civil-rights litigation. (252)

Proposition 227 passed overwhelmingly on June 2, 1998. The initiative essentially banned bilingual education and called for sheltered English immersion. Students were to be immersed in English for one year and then put into regular classes. This program had no research base. It had never been tried elsewhere, but the idea was appealing. Give students one year to learn English and then let them get on with their education. Who would vote against "English for the children"? The many advocates of bilingual education failed to get the message to the public about the effectiveness of bilingual education in time or in an organized way. Unz dismissed academic arguments referring to professors as "loonies." Unz got favorable newspaper coverage, but the press largely ignored arguments from academics.

Yvonne was teaching her bilingual methods course at the time of the Proposition 227 campaign. She commented in class that publicity that was pro-bilingual education was not appearing in the newspapers. She gave examples of how she and colleagues throughout the state had trouble getting articles printed that explained the value of bilingual education and how recent studies were being ignored by the press.

One of her graduate students, Jerry Sánchez, was a Hispanic coming to teaching after a business career. He was new to the program and still skeptical about bilingual education and its benefits. Jerry decided to do his inquiry project on local press coverage of Proposition 227. He collected all the articles related to Proposition 227 that were printed in the local paper, *The Fresno Bee*, over a six-month period. He categorized the articles by the perspective they took on bilingual education: pro, con, or neutral. He then counted how many column inches were devoted to each point of view. He also recorded where in the newspaper each type of article appeared (in the A or B sections of the paper) and he looked at headlines.

The results of Jerry's inquiry supported Yvonne's claims. The number of articles that were negative about bilingual education outnumbered those that were favorable. Forty-one (55 percent) of the articles were unfavorable, and thirty-four (45 percent) were favorable. Articles that were against bilingual education were longer, receiving far more space than favorable articles. The total space given to negative articles comprised 70 percent of the total space. The antibilingual articles were also more often in the front section. When the paper did include articles that showed the benefits of bilingual education, they were more often buried in the editorial section. Finally, headline space given to negative front-page articles was dramatically larger than headline space allotted to positive articles. Nearly 96 percent of the front-page headlines were negative. Jerry even found that sometimes a negative headline was given to an article whose content was actually positive. Yvonne, Jerry, and others in the community did go to the newspaper and show them Jerry's findings. The newspaper responded by printing more positive articles. However, this was at the end of the campaign and was far too late to have an effect.

Similar results have been found at the national level. McQuillan and Tse (1997) reviewed publications that appeared over a ten-year span and found that during the period, articles in newspapers and magazines supported bilingual education only 45 percent of the time, the same percentage that Jerry found. On the other hand, when McQuillan and Tse reviewed academic publications, they found that 87 percent supported bilingual education. For that reason, they titled their article "Does Research Matter?"

Newspapers reported public opinion polls during the Proposition 227 campaign. Krashen (1996) found that results to such polls are highly influenced by the way the question is asked. When pollsters ask, "Do you want your child in an all-English class so they can learn English faster?" the response, not surprisingly, is overwhelmingly positive. On the other hand, when the question is more general—"Do you support bilingual education?"—the results strongly favor bilingual programs. During the Proposition 227 campaign, many polls were reported that showed a negative public attitude toward bilingual education. However, as Krashen's research shows, the public is actually in favor of bilingual education. Positive surveys, however, were not widely reported by the press.

English Only campaigns like Proposition 227 are part of the agenda of many politicians across the country. English-only is an issue that appeals to the voters and helps politicians get elected. As educators, we must continue to inform ourselves and try to combat the disinformation that is prevalent. However, this is a hot issue and attracts readership, so the media feature stories about bilingual education, but most of them are negative, thus fueling negative attitudes toward a school program that has a sound research base and could have positive effects for English language learners.

Political issues, such as Proposition 227, that result in legal mandates form part of the societal context that impacts schools. This is a reality that teachers must face. Facing the reality, though, is not the same as accepting it as the final answer. We end this section on a positive note. There are teachers who are informed and who, like the readers of this book, are giving up their personal time to study how to better serve the diverse students we have in our schools. Toni, a bilingual kindergarten teacher whose first language was discouraged by "Speak English for Your Own Benefit" signs around the school, recently wrote the following:

> As I attend class after class, I am so encouraged to see the number of Anglo teachers taking courses and learning how to empower minority students. I'm encouraged by their care and concern and by their putting all their learning into real practice. This change has been long overdue.

Toni's observation is important. Teachers have found ways to change what is happening with bilingual students at their schools. Their understanding of bilingual education has made them stronger advocates for their students and for educational practices that work for those students. Rusty is an Anglo sixth-grade teacher who cares passionately about promoting a positive view of diversity:

> There is some satisfaction in knowing that in spite of the fact that we have ignorant politicians making foolish decisions, organizations and researchers being used for the promotion of self-serving agendas, and fellow teachers impacting student lives based on erroneous assumptions, there are thirty-three kids in my classroom that are getting the best they could get anywhere in the world. Now how is that for self-confidence?

Teachers like Rusty can make a difference for language-minority students in schools, especially if they become advocates for their students and help to inform their communities about bilingual education issues. If bilingual education is really viewed from a pedagogical perspective rather than a political one, and if the public learns about bilingual education research, more programs will be implemented. Recently, Secretary of Education Riley called for more dual-language programs. This kind of support from highly placed officials can help promote positive attitudes at every level.

Teacher Attitudes, Prejudices, and Perceptions

> During my student teaching experience, I had the opportunity to work with ESL classes in math, history, and English. In one of these classes the teacher was trying to give me some of her educational insight. She told me that the Asian students (Lao, Hmong, etc.) were much better students than the Mexican students. She went on to say that these children wanted to learn and were not a behavioral problem like the others. I do not think she knew that I was Mexican. Needless to say, I was extremely bothered by her remarks, and I immediately went home and shared this experience with my parents. They were both angered by her false statements. They felt that this new wave of immigrants are being treated much better than they were when they were in school.

The above quote comes from Loretta, the high school teacher who earlier commented on the "language mismatch" she experienced. The teacher she worked with during her student teaching reflected an attitude that teachers working in schools with large numbers of immigrant students may develop. Communities form attitudes toward schools, and school personnel develop attitudes toward members of different community groups. Teachers' opinions about students have an important influence on the school context. We believe that teachers may need to develop new attitudes for the new students in their schools (Freeman and Freeman 1990).

Throughout California and in other states with large numbers of immigrant students, teachers are responding in various ways to changes in the student population. We have worked with groups of teachers in states like Texas, New Mexico, and Arizona with long-term bilingual populations, those with new growth in immigrant populations like Iowa, Kansas, and Nebraska, those with indigenous as well as new immigrant populations like Alaska and North Dakota, and those with multilingual populations like Illinois, Alabama, and New Jersey. All teachers find these populations challenging, but some teachers are coping better than others.

Not all teachers are reluctant to work with multilingual students, but many are, at least initially. We have seen five common responses from teachers in schools with high populations of English language learners. In describing these responses we will use hypothetical situations that represent what we have observed. The scenarios help illustrate perceptions of failure we discussed earlier. In each situation, a number of factors come into play, and a single-cause explanation for success or failure is inadequate. And in each scenario, teacher attitudes and perceptions play an important role. We briefly analyze each scenario and then offer some possible positive responses.

"Teaching Isn't Like It Used to Be"

Mrs. Brown has taught kindergarten at Baker School in the south end of town for fifteen years. When she first began teaching there, the neighborhood was made up mostly of middle-class whites, but over the years large numbers of African Americans, Hispanics, and Southeast Asians have moved into the area, causing a "white flight" to the north. The majority of her present students arrive with little or no English. She complains that they cannot do what her students in the past could. She remembers the past fondly. On the first day of school, children arrived eager to learn, holding the hands of parents who offered support. Now, she complains, the students, especially the Southeast Asian children, enter the classroom reluctantly. They are either alone or with parents who don't speak English and seem anxious to escape as quickly as possible. Though she has an English-only rule for the classroom, she constantly has to remind students not to speak their native languages. Her biggest complaints are that the children don't seem motivated and the parents don't care.

Analysis

There are several reasons that Mrs. Brown may be responding as she is. In the earlier days, most of her students spoke English and came from a background similar to their teacher's. She now finds herself trying to teach students who not only do not speak the same language literally, but also do not understand her customs and values any more than she does theirs. Previously, Mrs. Brown had strong parent support, but now she is not sure how to communicate with the parents. Mrs. Brown does not know how to change her teaching to help students, and she responds by blaming them and their families.

Positive Responses

Many teachers who suddenly find themselves with large numbers of English-language learners make it a point to inform themselves about their new students. They read and discuss books and articles about other teachers working with non-English speakers. They talk with their fellow teachers and share materials and ideas that have been successful. They attend workshops offered by school districts and local colleges. They join professional organizations for teachers of bilingual and second language learners.

Once they learn more about English language learners, they become advocates for them. They seek people and materials who can provide first language support, and they promote school events that highlight different cultural traditions. In addition, they make an effort to include the parents of their new students, not only at special events but in the regular classroom day. Even if parents do not speak English, they are invited to class to read a book in their first language, cook, or do crafts. Though all of these things require extra effort, they make their classrooms exciting places where all their students learn.

"Language Minority Kids Make Me Look Like a Failure"

Ms. Franklin is a second-year second-grade teacher. Like most nontenured teachers in the district, she has been assigned to a classroom of diverse students, mostly Hispanic and Southeast Asian. Many of her students are classified as LEP. Ms. Franklin's teacher-education program included some coursework in second language acquisition, ESL methodology, and diversity. As soon as she began to work with her English learners last year, she fell in love with them. She read with the children, encouraged them to write often, and, in general, created activities that drew on their interests and background knowledge. The children responded well to this type of program, and she could see tremendous growth in their English.

Despite this success, Ms. Franklin has encountered problems. She teaches in a state and district where frequent skills-based tests in reading, writing, and math are mandated and the results are published. The test scores for her students have remained low, and the principal has talked about this with Ms. Franklin. Even though he did not threaten her directly, Ms. Franklin now feels her job is on the line. From the coursework she has taken and her own experiences, she realizes that standardized tests do not chart the progress of her bilingual students fairly. Still, she is tempted to try this year to "teach to the test," despite the fact that she does not feel that worksheets and drills are meaningful to her second language students. She is beginning to view her students as having deficits—deficits that could have direct consequences for her career. She is also beginning to wish that she could transfer to a school in the north part of town with fewer English learners.

Analysis
Ms. Franklin begins her teaching with enthusiasm and caring. Her college coursework prepared her to work effectively with English learners. However, Ms. Franklin is a new teacher and not really experienced enough to confidently defend her curriculum. The emphasis on test scores begins to erode her confidence in doing what is best for her students. She is beginning to view the students she once was trying to help as the source of her problems. Her solution is to try to get away from her present teaching situation.

Positive Responses
Many of the teachers who take our graduate courses are like Ms. Franklin. They are new teachers who want to help their students and have studied second language acquisition. However, they are concerned because they feel pressure from standardized testing and do not want to be judged by the poor performance of non-English speakers. After taking further graduate coursework, these teachers begin to understand how long it takes to speak, read, and write a second language with near-native proficiency and how critical first language support is for content learning. They begin to view their teaching and the testing of their students differently. Many of these teachers become confident enough in what they know to explain why they do what they do to administrators. They often become mentors in their school, advising other teachers who have multilingual students.

"It's Not Fair to the Rest of My Class to Give Those Students Special Attention"

Mr. Martin teaches in a farming community where he has lived since he was a child. At the beginning of the year, his sixth-grade classroom consisted of a nice group of Anglo and Hispanic children who were all fairly proficient in English and all reasonably successful learners. At the end of the first month of school, the principal called

Mr. Martin in to explain that five sixth-grade migrant children had just arrived from Mexico and that they would be placed in Mr. Martin's class.

Mr. Martin wasn't sure what to do with these new students, whose English was extremely limited. The district paid him to take training to learn new techniques, but he resented the idea that he had to attend extra classes and learn new ways to teach, especially when he had been successful for a number of years. Why should he be the one to change? If these students couldn't meet the expectations for his class, maybe they weren't ready for it.

Nevertheless, the students were in his class, and the principal was not about to transfer them out. Since he was a good teacher, Mr. Martin knew he should be doing something for them, and he felt guilty that they just sat quietly in the back of his classroom. On the other hand, it seemed to him that giving those students special attention wasn't fair to the rest of the class members, who were doing just fine with his traditional instruction. At the same time, the extra training he was receiving also made him feel guilty because it stressed that students should not simply be given busywork, but that they should be engaged in meaningful activities with other students in the classroom. However, Mr. Martin's teaching style did not include much student interaction. He became doubly frustrated, as he felt that he was not only being asked to deal with new students, but also to change his way of teaching.

Analysis

Mr. Martin, like Mrs. Brown, is a conscientious teacher in a school system that is changing. He has succeeded in the past and resents the fact that he has been designated to deal with the new students. It is probable that the principal chose Mr. Martin because she had confidence that he could do a good job. However, he feels picked on and resentful of the extra time and training necessary to work with second language students. In addition, he believes that giving them special instruction is actually going to be detrimental to his other students. At this point, Mr. Martin does not understand that what is good instruction for second language students is also good for his other students.

Positive Responses

Teachers we have worked with have come to realize that it is impossible to use a traditional transmission model of teaching to reach a very diverse student body. In addition, as they try interactive activities in which heterogeneous groups of students work on projects together, they see that all their students, including their native English-speaking students, learn more. Several teachers who entered our graduate classes determined never to change their teaching styles, later gave enthusiastic testimonials of how exciting teaching can be when it is organized around thematic units and includes literature studies, creative writing, and projects involving art, science, music, drama, and cooking.

"Who Wants to Be the Bilingual Teacher?"

Mr. González went into bilingual education because he himself had come to the United States as a non-English-speaking child, and he knew how difficult it was to succeed in school as a second language learner. His education classes had taught him that instruction in the first language helps children academically and actually speeds their success in English. During his first two years of teaching, he enthusiastically worked with his fourth graders, supporting their first language and helping them succeed in their second.

By the end of the third year when he was tenured, his enthusiasm began to wane. Mr. González was troubled by the subtle way his fellow teachers treated him. The bilingual program was considered remedial, and constant remarks in the teachers' lounge showed him that fellow teachers did not really believe bilingual kids were capable of the kind of success other students could achieve.

On top of that, Mr. González soon discovered that Hispanic children who were discipline problems were transferred into his class throughout the year even though they were not English language learners. When he objected, the principal always explained that since he was Hispanic, he could understand those children better. Mr. González's attempts to explain that his program was geared to work with Spanish speakers to help them succeed academically, not with discipline problems, fell on deaf ears. He began to feel that his expertise was not respected and that his classroom was becoming a dumping ground. He put in a request to be taken out of the bilingual program.

Analysis

Mr. González's situation is one that has repeated itself many times in different school districts. When there is little understanding of what bilingual education really is and why it is important, bilingual teachers feel isolated and misunderstood. Often, uninformed teachers make commonsense assumptions about bilingual learners and do not hesitate to express their opinions about the limited potential of that group of students. Administrators who have heard about the importance of ethnic and cultural role models but do not really know the theory behind bilingual education try to find quick and easy solutions to problems of minority students. In this case all Hispanics are lumped together, and Mr. González is asked to solve all the "problems" of the Hispanics at the school. Bilingual teachers such as Mr. González find themselves, like their bilingual students, suffering prejudice and a lack of understanding. It is no wonder that many bilingual educators drop out of bilingual education.

Positive Responses

Bilingual teachers we have worked with have not found an easy answer to this situation. Recently, attacks on bilingual education and negative public opinion have further undermined the efforts of schools and teachers trying to implement good bilingual programs. Because the general public often has a negative view of immigrants, bilingual teachers like Mr. González have the challenge of not only defending what they are doing but also keeping others from undermining the programs they have. A bright spot in the area of bilingual education is the rise of two-way bilingual programs. These programs have had positive results for native English speakers and those learning English, as both groups become bilingual and biliterate (Dolson and

Lindholm 1995). If Mr. González could teach in one of these programs or promote starting a program like this, he would probably have more support.

"Don't Expect Too Much of These Students"

Mrs. Williams is a pullout ESL instructor who works with children grades K–8. Most of her students are either Hispanics whose parents are migrant workers or Southeast Asians whose parents were peasants before coming to this country. The Southeast Asian and Hispanic children whose parents are well-to-do are seldom in these types of programs. Mrs. Williams likes teaching small groups of children and, in fact, volunteered to become a district pullout teacher because the idea of working with small groups of polite, respectful children appealed to her.

Mrs. Williams has had no special training in ESL teaching, but because she has seen lots of English language learners over the years, she feels she understands their problems. She firmly believes that many non-English speakers enter school with no language and that second language parents do not really value education. "After all," she explains, "their parents don't speak English, nor do they read or write in their first language. What these children need is lots of oral-language development in English."

In the pullout classes, the students get practice in pronouncing words, and they often do worksheets that focus on phonics. Since the students don't have control of the oral language, Mrs. Williams does not have them do much reading or writing. "They simply aren't ready," she concludes. Mrs. Williams and her students appear to have reached a sort of truce. She won't push too hard or expect too much, and they will be orderly and complete the assignments she gives them. The regular teachers from whose classrooms the students are pulled out don't complain. They are happy to be relieved of the responsibility of teaching these students for a part of each day, so this arrangement seems satisfactory to all concerned.

The parents of Mrs. Williams' students don't pressure the school to do more either. They seem reluctant to talk to her and do not show up for the conferences she schedules, thus reinforcing Mrs. Williams' belief that parents do not care about their children's school success. Since the students, their parents, and the other teachers are satisfied with her program, Mrs. Williams sees no need to change and resents the assertion from a new district specialist for second language students that she isn't really teaching her ESL students anything.

Analysis

Mrs. Williams is a classic case of a teacher who loves her students and perceives herself as doing the best she can for them. However, it is important to realize that a limited view of students' potential leads to a limiting curriculum. Often, people believe that simply knowing a language qualifies a person to teach it. Mrs. Williams does not see the need for any further education about English language learners or the teaching of a second language. If she had done some further study, she might have learned that students need lots of reading and writing as well as speaking and listening, and that worksheets and drills do not help with the natural acquisition of language. Mrs. Williams believes that the students' first language and culture are not really important for learning English. Stereotypes about the parents' lack of interest in the students' school success keep her from attempting to form links between the home and school. Perhaps most disturbing of all is the fact that the rest of the school is actually relieved that Mrs. Williams will take care of the "problem" of the second language children.

Positive Responses

Although it still happens, it is less and less possible for teachers like Mrs. Williams to be assigned to teach English language learners without professional preparation. In many states there are increasing numbers of programs at universities that help prepare teachers working with multilingual students. Quite a few school districts require that teachers have coursework in second language acquisition and methodology. California requires teachers who have English language learners in their classrooms to be certified, and certification is based on knowledge of second language acquisition, second language teaching, culture, and linguistics.

Coping with Change

Despite the positive changes that are taking place, there is still much to be done to improve the education of English language learners. Each time we read and discuss these five scenarios with the teachers in our graduate programs, we are saddened to learn how many of them tell us these situations are entirely representative of what is still going on in many schools. Rusty, the sixth-grade teacher mentioned earlier, reflected what he has seen in his school by writing a poignant poem (see Figure 9–4).

Although many teachers are learning about English language learners and are doing wonderful things in their schools, other teachers and schools still have a long way to go before they begin to meet their students' needs. With the growing number of second language students, the importance of developing new attitudes for the changing population becomes more critical daily.

For all teachers, though, coping with change is not easy. In their report on how California teachers are responding to an influx of immigrant students, researchers from the group California Tomorrow interviewed thirty-six teachers. Kate Duggan, a middle school teacher in a Los Angeles school district with a high second language population, expressed the views of many teachers across the country:

> Change in itself is extremely stressful, and teaching now immerses you in change. Changes in the student population and cultures and races who enroll. New kids coming in and out all the time. And because traditional methods don't work, you always have to be experimenting with different approaches so there are changes in what you're doing as a teacher. All this change affects the entire tone of the school. (Olsen and Mullen 1990, 9)

School Days, School Days

You can not see it,
So well it does hide,
Yet subtly it whittles,
Away all self-pride.

Through teeth straight and shiny,
You see the bright smile.
Yet no love is shown there,
Not even for a while.

The pros they can fake it,
They act like they care,
"No, Honey not here,
You sit over there."

"You don't speak our language,
I'm sure that will change."
She pokes little Susie,
"His home's on the range."

"Your mom calls you Carlos,
Now Charles is your name.
I'm sure that you realize
It all means the same."

"Oh, look at your free lunch,
Why, isn't that rice?
It's just like your home, dear,
Oh, isn't that nice?"

Yes, each day it happens
In room after room.
And kids really do wish
They'd stayed in the womb.

The talk, it is subtle,
It's impact so cruel,
Like slow-burning fire
when you've added some fuel.

It strikes at the heart
And pulls at the brain.
Like a strong locomotive,
That pulls the whole train.

We know what the law states,
and that is a start.
But can you really legislate,
Affairs of the heart?

We've had great examples,
In religions and creeds,
You'd think that would do it,
That's all we would need.

Yet man's basic nature,
His seeking of wealth,
Has caused him to stumble
All over himself.

And so often the children
They stand in the way.
And push comes to shove,
And the children, they pay.

Oh, teacher you must see,
You're the last hope
In helping that small child
With life just to cope.

His face may be dirty,
His clothes might have holes,
His stomach is growling,
He's had only stale rolls.

So reach out a hand please,
Bring a smile to his face.
Give each child a hug
Regardless of race.

No matter his language,
His color, his creeds,
As God is your witness
You must meet his needs.

And if you can't do it,
then please leave our ranks.
Go work in a factory
Or in one of the banks.

We're looking for teachers
With hearts big as stores
Who love *all* the children
And do a lot more.

So if you are willing
to look to the heart
Come quickly new teachers
We'll give you a part.

To show kids some justice
Some fairness and love,
With an abundant supply
That comes from above.

Challenges? Why yes,
Of course, that is true.
But no greater work
Can you ever do.
                    Rusty DeRuiter, 1992

FIGURE 9–4 *Rusty's Poem*

Change *is* stressful, but a number of teachers are not only coping with it, they are learning how to celebrate the growing diversity in their classrooms. These teachers find that the key to changing student and community attitudes toward schools is to develop a positive attitude themselves. They show faith in their diverse students as learners.

Teacher attitudes constitute an important component of the societal context for education. Equally important are the attitudes of immigrant group members toward school. Their feelings are shaped by the group's history and particularly its relationships with the mainstream culture. Differences among minority groups' school performance result in part from the way different groups view school and society.

Types of Ethnic Minorities

Ogbu (1991), an anthropologist from Nigeria, has examined how differences in the backgrounds and experiences of minority groups in various countries have affected their school performance. In the United States he has studied the discrepancies in the school achievement of Hispanics, Native Americans, and African Americans when compared with other minority groups from countries like Japan, Cuba, and China. Ogbu classified these minorities into two groups: immigrant minorities and involuntary minorities.

Immigrant and involuntary minorities now constitute the numerical majority in many school systems. (We should remember here Wink's [2000] objection to the label *minority*. However, for the sake of this discussion, we will retain Ogbu's terms.) Both groups frequently experience discriminatory treatment at the hands of the dominant group. Ogbu notes, however, that the response of the two minority groups to this negative treatment is quite different, and as a result, immigrant minorities tend to succeed in schools, while members of involuntary minority groups often fail. An important difference between these two groups is their attitude toward mainstream institutions, such as schools, and their perceptions of the benefits of education. These attitudes and perceptions form a part of the societal context that influence the school context.

When Ogbu reviewed the performance of different minority groups in school, certain patterns emerged. For example, he found that Chinese and Cubans, who generally meet the criteria for immigrant minorities, have usually done quite well compared with involuntary minorities, such as African Americans and Native Americans. However, it is important to note before further developing the differences between these two types of minorities that a number of factors determine whether any one person succeeds or fails in school. Further, it is not always possible to decide whether a particular individual falls into the immigrant or involuntary minority category. In fact, often students will fall under the category of immigrant minority in some areas and involuntary minority in other areas. Therefore, as one considers the differences between these types, it is important not to decide that certain students will fail or succeed if they belong to one group or the other. On the other hand, it is important to be aware of Ogbu's classifications, because an understanding of them is one factor that may help us to make informed decisions about how best to work with our students. Figure 9–5 summarizes key points from Ogbu's research.

Immigrant Minorities

Ogbu (1991) defines immigrant minorities as those who come from another country and retain their homeland as their reference point. Chinese, Cubans, and Japanese are examples of immigrant minorities. Immigrants are not highly influenced by majority-group treatment even when they are given low-status jobs, because they measure success by the standards of their homeland. As Ogbu writes, "The immigrants appear to interpret the economic, political, and social barriers against them as more or less temporary problems, as problems they will or can overcome with the passage of time, hard work, or more education" (11). Often they plan to return to their home, and they believe that they can return with new skills and degrees that will allow them to succeed there. They see themselves as outsiders in a new society and expect poor treatment and low status. They accept this treatment because they are still better off than they would be in their homeland, and the skills they are gaining will help them succeed later in their homeland.

The three teens from El Salvador, José Luis, Guillermo, and Patricia, profiled in Chapter 1, are fairly clear examples of immigrant minorities. When they arrived, they were fleeing for their lives. They felt lucky to be alive and to be given the opportunity to get an education. Their aunt, in fact, constantly reminded them that education was their only opportunity to succeed. All three fully expected to return to El Salvador and were preparing themselves to be leaders in the rebuilding of their country. Both José Luis and Guillermo studied engineering with this in mind. Guillermo's interest in politics was also related to a hope that he would someday be involved in the politics of his own country. Patricia studied medicine because she knew that there would be a need for medical workers when they returned to El Salvador.

All three suffered a great deal economically upon arrival. Their living conditions, their clothes, even their often meager diet reflected a dramatic change from their former lifestyle in El Salvador. Yet they rarely complained. In school, they separated themselves from Hispanics who had been here for a long time and had different attitudes and interests. To this day, they never admit to having experienced any discrimination or prejudice, though there were several incidents, especially at the beginning, when they were treated rudely or ignored because of their ethnicity and lack of English. Treatment by others simply did not matter that much to them. They had pride in their heritage. They were part of an important family in El Salvador, and they had confidence that they could succeed if they worked hard. Their confidence and hard work paid off.

Teachers working with immigrant minorities often find them to be willing to

Immigrant Minorities	Involuntary Minorities
Chinese, Cubans, Japanese	African Americans, Hispanics, Native Americans, Southeast Asians
not highly influenced by majority group attitudes and values	highly influenced by majority group attitudes and values
measure success by homeland standards	measure success by mainstream culture standards
believe they can go back home and use skills and degrees	can't go back home or export skills and degrees
can alternate behavior	can't alternate behavior
characterized by primary cultural differences	characterized by secondary cultural differences
Primary Cultural Differences	*Secondary Cultural Differences*
differences existed before cultures came into contact	differences came into existence after cultures came into contact
differences are specific, easily identifiable matters of content such as language, food, customs, and dress	differences are more a matter of style than content—different ways of walking, talking, and dressing
minority group members recognize the differences and are willing to work to overcome them to succeed in school or at work	minority group members have created the differences to distinguish themselves from the mainstream and will not attempt to cross self-imposed cultural boundaries
minority group members don't suffer emotionally as they work to overcome differences—they're motivated to learn the things that will help them to succeed—they can alternate— they develop a folk theory for success that places a high value on education	minority group members who try to overcome differences may suffer both emotionally and physically—group members may exert negative peer pressure against crossing boundaries— it is not possible for members to alternate—they develop a folk theory for success that puts a low value on education

FIGURE 9–5   *Classification of Minority Groups*

work hard and to be very responsive to even small bits of encouragement. José Luis, Guillermo, and Patricia still speak fondly of their first ESL teacher and give that teacher and our family, as their mentors, the majority of the credit for their success. When one considers the actual help that was provided, it was slight in comparison with their effort. Yet their positive attitudes, along with that assistance, seemed to make an important difference to them and increased their chances for success.

Yvonne remembers the first Hmong teacher-education candidate she counseled. She was impressed with Xe from the first moment she walked into her office. Xe was enthusiastic and eager. She wanted not only to be a Hmong/English bilingual teacher, but also to learn Spanish, "because there are so many Spanish-speaking people here." Though Xe was the only one of twelve children in a struggling Hmong immigrant family to attend college, she never felt sorry for herself. She resisted the pressure of her family to marry at a young age. She was, in fact, one of only a handful of Hmong women in the community to pursue a college education.

Yvonne counseled Xe through her college years, helped her apply for several scholarships, arranged for her to teach and be paid for a Hmong culture course for teachers, and made herself available when Xe needed advice and encouragement. When Xe saw Hmong teenagers—including her own relatives—failing in school, she often talked to Yvonne of "helping the Hmong community appreciate our culture" by setting up a Hmong culture center. When Xe was elected to give the commencement speech at her college graduation, Yvonne helped her edit the speech. Xe, however, had done all the hard work herself. Despite the fact that she encountered negative responses on several fronts during her college career, she maintained a positive attitude and even now hopes to author children's books in Hmong and write her life story, beginning with her escape from Laos as a young girl. Xe is a prime example of a successful immigrant minority.

Primary Cultural Differences COME TO U.S.A.

Ogbu identifies two kinds of cultural differences: primary and secondary. Immigrant minorities are characterized by primary cultural differences. These differences, such as language, food, and attire, are specific and easily recognizable. They existed before the dominant and immigrant groups came into contact.

Primary differences do not usually constitute barriers to students' educational success, because immigrants are able to alternate their behavior between the home culture and the mainstream school culture. For example, they may speak one language at home, but they recognize the importance of speaking English at school. They may give low status to women in the home culture but still accept and respect female teachers at school. Alternation between two worlds is not threatening to immigrant minorities. They want to gain as much as possible from schools and the majority society generally, and they also want to retain their primary culture. They see no contradiction in pursuing both these goals simultaneously.

Xe is a clear example of a student with primary cultural differences. Her family speaks Hmong, eats traditional Hmong food, and takes part in Hmong religious and cultural ceremonies. Although she is unusual as a college-educated Hmong woman, just before college graduation she did marry a Hmong man who holds a technical job working with photographic equipment. The two are a modern "American" couple in many ways, but they have chosen to live with his family following the tradition of the culture. They are living in both worlds and working to succeed in both.

Another of our case study subjects from Chapter 1, Sharma, is also an example of an immigrant minority with primary cultural differences. Her parents were educated in India, yet they were willing to come to the United States and take menial jobs in order to get a good education for their children. At home Sharma and her parents not only speak Punjabi and eat Punjabi food, they also practice the customs and religion of the people in their homeland. In fact, their school life and home life are kept very separate. While Sharma can dress in Western clothes for school, she wears traditional clothing during the weekends and holidays. Sharma's family maintains their culture and language and is not really interested in becoming part of mainstream American culture.

The perception in immigrant minority communities is that success comes from education. Students who come to school with this attitude generally do well. Immigrant minorities are able to acculturate, to take the best from the new culture without having to give up their own cultural identity or practices.

Involuntary Minorities BORN IN U.S.A.

Ogbu contrasts immigrant minorities with involuntary minorities. Examples of involuntary minorities are African Americans, Native Americans, Hispanics, and others who were born in the United States or arrived too young to identify with their heritage culture. They are often at least second- or third-generation Americans who have little connection with their ancestral homeland and lack a deep understanding of traditional cultural practices. Although immigrants have, to some degree, chosen to come to a country, members of involuntary minority groups have not. Immigrants may see their status as temporary, but involuntary minorities have become incorporated into a society quite permanently. The history of the relationships between involuntary minorities and mainstream society is often one of exploitation.

Tou, the Hmong junior high school student described in Chapter 1, seems to be a prime example of an involuntary minority struggling for identity. Unlike Xe, who remembers her childhood in Laos and her escape, Tou left the refugee camp as an infant. Xe's family strongly holds to traditional values and customs, but Tou's family seems to be unstable and certainly not the traditional Hmong family. In the Hmong culture, children live with their family even after marriage. Hmong families maintain close ties, but one of Tou's sisters has moved to Georgia, another lives in Sacramento with Tou's mother, and his brother, who is a known gang member, does not live with the family at all.

Tou, then, does not have strong support from his primary culture, and he struggles with his identity. Is he Hmong or American? As his teacher, Kathy, pointed out, he seemed to do a bit better after Kathy held a parent-teacher conference with his father, and lots of nagging did get him through the seventh grade. However, Tou's problems outside of school, including the fights between classes with students from other cultural groups, and his eventual transfer to "opportunity" classes, are discouraging. It is probable that Tou sees little hope, and he may try to find "family" through gang membership.

The major difference between immigrant and involuntary minorities lies in the ways they respond to discriminatory treatment and the folk theories for getting ahead that they develop. Immigrants are not highly influenced by majority-group treatment because they can alternate their behavior between home and school or workplace. In contrast, involuntary minorities are highly influenced by majority-group treatment. They strongly resent discriminatory practices such as tracking, exclusion from some social activities, and job ceilings. They resent the fact that they do not have what they see others as having. As a result, involuntary minorities develop a social identity in opposition to the dominant group. For example, members of involuntary minorities may adopt certain ways of talking or dressing to identify themselves with their cultural group in opposition to the majority culture. Many aspects of gang membership fall within this category. Members of involuntary minorities might also drive certain kinds of cars that they have decorated or changed to give their group a specific identity.

Secondary Cultural Differences

These differences between mainstream cultural groups and involuntary minorities are what Ogbu calls secondary cultural differences. They form after the two groups come into contact. In fact, according to Ogbu (1991), secondary cultural differences develop in opposition to the majority culture. As a result, members of involuntary minorities cannot alternate behaviors and be a "homeboy" at home but a "schoolboy" at school. They do not picture themselves exporting their skills and knowledge to some homeland, because *this* is their home. In addition, there may be considerable peer pressure for involuntary minorities to conform to group norms. "The secondary cultural system, on the whole, constitutes a new cultural frame of reference" (15).

Attempts by school personnel to correct or change aspects of this cultural identity may be perceived as attacks on the minority group by the dominant group rather than as efforts to help group members succeed. They "distrust members of the dominant group and the societal institutions controlled by the latter" (16). As a result, involuntary minorities develop a folk theory for success that places little value on education. Tou seems to fit into this category. He does not believe that his father and the school want the best for him. At this point, school just does not seem important to him.

It is important that teachers look carefully at their students to see if some of their characteristics are those of involuntary minorities. The idea is not to label them, but to understand the challenges these students face and then apply explorer principles of teaching to overcome some of the challenges. Susanne, the teacher we described in Chapter 6, responds to her first introduction to the ideas Ogbu presents:

> The distinctions Ogbu makes between different types of minorities begins to bring clarity to a huge gap in my understanding of minority populations in general. . . . Nearly all of my students are involuntary Hispanic minorities. Ogbu's theory gives me understanding as I look at my students and their parents. I see that many parents and their children can be described as belonging to *different* minority groups. My students share a surprising kinship with other involuntary minority groups: African Americans and Native Americans. . . . They came to this country "involuntarily," either before birth or shortly after, and were therefore too young to identify with their heritage culture. Unless these kids have parents who are themselves involuntary minorities, my students have vastly different worldviews than do their parents, a schism likely to grow and fester over time.

Both immigrant and involuntary minorities often face unequal treatment by the dominant social group. However, the two minority groups respond differently to this treatment, and they develop different folk theories for getting ahead. Immigrant minorities, like the El Salvadorans, Xe, and Sharma, are generally able to alternate their behavior between home and school. As a result, they can maintain primary cultural differences while still getting ahead or believing that they can get ahead in mainstream society. They value school because they are convinced that education provides the skills and knowledge that increase their possibilities for financial success, and they can use their accomplishments to improve their conditions.

Involuntary minorities are not able to alternate behavior because their secondary cultural differences such as manner of dress, their defiance of authority, or their way of talking were formed in opposition to the mainstream culture, and to give those up would be to abandon their identity. Folk theories of success place limited value on schools or other social institutions controlled by the dominant culture. Of course, some members of involuntary minorities do succeed in mainstream terms, but they often move out of their original neighborhoods to areas where they can fit in with the dominant group. Thus, those members of the community that might challenge the theory that schools do not lead to success are not there to argue the case.

Conclusion

In this chapter we have looked at ways in which three elements of the societal context—community attitudes, teacher attitudes, and student attitudes—affect the school context. Teachers should be aware of how factors from outside school impact their students. Explorer teachers work for change both in and out of school to afford their students the greatest chance for success.

Susanne, the teacher quoted above, is working to meet the needs of her fourth-grade students. She is convinced that her teaching can make a difference for them. We end this chapter with her passionate and hopeful plan for students to change their attitudes and their futures:

> While we, as teachers, cannot possibly engage in or affect all of the dynamic events shaping our students' lives, we can apply our knowledge of sound educational practice to begin to ameliorate some of the negatives pressed down on our children by the dominant culture. We can utilize our knowledge of social and economic pressures, as they define our students and their parents, to create inclusive and respectful learning environments. We have learned much about programs that succeed in empowering students to retain, maintain, or learn about the culture that connects and binds children to their parents, grandparents, and ancestors, that supplies a foundation for self-awareness and confidence. We are working with children "between worlds" whose life experiences could fill volumes. As we tap into these lives through relevant and meaningful curriculum, as we promote exchange and interaction among students and members of the school community, we can help bridge the gap that exists for many children who feel in some way homeless, a homelessness of the heart.

Applications

1. Three context-free interpretations for the school performance of second language students are genetic inferiority, cultural deficit, and cultural mismatch. In a small group, share any experiences you have had where minority students' failure has been interpreted in one of these ways. What would you now say to the person who took this perspective?

2. Look back at the case studies in Chapter 1, or look at the case study of a second language learner that you have carried out. What context-free interpretations could be given for the success or failure of the student on which you are focusing? How could a contextual-interaction perspective better account for the student's performance?

3. Read the letters to the editor in your local newspapers as well as the local and national editorials over several weeks. Clip any that have to do with the changing population. What is the general attitude expressed? What are the problems that are brought up? Share the articles with the class or a small group for discussion. What are the group conclusions?

4. In a group, make up a short series of interview questions about the immigrants in your community and/or beliefs about bilingual education. Interview seven to ten people, including people not in the field of education. Graph the group results. Discuss the findings.

5. How have schools in your community changed in the past ten years? How has the curriculum changed to meet new students' needs? Make a chart that reflects the relationship between the two.

6. Form groups of about four or five people each. Each group takes one of the five teacher-attitude scenarios described in this chapter. Each group can plan together a role-playing exchange of one to two minutes to show how they would interpret the scenario. (If there are ten groups, this is even more interesting, because there can be a comparison of how different groups choose to role-play the same scene.) After role-playing, discuss as a large group what impressed you. Finally, replay the scenarios, applying a solution your group feels might work to resolve the conflict.

7. Read Rusty's poem, "School Days, School Days" (Figure 9–4) and Susanne's final quote with a partner. Discuss.

8. Reflect back on one of our Chapter 1 case study students or the experience of some other language learner you know and think about whether that person would fall under Ogbu's immigrant or involuntary minority categories. Discuss with a partner.

9. Think about a case study student or another second language learner you know and list the primary cultural differences you see in that person's life. Are there secondary cultural differences? What are they?

10

How Can Teachers Help Schools Develop an Intercultural Orientation?

We have advocated an explorer orientation to language, teaching, learning, and curriculum. Teachers who adopt an explorer orientation celebrate learning and diversity, focus on the learner, make curriculum meaningful, organize for collaboration, encourage learning through different modes, respect learners, and celebrate students' first languages and cultures.

If school success for language minority students depended entirely on the efforts of individual teachers, it would be enough for teachers to focus on developing an explorer orientation. However, teachers do not work in isolation. Instead, they function within the wider societal context, as discussed in Chapter 9, and within a school system, an institution that represents the values and interests of the mainstream society. An individual teacher's orientation toward students and teaching may be shaped by the general school orientation. At the same time, the efforts of individual teachers may contribute to changes in the schoolwide orientation. In this chapter, we consider two orientations schools may develop toward language minority students. We also look at the different values conflicts that teachers and school systems must resolve as they attempt to work effectively with all their students.

School Orientations: Intercultural or Assimilationist?

Cummins (1996) defines two orientations that schools can develop: intercultural or assimilationist. These two orientations differ in four areas: <u>use of students primary</u>

languages and cultures in the curriculum, relationships with minority community members, approach to teaching, and methods of assessment. Figure 10–1 outlines the key points of difference.

As Figure 10–1 shows, when schools take an intercultural orientation, they encourage the use of students' primary languages and cultures, they attempt to involve minority parents in school activities, they encourage the use of current methods of collaborative critical inquiry, and they design assessment that allows students to demonstrate their competence. In contrast, when schools take an assimilationist orientation, they often ban the use of students' primary languages and pay little attention to the defining aspects of students' cultures, they exclude minority community members from active involvement in the schools, they teach using traditional methods and use forms of assessment such as tests and quizzes that help teachers justify the grades they give students.

Generally, schools that take an intercultural orientation see student diversity as an asset. Such schools find ways to incorporate diverse students into the institution and to provide programs that promote their success. Teachers who adopt explorer principles find those principles consistent with an intercultural orientation. On the other hand, schools that take an assimilationist orientation have as their goal the assimilation of diverse students into the mainstream. In the attempt to assimilate students, such schools often provide programs that disempower and marginalize second language students and the minority communities they come from. Explorer teachers find it difficult to work effectively in such schools because their individual efforts are often undermined by the general approach the school has adopted.

Rusty: Taking an Intercultural Orientation

Individual teachers can take an intercultural orientation, but changing the school itself is difficult. An example comes from Rusty, the sixth-grade teacher who authored the poem presented in Chapter 9. Rusty's class has many Hispanic as well as Anglo

	Intercultural Orientation	Assimilationist Orientation
Students' languages and cultures	add them to the curriculum	exclude them from the curriculum
Minority community members	involve them in the school	exclude them from the school
Teaching	use transformative methods	use traditional methods
Assessment	help students show what they know	use measures to justify grades

FIGURE 10–1 *Two Orientations*

students. In the farming community where the students live, the attitudes that Anglos hold about Hispanics, especially migrant Mexicans, is very negative. The little social interaction that takes place between Anglos and Mexicans is usually hostile.

Rusty has completed an MA in education, with a specialization in reading and a bilingual cross-cultural specialist credential. Through this coursework, his creativity, and his dedication to teaching, he has been able to develop a collaborative classroom where all his students work together to explore topics of interest. However, he is continually frustrated that his efforts have not resulted in change at the school level:

> It is really difficult to challenge the status quo at the individual school site, let alone the district's policies. Most principals are (or certainly seem to me) even more ignorant of the principles/concepts that are involved in bilingual education than teachers. And our resource teacher hasn't taken *any* classes (in reading or bilingual education) since I have been here and that covers fifteen years. The principal has been here for over twenty years. How do you bridge this gap without being very threatening or being seen as a "rebel"? My approach has been an effort to model what I believe are good practices in my own classroom. The problem is that my principal thinks that these things work "because Rusty is doing them," and does not wish to extend the principles/concepts to other staff.

Rusty has taken definite steps to try to change the attitudes of the students in his classroom. He uses a resource and activity book, *Portraits of Mexican-Americans: Pathfinders in the Mexican-American Communities* (Pérez 1991), which contains information about the significant Mexican American contributors in several areas, including the history of the Southwest, farmworkers, the arts, writers, educators, politicians, and sports figures. The book is designed for cooperative learning activities and includes several in both Spanish and English. Rusty has found these materials to be especially powerful because Hispanic students feel pride in their culture as they read about the history of the Mexican people in the United States. Several exercises involve students in linguistic investigations about the origins of Spanish words. In these activities, Rusty's Spanish-speaking students serve as experts.

When Anglo students in Rusty's class read about the rights promised Mexican Americans living in the United States by the Treaty of Guadalupe Hidalgo, the treaty written when the war between Mexico and the United States ended in 1848, they also feel the indignation of their Hispanic classmates over the broken promises. Students study the changing geography of the Southwest between 1810 and 1848, and they begin to understand the strong roots that Spanish-speaking peoples claim in this country. Studying about political activists like Cesar Chávez and Gloria Molina, as well as Latino writers and artists, gives Hispanic students a pride in their culture and people. In discussion about identity and labeling, students read about Chicanos and what that name implies as opposed to "Mexican American."

Rusty works hard to try to meet the needs of all his students, including his language minority students, but sometimes he admits to how overwhelming his students' needs are:

There is so much to learn/absorb/implement that sometimes I get a headache just thinking about it. I look at what I am doing in my classroom and at the needs of Placido and Nora and Rosalinda and I just become overwhelmed. Sometimes I also get very frustrated at the slow pace at which I seem to be making the changes that I need to make. I'm not berating myself, because I know that what I am doing really does make a difference in the lives of my students.

Even though Rusty is frustrated at the slow rate of change, he is making a difference for his students. However, students will only be in Rusty's class for one year, and he recognizes the importance of change at the school level. Rusty's students will face serious obstacles to academic success as they move into middle school and high school. At these levels, there may be less support for their primary languages and cultures, less attention given to collaboration with minority communities, and a tendency toward traditional methods of teaching and assessment that often results in low grades for English language learners. In other words, Rusty's students are likely to experience schooling from an assimilationist orientation in the higher grades.

Lucas (1997) has developed four principles for facilitating immigrant students' transitions into, through, and beyond secondary school. These principles are consistent with an intercultural orientation. Rusty's students would benefit from schooling that followed these principles. They include:

1. *Cultivating organizational relationships.* For schools to work effectively with immigrant students, they need to develop relationships with various organizations that can provide services to students. These include health and social service agencies, community-based organizations, businesses, and institutions of higher education.

2. *Providing access to information.* Students need to know about U.S. schools and culture, the resources and support services that are available to them, workplaces and career preparation, and opportunities for higher education.

3. *Cultivating human relationships.* Schools should foster positive relationships between immigrant students and adults, between students themselves, among the school staff, and between educators and the families of language minority students.

4. *Providing multiple and flexible pathways.* Schools should provide pathways into U.S. schooling and culture, into the mainstream, and beyond secondary school. These pathways should extend beyond the traditional avenues, because English learners often need more time and support to succeed.

In schools like Rusty's, there seems to be a resistance to adopting an intercultural orientation. Rusty's positive view of his students, their languages and cultures, and their parents, leads him to adopt methods of teaching that are consistent with explorer principles and forms of assessment that allow his students to demonstrate their knowledge and skills. However, even though he is considered an exemplary teacher, administrators and colleagues at his school do not share some of the basic beliefs about English language learners that Rusty holds.

For schools to adopt an intercultural orientation, it is important for administrators, teachers, and support personnel to examine the values they operate on. These values help determine how schools approach the education of English language learners. In the following sections, we examine five values conflicts that arise in schools with diverse populations. We also suggest solutions to these conflicts. Following that discussion, we describe in more detail the components of an intercultural orientation.

Recognizing and Resolving Values Conflicts

"All Asians are excellent students. Why aren't other minority groups as successful?"

"Juan started out the year way behind the other students. He's made great improvement, but I can't pass him because he only scored 55 percent on his final exam."

"At my school almost 80 percent of the students are Hispanics, but we have only two Hispanic teachers. We should hire more Hispanic teachers, but some of the applicants are not as well qualified as the Anglo candidates."

Comments such as these raise important questions. Are all Asians the same? Do all Asians do better in school than Hispanics? What do we do with a student who starts out way behind and makes great progress but still doesn't pass the final exam? Should we hire people because of their ethnicity? Often, the answers to these questions are based on underlying values.

We began this book by describing how John was "amazed" that so many of his students spoke Spanish and came from homes where Spanish was spoken daily. Like John, many teachers come from a different social context than their students, and they bring to their teaching certain attitudes toward students and toward school. These attitudes were shaped by the values they developed in their home communities, values that were not shaped by contact with diverse groups. By examining the values they hold, teachers can more consistently adopt practices that promote success for their students who are between worlds.

Sue and Padilla (1986) believe that for educators "many of the values relevant to ethnic minority issues are in conflict" (53). They examine five values conflicts that arise in schools with diverse populations. Some of these conflicts are also referred to as paradoxes, suggesting that some truth is contained in both views. For that reason, it is difficult to agree on which of the two positions is correct, and of course, this leads to difficulty in finding the solution. For our discussion, we have organized these five conflicts into two general categories: (1) differences and similarities and (2) minority and majority conflicts. For each conflict, we discuss the opposing views, the effects each view has, and some possible solutions. Figure 10–2 summarizes the values conflicts, lists the effects of adopting each point of view, and suggests solutions.

Conflicting elements	Effects	Possible solutions
Etic—Human beings are alike	Ignores cultural diversity	Coexistence Alternation
Emic—Human beings differ according to culture	Can't generalize or compare cultures	
Modal personality—study between group differences	Ignores within group variations	Alternation Divergent thinking Mediation
Individual differences—study within group differences	Ignores between group variations	
Equal opportunity—apply same color-blind criteria to all	Unequal outcomes	Mediation Alternation Higher level of abstraction
Equality of outcomes—see that minorities are proportionately represented	Differential treatment (discrimination)	
Presence of prejudice/discrimination—minorities are oppressed in society	Blame society; must eliminate discrimination	Coexistence Divergent thinking
Absence of prejudice/discrimination—opportunities are equal for all	Blame minorities; up to minorities to achieve	
Assimilation—become American and merge into society	Loss of ethnic cultures	Coexistence Divergent thinking
Pluralism—allow for and appreciate cultural diversity	Coexistence of separate and distinct groups	

FIGURE 10–2 *Values Conflicts*

Differences Versus Similarities: Etic or Emic?

The first conflict is truly a paradox. It involves two ways of looking at groups of people. One view values similarities, while the other values differences. These two views are referred to as etic (valuing universal similarities) and emic (valuing individual differences). The terms *etic* and *emic* are used in linguistics and anthropology. In linguistics, phon*etics* is the study of sounds in languages generally. All languages share certain sounds. In contrast, phon*emics* is the study of the meaningful sounds within a particular language. The phonemes of one language differ from those of another.

An etic view of people is based on the idea that humans are basically all alike. Certainly, up to a point, this is true. Humans have certain characteristics that distinguish them from other life-forms. An emic view, on the other hand, holds that humans differ according to culture. Hispanics are different from Chinese, for example. The etic/emic values conflict does represent a paradox, since both views can be justified.

Whether one values the etic or the emic view has educational implications. At a certain level, all students share some characteristics. However, students from different cultures have different views of school and act and use language differently. Teachers who value an etic view would focus on the similarities and ignore cultural differences. Such teachers might feel that any test is equally fair for all students and that norms of classroom behavior can be applied equally to all students. Teachers who value an emic view would maintain that students really are different, and would use different teaching techniques and apply different standards in assessing various groups of students. For example, they might resist giving English learners standardized tests because these students haven't acquired enough English to demonstrate their knowledge on this kind of test.

However, this emic view brings up a conflict. If students are never compared to others using standardized measures, schools will not know how well they are teaching and the English learners may develop a false sense of their abilities. They might be at the top of the class (or track) in their school, but good performance in one context might rank as only mediocre in another. In fact, we have seen second language learners graduate from high school without being able to read and write enough English to compete in junior college.

It is clear that this is not an easy conflict to resolve. Fermin, for example, writes about the dilemma he faces in his high school English department.

> There are some teachers who want standards, and then there are those like me who feel somewhat guilty using them because I know many of the second language learners are not ready for them. But as one of my colleagues says, if you do not use them, you will end up hurting the students in the long run. All you will be doing is giving them a false sense of their abilities, so when they go to college, they will be surprised when they find out how low their abilities are compared to the rest.

Fermin concludes by saying he tries to use his own best judgment in applying standards. There is no easy solution.

etic — focus on ways humans are alike.
emic — focus on the difference between cultural groups.

BETWEEN WORLDS

Summary and Possible Solutions

Those who value an etic view focus on ways humans are alike. Those who value an emic view focus on differences between cultural groups. The effect of valuing an etic view is to ignore cultural differences. The effect of valuing an emic view is the inability to compare groups and make generalizations. Two possible solutions to this values conflict are coexistence and alternation.

The coexistence solution would involve applying both etic and emic considerations in dealing with people. For teachers, that would mean preparing their English learners to be competitive on standardized tests and not simplifying their curriculum. At the same time they are doing this, they must use special techniques to make the curriculum comprehensible, and they must be sensitive to cultural difference and use strategies that help all their students become confident English users.

An alternation solution would be similar, but would be applied differently. In some cases, teachers of English learners would give students from various ethnic groups different kinds of assignments and would assess them differently. At other times, the teachers would expect all students to complete the same assignments and would assess them with the same measures. This is the solution Fermin chose. He alternates between holding all his students to the same standards and giving his English language learners assignments suited to their language proficiency.

Fermin's solution is consistent with the advice Sue and Padilla (1986) offer. They caution that "in the conflict between emic and etic positions, one must specify the exact standard, criteria, or issue being discussed" (56). That would lead to a context-specific solution. For example, if we say that all students must learn to speak and write standard English, we may wish to consider the contexts where standard English is appropriate and the situations where students could be encouraged to use other varieties of English or other languages. Journal writing, for example, is a place where English learners can be risk takers, try out English, and where teachers respond to the message. However, formal papers or articles to be published in a school newspaper would need to be in standard English.

Modal Personality or Individual Differences?

A related conflict involves looking at differences between groups or at differences within a group. When someone refers to Asians or Hispanics, that person is assuming that all members of the group are sufficiently similar to be grouped together. If we assume that members of a group share a significant number of characteristics, we can define a modal personality. For example, we might characterize Hispanics by saying that they value family, show respect for teachers and elders, love soccer, and speak Spanish. Defining a modal personality allows us to treat all members of a group the same. We can then study differences between groups. However, if we assume that considerable variability exists within any group, we would look more at individual differences. Certainly we know Hispanics who do not love soccer or, for that matter, speak Spanish!

The conflict between valuing the modal personality position or the individual differences position is complex. This conflict presents a true paradox because both points of view are valid. As teachers, it is possible, and sometimes even important, to attribute certain characteristics to groups in order to better plan for them and to meet their needs. For example, Sandra, the teacher we described in Chapter 6, developed the "From the Field to the Table" unit for her Mexican migrant students. She planned many hands-on activities and focused on familiar plants, such as corn, within the unit. This certainly showed that Sandra understood some things about her students, their background, and their culture. This required that she give more value to the modal personality position.

Stereotyping is a danger, but ignoring the language, values, and traditions of a particular culture may be equally harmful. For example, while she planned her unit around plants and corn, she was mindful of her indigenous Mixteco students as well as her Spanish-speaking Mexican students. She was careful not to assume that the customs of planting, harvesting, and preparing foods in both cultures would be exactly the same. In fact, it was her Mixteco students who were the leaders in the "From the Field to the Table" tortilla demonstration. In this respect, she gave more value to individual differences.

It is helpful for teachers to reflect on their practice to determine which point of view they take most often. In certain contexts it may be more useful to focus on group similarities; in others, to consider individual differences. Sue and Padilla relate a story that illustrates the problems inherent in assuming a modal personality for a particular ethnic group. A teacher who had attended a workshop that stressed incorporation of students' ethnicity into the curriculum asked a Japanese American fourth grader to demonstrate how she danced at home. When the child performed a typical American dance, the teacher was upset. She had expected that this student would perform a Japanese folk dance. She assumed that all Japanese-background students would know about typical Japanese dances.

Katie, the prefirst teacher we mentioned earlier, provided a similar example. One of her students, Chu, speaks only Hmong at home, although he speaks English at school. For a cooking activity, Katie's students made sticky rice and then ate it using chopsticks. When students who had never used chopsticks went to Chu for help, he got very upset and refused to talk to them. Later, Katie asked her students to write about this experience. In his response (Figure 10–3), Chu shows that despite his background, he doesn't fit the modal personality of an Asian, since he doesn't "no to uz chps."

As teachers are aware, many members of ethnic minority groups in the United States may not be familiar with the kinds of traditions (dances, clothes, foods) described in cultural handbooks or presented at cultural workshops. Many second- and third-generation Mexicans, for example, have no idea what Las Posadas, the Christmas celebration replicating Joseph and Mary's trip to Bethlehem, is. As Sue and Padilla point out, "The challenge for educators is to identify critical differences between and within ethnic minority groups and to incorporate this information into

FIGURE 10–3   *Chu's Chopsticks*

classroom practice" (62). Schools that adopt an intercultural orientation make a point of including students' languages and cultures in the curriculum.

Summary and Possible Solutions

A modal personality is an average or representative individual who carries the traits of a whole group. The effect of valuing the modal personality is that one must ignore variations within a group, while the effect of looking at individual differences is that one must ignore differences between groups. Three possible solutions for this values conflict are alternation, divergent thinking, and mediation. Alternation would involve shifting the focus from the whole group to individuals and back again. Sandra planned for all her Mexican migrant students. However, she took into account her Mixteco students and their talents when she called on them to be experts. Nevertheless, the entire unit assumed that the migrant students would have certain general characteristics.

At times, using divergent thinking can help solve values conflicts. Most schooling leads to convergent thinking; that is, getting students to think in the same way to come to the same conclusions. Divergent thinking requires people to think outside the box and come up with novel solutions. An example of divergent thinking is the Learning Edge program for Project VOICE students that we described in Chapter 7.

The students from Project VOICE are Hispanic and Hmong paraprofessionals returning to school to become teachers. Bobbi Jentes Mason, the director of the Learning Edge workshop, decided to do something different for these language minority students. In order to meet their needs, she had to understand that they were English language learners, unaccustomed to the university coursework demands, and that their cultural backgrounds differed from those of traditional university students.

Despite the similarities they shared, the Project VOICE students also differed in significant ways. Some students were excellent readers and poor writers. Some had families and others did not. Some were very connected to their cultural background and others were not. Some were Hispanics and others were Asians.

To plan an effective program, Bobbi had to assume that the students shared certain similarities in spite of their obvious differences. She gathered a small group of dedicated and innovative teachers who had been studying recent research and theory for language learning. One was an experienced, creative Hispanic male who had begun his career as a paraprofessional and who was talented in music and Mexican dance. The teachers worked with Bobbi to plan an intensive two-week session. During the two weeks, students read, wrote, and discussed topics of interest to them as future teachers. They did literature studies using books which connected to their cultures and experiences. They wrote back and forth in learning logs with the teachers, and published their stories in an anthology that they all received at the end of the course. All the activities, including lunch together and planned outdoor games, led to the building of a strong community.

Bobbi certainly used divergent thinking to devise a curriculum for students who needed extra support if they were to succeed as teachers. Instead of drills or exercises on standard English, she and the other teachers gave the students real reading and writing and caring responses. She understood the students as a group (modal personality) and as individuals. The results have been positive. The Learning Edge experience has given the Project VOICE students the extra boost they needed.

Sandra's fourth-, fifth-, and sixth-grade newcomers class offers an example of a third possible solution for this values conflict: mediation. When both sides of a values conflict are valid, it is often difficult to find a middle ground. However, mediation may be a possible solution. Sandra teaches in a farming community with a high Hispanic population. Many of the students attending the school where she teaches, like Sandra's students, speak Spanish at home. They have the same language and cultural background as her students. One could, in some ways, say that Sandra's students fit the modal personality of the other Hispanics in the school.

However, there are also some important individual differences between Sandra's students and other Hispanic students at her school. Sandra's students are all newcomers to this country. In addition, although they are older students, they have had little to no previous schooling. Even the little schooling they have had has often been interrupted. These differences make it difficult for her students to compete in regular classrooms.

Several years ago, the school district where Sandra teaches had a problem when the numbers of these students became quite large. There were those who wanted to develop individual educational plans for these students within a special education setting. Others thought that these students shared many characteristics with other English learners and should be put into regular ESL classes. Neither of these solutions was really appropriate; so after some discussion, the district created the newcomer class for these students. In doing so, the district found a middle ground between the two alternatives. The solution was to create a special class that was unlike either of the alternatives. In this case, mediation solved the values conflict.

Minority and Majority Conflicts

A second set of values conflicts centers on the relationships and interactions between minority and majority group members. If a school values homogeneity, it may adopt an assimilationist orientation. If, on the other hand, heterogeneity is seen as desirable, the school may promote diversity and take an intercultural orientation. The three minority/majority values conflicts are (1) equal opportunities or equal outcomes, (2) real or imagined discrimination, and (3) assimilation or pluralism.

Equal Opportunities or Equal Outcomes?

The conflict between equal opportunity and equality of outcomes is one of the most difficult and emotional of the values conflicts and paradoxes. If we believe solely in equal opportunity, we apply the same criteria for all. In hiring practices, for example, employers would consider job-related skills and degrees only and not look at factors such as an applicant's ethnicity or gender. In college admissions, students' grades and activities would be considered, but not their race, socioeconomic status, gender, or ethnicity.

In contrast, those favoring equality of outcomes would consider ethnicity in hiring because their goal would be to ensure that underrepresented groups be represented proportionately. A school with large numbers of Hispanic students, for example, might feel that the ethnicity of a candidate for a teaching position is more important than other factors and hire a Latina to increase Hispanic representation on the staff. The goal would be to achieve an equality of outcomes. In this case, the outcome would be more of a balance in ethnicity between the percentage of Latino teachers and the percentage of Hispanic students that the school serves. This type of hiring often upsets people, and there are often accusations of reverse discrimination when whites are not considered for certain positions.

Teachers are frequently faced with decisions that involve this values conflict, and they have to choose between two valid alternatives. This becomes quite complex. Consider the following dilemma. Some students come to school with more knowledge and better skills because of their background experiences and socioeconomic status than others. Should the teacher treat all students equally by giving them the same assignments and the same tests even though it is clear that the students are not equal? Should the teacher provide experiences for the students who come not so well prepared to help them compete in the future, and thus give special treatment to certain students?

Teachers who decide that all students should be treated the same may simply be serving to maintain the status quo. Students who enter school with more of the attributes schools value succeed while those who enter lacking those attributes fail. In this case, an equal opportunities approach results in unequal outcomes. On the other hand, teachers may fear that if they try to ensure that all students succeed, the better students will be ignored. This could constitute a kind of discrimination against certain students.

This values conflict raises important questions. If students grow up in poor neighborhoods and attend inadequate schools, do they have equal opportunities when they apply for colleges or jobs? Do these same students have equal opportunity when they take standardized tests meant to give schools a valid measure of how schools are doing? Books such as Kozol's *Savage Inequalities* (1991) suggest that opportunities for students from different backgrounds are not equal. Kohn's book, *The Case Against Standardized Testing: Raising the Scores, Ruining the Schools* (2000), shows that standardized tests are most damaging for low-income and minority students.

A question to ask ourselves is, "At what point do equal chances begin?" Proponents of equality of outcomes argue that current practices in areas such as hiring must discriminate in favor of minorities now to compensate for discrimination against minorities in the past. Of course, this raises a means-justifying-the-ends question. Are short-term discriminatory practices necessary to correct the results of long-term discrimination? Again, solutions to this conflict are not easy. Effective solutions must be specific to the situation. However, we agree with Sue and Padilla that "only after opportunities become truly equal can a color- or ethnic-blind system have any meaning" (60).

The conflict between equal opportunities and equality of outcomes often arises in discussions about bilingual education. Although there are some excellent bilingual programs in which the second language is other than Spanish, the vast majority of the bilingual programs that are fully implemented are for Spanish speakers. We often have teachers ask us questions such as the following about equality: "Is it fair to give first language support to the Spanish-speaking students when we cannot provide it for Khmer, Vietnamese, Hmong, Punjabi, or Russian speakers?"

This is an interesting application of the "equal opportunity" value. Our response is with another question: "If you know that many children in the world are hungry, but you only have food for some, do you withhold the food you can supply because it is not fair to the others that only some children be fed?" In the same way, if we can provide first language support to some children, do we withhold it because we cannot give it to all the children? Added to that is the argument that about 80 percent of the English learners are native Spanish speakers.

Summary and Possible Solutions

Those who value equal opportunity attempt to judge all people the same way without regard for race, gender, socioeconomic status, or ethnicity. Those who favor equal outcomes take those factors into account in order to produce certain results. Historically, the effect of giving equal opportunities has been unequal outcomes. Certain groups maintain positions of wealth and power. On the other hand, the effect of valuing equal outcomes is that some groups will be given preferential treatment.

Three possible solutions to this conflict are mediation, alternation, and moving to a higher level of abstraction. Mediation would involve finding a compromise between the two positions. This might involve hiring a Hispanic teacher if two candidates are evenly matched in other respects. Mediation comes into play because those who value equal opportunities would insist on ignoring ethnicity, while those who value equality of outcomes would insist on hiring a Hispanic. The compromise would be to specify certain conditions any candidate must meet and then agreeing that if several candidates meet these conditions, the Hispanic would be hired first. Alternation, on the other hand, would mean considering ethnicity for one hire and not for the next.

A third solution for this values conflict is moving to a higher level of abstraction. This involves looking at the big picture and considering eventual outcomes. In the case of college admissions, for example, we might consider the effects of a policy of equal opportunities as opposed to a policy of equal outcomes when applied over several years. If minorities were given preferential admissions treatment, for example, that might result in more minority graduates, which, in turn, could change minority communities. By starting to consider the long-term social effects of a policy, we are moving to a higher level of abstraction, and this could guide our decision making.

Discrimination—Real or Imagined?

A second conflict that involves majority and minority group members is equally emotional and difficult to discuss. This is the conflict between the presence or absence of discrimination. Some people believe that prejudice exists and that minorities are oppressed. Others feel that prejudice is no longer a factor, and that all people have equal opportunities.

It is helpful to consider this conflict from the point of view of minorities as well as from the point of view of members of the majority culture. For many minority group members, prejudice is a painful reality. This is shown in Paulina's story. She wrote of her experiences as a child in a small rural community in California:

> As a migrant child in P——, I was well aware of the town's prejudice. The movie theater had segregated seating along color lines. That was no cause for alarm, we accepted it. When I had my own experience, it was traumatic.
>
> In our third-grade class, we had seating arrangements in the traditional rows, and the five to six Hispanic students in that class sat in one row apart from the class. I didn't mind, I felt secure with my fellow brown-skinned peers. Our teacher was the traditional strict disciplinarian common in those days, and one day an active Anglo boy named Timmy was too much for her. In her desperate attempt to control him, she punished him by asking him to get a chair and to sit next to me. The class giggled as he obeyed her. When he sat next to me, I immediately got a stomach ache, and when he started sobbing, I felt that I must have been the worst person in the world. Why else was he sobbing so painfully?
>
> I can't recall much, but I do remember suffering stomach aches every time I walked into class. When I went home, I recall I took a bath and tried to wash my brown color off. I scraped so hard that when my mother asked what happened, I told her I scraped myself on the playground. I didn't have the courage or heart to

tell her the truth. I wanted to spare her the pain I had felt. One of the many reasons I decided to teach was to put an end to the ignorance about different ethnic groups.

Pauline's story is a powerful one. We would hope that no school would now tolerate such practices.

However, there are those who would say that prejudice does still exist. We talked recently with Francisco, one of the case study students in Chapter 1. He commented that he is almost always asked for identification when he uses his credit card, even when younger and poorly dressed Anglo customers in the same store are not questioned. A colleague of ours who has a Ph.D. and is a college professor described how she is almost always followed in discount stores by the store detective. She is Hispanic and often wears her hair in a long braid. She believes her appearance is why she must suffer such scrutiny.

For minorities, the question to be asked about discrimination is not simply whether migrant workers in Arizona or Cambodians in Los Angeles face discrimination, but whether *they* think they face discrimination. What matters here is the perceptions of the groups involved.

Ogbu points out that immigrant and involuntary minorities respond differently to prejudicial treatment. Immigrants expect to face discrimination and find ways to circumvent unequal treatment. In some cases, they may not even notice it. The three teens from El Salvador, for example, refused to see what we perceived as discrimination against them in their high school. Involuntary minorities, in contrast, are very aware of prejudice and may even assume that someone is discriminating against them in situations where no discrimination exists.

A student's belief about the presence or absence of prejudice helps shape his or her attitude toward school, and this can have a strong impact on their school performance. It is the student's perception that counts, not the presence or absence of specific discriminatory acts.

This conflict also may be considered from the point of view of members of the majority culture, including many teachers. If teachers believe that prejudice exists and that minorities are oppressed by society, the teacher may work to eliminate prejudice. This may include involving students in investigations of social issues.

On the other hand, if majority group members believe that prejudice no longer exists and that all members of society have equal opportunities, they may blame minorities for their failure to achieve. After all, in a just and equal society, everyone has an equal chance.

Summary and Possible Solutions
Those who consider that prejudice and discrimination are social realities believe that minorities are oppressed. As a result, they attempt to change society and eliminate discrimination. Those who decide that discrimination no longer exists believe that all individuals have equal opportunities. If minority groups are not succeeding, then it is their fault.

Two possible solutions for this conflict are coexistence and divergent thinking. One could decide that prejudice still exists and find ways to combat it. In institutions, such as schools and businesses, glass ceilings do exist. Most superintendents of large districts and most CEOs of big companies are white males, although this is changing. In the 2000 presidential election, neither major political party backed a woman or ethnic minority presidential candidate. These practices could be challenged. At the same time, success of minority groups depends on their willingness to work and take advantage of any opportunities they are afforded. Coexistence would involve holding a belief that prejudice exists and trying to combat it, while at the same time acting as though opportunities were equal and striving to succeed.

An example of a solution to this conflict in the educational arena is a two-way bilingual program. Many native English-speaking parents have opposed bilingual education, saying that bilingual students get special treatment and that their own children are not given any special programs. They point to this as a kind of discrimination. On the other hand, bilingual educators say that all English programs discriminate against English learners because such programs do not give students access to content in their native languages while they are learning English. Two-way bilingual programs are a solution because all students acquire a second language, and both groups of students also excel academically. The children in both groups coexist as they learn together in two languages. Such programs answer the concerns of both mainstream parents and bilingual educators.

Another possible solution for conflicts of presence or absence of discrimination is divergent thinking that produces new programs. Dolson and Mayer (1992), in their discussion of effective programs for language-minority students, include a component that addresses prejudice. "Minority students, regardless of the efforts of the school to promote equal educational opportunities, will be faced with manifestations of discrimination and prejudice at school as well as within the larger community" (143). These authors suggest that schools include a "survival" training component that would help all students deal with instances of discrimination and prejudice. "The training should consist of information on the presence of racism in the general society, how it effects minority and majority peoples, and schemes minority individuals can tap to counteract the negative influences it may have on their spirit and self-concept" (142). Dolson and Mayer advocate involving students in studying attitudes toward minorities, their language, and culture as a part of the school curriculum.

Klassen (1993) used divergent thinking by helping her students understand discrimination and its effects. She engaged her students in a peace and conflict unit after two students got into a fight and called each other racially charged names. She developed a literature study with books that dealt with resolving conflicts among different ethnic groups.

Literature studies can be an excellent way to help students deal with issues of discrimination. In fact, one chapter in Samway and Whang's book, *Literature Studies in a Multicultural Classroom* (1996) is entitled, "'I Think I Might Have Been a Little Bit Racist Before Coming to Hawthorne': The Influence of LSC's [literature study circles] on Cross-Cultural Understanding." The authors show how to use literature study circles in multilingual settings to help students learn about other cultures and avoid stereotyping. This book offers excellent suggestions for teachers who wish to implement literature studies in classes with English language learners.

In the next section, we look at how another teacher used divergent thinking to develop an innovative curriculum unit to help her students approach racial differences.

Helping Students Deal with Prejudice

Yvette was a high school English teacher in a large, inner-city high school with a very diverse student body. She was disturbed by the lack of community within her classroom. She noticed that the different ethnic groups kept to themselves and lacked respect for one another. She suggested to her students that they might investigate the cultures represented in their class. The students' initial responses were less than enthusiastic. No one thought the idea would work. Yvette, however, persisted. She began by asking students to do a quickwrite on the question "What is a stereotype?" One of her students, who now laughs sheepishly at his ignorance, was serious in his response: "You listen to a stereo and type" (see Figure 10–4).

Yvette was somewhat shocked to learn how little her students knew about stereotyping and how close-minded they were. She had them read an article from the *Los Angeles Times*, "The Stereotyping Habit: Young People Try to Fight It" (Robinson-Flint et al. 1992). In this article, thirteen teenagers tell about their personal experiences with stereotyping. Through class discussion and written responses, Yvette discovered that many of her students, like the teenagers in the article, suffered from being stereotyped. Youa, a Hmong girl, told how a clerk had treated her rudely in a store while she was looking at magazines. She was told, "You can't look at them!" Yet another teenager who came in and did the same thing was left alone. Vicki went on to describe how poorly she and other Asian students were always treated by office staff. Martín, a Hispanic, wrote about how, after being followed in stores so often in

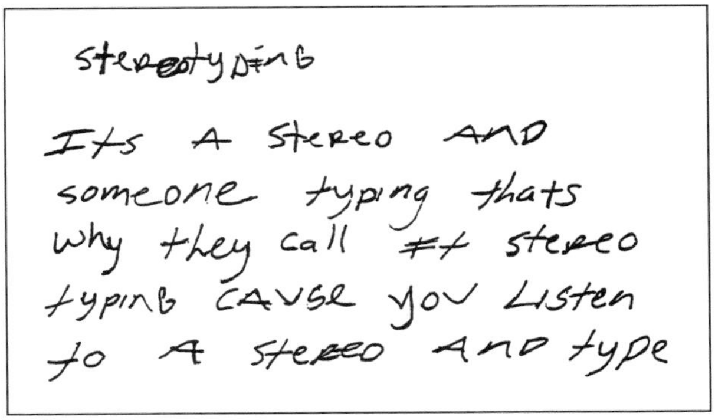
stereotyping

Its a stereo and
someone typing thats
why they call it stereo
typing cause you listen
to a stereo and type

FIGURE 10–4 *Stereotyping*

the past, on one excursion, he went to the register first to explain that he wanted to buy something. The clerk's response was to call security guards. (See Figure 10–5.)

As the students discussed and wrote about stereotyping and beliefs about other cultural groups, it became clear that the Hispanics and African Americans believed that all the Asians were alike, even though there were Vietnamese, Cambodian, and Hmong students in the class. The Asians were denigrated for being on welfare and "mooching off" the government. Though the students held stereotypes about all the groups represented, Yvette began the unit with readings about Asians. She brought in articles about how the U.S. government had used the Southeast Asians, especially the Hmong, during the Vietnam War. Students learned that Hmong boys as young as twelve were killed fighting for the U.S. cause. The students read how when the United States left Laos, all Hmong were condemned to death by the Vietcong if they were found in their own country.

Students read about and discussed the other cultures represented in their class and school, including the different Hispanic cultures and African American culture. The students were encouraged to write about what they had learned from doing the unit. Several wrote about how they learned that all groups were not alike and that

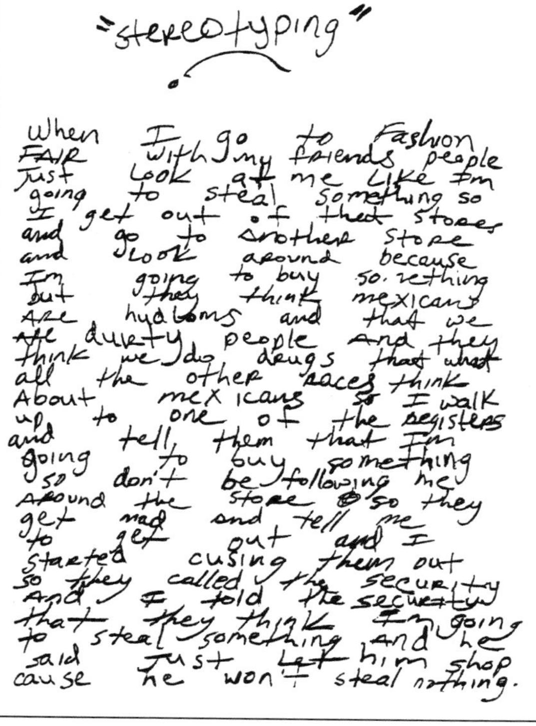

"Stereotyping"

When I go to Fashion Fair with my friends people just look at me like Im going to steal something so I get out of that store and go to another store and look around because Im going to buy something but they think Mexicans are hudloms and that we are durty people and they think we do drugs that what all the other races think about Mexicans so I walk up to one of the registers and tell them that Im going to buy something so don't be following me around the store so they get mad and tell me to get out and I started cusing them out so they called the security and I told the security that they think Im going to steal something and he said just let him shop cause he won't steal nothing.

FIGURE 10–5   *Martín's Response*

there were two sides to all stories. Others mentioned how they would judge more carefully another time and how they were glad to have new friends now. Juana's summary demonstrates how the five-week unit changed her attitudes (Figure 10–6).

Yvette gave her students a voice. Through the reading, writing, and discussion in the class, students began to look at their beliefs and their values. Sometimes, as in the case of Juana, their values changed; other times students were simply given an opportunity to express what was important to them. By using divergent thinking, she was able to develop innovative curriculum to get at the conflicts surrounding prejudice.

Assimilation or Pluralism?

The final values conflict is between assimilation and pluralism. The assimilation view holds that minority groups should merge into the mainstream culture. The traditional image for this has been the melting pot. The effect of assimilation can be a strengthening of the mainstream culture at the expense of ethnic cultures. Organizations like U.S. English hold this extreme view of assimilation and raise fears of a fragmented society

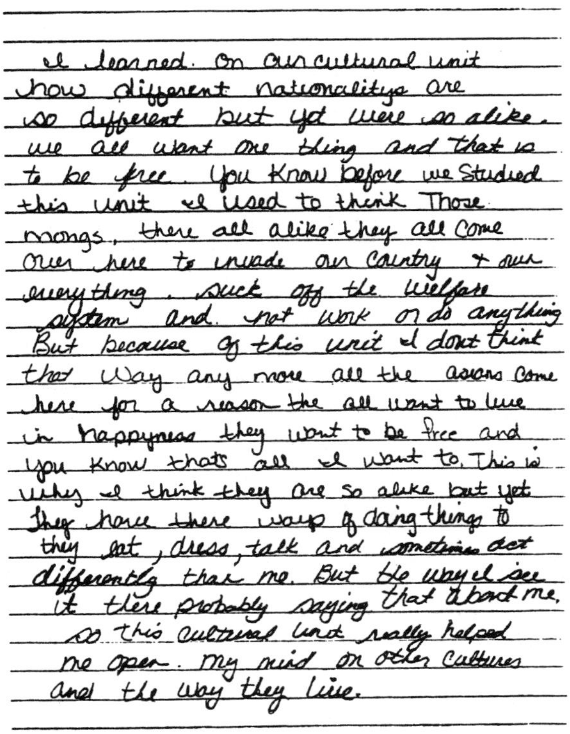

melting pot

I learned on our cultural unit how different nationalitys are so different but yet were so alike. We all want one thing and that is to be free. You know before we studied this unit I used to think Those Mongs, there all alike they all come over here to invade our country and own everything. suck off the welfare system and not work or do anything But because of this unit I dont think that way any more all the Asians come here for a reason the all want to live in happyness they want to be free and you know thats all I want to. This is why I think they are so alike but yet They have there ways of doing things to they eat, dress, talk and sometimes act differently than me. But the way I see it there probably saying that about me, so this cultural unit really helped me open my mind on other cultures and the way they live.

FIGURE 10–6 *Juana's Cultural Unit Response*

that would result from allowing a multiplicity of languages to be used. They advocate for laws making English the official language (Crawford 1999). Sometimes people point to Canada, where both French and English have official status, and the problems and resentment that has caused. They believe that Canada is an example of a country that would be stronger if all citizens were forced to speak the same language and agree on one cultural perspective.

A pluralistic stance allows for and appreciates cultural diversity. However, the result may be the coexistence of separate groups and a weakening of the mainstream. A society benefits from having distinct ethnic groups represented, but risks a loss of unity.

We see this conflict between assimilation and pluralism in other countries besides the United States. Refugees have come to a number of countries due to the breakup of Yugoslavia. A sudden influx of refugees raises this conflict. Megan, an MA student in TESOL, teaches German and English in Switzerland. She explained what she has seen there.

> "Switzerland Plagued by Growing Yugoslav Threat" and "Why Must We Bear the Wrongs of Other Nations?" are two examples of headlines that I have seen recently. The wars in Yugoslavia have forced many people to leave their homes and seek refuge in Switzerland. Many Serbs, Bosnians, and Kosovo Albanians now live in Zürich and in other cities throughout Switzerland. They work in low-status jobs but believe that they are truly better off in Switzerland than in their homeland. What will be interesting to follow, however, is if their children will assimilate and be accepted by the Swiss.

Unlike the other values conflicts we have discussed, the assimilation/pluralism conflict does not seem to present two equally valid options. In the educational context, assimilationist views do not seem productive and may be harmful. We advocate an intercultural orientation, one that incorporates students' languages and cultures, rather than an assimilationist orientation.

The melting pot metaphor suggests that different linguistic and ethnic groups succeed in the United States as they assimilate into the mainstream culture. Over time, these groups lose their distinctive ethnic characteristics, blend in, and achieve success. We have seen the almost literal realization of the melting pot metaphor as many minority students strive to blend in and avoid being different. Vince, a fourth-grade teacher in an inner-city school, recalls the Southeast Asian girl who couldn't wait to be old enough to bleach her beautiful long black hair and buy blue contact lenses.

Toni, a bilingual kindergarten teacher, wrote of her own similar experience growing up in a small farming community:

> It was my deepest desire (as I was growing up) to become completely assimilated into the American culture as quickly as possible. I did not care to use the language of my

parents except when I absolutely had to. Of course, the school I attended had a lot to do with developing this attitude, especially when there were signs in the hallway that read "Speak English For Your Own Benefit" and you were punished for speaking Spanish. I was not proud to be Mexican American, and in fact, I always had an inferiority complex, especially being the darker-skinned version.

A third example of the pressures to assimilate comes from Cándida, a bilingual teacher from Puerto Rico, mentioned in Chapter 1. Cándida's story is both sad and humorous.

> When I was very young, I assumed that being a Puerto Rican automatically meant that I would have to endure an accent. I prayed that I wouldn't sound like my parents or relatives that had come from Puerto Rico. Little did I know that being raised in the Bronx would endow me with an accent that was just as ridiculed, if not more, than a Spanish accent! As my mom would say, it's the *Castigo de Dios* (God's punishment).

Although individuals such as these may wish to blend into the mainstream culture, a closer look at the history of schooling for ethnic minority groups suggests that the melting pot metaphor may not be appropriate. For one thing, not all groups have been assimilated. Native Americans, for example, have not done well in schools and have not generally been assimilated. For another, assimilation may not be desirable and may not be the only route to success. Cultural pluralism benefits both the nation and the various groups that contribute aspects of their heritage.

Cortés (1986) suggests that when we consider the history of schooling for language minority students, a new metaphor is needed:

> In short, rather than a melting pot a more cogent metaphor for the United States is that of a mosaic, a constantly-shifting mosaic in which the multihued pieces do not always fit together perfectly, as if an on-going historical earthquake has been challenging the society to attempt to resolve the unresolvable. (6)

In a mosaic, individual pieces maintain their shape, form, and color. They do not have to melt together. Yet, as Cortés suggests, these pieces may not always fit together neatly. His image is a dynamic one, reflecting the social upheaval caused by waves of immigration into the United States. It may well be that schools have been given the impossible task of resolving the unresolvable. And new pieces are being added to the puzzle all the time.

Sue and Padilla (1986) point out that "the assumption underlying assimilation, effective functioning can occur only if one assimilates, is not valid" (58). Those cultural groups or individuals that can function effectively in two different frames of reference by alternating home and school behavior, for example, can succeed in both contexts, as Ogbu points out. They do not need to assimilate to do well in school. In fact, when they are forced to assimilate, students sometimes become alienated from both groups.

This values conflict is unlike the others. In schools that promote pluralism, all students come to be valued. These schools take an intercultural orientation, and students are encouraged to add English to their native language and to add mainstream culture to their native heritage. This process is often referred to as acculturation. Cortés (1994) explains the difference between acculturation and assimilation in this way: "[A]cculturation means learning to adapt to mainstream culture while assimilation means attempting to adopt it as yours" (26).

Cortés identifies four kinds of acculturation that can serve as goals for English learners and their teachers. The four elements of the "multiculturation" model are:

1. *Mainstream empowerment acculturation.* Refers to the development of the ability to function effectively as part of the mainstream.

2. *Intergroup understanding acculturation.* Refers to the development of "intercultural knowledge, understanding, and sensitivity in an increasingly racially, ethnically, culturally, and linguistically diverse society" (25).

3. *Group resource acculturation.* Refers to the development of the different resources of students who come from diverse backgrounds.

4. *Civic commitment acculturation.* Refers to the development of a sense of "concern for and commitment to others and willingness to act on the basis of that caring in order to work toward a more just, equitable society" (25).

Freeman and Freeman (1999) show how this model can be applied with secondary students. They provide examples of teachers working with students toward the goal of multiculturation. Some educators with assimilationist attitudes, such as the teachers described in the previous chapter, may not realize that the goals of an intercultural orientation include full adaptation to the mainstream as well as the maintenance of the first language and culture.

Summary and Possible Solutions

Those who hold an assimilationist view want minorities to merge into the mainstream. The result for many minority groups has been the loss of ethnic cultures and primary languages. In fact, looking at the world's existing languages presents us with an alarming picture of assimilation happening through language loss. Baker (2000) reported on Krauss's 1992 study that showed that there are presently sixty-seven hundred languages used in the world. There is the prediction that 20 percent to 50 percent of those will die in the next one hundred years and that, eventually, 90 percent of the world's languages will be lost. With the loss of the languages, we will also lose the cultures.

In the United States, Krashen and colleagues (1998) have documented the prevalence of language loss even among cohesive ethnic groups. Most immigrant families lose the native language by the second or third generation. As Krashen notes, "[H]eritage languages are typically not maintained and are rarely developed. They are, in fact, victims of language shift, a powerful process that favors the language of the country over the language of the family" (3).

Those who value pluralism encourage the incorporation of students' languages and cultures into the school. However, a fear of those who support an assimilationist view would be that attempting to acknowledge and celebrate different cultural groups within a school or a community encourages the formation of separate groups and a weakening of the institution, community, or country.

Two possible solutions to the assimilation versus pluralism conflict are coexistence and divergent thinking. Two-way bilingual programs are a good example of coexistence. These programs attempt to help students develop proficiency in two languages. English speakers learn in English and a second language and second language learners study in their first language and English. Both languages are equally valued and thus both cultures become valued. Second language learners in two-way programs can function in both their first language and in English. As Sue and Padilla (1986) note, "The continual challenge before us is to . . . explore ways in which individuals can develop educational competencies without losing the language, values, and identification with ethnic minority culture" (58). Two-way bilingual programs accomplish these goals. In well-implemented programs, all students add a language and knowledge of a culture to the language and culture they bring to school. An added benefit that researchers have found is that students who become bilingual are more tolerant of other cultures and more able to function in multicultural settings (Christian et al. 1997). A two-way program has also been for many schools an example of divergent thinking. When some Anglo parents objected to bilingual education, school officials asked them if they wouldn't see it as positive to have everyone learn a second language. The parents did want their children to learn a second language, so they agreed.

The Cambodians described in Chapter 1—Chham, Navy, and their family—are a good example of immigrants using both coexistence and divergent thinking to solve their conflict between assimilation and pluralism. Chham realized that he and his wife needed to learn English and American customs, so they attended adult ESL classes faithfully. Despite the fact that they had to take menial jobs in this country, they worked cheerfully and looked to the future rather than dwelling on the past.

The tragedy of the genocide in Cambodia, however, brought the conflict of assimilation versus pluralism to the surface for Chham and his family. With the realization that they needed to maintain the Khmer culture in this country, since it was being systematically eliminated in their own, Chham and Navy began to question whether their own children should attend public schools. They realized that their children were losing their first language and adopting cultural values of their American peers. Chham and Navy's Cambodian friends also feared that assimilation would lead to cultural extinction, but at the same time they recognized the need to fit in to survive economically. Conflicts arose as older children were pressured to marry fellow Cambodians to preserve a culture they did not really understand or appreciate.

The Cambodians continued to coexist with Americans as they worked to learn English and help their children in public schools. At the same time, they formed a Cambodian organization which became part of a statewide group to maintain their culture and language and to link Cambodians around the state and country together. They held social events so that their Cambodian children could get to know each other and learn to appreciate their heritage.

Sue and Padilla warn against adopting quick answers to values conflicts. As they put it, "These solutions may require change over time since single, overall solutions may not always fit a changing context. Otherwise, today's solutions may well become tomorrow's problems" (53). This is an important caution. Solutions must be flexible and context-specific. However, unless schools recognize that these values conflicts exist and unless they consider the possible effects of the conflicts, no solutions can be considered. It is important for teachers to think about where they stand on these issues, so that they can help influence the schools where they work by offering informed and thoughtful advice.

The orientation a school adopts is often dependent on how administrators, faculty, and support personnel resolve values conflicts. Their views on key issues, such as those described in the previous sections, help determine their stance toward English language learners and their parents. At the beginning of this chapter, we introduced two orientations: intercultural and assimilationist. An intercultural orientation is consistent with the explorer principles we outlined. In the sections that follow, we discuss in more detail the four key components of an intercultural orientation: (1) including students' languages and cultures, (2) involving minority community members in the school, (3) implementing transformative pedagogy, and (4) taking an advocacy role in assessment.

Including Students' Languages and Cultures

In schools that adopt an intercultural orientation, students' primary languages and cultures are included in the curriculum. For example, schools may develop bilingual programs. This is an additive approach because new students add "a second language to their repertory of skills at no cost to the development of their first language" (Cummins 1996, 105).

For teachers who follow an intercultural orientation, students' languages and cultures serve as a rich resource for curriculum. In Chapter 7 we introduced Shelly's unit, "Culture: A Pattern of Civilization," which she planned with her seventh- and eighth-grade social studies ESL students. Shelly stated the following four goals for the unit:

1. To increase student self-esteem/self-awareness.
2. To build mutual respect and self-understanding.
3. To increase an awareness of why we study about others.
4. To learn about the past and to be prepared for the future.

In her rationale statement for her unit, Shelly emphasizes the importance of incorporating all students' cultures into the curriculum:

234

> The unit activities are hands-on and accommodate second language students, giving them an opportunity to actively participate in projects. Also, because these activities are centered around validating their culture, it will help make second language students more comfortable with their culture in the classroom. They will develop clear concepts of cultural diversity and a true appreciation and respect for the wonderful differences in people of the world.

To launch her unit, Shelly discussed with her students the job descriptions for an archaeologist and an anthropologist. Next, she told them that *they* would be archaeologists and anthropologists. She shared examples of fossils, artifacts, legends, pieces of art, folk beliefs, and old written documents to give students ideas about how scientists research the past. The students then brainstormed what aspects of their own cultural background they would explore during the unit. The following seven items were chosen:

1. *Customs/Traditions*. Discuss five cultural traditions/customs.
2. *Religious Traditions* (if applicable). Discuss five religious traditions.
3. *Recipes/Food*. Share five favorite family recipes.
4. *Legends*. Record three legends.
5. *Music*. Share the lyrics of three songs or list names of musical compositions.
6. *Holidays*. Discuss five holidays.
7. *Values*. Discuss family values and important issues.

After each student had picked a topic from the list, they interviewed their families to find out about coming to the United States and California. This information was compiled for a class map so that students could compare their migrations with those of others in their class. In addition, students brought in "artifacts" from their homes and created a class museum of cultural pieces.

After completing this first activity, students worked in pairs or individually to complete projects based on the list they had brainstormed. Examples from two projects demonstrate both what students had learned and the pride they had developed in their own culture. Patricia and Suiem coauthored a bilingual Spanish/English book on Mexican holidays. Figure 10–7 shows the page that describes the Mexican cultural practice for January 6, the Epiphany. The two students also researched

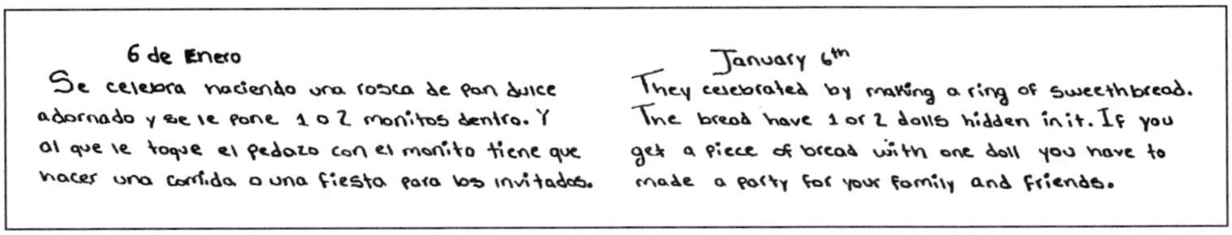
6 de Enero
Se celebra naciendo una rosca de pan dulce adornado y se le pone 1 o 2 monitos dentro. Y al que le toque el pedazo con el monito tiene que hacer una comida o una fiesta para los invitados.

January 6th
They celebrated by making a ring of sweethbread. The bread have 1 or 2 dolls hidden in it. If you get a piece of bread with one doll you have to made a party for your family and friends.

FIGURE 10–7 *January 6*

information about Mexican history for their project. Figure 10–8 contains their drawings of five important leaders of the Mexican revolution.

Each student also completed an individual project. One of the most powerful examples of the positive results from this project came from Patricia's book, titled "My Culture of México." In this project of over twenty neatly handwritten pages in Spanish, Patricia included the national hymn of Mexico, selected pieces of poetry, two legends, summaries of holidays, traditions, religious customs, and values and attitudes of the Mexican people. The section "Valores Familiares en México" (Family Values in Mexico) is a clear demonstration of how a project such as this can help students not only understand their culture but have pride in what that culture represents. (See Figure 10–9.)

The final projects were published for other students to read. Each project included an author's page with a picture of the student author and some biographical information. Figure 10–10 shows Patricia's author's page.

Shelly's unit served to help her students learn through reading, writing, and sharing in several different content areas. In addition, an activity that offers choice can build on what students already know or can discover from their families, assuring

FIGURE 10–8   *Figures of the Revolution*

Valores Familiares en México.

Son aquellos que nos han venido dejando nuestros antepasados, como nuestros bisabuelos, abuelos, padres y así de generación a generación. Y son primeramente el
Respeto a nuestros padres,
El respeto a toda persona mayor,
El vestir y hablar correctamente o decentemente delante de personas mayores.
El ~~────~~ procurar que la mujer siempre vaya virgen al matrimonio.
El tener siempre una diciplina rígida tanto para el hombre como para la mujer.
El conservar siempre la dignidad y la honradez delante de todo.
El seguir siempre el ejemplo familiar.
El saber elegir a nuestras amistades y saber destinguir lo bueno y lo malo.
El tenerle amor y respeto a nuestra Bandera y nuestra patria, Así como a la escuela y nuestros maestros.

Family Values in Mexico
They are those that have been passed on to us by our ancestors, such as our great-grandparents, grandparents, parents and so forth from generation to generation and are primarily the following
Respect for our parents
Respect for all older people
Dressing and speaking properly or decently in front of older people
Being sure that a woman always is a virgin upon getting married
Discipline should be strictly maintained for both men and women
Above all else conserving always dignity and honesty
Always following the example of the family
Knowing how to choose our friends and knowing how to distinguish between good and evil
Having respect and love for our flag and our country as well as for our school and our teachers

FIGURE 10–9   *Family Values*

success for all students. In fact, Shelly's self-evaluation illustrates why a project such as this one is important for second language learners:

> This project worked exceptionally well in my ESL class since all the students are at so many levels. Although some of the projects may appear to show little work in comparison to others, each student worked very hard. I was able to assess each student's work based on his abilities, since the projects were individual.
>
> The class really developed sophisticated concepts about culture. As we have continued to study other cultures it is obvious that they have a framework within which to work. By having them study their own culture first, they were able to personally define the meaning of custom, tradition, culture, religion, family, values, and perspective.

By beginning with the students' cultural backgrounds, Shelly was able to build a conceptual base for future studies. The students were proud of their finished projects and developed a positive attitude toward Shelly's class.

In schools that take an intercultural orientation, students' languages as well as their cultures are incorporated into the curriculum. In the same way that students

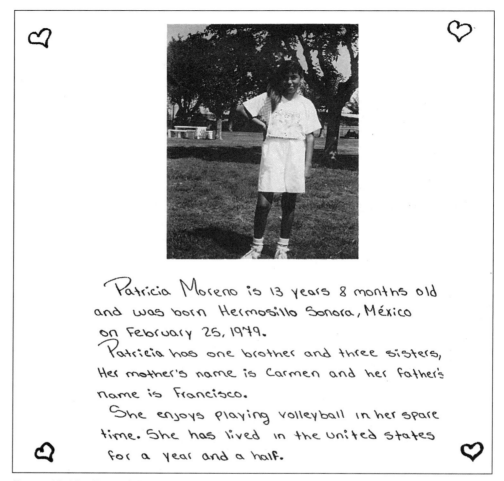

Patricia Moreno is 13 years 8 months old and was born Hermosillo Sonora, México on February 25, 1979.

Patricia has one brother and three sisters, Her mother's name is Carmen and her father's name is Francisco.

She enjoys playing volleyball in her spare time. She has lived in the United States for a year and a half.

Figure 10–10   *Patricia's Page*

study about their cultures, they can study about their languages. In addition, English language learners can compare their language with English and become more proficient users of their new language, English. Besides valuing bilingualism and biculturalism in an intercultural orientation, it is also important for native speakers of English to consider the benefit from a study of dialects. The goal is for students to recognize that all languages and all language varieties have value.

Valuing Language Varieties

Wolfram (1991) has written about how important it is for teachers to know about language varieties. He claims that teachers need to develop "an informed perspective

demonstrate language and in what situations to use the language.

on dialects." This involves an appreciation for "the complexity and naturalness of community language patterns" (265). It is the attitude toward student language that is important here. Wolfram is concerned that teachers adopt positive attitudes toward the language varieties that students bring to the classroom. In addition, he encourages teachers to develop a more thorough understanding of different language varieties. "Knowledge of community language must, of course, extend beyond respect for the naturalness and complexity of community language systems. It should also involve knowledge of the structural details of the community language system" (265). Wolfram's book provides the basic information necessary for teachers to conduct language study. That knowledge base helps prepare teachers to study the particular language varieties their students speak.

In a second useful book, Wolfram and Christian (1989) state, "It is clear that teachers need to know about dialects in order to understand the oral and written language behavior of their students." They then ask, "Would any of this information be useful to students as well?" (77). They describe ways teachers can involve students in the study of the language varieties of their own communities. As they note, "The study of community language and culture allows for the development of a full range of academic skills through meaningful content, lessening the gap between home and school. Students at all levels can conduct ethnographic and linguistic research, gathering information, testing hypotheses, and writing reports" (78).

Another excellent resource for teachers interested in learning more about dialects is *Spreading the Word: Language and Dialect in America* by John McWhorter (2000). This book addresses questions often raised by educators and by students. What is the difference between a language and a dialect? What is slang? Why do people code switch? What about black English? What are some of the roots of English? This book is easy to read. Teachers and students could use it as a resource for collaborative inquiry into language. In the process, students could gain a greater appreciation of the different languages and dialects their classmates speak.

Delpit (1990) points out that teachers can affirm students' primary languages and dialects and still help them acquire academic English by conducting lessons that contrast the two. She gives the example of Martha Demientieff, a native Alaskan teacher of Athabaskan Indian students. Martha divides a classroom bulletin board in half. On one side she lists words and phrases taken from student writing that represent what she calls "Our Heritage Language," and on the other side she provides translations into "Formal English." Martha and her students discuss the differences between the two styles. As Delpit points out, "It is possible and desirable to make the actual study of language diversity a part of the curriculum for all students" (253). The Athabaskan students conclude their unit of study with a formal dinner at which they speak only formal English and a picnic where they speak their heritage language. In this way, students begin to understand that different kinds of language are appropriate for different contexts. In Halliday and Hassan's (1976) terms, language is coherent when the kind of language used fits the context. Martha is increasing her students' language proficiency by increasing the range of contexts in which they can use language appropriately. She is not only teaching them language, but also showing them which language varieties to use in different situations. In this way, she is taking an intercultural orientation.

Involving Minority Community Members in the School

A second characteristic of schools that adopt an intercultural orientation is that minority community members are involved in school activities. These schools develop programs that encourage collaboration between the school and the minority community. In Chapter 11 we discuss the importance of involving parents of English language learners in the schools. We describe successful projects teachers have developed to include minority parents in school activities. Schools that take an intercultural orientation foster strong home-school relationships with all parents, including parents of English language learners.

Implementing Transformative Pedagogy _relate curriculom to experier.

When schools adopt an intercultural orientation, teachers move toward transformative pedagogy. As Cummins (1996) explains,

> Transformative pedagogy uses collaborative critical inquiry to enable students to relate curriculum content to their individual and collective experience and to analyze broader social issues relevant to their lives. It also encourages students to discuss ways in which social realities might be transformed through various forms of democratic participation and social action. (157)

Shelly's unit reflected several aspects of transformative pedagogy. She involved her students in collaborative projects related to their own experiences. Cummins would probably classify her unit as an example of progressive pedagogy.

> Progressive approaches highlight the role of collaborative inquiry and the construction of meaning as central to students' academic growth. The classroom is seen as a community of learning where knowledge is generated by teachers and students together. (156)

The difference between progressive and transformative pedagogy is that transformative pedagogy includes critical inquiry (Wink 2000). Students are encouraged to consider how social realities might be changed through social action. Shelly's unit, for example, might have been expanded to include an analysis of current relations between ethnic groups in their town and a plan to improve relationships.

Faltis and Hudelson (1998) describe how students in a fourth/fifth-grade classroom of Spanish speakers and English speakers worked collaboratively in a "Community Kids" project that is a clear example of transformative pedagogy. The project began with students involved in activities that led to self-awareness. Next they became aware of needs in the school community, and finally, in the larger community. During the project, students wrote to their principal asking for paint to cover graffiti on their classroom building and then organized a work party to paint, including parents and school staff. Later, after discovering a preschool in the community for homeless children, they began regular visits and became big brothers and sisters for the younger children. For another example of transformative teaching with second language students, see Freeman and Freeman (1991).

The Center for Research on Education, Diversity, and Excellence (CREDE) reports on five principles for sound pedagogy (Saunders and Goldenberg 1997). These principles can help guide teachers as they implement transformative education. They comprise the following:

1. *Facilitate learning through joint productive activity among teachers and students.* Learning occurs when experts and novices work together on projects of interest and when they talk about what they are doing.
2. *Develop students' competence in the language and literacy of instruction throughout all instructional activities.* Students continually develop language and content-area knowledge in every activity they undertake.
3. *Contextualize teaching and curriculum in the experiences and skills of home and community.* Patterns of classroom interaction and curriculum topics and materials should reflect the patterns and values of the second language learners' communities.
4. *Challenge the students toward cognitive complexity.* Even though students are limited in English, they are not limited in thinking. They need to be engaged in curriculum that challenges their thinking.
5. *Engage students through dialogue, especially the instructional conversation.* The instructional conversation is the means by which teachers and students relate formal, schooled knowledge to the student's individual, community, and family knowledge (Goldenberg 1991). Classroom talk is key for cognitive and language development.

Taking an Advocacy Role in Assessment

Cummins (1996) points out that schools with an intercultural orientation promote the use of alternative forms of assessment rather than emphasizing scores on standardized tests. Standardized tests do not fairly evaluate English language learners. Because what students are learning is not valued, students' self-esteem is lowered. Transformative teachers view assessment as an opportunity to advocate for their students. They find ways to help students show what they know.

Shelly took an advocacy role as she assessed her students. She evaluated the students' learning by having them do a project rather than giving them a test. She gave students several choices, including making a home video; doing a mural or illustration of their family or culture; compiling a book or report on family myths, legends, traditions, or recipes; producing a family newsletter, including not only history and present-day gossip but also articles written by family members; creating and performing a drama; or putting together a scrapbook or collection of articles, advertisements, or pictures that displayed aspects of their culture.

Shelly explained why this alternative form of assessment was so successful:

> The project was the culmination of the students' self-exploration of their own culture. Most of the students were very eager to do something with the information they had spent four weeks gathering. Since the class had developed particular guidelines that everyone used to explore his/her culture, I could have given them an essay exam based on these questions. In fact, the students were surprised that I did not give them a test. I think that this project worked much better.
>
> The students completed a variety of projects, utilized their talents, and practiced reading, writing, and verbal language skills. They were able to work in groups and share their knowledge. I believe that they learned so much more by sharing than if they had simply studied for a test. Many of them continued to record new information long after I had made my final check of their research notebooks.

It is important to note that Shelly allowed her ESL students to use both English and their first languages. This not only validates their first language and culture, it makes it easier for students to show what they do know and to share that information. The students were proud of their work and viewed it as important.

Outcomes of the Two Orientations

In schools that adopt an intercultural orientation, there is a positive attitude toward English language learners. According to Cummins (1996), when schools adopt an intercultural orientation, the result is students who are academically and personally empowered. Students in Shelly's class, like Patricia, developed academic skills and raised their self-esteem by completing their projects. However, when schools choose an assimilationist orientation, many English language learners are academically disabled or at least resistant.

Schools that take an intercultural orientation help change the societal context for schooling in ways that improve English learners' chances for academic success. As Cummins (1989) points out, "Minority students will succeed educationally to the extent that the patterns of interaction in school reverse those that prevail in the society at large" (58). Historically, minority groups have received discriminatory treatment at the hands of majority group members. This treatment has led to the development of a folk theory for success that puts little value on schools for involuntary minorities. To reverse this pattern, schools can take an intercultural orientation.

Individual teachers like Shelly can help schools move toward an intercultural orientation. Teachers who adopt an intercultural orientation find ways to incorporate students' languages and cultures into the school program. They encourage parent involvement. They adopt transformative pedagogical approaches and take an advocacy-oriented approach to assessment.

Applications

1. Read the following descriptions of two Hispanic college students. In groups, discuss the values conflicts and paradoxes as described by Sue and Padilla (1986) that might arise in each case.

   Carmela is from a low-income Hispanic family. Her mother had six years of schooling and her father eight. There were four children in the family. Carmela attended school in a small rural farming community in the San Joaquin Valley. The family is devoutly Catholic. Her grades in high school were high, and she qualified for grants and loans. She not only did well at a small Christian (Protestant) college, but she excelled. She presently is teaching successfully and has begun working on a master's degree. Eventually she plans to work on a doctorate.

   Pedro attended the same Christian college as Carmela though he is from a Protestant background. Unlike Carmela, his high school work was only average. Despite this, Pedro received financial support for college studies. Pedro was a bit older than the traditional college student, married with children, and had health problems. He struggled constantly with his courses. Professors said he was intelligent, but he just couldn't "get it together." He graduated, but with a struggle, and he does not have a high enough grade point average to continue into the teacher-education program as he had planned.

2. The following statements are often heard in schools and the community. Which of the values conflicts or paradoxes do you see present in each statement? Jot down some notes and then share in small groups.

   All the Hmong students are quiet and hate to participate in class discussions.
   Hispanics should be given scholarships for college because their group has experienced prejudice.
   It doesn't matter if we are black or white, Catholic or Protestant, male or female. We are all basically alike.
   I don't notice if a person is a minority or not. I just look at the results.
   They came to this country. They need to learn English and act American.
   African Americans are athletic. Asians are intellectual. Hispanics are friendly.
   We need to celebrate and appreciate our multicultural and multilingual society.
   Everyone in my class gets the same chance to succeed.
   Every person is unique. It doesn't matter where he or she came from.
   If Mexican parents only cared, their children would have a chance.
   How can you expect them to do well in school? Their parents are illiterate.
   Those immigrants don't even try to learn English!
   The college provides tutors free of charge to minority students.
   Kids from the ghetto are behind before they even start.

3. Discuss with three other people a unit and/or materials that would support an intercultural orientation.

4. Bring to class an adult book (fiction or nonfiction) that you have read that informed you about another culture. Do a book talk in a group about your book.

5. Bring a literature book appropriate for your students that supports an intercultural orientation. Share the book with a group.

11

How Can Schools Involve Parents?

Teachers have been heard to say the following:

"The problem is these parents. They just don't care about their child's education."
"There is no parent participation. They don't come to Open House. I know one parent who didn't even come to his son's graduation!"
"The parents don't even want to learn English! No wonder their kids aren't learning. How can I communicate with them?"
"What have the parents been teaching them at home? They don't even know their numbers or colors!"

And the parents respond:

"I only had two years of school in a pueblo. How can I tell the teacher anything?"
"In my country the teacher is very respected. In my country teachers don't like parents to interfere."
"I can't understand anything what anyone says anyway. Why should I go to school meetings?"
"We work very hard and long hours to get food on the table. Anyway, we don't have anything to say to the teacher."

"My son asked me not to attend his graduation. He said it was because I wouldn't understand and would be bored, but I know it is because he is ashamed of me."

"Teachers come up to me and shout. They are so rude! I can't understand English. Shouting doesn't help!"

"No quiero que mi hijo hable español en la escuela. Yo quiero que él aprenda hablar inglés bien." (I don't want my son to speak Spanish in school. I want him to learn to speak English well.)

These sentiments are typical and reflect the misunderstandings and frustrations of both teachers and parents. However, we know of schools where these kinds of comments are being made less and less frequently. At these schools, teachers, counselors, administrators, and other personnel have adopted an intercultural orientation. They encourage community participation, and they develop effective programs to involve parents of second language students. As Cummins (1996) points out, when schools take an intercultural orientation, they promote positive relationships between the school and the community. By doing this, schools create a supportive societal context for the education of students between worlds. In this chapter we look at some of the ways schools and teachers have been able to work successfully with parents of second language students.

"Second Language Parents Just Don't Care"

Some of the teacher remarks indicate that parents of bilingual students are indifferent. Why do so many teachers feel that second language parents don't care?

Our basic assumption is that all parents want their children to be successful. However, some parents of English language learners do not appear to show interest in their children's school lives. Francisco, whom we described in Chapter 1, provides us with some insights. Francisco came to the United States at age fourteen. In El Salvador, Francisco was in danger of being picked up by the army of either side of the war and forced to fight. Concepción, his mother, viewed his arrival in Fresno as the end of her long struggle to get him to the United States legally. Concepción spoke no English and had not been educated in El Salvador. She saw her responsibility as providing food and shelter for her children. Now that Francisco was in the United States, his job was to succeed here—to accomplish the American Dream. She certainly cared about his schooling, but she was not prepared to approach his teachers to discuss his schoolwork and progress. The large inner-city high school of over three thousand was overwhelming to her. Later, when Francisco's college coach, who could speak Spanish, came to her home to talk to Concepción about his concern that Francisco would drop out of college, she talked to her son long and hard. However, Francisco still remembers thinking, "You don't know how hard it is. You have no idea." He did not lack respect for his mother. He was simply living in a world that she was not part of and could never be part of. She was not a negligent parent. She was just not able to help him in that part of his life and she did not see that as her role.

Tou, the Hmong student, came from an immigrant family that had suffered greatly because of the move from Southeast Asia to the United States. Tou's parents had separated, and he lived with his father, who could not find work and who did not speak English. His father only came to school for a conference at the request of school personnel. He would probably not have felt comfortable coming to parent meetings or participating in parent groups.

José Luis, Guillermo, and Patricia, the three teens from El Salvador, lived by themselves. Their only relative in the United States was their aunt. Unlike Francisco's mother, she was very well educated, studying for a doctorate. She was a wife, a graduate student, and a teacher of Spanish at both the university where she studied and at the local community college. Like Tou's father, she would come to a school meeting, but only if a serious problem arose. She provided the teens with family love and shelter. Her nieces and nephews knew what they needed to do to succeed, and it was up to them to do it.

Caretakers of English language learners like Francisco, Tou, and the three siblings from El Salvador realize that school may be the only road to success for the young people. Sometimes they do not know how to help their relatives succeed, especially if they do not speak English and have had very little schooling themselves. Even if they received an education, it may have been in a school system very different from the system in this country, and they do not understand the roles expected of them here. Immigrant parents' expectations of schools and their attitudes toward teachers may differ considerably from the expectations and attitudes of mainstream parents (Valdés 1996). As a result, immigrant parents may give the impression that they don't care, even when they are in fact very concerned.

So it is not surprising when some teachers conclude that parents of bilingual students aren't interested in what happens with their children in school. Teachers who criticize parents for not trying to learn English and for not spending more time with their children, however, may not realize how difficult it is for immigrant parents to adjust to life in a new country, to understand the school system, and to comprehend the expectations schools have of parents.

Our own family's experiences while living in Mexico have helped us to more fully appreciate the problems language minority parents face. When we first moved to Mexico City with two children in elementary school, we did not realize how difficult this change would be for all of us. Everything took longer. Simple errands were never done easily. Day-to-day living became a real challenge. In addition, even though we are both teacher educators and had quite a bit of travel experience, we were often bewildered by the school system our children were in. Teachers at our children's school must have concluded that we just weren't interested.

Two experiences stand out. About a month after their bilingual Spanish/English school had started, our kindergartner, Ann, brought home an invitation to her class' Spanish *asamblea* (assembly). Each class gave one *asamblea* in English and one in Spanish yearly. On the invitation was glued a magazine picture of a Native American in an elaborate buckskin outfit, complete with headdress and bow and arrow. Both of us asked Ann about her part in the *asamblea*. She was a bit confused. She knew that her friend, Erica, was to be a Spanish dancer. Ann said she was going to be a Native American Indian and that she needed a costume. We were surpised that Ann was being asked to dress up as an American Indian for a Mexican program, but we rummaged around in our closets and put together a long colorful skirt and a peasant blouse.

We arranged our schedules to attend the event and thought little more about it until the day before the assembly, when we received a telephone call from the director of the school. Ann was in her office in tears. The director coldly asked us about Ann's costume. We explained what we had in mind, but the director said that it would definitely not do. The school had, after all, sent a picture of what the costume must look like several weeks before! We were shocked. To find a costume like that in Mexico City at this late date was going to be impossible. Besides, we did not consider the expense involved as justified, and we were uncomfortable with the stereotyping of the costume anyway. The school was wrong in our view. They had seen American movies with Indians and were asking for a stereotypical costume.

The situation did turn out all right for Ann. Fortunately, another child slated to be a Native American Indian was unable to attend, and he loaned Ann his costume. It really did look like the picture. His parents had bought the material and hired a seamstress to make the buckskin outfit. However, the school personnel knew that we hadn't provided the costume ourselves, and they began to think that we were negligent parents.

Another incident with Ann must have convinced them that they were correct. We had arrived in Mexico City in December, two months before the Valentine's Day holiday. The day before the holiday, Ann came home at 5:00 P.M. and told us that she needed red velvet paper, shiny red paper, and glitter and glue for school the next day. We could not imagine a teacher asking for all those supplies at the last minute, and anyway, we had no idea where we would get them. Ann was insistent, but we were equally so. The next morning Ann complained that she had a terrible stomach ache and could not go to school. When we questioned her further, she burst into tears and told us that the teacher would get very mad at her if she came without her supplies, and she was scared to go to school. We let her stay home, asked neighbors about where to buy what she needed—we discovered the world of the *papelería* (paper supply store)—and determined to inform ourselves better in the future.

The only reason that we were not permanently labeled terrible parents by the school personnel and the other parents at the school our children attended was that one of us, Yvonne, began to work there. Because she was on site, she could ask questions and see for herself what was needed for our two daughters. However, there were many differences in expectations from what we had known before, including uniform requirements, the need for parent signatures on homework, the purchase of many supplies, and mandatory gifts for teachers and administrators. Few of the people at the school ever understood our early confusion, even when we tried to explain later. Our worlds were different, and they had trouble accepting that their world was not the only real and reasonable one.

Understand Families Through Home Visits

Our own experiences have helped us understand the gulf that can exist between parents' beliefs about school and school's expectations of parents. Even when parents really do care, they may do things that lead teachers and other school personnel to conclude that they do not. Valdés (1996), in her study of ten migrant families over a three-year period, found that the gap between home and school was, indeed, wide. The school did not understand the families, and the families did not understand the school. She explains the problems in communication from the school's perspective:

> Schools expected a "standard" family, a family whose members were educated, who were familiar with how schools worked, and who saw their role as complementing the teacher's in developing children's academic abilities. It did not occur to school personnel that parents might not know the appropriate ways to communicate with the teachers, that they might feel embarrassed about writing notes filled with errors, and that they might not even understand how to interpret their children's report cards. (167)

The lack of communication between home and school was further complicated by the parents' lack of understanding of the school. In fact, not only did the parents not understand the expectations of the school, they did not conceive of a worldview different from theirs. Therefore, when teachers or administrators responded in ways they found insulting or uncaring, they took those responses at face value and were angry or hurt. While the school thought the parents were indifferent, Valdés found a very different perspective:

> The parents, on the other hand, were living lives that required large amounts of energy just to survive. They had little formal schooling and few notions about what schools expected of them and their children. And yet, they valued education. The collective family wisdom had already instilled in them a sense of the importance of high school graduation. They wanted their children to have good jobs, and they wanted them to have whatever education they would need in order to get such jobs. (167)

The home and the school can really be two different worlds. What can teachers and other school personnel do to bridge the gap? Valdés, in her study, spent a great deal of time in the homes of the families. It was only through these home visits that she came to understand their worldview. One way teachers can begin to understand the world of their immigrant students is to visit their homes. Power (1999) comments, "While home visits are time-consuming, in homes where English is the second language a visit can provide more information than any other experience" (24). Several school districts have made it mandatory for teachers to visit their students in their homes either before school starts or at the end of the first grading period.

Kristi was in her first year of teaching when she visited her students' homes at the end of the first grading period. Before she went, she complained about the time and effort such an endeavor was going to take. Afterward, however, she realized how much she had learned. Her students' homes were modest, located around the small farming community where she taught. She came away from each visit with respect for both the parents and the children. She saw that many parents were struggling to get food on the table for their children. She found out that many of her first-grade children often took on responsibilities at home, while parents and older siblings worked extra hours to make ends meet. Perhaps what touched her most, however, was the eagerness and respect with which she was received in the homes, and the interest, pride, and hope the parents showed for their children's futures.

Even when it is not a school requirement, several teachers we work with have made home visits because this has helped them understand their students and parents so much better. Peter sends an introductory letter to all the children in his class, and their parents, two weeks before school starts. He tells them in the letter that he will be visiting their home to get to know them in the following week. Then he makes short visits to as many homes as possible. Even though he does not speak the first languages of many of his students, he is welcomed into the homes and has a chance to see something of his students' home life. He has found that those visits have a made a big difference for students during their first days of school, and that after meeting their children's teacher, parents are much more comfortable with both him and the school. The visits have often given him ideas about how parents can become involved in his class. One parent, for instance, played a musical instrument, and another did wood carving. Peter would never have known this had he not been in the students' homes, and since the parents have met him, they are more responsive to his invitations to come and share their skills. This personal contact, undertaken before school even starts, has made a big difference for Peter in the home-school relationship.

Susanne, the teacher who gave suggestions for changing student attitudes at the end of Chapter 9, described in her case study how much she learned about family and family values from doing a home visit. She described the beginning of the visit as follows:

> The family of nine occupies half of a small stucco house, which at some point was haphazardly divided into two units. The house was easy to spot, as Juan was playing just outside the front gate, waiting. At first glimpse of the car, he flew into the house to announce my arrival. . . . Colorful quilts, clothing, and sheets hung from lines strung parallel to the short walkway leading to the outer security door. My immediate impression of the home was one of choked clutter. . . . It seemed more a picture of Mexican poverty than of any American dream fulfilled.

Susanne's interview with Juan's parents showed her that they were classic immigrant minorities, convinced that their life here in this country offered many opportunities. They hoped that Juan might go to college some day. At the same time, they were worried about young Juan, because the neighborhood had much gang activity and in fact, a man who had tried to get out of a gang had been killed on their street recently. During her visit Susanne learned how the older children cared for the younger children, how Juan's mother taught daughters how to cook, sew, and crochet, and how his father taught boys how to do yard work and pick grapes in the field. The visit gave Susanne a new perspective on her student and his life:

> It wasn't until our meeting ended and I was leaving that I realized how radically the lens through which I had been looking had changed. As I left the house, I was able to take in the details. I saw the front yard through very different eyes. I could still see the crowding, but now I saw the care and pride. Small clay animals huddled on narrow strips of mown lawn. Deep red rose blooms flanked one side of the walkway. . . . Topalo cacti rose up with new prickly pads, nearly ready to be cut, shaved, parboiled, and cooked with meat. "Have you ever tasted it?" Juan's mother asked as we walked out. "Not yet!" I answered with a wave good-bye to the assembled family. The visit left me with a new consciousness, a new way of looking. I could see the details, both concrete and ephemeral, of the lives that grew and struggled and lived within this home.

Cultural Experiences and Proverbs

Home visits are one important way for teachers to develop a greater understanding of their students. In addition, teachers can attend community cultural celebrations to learn about the traditions and beliefs of the parents of second language students. There are many diverse cultures living in our city; yet, many people never move beyond their own cultural group. While educators accuse immigrants of speaking only their native language and socializing only within their own cultural group, they often do the same thing.

In order to encourage present and future teachers to move out of their own comfort zones, Mary Ann, a professor who teaches undergraduate and graduate courses in cultural diversity at our university, assigns her students to do more than read about other cultures. She requires them to experience other cultures. Her students work all semester with an informant who must be from an ethnic and cultural group different from their own. Her assignment shows the goals that she has for her students:

Participant Observer Project

To gain expertise in one of the minority groups we are studying this session and to get to know a person from a cultural or racial group other than your own on a personal basis, you will engage in a participant observer research project. You will interact with this person on a regular basis (choose someone from work, church, or neighborhood). You should plan to immerse yourself into the group you are studying as much as possible: you may attend "cultural events" with the person (wedding, birthday party, funeral, worship service, etc.), watch a video or movie about the target culture with the person and discuss the differences in perceptions you have,

immerse into the Culture of your students

attend a concert or go to a party, etc. The important thing is for you to experience being the "outsider" and to discover the different perceptions you have of the same experiences. Keep a journal in which you record what you do, what you talk about, and your reflections on how you feel and see things differently. Summarize at the end of the journal what you learned from this project and how you might use this as a research tool in your teaching.

This project is often a life-changing experience for these teachers and future teachers. It helps them see the world from a different perspective and makes them much more sensitive to the diverse students in today's classrooms.

Ouk (1993) has suggested other ways that teachers can gain valuable information about their students' backgrounds. One is through the study of traditional proverbs. Ouk has analyzed Cambodian proverbs to show how they help form student and parent attitudes toward "proper" behavior at school. These proverbs, with Ouk's commentary, provide clear examples of the importance of Ouk's suggestion:

> **"When not invited, it is not appropriate to attend; when not asked, it is not proper to answer."**
> Educators need to understand the diversity in the Cambodian community and employ multiple strategies for reaching out and communicating with parents. Some parents may respond to written notices; others may need to receive a follow-up telephone call or a home visit by school staff members. If parents are expected to be at a school event, it is important that they be *invited* to participate. A simple notification may not convey the importance of their attending.

> **"Silence is better than speech."**
> Americans believe in freedom of speech; Cambodians believe in freedom of silence. Silence is a sign of humility and deference, a way to show one's respect for others. (5)

By making the effort to visit parents at home, to get to know people who speak other languages, to experience cultural celebrations, and to study cultural beliefs, teachers and other school personnel take an intercultural orientation. Rather than trying to change parents, teachers can work with them. This attitude can lead to greater parent involvement in schools.

Power (1999) has written a very useful book for teachers who want to work effectively with parents. This book, *Parent Power: Energizing Home-School Communication*, includes several useful suggestions for working with English language learners. These include visiting the home, translating key information from newsletters into the native language, providing translators at school events, and purchasing additional materials for non-English speakers in their native language.

Power lists two clearinghouses for materials for connecting Hispanic parents to schools:

ASPIRA Association Inc.
Parent Leadership Programs
1444 Eye Street NW, Suite 8000
Washington, DC 20005
Phone: 202-835-3600
Fax: 202-835-3613
E-mail: aspira1@aol.com
URL: www.incacorp.com/aspira/

Hispanic Policy Development Project
1001 Connecticut Avenue NW
Washington, DC 20036
Phone: 202-822-8414
Fax: 202-822-9120
E-mail: jlgar@erols.com

She also includes a resource for working with immigrant children:

Clearinghouse for Immigrant Education (CHIME)
c/o National Coalition of Advocates for Students
100 Boylston Street, Suite 737
Boston, MA 02116
Phone: 1-800-441-7192

Power's book is geared for teachers working with K–3 students. She includes many different essays teachers can use to communicate with parents. The essays cover a range of topics such as writing at home, helping your child enter a new school, and reading around the house. One essay talks about Internet use and lists two Internet sites especially useful for parents:

Family Education Network: www.familyeducation.com

Parent Soup: www.parentsoup.com

Each essay is presented as a one-page master a teacher could photocopy and send home. The essays are written in both English and in Spanish. The essays are also available on a CD that accompanies the book. Power includes a sample schedule of when to send home the different essays. The sample essays can be very useful to teachers. This book is an excellent resource for any teacher who wants to improve communication with parents.

Parent Involvement

Valdés (1996) concludes her book about the ten migrant families with a chapter titled "Changing Families." She expresses some concerns with traditional parent involvement programs which do not take the cultures and values of families into consideration. She makes specific suggestions about what parent programs should look like to be helpful. Valdés explains that the families she studied did not really understand parent involvement:

> As might be expected, very few families had any concept of "involvement" in their children's education as defined by the schools. . . . parents in the study did not impress teachers with their willingness to "help the schools educate their children." (160)

Valdés defines three possible types of programs for parents:

1. *Parent education.* These programs, which have been used for some time, are meant to give parents information on how best to raise their children. At meetings, parents receive information on topics such as nutrition, discipline, and early-learning activities.
2. *Parent involvement.* This is a more recent trend in schooling. Parent involvement programs emphasize the importance of parents helping children with homework, volunteering in school, and attending school functions. A key difference between parent education and parent involvement is that parent involvement is specifically meant to help children succeed academically, to become better at math, to have better study skills, or to become better readers.
3. *Parent or family empowerment.* Empowerment programs draw on Freire's (1970) idea of conscientiation, "a bringing to participants' awareness the realities of the structural inequalities in the society in which they live" (Valdés 1996, 194). These programs help parents reflect on the social realities of their community and involve them in social change. Valdés worries that programs with this name may be led by well-meaning educators who do not understand the complexity of the parents' lives and the home school interactions. Valdés explains that if empowerment programs were well conceived, parents would not blame themselves "for being 'uninvolved,' 'uninformed,' or 'uneducated' parents" (194). Instead, they would learn how they could be involved in ways that improve schooling for their children.

Teachers we have worked with have made an effort to follow some of Freire's key ideas about parent empowerment. These teachers help parents and families to analyze their social situations and to take action to improve their lives and the lives of their children. One way to give the immigrant community power is to offer adult ESL and first language literacy programs to parents. However, even when parents can get to school, it is often difficult for them to concentrate because of the many other concerns and responsibilities they have. In addition, their attendance is often sporadic, as job opportunities, family illnesses, and child care responsibilities take priority.

Steve, an adult ESL teacher, was well aware of the fact that his students needed English, but they also needed to cope with many problems as they adjusted to a new country and culture. He decided to adopt a method, derived from the work of Freire, that would enable his students to learn English in the process of discussing the problems they faced.

Problem Posing: Steve

Steve was teaching beginning English to Southeast Asian immigrants living in the inner city when he first read about Freire's idea of problem posing (Freire 1970). Freire had developed this method for teaching reading to peasants in Brazil. Steve also read how Wallerstein (1987) had adapted Freire's idea to teaching adult ESL, and he decided to try it with his students. He began by asking the students to list some of their problems. During the course of the discussion, the topic of inadequate housing came up several times. Almost all the Southeast Asian students lived in large apartment complexes, and the apartments had many defects.

When Freire developed problem posing, he brought pictures of peasants' homes into the classroom to get students to talk about their living conditions. The pictures, which Freire calls "codes," serve as a catalyst to help the peasants identify problems. Steve didn't have pictures, so he asked his students to draw a picture of the problems they had and to label the problems in English. Chao's picture shows that a poorly functioning sink with no plug and cockroach infestation were very serious problems for him and his family (see Figure 11–1). Kong identified many problems including a sink with no plug, children running and yelling, no air conditioner, a broken window, a leaking roof, a broken door, a broken stove burner, a plugged-up shower head, and a broken (extinct!) oven coil (see Figure 11–2).

Steve decided that his students' drawings could be the codes for class discussion. The conversation was lively, and both Steve and his students began to talk not only about the problems, but also the solutions. Steve then had his students identify one specific complaint, consider why it was troublesome, what caused it, and what could be done about it. Solutions included talking to the landlord, contacting the owner, writing a letter, and as the next example shows, moving to a better apartment. Kia and her husband Txong, Mien people from Laos, first answered a class-generated list of questions about their problem and then wrote about it along with their solution (see Figure 11–3). It is interesting that these beginning ESL students with no first language literacy were able to understand and answer

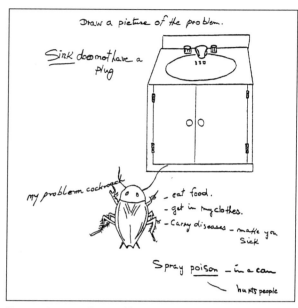

Draw a picture of the problem.

Sink does not have a plug

my problem cockroach
- eat food.
- get in my clothes.
- Carry diseases - make you sick

Spray poison - in a can
- hurts people

FIGURE 11–1   *Chao Problem Posing*

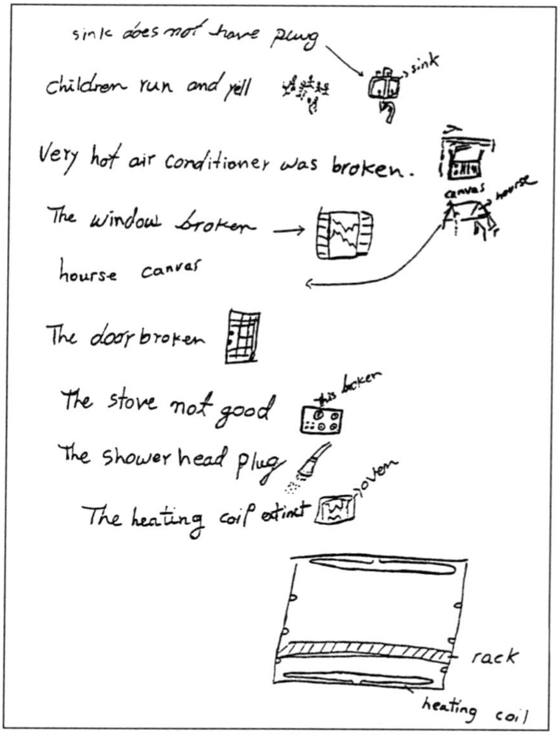

sink does not have plug → sink
children run and yell
Very hot air conditioner was broken.
The window broken →
hourse   canvas
The door broken
The stove not good → baker
The shower head plug
The heating coil extinct → oven

rack
heating coil

FIGURE 11–2   *Kong Problem Posing*

256

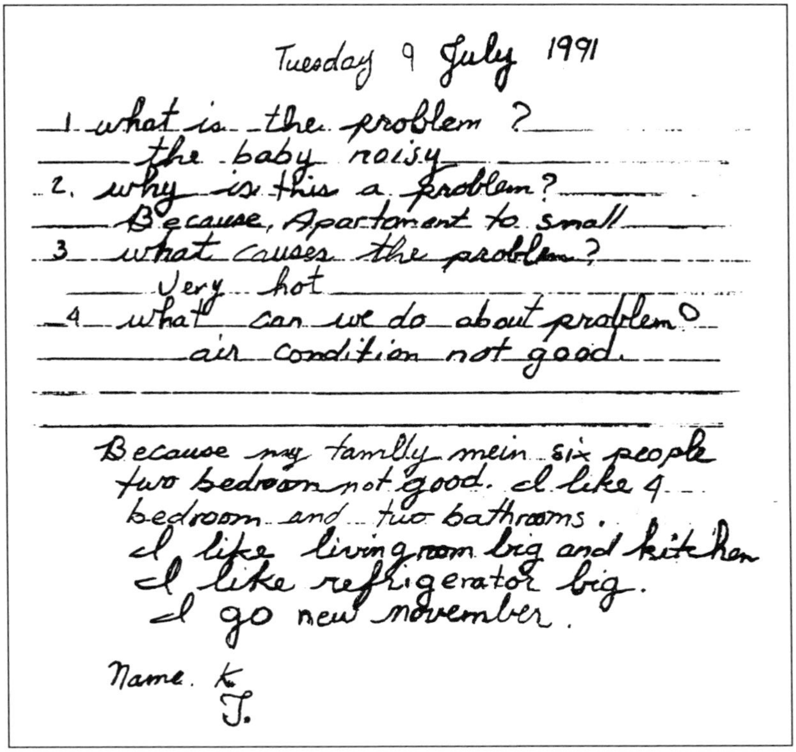

Tuesday 9 July 1991

1. what is the problem?
   the baby noisy

2. why is this a problem?
   Because, Apartment to small

3. what causes the problem?
   Very hot

4. what can we do about problem?
   air condition not good.

Because my family mein six people
two bedroom not good. I like 4
bedroom and two bathrooms.
I like living room big and kitchen
I like refrigerator big.
I go new november.

Name. K
       J.

FIGURE 11–3   *Kia and Txong Problem and Solution*

the first three questions, though they were confused about number four. In addition, their solution is clear.

Problem posing served as a way for Steve's students to both increase their English and solve real-world problems. The vocabulary they were learning was meaningful and important to them. Problem posing is a method of teaching ESL that is consistent with an intercultural orientation and an explorer image of teaching and learning. Using this method, Steve's students learned English as they explored ways to cope with the daily problems of living that they faced in adjusting to a new culture.

Because of the hardships they face, immigrant parents may find it difficult to attend classes. Some districts have solved this problem by offering ESL and literacy classes to adults at the same location where their children attend school. Classes may be held either during regular school hours or after school. When they study at their children's school, parents tend to feel more comfortable and are more willing to participate in classroom activities or attend parent meetings.

In addition, these programs for parents serve two purposes. They provide ESL and primary-language literacy to parents, and this education enables parents to help their children with school-related activities. Parents who are not literate themselves can learn how to encourage their children to read and write at home. In the same way that Steve was able to teach English through the meaningful content of daily life, these programs teach both English and first language literacy through the content of school and family relations.

Improving Home/School Communication: Claudia

Claudia is a Spanish/English bilingual teacher who teaches at a charter school with a high immigrant population. Claudia and her colleagues work closely together to meet the academic, social, and personal needs of their students. Several years ago, it came to the attention of Claudia that there were no school personnel in the front office who could speak Spanish and that communication from Hispanic parents was almost nonexistent. Claudia explained her concern:

> Though the teaching staff at the school had made considerable efforts to bring parents into the life of the school, few Spanish-speaking parents played an active role in the school. My belief was that in order to bring Spanish-speaking parents into the life of the school, we would have to give them the opportunity to participate in a way that was personally meaningful.

At the time, Claudia was doing graduate work in bilingual education and beginning to work on her MA thesis. She was interested in parent involvement and had read about workshops for Hispanic parents (Vopat 1994) which validated parents and families. She had read the work of Freire as well and decided to develop a family program for the Spanish-speaking parents at her school and report on the results for her thesis.

The first night the "Los padres como socios" (Parents as Members) met, Claudia welcomed the parents and started the meeting with the following question in Spanish: "What are the questions you have about how you can best help your children?" Claudia described what happened next:

> With hardly a pause, the questions flowed from parents, reflecting the depth of their concerns and worries about their children. They had questions about bilingual education and repeating grades. They wanted to know if they should encourage their children to speak English or Spanish at home, how they could help their children in math when they learned math differently, how to motivate their children to do their homework and chores. They also wanted to know how they could learn more English.

At the end of the evening, not only did Claudia have more than enough questions than could be answered in the six weeks of planned workshops, but she had learned wonderful things about her students and a community of parents had been formed. They were excited about coming the next time to share and get answers to the questions they had had for some time.

Based on the questions raised that first night, Claudia invited guest speakers and planned discussions to deal with parents' concerns. Over a period of six weeks, meeting each week, the community grew. Because there was free discussion, the parents told stories of their children and school. In their time together parents shared information and supported one another in their efforts to help their children grow and learn.

Toward the end of the year, the parents got involved in the same kind of writing process their children were doing in school. Volpat suggested having the parents write poetry, and Claudia decided to try this with her parents. "The parents were a little nervous about writing and others seeing their writing, but as they went through the process of writing, editing, and then sharing, they were more confident and got excited. The parents wrote poems about their children's learning at home and at school *Poemas de nuestros hijos* (Poems about our children)" (Socios 1996). The poems were typed up, and the children illustrated them. Then the poems were assembled into a book, which was spiral-bound. Each family received a book to take home. Figures 11–4 and 11–5 are examples of two of the poems. The first was written about Alvaro by his mother and the second is an acrostic about Robert, written by his father, Roberto.

Trust Parents to Help

> Parents from every culture need to know that you care, respect, and value their families and are doing your best to educate their children for success.

The above was written by Cándida, Eugenia's bilingual kindergarten teacher. She was responding to her reading and class discussion about parents and how to involve them. A key to involving parents is to trust them to help. This may sound simplistic, but it is too often the case that teachers or other school personnel decide that parents cannot help when they really can.

In fact, a common misconception about non-English-speaking parents is that they cannot help their children because they do not speak English. One of the worst recommendations that has come from schools in the past is "Speak English at home." This advice not only negates the value of the students' first languages and the importance of family discussions for building concepts, but it effectively cuts off important family communication. Hispanic parents, for example, have been made to feel guilty for speaking to their children in Spanish, so they encourage their children to watch television instead of talking to them. The children, in turn, lose their ability to speak and understand their first language with any facility. Hispanic and Hmong graduate students have told many stories of family members not being able to communicate with grandparents and even parents. Mothers tell of how the only thing their children understand is the language of food. Valdés (1996) writes about the values and the important *consejos* (bits of wisdom) parents pass on to children. These are all lost when first language communication in the home is discouraged.

Translation into English of "Alvaro Mercado"

Alvaro Mercado,
Is our son.
He has a beautiful smile.
He is very interested in school.
He gets up very happy
And gives his dad
And mom a kiss,
He says
Tomorrow is Monday
I get to go to school
Because he misses his classmates,
And his teacher very much.

Alvaro Mercado,
es nuestro hijo.
Tiene una sonrisa muy bella.
Tiene mucho empeño en la escuela.
Se levanta muy contento
y le da un beso a papá
y a mamá,
dice que
mañana es lunes
para irse a la escuela
porque extraña mucho a sus compañeros, y
a su maestra.

por Andrea Mercado

FIGURE 11–4 *Alvaro Mercado Poem*

Robert es mi niño más pequeño

Obediente aveces, a veces travieso

Bueno es con nosotros

En todo momento

Revisa sus libros y nos encuentra cuentos

Terminando, todas quedamos contentos.

por Roberto Jimenez

Translation of "ROBERT"

Robert is my youngest son
Obedient at times, sometimes naughty
Good with us
All the time
He looks over his books and finds us stories
Finishing, we are all happy.

FIGURE 11–5   *Roberto Poem*

In Chapter 8 we stressed the importance of first language support for academic success. Though parents may ask themselves how they can help when they do not speak English, what children need to learn are ideas, concepts, and processes, and it does not matter in which language they learn these things (Cummins 1996; Krashen et al. 1998). Parents should teach their children about the world. Once children understand ideas, form values, and solve problems in their first language, they transfer those basic understandings to their second language.

Collier and Thomas (1996) have written about the importance of cognitive development at home. They makes specific suggestions to parents about how they can capitalize on interactions in the home using the primary language. They encourage parents to stimulate their children's cognitive growth through daily interactive problem solving such as discussing daily activities, asking questions and sharing values, talking about household chores, including shopping, cooking, and cleaning, and family activities such as celebrations and storytelling.

When parents talk to their children and read and write with them in their first language at home, children build important background that leads to school success. Yvonne has often been asked to present to parent groups in Spanish. She has developed some suggestions that, like Collier and Thomas', are things parents can do in the native language and seem practical to parents. Below are three simple suggestions teachers can make to parents, with some clarification of each and extension ideas. It is important to note that not all parents are literate, even in their native language. However, suggestions can be worded in ways that give parents things they can do with their children to support their children's literacy development.

Parents can support their children's school success in the following ways:

1. *Talking*. Parents who play with their children and have conversations with them are helping them to think and to explore their world. In this process children learn to use language for a variety of functions.
2. *Reading*. Parents who read with their children and take them to the library are giving them experiences with books that they need for school success. If parents are not confident readers, they can ask their children to do the reading, or parents and children can follow a story while listening together to a tape-recorded reading. If the children read a book in English to their parents or if the children and parents listen to an English book on tape, the children can then explain the story to the parents, and they can discuss it as they look at the pictures.
3. *Writing*. Parents who encourage their children to draw and write are teaching them to express themselves in writing. Parents can also make children aware that adults use writing for a variety of purposes every day, including writing letters, making out checks, jotting notes, and making shopping lists. If parents do not write frequently themselves, they can have writing materials including paper and marking pens around for children during play time.

Goldenberg and Gallimore (1991) worked over several years on a project to improve reading achievement of Spanish-speaking children. One of the aspects of the study included parent involvement. The teachers at the school where the research was conducted were hesitant about parent involvement because they believed that there was no literacy in the home, that parents were not interested in the children's achievements, and that because of their minimal academic background, parents could not help their children. As stated below, Goldenberg and Gallimore found these assumptions to be false.

> Although literacy did not occupy a prominent place in most homes, it was not entirely absent. Virtually all homes, for example, sent and received letters to Mexico or Central America. All homes received printed flyers or advertisements . . . most parents reported (and subsequent studies have confirmed) that children consistently asked about signs, other "environmental print," or the contents of letters to or from relatives. None of this would be possible if literacy did not exist in the homes, at least at some level. (8–9)

In interviews with parents, Goldenberg and Gallimore found that parents "saw themselves as playing a key role in their children's school success, particularly while their children were young" (9). In addition, when asked, parents expressed great interest in helping their students at home, though many "expressed fear of confusing their children" because they were "unfamiliar with 'the system' here" (9).

The researchers found that "although the overall educational levels of parents were indeed low," most of the parents could read books with limited text and several were able to read quite well (8). Despite the doubts teachers had about the parents' ability to help their children, story books and other literacy materials were sent home with the children. Some teachers developed activities for parents to do with their children at home that would reinforce what was being done in the classroom. These activities were similar to the *tarea* (homework) that parents were familiar with from their native countries. Some of the activities were actually quite fragmented. However, the important finding from this study was that parents did get involved. They wanted to help their children at home, and they *could* help them. Teachers need to trust that parents will engage in talking, reading, and writing with their children. These activities all contribute to English language learners' school success.

Pulling Parents In

Home visits, ESL classes, and parent programs can be important steps for educators to take in working with parents. However, school personnel must take additional steps to pull parents in and involve them actively in school events.

Carolina

Parents of second language students may attend ESL or special programs for them, but often they do not attend regular school meetings, school functions, or parent-teacher conferences. This pattern can be changed. Carolina, a bilingual teacher for several years, offered the following ideas:

> As bilingual teachers, we are often frustrated by conditions which we *perceive* as being unchangeable. For instance, our site's Parent/Faculty Club has been frustrated by the fact that our Hispanic parents do not actively participate in the Fall Carnival or in the Spring Chicken Barbecue Sale. Why should parents come when they can't understand the meeting's agenda or when they feel uncomfortable because we're having to whisper our translations? Why not have the meeting conducted in two different languages for part of the time so that both groups can meet and share their results? I believe our English language parents would be surprised as to how our Hispanic parents would respond.

[handwritten margin note: meeting in primary language]

Tammy

Unfortunately, Carolina's observation of Hispanic parents feeling uncomfortable and not part of the meeting is not uncommon. Tammy, a relatively new teacher, wrote about a parent meeting she attended in another farming community with a high Hispanic population:

> I walked in and took a seat at what would be my first experience at attending a Parent-Teacher Association meeting. As I sat down, I observed the association president sitting next to last year's president, two white, middle-class women. I watched as three more women of the same type came and took their usual seats. I sat, feeling a little strange to not see any Hispanics, especially since the school is at least 90 percent Hispanic. Then, four Hispanic women came in escorted by one of our bilingual teachers. What a relief! The four "new" women spoke only Spanish and were looked on by the others as "out of place." In fact, one of the regular attendees (a middle-class Asian woman) walked in late and turned around to leave because the sight of the Hispanics at the meeting led her to believe that she was in the wrong place.

Fortunately, some districts have found ways to involve parents. In a school district near Tammy's that has an equally high Hispanic population, two different school sites have held bilingual parent meetings in the evening. At both schools, the meetings were well publicized. Emphasis was given to the fact that the presentations would be in both Spanish and English and that the speakers would discuss ways parents could help their students succeed. In both cases, teachers and administrators were overwhelmed by the response of the Hispanic parents. In fact, Hispanic parents outnumbered Anglo parents ten to one. Both meetings were so crowded that there was standing room only. At one site, the meeting was held on Back to School Night, and the principal announced that it was the best-attended Back to School Night the school had ever had.

Kay

Parents get involved when schools take specific actions to include them. Kay is a resource teacher in a district with a high Hispanic population. In the past, the district did little to include minority parents, but recently district administrators have made parent involvement a priority. The district commitment has extended to hiring experienced bilingual teachers like Kay to work with parents. When Kay started working for the district, she observed that Hispanic parents were largely left out of activities for parents. The Anglo parents complained that the Hispanics did not want to help, but the Anglos never made an effort to include them.

Kay initiated an event that she thought would be of particular interest to Hispanic parents. The Mexican American farmworkers in the small community always celebrated the Cinco de Mayo (Fifth of May), so Kay decided to have an all-school Cinco de Mayo celebration. She called a meeting of Spanish-speaking parents to discuss a Cinco de Mayo school celebration and promised to conduct the meeting bilingually. When only Spanish-speaking parents showed up, she talked about her idea in Spanish and asked them what they thought. They were very enthusiastic. They offered to bring food, to teach the students how to perform traditional dances, and to decorate the school.

Kay admits that she was nervous that first year. Others at the school, including the administration, were skeptical about whether the parents could be counted on to help, but they did agree to set aside a day for the activities once Kay showed them the plans that she and the parents had developed. Kay spent long hours coordinating the activities, and the results were fantastic. Hundreds of migrant families attended the all-day celebration, which included dancing, singing, crafts, and a huge lunch. Almost all the parents contributed something, and many took on the role of teachers of their culture as they instructed whole classes in art and music. The day was so successful, it became an annual school and community event.

Lisa

Lisa helps coordinate the Migrant Education program in a large urban district. This program helps Southeast Asian parents, who historically have never participated. In order to receive Migrant Education funds, the district is mandated to hold at least six council meetings yearly with representatives from each school. The Migrant Education staff organized school-site meetings in which they provided translators so that parents could raise concerns. Having translators at these meetings allowed the Asian parents to gain a stronger voice in district decisions. Further, the migrant staff encouraged parents to seek solutions by working with school personnel. In just three years, there has been a tremendous difference in parent participation and empowerment. Lisa reports an example of how parents are taking the responsibility for initiating change:

> We are finding more and more parents initiating meetings at their schools without our help or involvement. An example of this was when a Southeast Asian parent typed an invitation to the district superintendent inviting him, administrators, teachers, and parents from his school to a luncheon at his house. The purpose of this meeting was to bring together the diverse cultures at the school. (Marasco 1993, 17)

According to Lisa, an additional benefit of these school-site meetings has been increased communication between Southeast Asians and Hispanics, groups who had previously resisted working together:

> Another positive outcome from this council is that with the help of translators I have also seen the Hispanic and Southeast Asian parents come *together* to brainstorm solutions to their concerns. At the last meeting our Southeast Asian president and Hispanic vice-president expressed a belief that all our children have to learn to live peacefully with one another and their role as parents is to model this. (17)

Linda

Linda works in a rural school district with a high Hispanic population. Her school wrote a grant that allowed teachers to reach out to parents more effectively. Linda wrote:

One of our major priorities was to create a parent center at our school, staffed with a bilingual person who could offer services to parents and provide a place where parents could find out about school policies and make them feel more in touch and in tune with our school.

Teachers and administrators at Linda's school found additional ways to make parents feel welcome. For Back to School Night, all the families were invited to bring a picnic and blankets. In the early evening, students, parents, teachers, and administrators had dinner together on the lawn outside. After dinner, parents visited booths where they could find information in English or Spanish about the various programs at the school. Later, the parents met with individual teachers in the classrooms. Linda reported, "It was a huge success and the comment made most often was that the parents felt welcome and at ease at school."

At schools such as the ones we have described above, minority-parent involvement is a priority. Specific events and programs are planned to pull all the parents in, to make them feel welcome, and to give them a voice in decisions that affect their children. These schools send out a clear message to parents: "We want you to help us provide the best possible education for your children."

Getting Parents Involved in the Classroom

Schools can change community attitudes by reaching out to parents, by working with parents, and by pulling parents in to meetings and other school functions. In addition, a number of teachers have found ways to involve parents even more directly in daily classroom activities. For these teachers, parents of second language students are a valuable resource.

One project that involved an entire school but also pulled Spanish-speaking parents into the curriculum was the *Math Story Book* (Zanger 1996) project in Boston, Massachusetts. In an effort to help parents understand and participate in the math curriculum, the school produced a book of math story problems in Spanish and English. School administrators, classified personnel, teachers, students, and parents were encouraged to write math problems to be included in the book. Sample problems were sent home and children and parents wrote problems together. The results were exciting. The problems reflected not only the bilingualism of the school community but also biculturalism. For example, one boy and his mother wrote and illustrated a math problem about a family baptism, an important social event in the Hispanic community. They listed who brought how many items and included the very important cake in the problem and illustration. No baptism is complete without an official bakery cake. Problem solvers were asked to count up the total number of items. In another, two brothers collaborated on a problem in which they had fifty cents, spent part of the money and lost some. They asked for the amount of money that was left. Probably our favorite problem in the book, however, is one in which the author depicts six stick-figure mothers with two small stick-figure children beside each. The question posed was, "Six ladies had two babies each. They all had real good kids. How many babies did they have?" (38). An interesting question that comes from this and other student- and family-generated story problems would be, "What information is not necessary to solve the problem?"

At Fipps Primary School in rural Riverdale, California, teachers instituted a plan to involve parents in their children's reading by starting a program they call Book Bags. The idea was to find a way to get books into the homes. The teachers first collected a number of books. Then teachers and parent volunteers sewed book bags using a heavy canvas material. They decorated them with an appliqué to represent each book. For example, *The Little Red Hen* bag had an appliqué of a hen. The teachers first shared books in Spanish or English in class and then put them inside one of the book bags for students to take home. They also put storytelling props, when appropriate, into the bags. These props helped the children share their books in different ways with their parents. Rojas (1993) describes the importance of the Book Bags project:

> Teachers decided that the best way to encourage literacy was to send home books that the parents and children could enjoy together on a daily basis. Without the opportunity to take books home daily, many of these students would not read at home due to the lack of materials. Besides the benefits for the kindergarten students, the book bags have also provided the preschool siblings of these students some of their first opportunities with books. (8)

Projects such as this one show that parents are interested in improving their children's literacy and that they are willing to help their children when the school provides them with the necessary resources.

Finding ways to involve bilingual parents can be a special challenge for teachers who are not bilingual themselves or who have students from several language backgrounds. Nevertheless, as the following examples show, the effort is well worth it.

Gayleen, a first-grade teacher, set up a schedule for her bilingual parents to come into her classroom and participate in class events. She had children whose first languages included Spanish and several Southeast Asian languages. She was especially excited about the involvement of one husband-and-wife team. The father of a Spanish-speaking child agreed to come into the class and read books to Spanish-speaking children in Spanish. Gayleen encouraged the father to read the books in Spanish to the entire class. At first he was reluctant to do this, but when Gayleen let him choose the book ahead of time and take it home to practice first, both the father and the children had a positive experience with the reading. The wife was not comfortable reading in Spanish, but she also wanted to do something in the classroom. Gayleen asked her to help with cooking and crafts and encouraged her to speak Spanish with the children as she did this. All of the students in Gayleen's class benefited from these experiences, even though only a few spoke Spanish.

Gayleen also had a Southeast Asian grandfather who was literate in Hmong come into her classroom as a volunteer. He worked with the Southeast Asian children as they published bilingual books in Hmong and English. This increased Gayleen's resources in Hmong and helped her Hmong students take pride in their first language.

Sharon, another first-grade teacher, wanted more of her parents to participate in the classroom. She knew that many non-English-speaking parents were reluctant to come to school because they did not speak English, and they did not really understand the school system. She decided to have community aides invite parents personally to a meeting, promising to have translators available.

On the night of the meeting, Sharon and the aides, who were able to speak Spanish, Lao, Mien, Hmong, and Khmer, waited anxiously for parents to arrive. Sharon describes what happened:

> The time came for the meeting and only two parents were there, so I told the interpreters they could leave. Ten minutes later about ten more parents showed up and there were representatives of every language in my classroom! I visited around the room and discovered there was at least one parent from each different culture represented who could speak English. Each one of these became an interpreter for several new friends. At times you would hear them laughing together at things I said or they interpreted. They all seemed to have a great time sharing and laughing together. At the end of this meeting they decided they wanted to meet together on a regular basis. There were smiles on their faces and new friends made.

Sharon's parent group met about five times that year, working on strategies to help their children at home. Sharon showed them how she used big books, predictable books, journal writing, and themes, and through their sharing, the parents helped teach each other. They became active at school and helped with field trips and class activities. Working with this parent group was one of the most rewarding experiences Sharon had ever had. Parents from different language and culture groups worked together to learn, and because they helped each other and set the agenda themselves, they felt good about themselves and their involvement in school.

In each of these cases, teachers believed that parents could and would help. Rather than accepting negative stereotypes of language minority parents, these teachers took a positive view and found ways to utilize the parents' talents.

Conclusion

Working effectively with parents has never been easy. When the cultural and linguistic backgrounds of teachers and parents differ, the challenge becomes even greater. Teachers are busy people, and establishing positive relationships with second language parents takes time and effort. When the effort is schoolwide, supported by administrators and, often, by outside agencies or by funds and personnel supplied by grants, there is even more possibility of success.

In schools that take an intercultural orientation, involvement of language minority parents is a priority. Parent involvement fosters a positive relationship between the community and the school and helps create a supportive societal context for the schooling of students who move between two worlds. The societal context strongly influences the educational context, so teachers and other school personnel must work to develop a supportive societal context. At the same time, teachers must continually refine their own practices to meet the needs of their students. In our final chapter we turn again to the school context as we consider ways teachers can reflect on and continually improve their educational practices through classroom-based research.

Applications

1. "They just don't care" is a common assumption made about the parents of English language learners. What have you observed that might support this statement? How could you further investigate to challenge its validity?

2. Group yourselves according to the age level of the students you are teaching or plan to teach. How can parents or other community members be involved at your school? If you teach adults in this country, how can you help them feel more a part of the schools their children attend or more a part of the community in general? If you plan to teach EFL in a foreign setting, discuss the kinds of parent involvement that are encouraged.

3. Interview the parent or parents of a second language learner. Try to determine the parents' expectations for the student. Do they agree with what the school's goals are?

4. Review the three types of parent involvement programs that Valdés describes. Which type(s) of programs have you observed being used in schools? How did those programs work? Were there problems? Discuss with a small group, and then share your conclusions with the larger group.

5. What successful family or parent programs or experiences have you had or observed? List as a class ideas that have worked.

6. Make a visit to the home of one or more of your immigrant students. What did you learn from the visit?

12

How Can Teachers Improve Their Practice Through Classroom-Based Research?

I work through the needs of limited English students a majority of my teaching (and nonteaching) day. The concerns and recommendation of the California Tomorrow report are fought out in the battleground of my classroom with parents, administrators, students, other teachers, and even in the confines of my own consciousness. But because of this, in the last year I have come to understand my best ammunition is in working *with* students, allowing group process/social interaction, increasing and refining comprehensible input for context-reduced academic tasks, letting students come to an understanding that they can achieve in their own way and time—providing a safe environment . . . and wrapping this in a format that celebrates students' personal experiences.

Rhoda, the teacher of our case study student Sharma, reflects here on how she works to improve schooling for her second language students. Teaching for Rhoda, and for many committed explorer teachers, extends well beyond the normal school day. She has read reports put out by the California Tomorrow organization (Olsen and Mullen 1990) that help inform her about her immigrant students. Rhoda has adopted an intercultural orientation and an exploratory teaching style. She has studied theories of language, learning, teaching, and curriculum. She has considered factors both inside and outside the school that affect her students who move between worlds. In the process, she has become a teacher researcher who can reflect on and refine her own practice in a continuous attempt to improve learning for all her students.

In this final chapter, we will look more closely at the idea of teacher research as a way to find context-specific solutions to the challenges of teaching English language learners. Teacher researchers are aware that in any situation, a number of different factors interact to influence the school performance of English language learners. These teachers reject single-cause explanations for success or failure. Through awareness of the world outside school, the societal context, and through reflection on their own teaching, the world inside school, teacher researchers attempt to discover practices that fit their particular contexts and help all their students succeed.

Models of Teacher Research

Case Studies

Teachers who wish to understand the complex interaction of factors that affect the performance of their students benefit from conducting case studies such as those presented in Chapter 1. These studies take into account factors from both the world of the school and the world of the community outside school. The way that students interact with one another and with teachers, the students' and teachers' attitudes, expectations, and goals, as well as the attitudes and values of the community, all shape the outcomes of learning experiences for students between worlds.

Case studies can reveal possible courses of action teachers can take to change situations in which students are not succeeding. In the process of carrying out these studies, teachers become teacher researchers who analyze the effectiveness of the teaching strategies they use. Teacher research provides insights that enable teachers to modify their practices in ways that result in greater success for their students. Case studies of individual students or studies of classroom practices constitute a context-specific response to educational questions. By conducting classroom research, teachers can gain greater understanding of the different factors that impact student performance. At the same time, this sort of research can help teachers reflect on and make changes in their own daily teaching practice.

Conducting case studies helps teachers understand their students, and it also helps them evaluate their own teaching. The case studies we have described comprise one model of teacher research. Our students collect data on their case study student from sources both inside and outside the classroom. They analyze the data by applying concepts they have studied in their university classes. Then they share their results and get feedback from their peers in their university classes. Case studies are just one kind of classroom-based research. In the sections that follow, we describe two other possibilities: individual action research and collaborative action research.

Individual Action Research *TCACHEK*

Nunan (1993) has worked extensively on staff-development programs. These programs help teachers conduct action research, particularly in ESL and foreign language classes. He identifies the following steps in an action research cycle:

1. problem identification
2. preliminary investigation
3. hypothesis
4. plan intervention
5. outcome
6. reporting

An action research cycle begins with the teacher identifying a problem or puzzle. For example, a teacher might notice that students don't like working in cooperative groups. The teacher then does some preliminary investigation. This would include making systematic observations. The teacher might tape the class sessions when students are given group tasks. The next step is to form a hypothesis. For example, the teacher might hypothesize that the top students don't feel they learn anything in the groups and that they are doing all the work because they don't want to get a bad grade.

The fourth step in an action research cycle is for the teacher to plan an intervention. An intervention involves some change in practice. The teacher could change the way students are graded on group projects to include both individual and group grades. Or the teacher could change the composition of the groups. This intervention results in some outcome that is then reported. If action research is part of staff development, the report could come at the next staff meeting as teachers share the results of their research.

Action research has important potential for positive teacher change. Rather than listening to an outside expert who has all the answers, teachers identify puzzles, investigate them, try out new practices, and report the results to a supportive group of colleagues. This approach to staff development encourages teachers to become explorers in their own classrooms. The process is cyclical, because the results of one investigation often lead to new questions.

Teachers can learn more about classroom research through professional reading. A good starting point would be the practical and easy-to-follow book *The Art of Classroom Inquiry* (Hubbard and Power 1993). Power and Hubbard (1999) have also written an excellent article that includes clear examples of how teachers can become researchers. *Ethnographic Eyes* by Carolyn Frank (1999) provides more detailed instruction on how to carry out classroom observations from an ethnographic perspective. *Engaging Teachers: Creating Teaching and Researching Relationships* (Bisplinghoff and Allen 1998) includes chapters by classroom teachers and university researchers who have worked to conduct classroom-based research. Another excellent resource for schools that can guide professional development is González and

Darling-Hammond's *New Concepts and New Challenges: Professional Development for Teachers of Immigrant Youth* (1997). The authors begin by reviewing the changing context for educating immigrants. Next, they look at changes in professional development. Then they turn to structures, models, and practices in professional development that promote collaboration. Finally, they review specific programs that are effective in preparing teachers to work with immigrant students.

Collaborative Action Research

TEACHER + STAFF (PRC)

In some cases, teachers may work with researchers from colleges or universities as they engage in action research. A number of benefits can result from teachers' collaborating with researchers from colleges and universities. A college researcher may have a fresh perspective, time, and resources that a teacher lacks. The college researcher can come into the classroom and view the class with fresh eyes. It often happens that discussion with the teacher afterward reveals that the researcher saw things that the teacher, distracted by other concerns, never noticed. It is also possible that a college researcher would have more time or a more flexible schedule to do things like interview parents or other community members. Finally, the researcher can identify books or articles about situations similar to the ones the particular teacher is facing and bring those to the teacher's attention.

Allwright (1993) lists seven major aims for any project for collaborative research involving a teacher and a college researcher:

1. relevance
2. reflection
3. continuity
4. integration
5. collegiality
6. learner and teacher development
7. theory building

Any research proposal should meet all seven of these aims. Concerning relevance, Allwright states the following:

> The least to hope for from our work is that teachers bringing research into their own teaching will ensure that what they explore is relevant to themselves regardless of what concerns academic researchers, and that it is also relevant to their learners, who may well have interesting puzzles of their own to explore. (128)

Allwright is an advocate of exploratory teaching and learning. He sees classroom research as a way in which both teachers and students can explore aspects of their situation together with assistance from academic researchers. This call for relevance is particularly important. Too often outside researchers have conducted studies that were not relevant to the teachers and students in the classrooms where they worked. Allwright's call for relevance also points to the need for true collaboration. The academic researcher and the classroom teacher, along with the students, are exploring matters of mutual interest. The outsider is not coming in to offer expert advice or to conduct a study whose only purpose is to advance the researcher's career.

In addition to relevance, Allwright proposes that classroom research promote reflection by both teachers and learners. He also stresses that integrating research and pedagogy should be a continuous enterprise. If the research is relevant, and if teachers and students reflect on what they are discovering, then the results can be integrated into daily practice. In addition, Allwright feels that integration of research and pedagogy should encourage collegiality among teachers and also bring teachers closer to their students. Finally, Allwright points out that any proposal for integrating research and teaching should have the aims of learner development, teacher development, and theory building.

Allwright notes that certain problems are to be expected. Action research requires time, new skills, and a willingness to change ineffective practices. First, "doing research in the language classroom is time-consuming" (129). Teachers need more time to prepare lessons to try out new ideas, and more time is needed for reflecting on the questions being explored. Our students conducting case studies, for example, took extra time to talk, read, and write with individual students, and then they took time to think and write about what they were learning. However, as we explained earlier, most teachers conclude that this is time well spent.

Teachers involved in action research also need to learn new skills. For example, teachers may need to learn how to develop effective questionnaires or how to record daily observations. In addition, the research may show that certain practices teachers have been following are not effective, so research can be a threat to a teacher's self-esteem. This threat is minimized when there is true collaboration between the teacher and the researcher. It is maximized when the outside expert comes in to critique the teacher's practices. Despite these potential problems, collaborative research is extremely effective in helping teachers refine their educational practice in ways that benefit all their students.

Yvonne and Sam's Experience

Yvonne spent time working in Sam's combination first- and second-grade bilingual classroom (Freeman and Nofziger 1991). Their work together was consistent with Allright's list of aims for a research project. Both Yvonne and Sam found that this collaboration was not always easy, but that it was very beneficial. The two met through their church, and after preliminary discussion they agreed to work together over time to see how curriculum could be organized around themes in Sam's class. Both Yvonne and Sam were a bit nervous at first, and both went through stages of wondering how the collaboration would really work. Yvonne shared her feelings as the project began and the two were in the planning stage:

On the day of my first visit to Sam's classroom, I was nervous. I worried that my convictions about the most effective practices for English language learners might not really work with these bilingual children. I wasn't certain that I would be able to communicate honestly with Sam. Before the end of the first hour, my fears were being replaced with excitement. Things I noticed about the children and things Sam pointed out to me helped me realize we had similar interests and concerns: We both showed similar interest in student journal responses that were intriguing; we both noticed the same strengths in the children as they interacted; we both had similar concerns about students who were not involved enough in the classroom community. After school that first day, we sat and talked for over two hours discussing our philosophies about learning for bilingual students and considering where we might begin. (66)

It was important to both Sam and Yvonne that they decide together the direction the classroom research should take. Yvonne explained how they reached their decision:

Sam was already using literature in English and Spanish instead of basals, and he had his children doing daily journal writing and also writing stories in the language of their choice. However, he wasn't comfortable with the organization of his classroom and wasn't sure how to begin working on that. After some discussion we decided to see if working with a broad theme that included comparison and contrast would give us a start. (66)

Sam reflected on his perspective as he began the project and also on some of the limitations in what he was willing to do with the researcher:

When Yvonne's visit began, so did our adventure. Although I was using some activities consistent with current research, I knew that I did not completely understand how to implement the most effective practices. . . . While there were parts of our classroom schedule I was anxious to work on, there were areas within the day that Yvonne and I decided not to modify because I felt that these were important times for the students. I was not willing to change the morning opening time, the time spent in small groups with Mrs. Romero, the bilingual aide, or our daily share time. Yvonne supported my decision, reinforcing the idea that I was the teacher and I had to decide what I wanted to change and how I wanted to try to change it. (67)

This element of the collaboration was very important. Sam had to feel that he was in charge of his own classroom and that, at any time, he could make decisions. Sam recalled one incident early on where he had to pull back from the new things he was trying to do. He was instituting more choice for his students, but it did not run as smoothly as he would have liked.

Once I began giving students choice, there was stress. That first day with Yvonne's help and the help of the aide, all went quite smoothly even though two or three children could not make their own choices. However, by the third day, I felt myself losing control. Students in some centers were involved but at others they seemed to get bored quickly, and relied on me to make their choices for them. The more things changed, the more I feared I was losing control. I called Yvonne, telling her I could not do this. She assured me that it was my classroom, and that I should do what I needed to do. At this point in my learning, I realized a very important thing: Too much change too quickly hurts the students as well as the teacher. (71)

Sam and Yvonne learned that collaborative classroom research is both challenging and exciting. As they reflected together, they learned about the structure needed for an explorer classroom, they learned what helped bilingual children read and write, they learned that change was hard but worth it. As Sam commented, "We were not 'traditional' teachers anymore. Over the past months, our roles had changed. We liked our new roles better" (83). Sam and Yvonne also followed up with one more step from their research. They wrote a chapter for a book together (Freeman and Nofziger 1991). This practice of classroom teachers and researchers writing and publishing together is one more act of true collaboration.

Since working with Sam, Yvonne has had the privilege of collaborating with several excellent explorer teachers. She has found that working in teachers' classrooms is critically important for her too. The classrooms she is in give her questions to answer and answers to questions. Almost weekly, her graduate students bring up problems in class that she can respond to because of the time she spends in classrooms. Recently, for example, she spent time in Sandra's classroom. Sandra is the teacher working with the newcomer students. As a result of their work together, Sandra and Yvonne have presented together at conferences. They also have published articles together and separately (Freeman et al. in press; Mercuri 2000).

Despite the potential problems and extra work, collaborative classroom research can benefit academic researchers, teachers, and students. Academic researchers can learn more about the different factors that affect students' academic success. Teachers can learn more about the practices that work for them and their students and also gain a greater understanding of why those practices work. Students can gain insights into their own situation and start to learn more about what they can do to help themselves be more successful learners.

All three models of teacher research we have discussed hold great promise. Teachers from different schools can conduct individual research, such as case studies, and then share their results in graduate classes. Teachers can launch individual action research projects. Or teachers can collaborate with college researchers to explore problems and puzzles in their classrooms. The result in each case is a context-specific solution to particular problems that teachers identify. As teachers conduct research, they reflect on their practice and build an integrated theory of language, learning, teaching, and curriculum.

What Makes an Effective Teacher?

We have described various models of classroom research that involve teacher researchers in examining their own practices in an attempt to improve the learning situation for their students. Teachers do want to improve their teaching. Whether or not they are effective in instituting change depends on a number of factors. Erickson (1993) observed and interviewed teachers working with English language learners at different grade levels from elementary through adult. Some followed traditional approaches. Others used an interactive, exploratory approach.

In her interviews, Erickson asked the following questions:

1. What makes teaching second language students difficult for you?
2. What has helped?
3. What would help?
4. What do you like about teaching?
5. What do you think is the most successful thing you've done?
6. Why or how did it come about?
7. What kinds of things would you like to try next? (60)

After discussing these questions, Erickson asked, "What else would you like to comment on?" She was interested to find that teachers had a great deal to talk about. Many teachers are isolated. They are often doing wonderful things, but they may not have anyone who is truly interested in listening to their stories. Perhaps they fear that if they tell about their failures, they will be criticized. If they tell about their successes, they might appear to be bragging. Having someone who was interested but who wasn't directly part of their school ask them to talk provided the teachers with the sounding board they needed. Erickson commented as follows:

> All of these teachers work under different circumstances. Each one faces budget constraints, facility challenges, and scheduling problems. Yet each teacher worked within those constraints to creatively reach the students, and every one in a different way expressed that it was the students themselves who make their job worthwhile. (70)

In her conclusions, Erickson listed five characteristics of effective teachers:

1. Teachers are effective when they assume an advocacy role for their students.
2. Teachers are effective when they have an adequate theoretical preparation for working with second language students.
3. Teachers are effective when they have professional support.
4. Teachers are effective when they assume control over their physical environment.
5. Teachers are effective when they have a sense of mission.

In the process of conducting classroom research, teachers often take on these characteristics. The decision to conduct research in their own classrooms is a first step toward taking an advocacy role for students.

Teacher researchers also read about theories of learning and second language acquisition as they attempt to explain what they observe in their classes. Teacher researchers gain support from colleagues or university researchers. As they reflect on their practice, they often begin to take control of the classroom and make changes in the learning environment. Teachers willing to take the time and make the effort to conduct research with their own students do so out of a sense of mission. They are true professionals who do everything they can to improve the chances for school success for all their students.

Throughout this book, we have shared examples of how explorer teachers take an intercultural orientation to meet the needs of English language learners. For many of these teachers, this has required a change in their attitudes, assumptions, and daily practices. We close the book with the story of Bunny, a second language teacher, who engaged in action research, critically reflected on her traditional teaching, and, as a result, changed her practice drastically. Bunny was, in fact, one of the teachers interviewed in the Erickson study and exhibits all the characteristics of an effective teacher.

Change Through Action Research

Bunny became involved in action research when her life circumstances changed and she decided to return to college for a master's degree. Bunny was a teacher with many years of experience. She used traditional grammar-based lessons with vocabulary lists and spelling lessons with her English language learners. Bunny believed that students needed the basic building blocks of English before they could hope to communicate either orally or in writing. Activities in Bunny's ESL classes were geared to improve students' grammatical competence and their ability to manipulate linguistic units, rather than their communicative competence (Hymes 1970).

However, when Bunny took her first two graduate courses, Introduction to Reading and Miscue Analysis, she was introduced to a sociopsycholinguistic view of learning. Though she resisted some of the things she was learning and did not institute change in her classes immediately, Bunny began to question whether her traditional methods were really helping her students.

When Bunny was asked to do a case study of one of her students for her graduate Language Acquisition and Cross-Cultural Communication class, she chose an eighteen-year-old Hmong woman who had shown little progress in her class. In fact, at the time of the case study, Pa was in her second year of beginning ESL. Bunny described her impressions of Pa at the beginning of the study:

> When Pa first entered school, she was shy and silent. Although she tried faithfully to do all the work, her comprehension level was very low, requiring much tutorial assis-

> tance and translation. She seemed to be withdrawn and uncomfortable. I felt she was not feeling very good about herself, and she appeared lonely and insecure with little evidence of any friends.

Bunny's early impressions of Pa were consistent with the labels Pa brought with her. Based on her reading test scores, Bunny had placed Pa in a low level for reading, and the types of activities that Pa was engaged in reinforced a kind of deficit view of her abilities. Bunny viewed Pa as a student with little self-confidence who required much individual help.

The assignments Bunny gave did not seem to inspire either Pa or Bunny. Figure 12–1 shows a typical assignment of Pa's that Bunny had given her students before doing the case study. Bunny first dictated the spelling list and then asked students to write the words in sentences. The words for the spelling list were chosen because

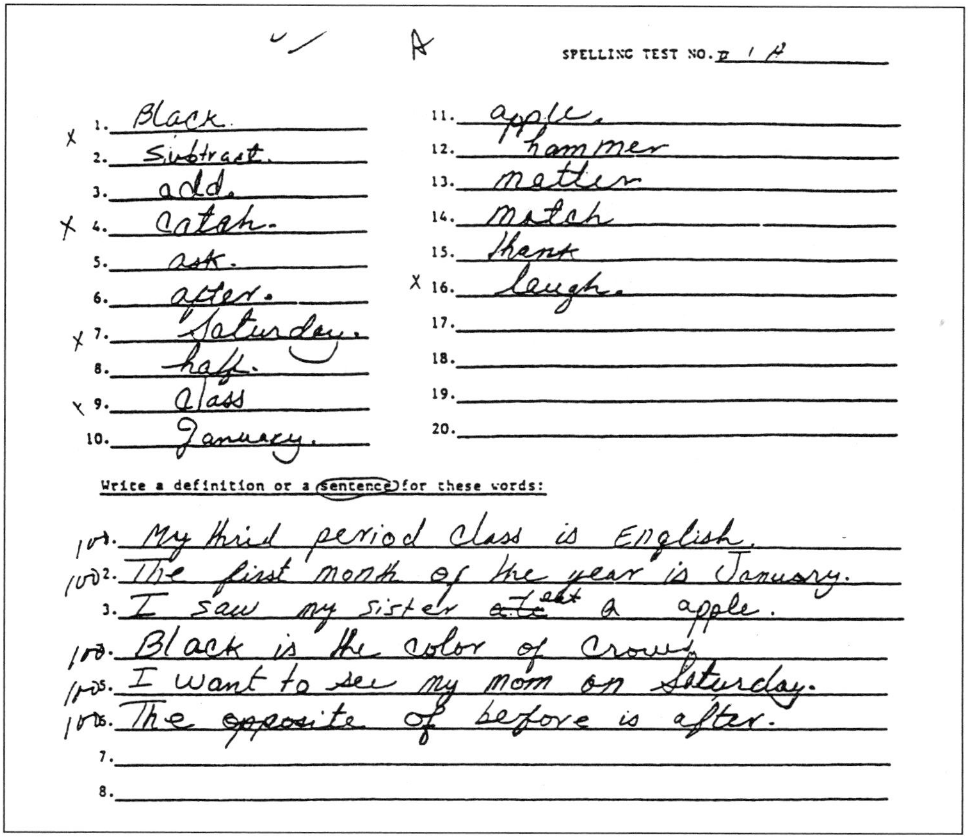
SPELLING TEST NO.

1. Black.
2. Sibtract.
3. add.
4. catah.
5. ask.
6. after.
7. Saturday.
8. half.
9. class
10. January.
11. apple.
12. hammer
13. matter
14. match
15. thank
16. laugh.
17.
18.
19.
20.

Write a definition or a sentence for these words:

1. My third period class is English.
2. The first month of the year is January.
3. I saw my sister ate a apple.
4. Black is the color of crow.
5. I want to see my mom on Saturday.
6. The opposite of before is after.
7.
8.

FIGURE 12–1 *Spelling Test*

they all contain a short *a* sound. Grading of the sentences was related to grammatical correctness only.

In the graduate language-acquisition class, Bunny read about theories of second language acquisition, including the importance of supporting the first language and lowering the affective filter (Cummins 1981, 1989; Krashen 1982, 1985). As she read and discussed these ideas with other teachers in her graduate class, Bunny started to realize that her spelling assignment represented learning rather than acquisition. Bunny began to introduce activities that would encourage a more exploratory type of learning. She wanted to build her students' independence and increase their self-confidence. The case study assignment provided Bunny with the impetus to begin to make changes.

As she observed Pa closely and carefully examined the work Pa turned in, Bunny began to reflect upon Pa's overdependence, loneliness, and insecurity:

> She usually was waiting for me when I arrived each morning and seemed to look forward to standing near me chatting haltingly about things that happened last year. Then I noticed little messages she was slipping to me in her written work hinting at her loneliness and homesickness. In a classroom writing assignment on a topic not at all related to personal feelings, Pa wrote, "I am lonely every day."

This writing assignment was another set of sentences based on the weekly spelling words. One of the words was *lonely,* and that prompted Pa's sentence, "I am lonely every day." Rather than marking grammatical errors as she might have done in the past, Bunny wrote a personal response to Pa, "I am sorry you are lonely. I want to be your friend." Bunny was beginning to see Pa not simply as a student needing lots of assistance to improve her language, but also as a person with human needs.

When Bunny asked Pa if she could be her case study subject, Pa was "delighted and very cooperative." Bunny decided that she wanted to reduce Pa's anxiety and increase her self-confidence and sense of self-worth through personal attention and encouragement. Because Bunny had been reading about the importance of first language support, she asked the primary-language tutor to encourage Pa to use her native-language skills to help other Hmong students in group settings. Over time, this led to a change in Pa's self-perception and interactions with all her peers, including those of different cultural backgrounds. In one of her anecdotal notations, Bunny described how Pa was changing as the result of this new role:

> She has assumed a leadership role in tutoring and translating for other students. . . . Interestingly, I have noticed her moving out of her seat to help not only girls of other cultural backgrounds, but boys with a different first language as well, unusual for a Hmong girl.

These interactions in class led to the building of friendships that Bunny noticed extended outside the classroom. "Another change is her happiness with her new friends. I now see her almost daily sitting in the hall, studying with them before class instead of sitting silently by herself."

Pa's use of her first language had other advantages. Bunny became more aware of Pa's academic competence:

> She knew more than I assumed. Recently, as I began reading a Hmong folktale to the class, Pa volunteered to read the Hmong translation as I read the English, and did so with ease and enjoyment. My surprise shamefully revealed a serious judgment error on my part by supposing that because Pa had not developed fluency in English, she lacked cognitive proficiency in her first language.

In addition to encouraging Pa to use her first language, Bunny initiated authentic writing activities with all her students. She began with a dialogue journal (Peyton 1990) and was particularly pleased with Pa's responses: "Immediately, she responded by writing a whole paragraph in comprehensible English. Subsequently, she began to share with me more information about herself and her background." Figure 12–2 shows Pa's first entry and Bunny's response.

The dialogue journal writing freed Pa from having to use the week's spelling words. In the journal, Pa was able to create a coherent text with related sentences. She reminded her teacher of a picture Bunny had given her last year and explained that she kept the picture at home. In her response, Bunny recalled the present Pa had given her last year at Christmas and pointed out that she had displayed it in the classroom. She did not comment on or mark the grammatical errors in Pa's journal as she had done with the spelling tests. Instead she focused on the content and established rapport with Pa.

Bunny's work with Pa was a catalyst that led her to change her teaching practices with all of her students. An early anecdotal record for this case study reflects how impressed Bunny was by the effect of personal attention on Pa:

> Due, I think, to the effect of the special attention focused on her by this study, I have noticed in recent weeks some changes in Pa's classroom behavior and progress. Most evident is her willingness to participate in all activities. She now volunteers information and comments regularly.

In addition to implementing authentic writing activities, Bunny made changes in her reading program. She found that the difficulties Pa experienced with reading were a reflection of the "very poorly condensed and difficult version" of the novel she had asked her class to read. In other words, Bunny began to critically examine reading materials rather than blaming the students. She asked Pa to read a complete short story and retell it. Bunny found that Pa made very few significant miscues in her reading and "in the retelling she covered all of the important details adequately and clearly."

Encouraging the use of the first language, beginning a dialogue journal, using complete stories, and responding to Pa personally were all steps toward more effec-

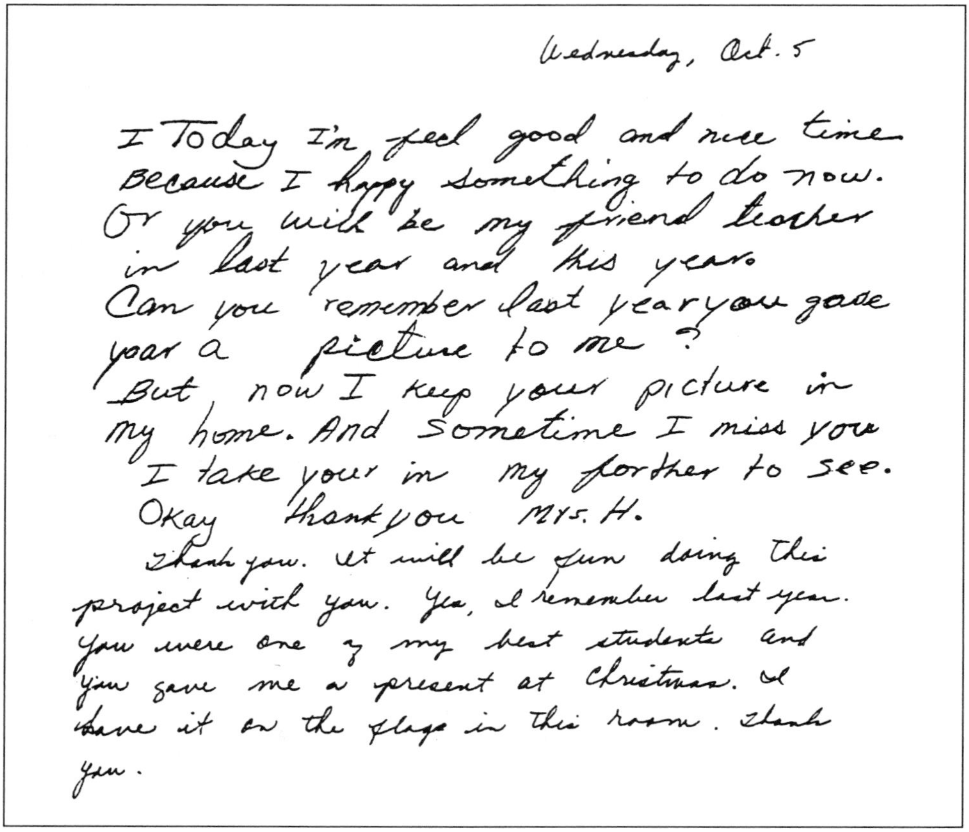

Wednesday, Oct. 5

I Today I'm feel good and nice time
Because I happy something to do now.
Or you will be my friend teacher
in last year and this year.
Can you remember last year you gave
year a picture to me?
But, now I keep your picture in
my home. And Sometime I miss you
I take your in my forther to see.
Okay thank you Mrs. H.
Thank you. It will be fun doing this
project with you. Yes, I remember last year.
You were one of my best students and
you gave me a present at Christmas. I
have it on the flag in this room. Thank
you.

FIGURE 12–2   *Pa's Journal Entry*

tive teaching for Bunny. She was willing to begin making changes in her classroom practices because she could see the difference these practices were making for Pa. She concluded, "At this point Pa seems to be feeling pretty good about herself and her progress. . . . I believe Pa is well on her way to developing adequacy, perhaps even fluency, in English rather soon."

Using dialogue journals instead of spelling lists was a big first step for both Bunny and her students. When we saw Bunny and several students at Back to School Night the next fall, we were delighted to find that they had taken a new step. Her high school ESL students had put together a collection of their personal stories around the theme of "The Big Experience." They wrote about coming to the United States, their first days at school here, or things they had experienced previously, such as the Mexico City earthquake. They typed the stories, planned the artwork, and designed a cover for their "published" book. The class book became a reading resource for all the ESL classes in the school, and students took their copies of the book home to read to family and friends.

Authentic writing activities such as the publishing of their own stories as a book also led the students to other kinds of authentic language-development activities. Once the students decided to publish their book, they realized that they needed money to do so. Bunny allowed the class to decide what they wanted to do. They elected to put on a spaghetti dinner to make money. The students planned the menu, sought out recipes, calculated ingredients, figured out how much money was required in advance to buy what they needed, arranged to use the school facilities, made the advertisements, and put on the dinner. Bunny's enthusiasm for this activity could hardly be contained as she observed not only the varied language students were using as they planned and worked, but also the students' enthusiasm as they completed a project in which they used English for real purposes.

Bunny's teaching changed dramatically. She moved from traditional vocabulary lists and spelling tests to dialogue journals, meaningful literature, and content-area units. Bunny considered many different factors that influenced her students. When Bunny looked closely at Pa as she carried out a case study, she realized the complexity of Pa as a person. She started to take into account both academic and social factors as she worked with Pa. This experience led Bunny to view all her students in a new way.

Bunny took an explorer approach to teaching. She and her students celebrated learning and celebrated their diversity. She focused on her students and built on their strengths by providing choice, building curriculum around their questions, making learning meaningful, encouraging collaborative learning, and allowing students to learn and express their learning through different modalities, including their first languages. She showed respect for her students by valuing their opinions

Bunny also continued to grow professionally. She joined a team of teachers at her school who worked together, creating curriculum and exchanging ideas for working effectively with their immigrant students. Their collaboration and joint projects led to the creation of a "graffiti-free zone" in the hall where ESL classes were held. Instead of graffiti, students and teachers put up writing, artwork, photos, and posters that are related to their classwork. The graffiti-free zone attracted other students and teachers to the ESL area of this large high school. The second language students' work drew attention and was appreciated.

Bunny continually planned new projects and got involved wherever she could to improve her teaching and to help her students. Her sense of mission led her to become a member of the California Literature Portfolio Assessment Project for high school ESL assessment. This work contributed to her master's thesis project on portfolio assessment for second language learners. When she graduated with her master's degree, she received the Dean's Award as the Outstanding Master's Student, not only because of her thesis but because of her involvement and dedication. Bunny told us afterward that she was surprised by the award, that she was "overwhelmed," and that she still had much to do. She planned to write a book on secondary ESL teaching, outlining the projects she and her colleagues were working on with their students.

Bunny is a classic example of Erickson's five characteristics of an effective teacher.

1. Beginning with the case study and her close look at Pa, Bunny became an advocate for her students. She saw them as having potential and was as excited as they were when they succeeded.
2. Bunny's graduate work provided her with a theoretical base that supported the successful practices she was implementing in the classroom.
3. Through friends she made in the graduate classes, an encouraging school administration, and the team she worked with at her school, Bunny found support for what she was doing.
4. Despite the fact that Bunny worked in a large inner-city high school that was poorly maintained and often dangerous, she and her colleagues made an attempt to improve the physical conditions in which they worked with projects like the graffiti-free zone.
5. Certainly, Bunny had a sense of mission. This was shown by her dedication to and enthusiasm for her work and her students.

Final Words

In this book we have examined the different factors inside and outside of classrooms that affect the second language acquisition and academic development of students caught between worlds. We have based our analysis on Cortés' Contextual Interaction Model. Cortés argues that the societal context affects the educational context in a number of ways. Effective teaching requires an understanding of both social and school factors that influence second language acquisition and academic development.

We have proposed an orientation to teaching, learning, language, and curriculum that is interactive and exploratory. Throughout the book we have provided examples of explorer teachers who take an intercultural orientation with the goal of multiculturation. In this last chapter, we have suggested that classroom-based research, which results in context-specific solutions and takes into account factors from both worlds—the school world and the societal world—offers the best possibility for creating meaningful and effective classrooms for English language learners. Effective teachers, as Erickson points out, are advocates for their students, they have a knowledge of theory, they have support, and they have a sense of mission. Teaching, and especially teaching English language learners, does require a sense of mission. It is a changing profession in a changing atmosphere as student populations and the community contexts both shift rapidly.

We see teachers meeting the challenges of the ever changing contexts daily. These teachers effectively promote optimal learning situations for second language students. It is exciting to see the kind of work they are doing, and it is our hope that their examples can provide support and inspiration for other teachers of English language learners. We hope that other teachers will conduct research in their classrooms and share their results, so that all of us can continue to grow in our understanding of how best to promote educational success for all our students, and especially for those living between worlds.

Applications

1. Different models of teacher research are discussed in this chapter. Have you ever been part of any of these models? In a group, share your teacher research experiences and/or how you see yourself doing teacher research in the future.

2. Allwright states three potential problems with teacher collaborative research. Have you or any of your peers ever experienced these problems? Discuss.

3. Erickson's research suggests five characteristics of successful teachers. Do you agree with her conclusions? Would you add others? Discuss.

Appendix
Websites for ESL Teachers

Classroom Ideas and Resources

Adult Education ESL Teachers Guide
humanities.byu.edu/ELC/teacher/TeacherGuideMain

Classroom Handouts
www.englishclub.net/teachers/handouts/index.htm

Clip Art Collection for Foreign/Second Language Instruction
www.sla.purdue.edu/fll/JapanProj/FLClipart

Conversation Questions for the English as a Second Language Classroom
www.artech.ac.jp/~ckelly/sub/questions.html

Dave's ESL Cafe
www.eslcafe.com

ESL Classroom Ideas
members.aol.com/Lingoteach/index2.html

ESL Lesson Plans and Resources
www.csun.edu/~hcedu013/eslplans.html

ESL Resources, Games, Songs, Chat, and Books
www.nanana.com/esl.html

Free Edutainment Games
www2.gol.com/users/language/games.html

Teacher Corner: BYU English Language Center
humanities.byu.edu/elc/teacher/teacherCorner

The ESL Center
members.aol.com/eslkathy/esl.htm

Teacher-Generated Subjects

Teacher Resource Site
www.forumeducation.net

Comenius English Language Center
www.comenius.com

Global Schoolhouse
www.gsh.org

Culturgrams Available
www.culturgram.com

ESL K–12 Resources
www.doe.k12.ga.us/resources/esol.html

ESL Teacher Resources and Lesson Plans
www.csun.edu/~hcedu013/eslplans.html

Teaching Tolerance
www.splcenter.org/teachingtolerance.html

Language and Linguistics

ERIC Clearinghouse on Language and Linguistics
www.cal.org/ericcll

Language Census Data
www.cde.ca.gov/demographics/reports

Net-Language
www.net-language.com

The Human Languages Page
www.june29.com/HLP

The Applied Linguistics WWW Virtual Library
alt.venus.co.uk/VL/AppLingBBK

Encarta Lesson Collection
www.encarta.msn.com/schoolhouse/default.asp

Organizations and Government Resources

Professional Associations
www.csun.edu/~hcedu013/eslprof.html

National Association for Bilingual Education (NABE)
www.nabe.org

National Council for Bilingual Education
www.ncbe.org

National Clearinghouse for Bilingual Education (NCBE)
www.ncbe.gwu.edu

Index of Publications
sf.bilingual.net/publications/newsletter/2_99

Teachers of English to Speakers of Other Languages (TESOL)
www.tesol.org

NCLE National Clearinghouse for ESL Literacy Education
www.cal.org/ncle

United Nations High Commisioner for Refugee (UNHCR)
www.unher.ch

Center for Multilingual Multicultural Research
www.usc.edu/dept/education/CMMR

California State Dept. Resources for English Learners
www.cde.ca.gov/cilbranch/bien/bien.htm

Sites of Professionals in the Fields of TESOL and Bilingual Education

Language Policy Web Site and Emporium by James Crawford
ourworld.compuserve.com/homepages/jwcrawford/

Communicative Language Teaching by Ann Galloway
www.cal.org./ericcll/digest/Gallow01.htm

Language Learning Strategies by Joann Crandall
www.cal.org/ericcll/digest/Cranada01.htm

Articles and Commentary by Stephen Krashen
www.languagebooks.com/2.0/articles/default.html

References

Adair-Hauck, B., R. Donato, and P. Cumo. 1994. "Using a Whole Language Approach to Teach Grammar." *Teacher's Handbook: Contextualized Language Instruction*, ed. J. Shrum and E. Glisan. Boston: Heinle and Heinle.

Allwright, D. 1993. "Integrating 'Research' and 'Pedagogy': Appropriate Criteria and Practical Possibilities." *Teachers Develop Teachers Research: Papers on Classroom Research and Teacher Development*, ed. J. Edge and K. Richards, 125–35. Oxford: Heinemann International.

Auerbach, E. 1993. "Reexamining English Only in the ESL Classroom." *TESOL Quarterly* 27(1): 9–32.

August, D., and K. Hakuta. 1997. *Improving Schooling for Language-Minority Children: A Research Agenda*. Washington, DC: Commission on Behavioral and Social Sciences and Education.

Baker, Colin. 2000. "Different Perspectives on Bilingual Education: The Agendas of Language Planning, Pedagogy, Economics and Politics, and the Need for Language Marketing." California Association of Bilingual Education (CABE) conference, San Francisco.

Beebe, L., ed. 1987. *Issues in Second Language Acquisition: Multiple Perspectives*. New York: Newbury House.

Bennett, W. 1985. Press release of Address to Association for a Better New York. New York.

Bisplinghoff, B. S., and J. Allen, eds. 1998. *Engaging Teachers: Creating Teaching and Researching Relationships*. Portsmouth, NH: Heinemann.

Bliatout, B. T., B. T. Downing, J. Lewis, D. Yang. 1988. *Handbook for Teaching Hmong-Speaking Students*. Folsom, CA: Folsom Cordova Unified School District.

Brisk, M., and A. Bou-Zeineddine. 1993. *It Feels So Good: Native Language Use in ESL*. Atlanta, GA: TESOL.

Brisk, M. E., and M. Harrington. 2000. *Literacy and Bilingualism: A Handbook for ALL Teachers*. Mahwah, NJ: Lawrence Erlbaum.

Brown, H. D. 1980. *Principles of Language Learning and Teaching*. Englewood Cliffs, NJ: Prentice Hall.

Bruner, J. 1985. "Models of the Learner." *Educational Researcher* 14(6): 5–8.

Bunting, E. 1988. *How Many Days to America?* Boston: Clarion Books.

Cary, S. 2000. *Working with Second Language Learners: Answers to Teachers' Top Ten Questions*. Portsmouth, NH: Heinemann.

Cazden, C. 1992. *Whole Language Plus: Essays on Literacy in the United States and New Zealand.* New York: Teachers College Press.

Chomsky, N. 1959. *Syntactic Structures.* Cambridge, MA: MIT Press.

Christian, D., C. Montone, K. Lindholm, and I. Carranza. 1997. *Profiles in Two-Way Immersion Education.* Washington, DC: ERIC.

Cochrane, O., D. Cochrane, S. Scalena, E. Buchanan. 1984. *Reading, Writing, and Caring.* Winnipeg: Whole Language Consultants.

Cohen, A., and E. Olshtain. 1993. "The Production of Speech Acts by ESL Learners." *TESOL Quarterly* 27(1): 33–56.

Cohen, B. 1983. *Molly's Pilgrim.* New York: Lothrop, Lee & Shepard.

Collier, V. 1989. "How Long? A Synthesis of Research on Academic Achievement in a Second Language." *TESOL Quarterly* 23(3): 509–32.

———. 1995. "Acquiring a Second Language for School." *Directions in Language and Education* 1(4).

Collier, V. P., and W. P. Thomas. 1996. *Effectiveness in Bilingual Education.* Orlando, FL: National Association of Bilingual Education.

Condon, M., and M. McGuffee. 2001. *Real E-publishing, Really Publishing!* Portsmouth, NH: Heinemann.

Cortés, C. 1986. "The Education of Language Minority Students: A Contextual Interaction Model." *Beyond Language: Social and Cultural Factors in Schooling Language Minority Students,* ed. D. Holt, 3–33. Los Angeles: California State University Evaluation, Dissemination, and Assessment Center.

———. 1994. "Multiculturation: An Educational Model for a Culturally and Linguistically Diverse Society." *Kids Come in All Languages: Reading Instruction for ESL Students,* ed. K. Spangenberg-Urbschat and R. Pritchard, 22–35. Newark, DE: International Reading Association.

Crawford, J., ed. 1992. *Language Loyalties: A Source Book on the Official English Controversy.* Chicago: University of Chicago Press.

———. 1999. *Bilingual Education: History, Politics, Theory and Practice.* Los Angeles: Bilingual Educational Services.

Criddle, J., and T. B. Mam. 1999. *To Destroy You Is No Loss: The Odyssey of a Cambodian Family.* Dixon, CA: East/West Bridge Publishing.

Cummins, J. 1981. "The Role of Primary Language Development in Promoting Educational Success for Language Minority Students." *Schooling and Language Minority Students: A Theoretical Framework,* 3–49. Los Angeles: California State University Evaluation, Dissemination, and Assessment Center.

———. 1984. "Language Proficiency and Academic Achievement Revisted: A Response." *Language Proficiency and Academic Achievement,* ed. C. Rivera, 71–76. Clevedon, England: Multilingual Matters.

———. 1989. *Empowering Minority Students.* Sacramento, CA: California Association of Bilingual Education.

———. 1996. *Negotiating Identities: Education for Empowerment in a Diverse Society.* Ontario, CA: California Association of Bilingual Education.

DeBruin-Parecki, A., and C. Timion. 1999. *Building Intercultural Friendships Through Story Development and Socialization: A Middle School/University Partnership*. Orlando, FL: National Reading Conference.

Delpit, L. 1990. "Language Diversity and Learning." *Perspectives on Talk and Learning*, ed. S. Hynds and D. Rubin, 247–66. Urbana, IL: National Council of Teachers of English.

Dewey, J., and A. F. Bentley. 1949. *Knowing and the Known*. Boston: Beacon Press.

Díaz, S., L. C. Moll, and H. Mehan. 1986. "Sociocultural Resources in Instruction: A Context-Specific Approach." In *Beyond Language: Social and Cultural Factors in Schooling Language Minority Students*, 187–230. Los Angeles: California State University Evaluation, Dissemination, and Assessment Center.

DiCerbo, P. A. 2000. "Transforming Education for Hispanic Youth: Broad Recommendations for Policy and Practice." Report from National Clearinghouse for Bilingual Education, Washington, DC: 1–7.

Dolson, D., and K. Lindholm. 1995. "World Class Education for Children in California: A Comparison of the Two-Way Bilingual Immersion and European Schools Model." *Multilingualism for All*, ed. T. Skutnabb-Kangas. Lisse, Netherlands: Swets and Zeitlinger.

Dolson, D., and J. Mayer. 1992. "Longitudinal Study of Three Program Models for Language Minority Students: A Critical Examination of Reported Findings." *Bilingual Research Journal* 16 (1–2): 105–57.

Dulay, H., and M. Burt. 1974. "Natural Sequences in Child Second Language Acquisition." *Language Learning* 24: 37–53.

ERIC (Educational Resources Information Center). 1997. *From At-Risk to Excellence: Principles for Practice*. Washington, DC: ERIC.

Elley, W. 1989. "Vocabulary Acquisition from Listening to Stories Read Aloud." *Reading Research Quarterly* 24: 174–87.

———. 1991. "Acquiring Literacy in a Second Language: The Effect of Book-Based Programs." *Language Learning* 41(2): 403–39.

———. 1998. *Raising Literacy Levels in Third World Countries: A Method That Works*. Culver City, CA: Language Education Associates.

Ellis, R. 1990. *Instructed Second Language Acquisition*. Oxford: Blackwell.

———. 1998. "Teaching and Research: Options in Grammar Teaching." *TESOL Quarterly* 32(1): 39–60.

Enright, D. S., and M. L. McCloskey. 1985. "Yes, Talking!: Organizing the Classroom to Promote Second Language Acquisition." *TESOL Quarterly* 19(3): 431–53.

———. 1988. *Integrating English: Developing English Language and Literacy in the Multilingual Classroom*. Reading, MA: Addison-Wesley.

Erickson, J. 1993. "Teachers' Voices: An Interview Project." Fresno, CA: Fresno Pacific College.

Faltis, C., and S. Hudelson. 1998. *Bilingual Education in Elementary and Secondary School Communities*. Boston: Allyn and Bacon.

Ferreiro, E., and A. Teberosky. 1982. *Literacy Before Schooling*. Portsmouth, NH: Heinemann.

Fitzgerald, J. 1993. "Literacy and Students Who Are Learning English as a Second Language." *The Reading Teacher* 46(8): 638–47.

Flint, D. 1998. *Where Does Breakfast Come From?* Crystal Lake, IL: Rigby.

Frank, C. 1999. *Ethnographic Eyes: A Teacher's Guide to Classroom Observation*. Portsmouth, NH: Heinemann.

Freeman, A. 2000. "Considerations for the Selection of Culturally Relevant Text." *Language, Literacy and Culture*. Occasional paper 85. Tucson, AZ: University of Arizona.

Freeman, D. E., and Y. S. Freeman. 1990. "Case Studies: Viewing New Students in New Ways." *California English* 26(3): 8–9, 26–27.

———. 1991. "Doing Social Studies: Whole Language Lessons to Promote Social Action." *Social Education* 55(1): 29–32, 66.

———. 1993. "Strategies for Promoting the Primary Languages of All Students." *The Reading Teacher* 46(7): 552–58.

———. 1997. *Teaching Reading and Writing in Spanish in the Bilingual Classroom*. Portsmouth, NH: Heinemann.

———. 1998a. *ESL/EFL Teaching: Principles for Success*. Portsmouth, NH: Heinemann.

———. 1998b. *La Enseñanza de la lectura y la escritura en español en el aula bilingüe*. Portsmouth, NH: Heinemann.

———. 1999. "School Success for Secondary English Learners." *Reading and Writing in More Than One Language: Lessons for Teachers*, ed. E. Franklin, 1–28. Alexandria, VA: TESOL.

———. 2000. *Teaching Reading in Multilingual Classrooms*. Portsmouth, NH: Heinemann.

Freeman, Y. S., S. Mercuri, and D. Freeman. In press. "Keys to Success for Bilingual Students." *NABE Research Journal*.

Freeman, Y. S., and S. Nofziger. 1991. "WalkuM to RnM 33: Vien Vinidos al cualTo 33." *Organizing for Whole Language*, ed. K. Goodman, Y. Goodman, and W. Hood, 65–83. Portsmouth, NH: Heinemann.

Freeman, Y. S., and L. Whitesell. 1985. "What Preschoolers Already Know About Print." *Educational Horizons* 64(1): 22–25.

Freire, P. 1970. *Pedagogy of the Oppressed*. New York: Continuum.

Freire, P., and D. Macedo. 1987. *Literacy: Reading the Word and the World*. South Hadley, MA: Bergin & Garvey.

García, E. 1999. *Student Cultural Diversity: Understanding and Meeting the Challenge*. Boston: Houghton Mifflin.

Gardner, H. 1984. *Frames of Mind*. New York: Basic Books.

Garza, C. L. 1990. *Family Pictures: Cuadros de familia*. San Francisco: Children's Book Press.

Gee, J. P. 1988. "Count Dracula, the Vampire Lestat, and TESOL." *TESOL Quarterly* 22(1): 201–25.

———. 1992. *The Social Mind: Language, Ideology, and Social Practice*. New York: Bergin & Garvey.

Goldenberg, C. 1991. "Instructional Conversations and Their Classroom Application." Los Angeles: National Center for Research on Cultural Diversity and Second Language Learning.

Goldenberg, C., and R. Gallimore. 1991. "Local Knowledge, Research Knowledge, and Educational Change: A Case Study of Early Spanish Reading Improvement." *Educational Researcher* 20 (8): 2–14.

González, J., and L. Darling-Hammond. 1997. *New Concepts for New Challenges: Professional Development for Teachers of Immigrant Youth*. McHenry, IL: Delta Systems and the Center for Applied Linguistics.

Goodman, K. S., Y. M. Goodman, B. Flores. 1979. *Reading in the Bilingual Classroom: Literacy and Biliteracy*. Rosslyn, VA: National Clearinghouse for Bilingual Education.

Goodman, Y. 1982. "Retellings of Literature and the Comprehension Process." *Theory into Practice: Children's Literature* 21(4): 301–307.

Goodman, Y. M., and K. S. Goodman. 1990. "Vygotsky in a Whole Language Perspective." *Vygotsky and Education: Instructional Implications and Applications of Sociohistorical Psychology*, ed. L. Moll, 223–50. Cambridge: Cambridge University Press.

Goss, J. L., and J. C. Harste. 1985. *It Didn't Frighten Me*. Worthington, OH: Willowisp Press.

Graves, D. 1994. *A Fresh Look at Writing*. Portsmouth, NH: Heinemann.

Greene, J. 1998. *A Meta-Analysis of the Effectiveness of Bilingual Education*. Claremont, CA: Tomas Rivera Policy Institute.

Hakuta, K., Y. G. Butler, and D. Witt. 2000. "How Long Does It Take English Learners to Attain Proficiency?" Policy report 2000–1. Los Angeles: University of California Linguistic Minority Research Institute.

Halliday, M. A. K. 1984. "Three Aspects of Children's Language Development: Learning Language, Learning Through Language, and Learning About Language." *Oral and Written Language Development Research: Impact on the Schools*, ed. Y. Goodman, M. Haussler, and D. Strickland. Urbana, IL: National Council of Teachers of English.

Halliday, M. A. K., and R. Hassan. 1976. *Cohesion in English*. London: Longman.

Harste, J., V. Woodward, C. Burke. 1984. *Language Stories and Literacy Lessons*. Portsmouth, NH: Heinemann.

Hatch, E. 1983. *Psycholinguistics: A Second Language Perspective*. Rowley, MA: Newbury House.

Heath, S. 1986. "Sociocultural Contexts of Language Development." *Beyond Language: Social and Cultural Factors in Schooling Language Minority Students*, ed. D. Holt, 143–86. Los Angeles: California State University Evaluation, Dissemination, and Assessment Center.

Heath, S. B. 1983. *Ways with Words: Language, Life, and Work in Communities and Classrooms*. Cambridge: Cambridge University Press.

Holmes, D. 1993. "IATEFL 1993: Are Politicians Seized by Linguistic Panic?" *TESOL Matters* 3(3): 1, 8.

Holt, D., ed. 1993. *Cooperative Learning: A Response to Linguistic and Cultural Diversity*. Washington, DC: Center for Applied Linguistics.

Hubbard, R. S., and B. M. Power. 1993. *The Art of Classroom Inquiry*. Portsmouth, NH: Heinemann.

Hudelson, S. 1984. "Kan yu ret an rayt en ingles: Children Become Literate in English as a Second Language." *TESOL Quarterly* 18(2): 221–37.

———. 1986. "ESL Children's Writing: What We've Learned, What We're Learning." *Children and ESL: Integrating Perspectives*, ed. P. Rigg and D. S. Enright, 23–54. Washington, DC: TESOL.

———. 1987. "The Role of Native Language Literacy in the Education of Language Minority Children." *Language Arts* 64(8): 827–40.

Hymes, D. 1970. "On Communicative Competence." *Directions in Sociolinguistics*, ed. J. Gumperz and D. Hymes, 35–71. New York: Holt, Rinehart and Winston.

Johnson, K. E. 1995. *Understanding Communication in Second Language Classrooms*. New York: Cambridge University Press.

Jones, R. 1976. *The Acorn People*. New York: Bantam

Kagan, S. 1986. "Cooperative Learning and Sociocultural Factors in Schooling." *Beyond Language: Social and Cultural Factors in Schooling Language Minority Students*, 231–98. Los Angeles: California State University Evaluation, Dissemination, and Assessment Center.

Kaplan, R. 1966. "Cultural Thought Patterns in Intercultural Education." *Language Learning* 16: 1–20.

Klassen, C. 1993. "Exploring 'The Color of Peace': Content Area Literature Discussions." *Cycles of Meaning: Exploring the Potential of Talk in Learning Communities*, ed. K. Mitchell Pierce and C. Gilles, 236–59. Portsmouth, NH: Heinemann.

Kohn, A. 2000. *The Case Against Standardized Testing: Raising the Scores, Ruining the Schools*. Portsmouth, NH: Heinemann.

Kozol, J. 1991. *Savage Inequalities*. New York: Harper

Krashen, S. 1982. *Principles and Practice in Second Language Acquisition*. New York: Pergamon Press.

———. 1985. *Inquiries and Insights*. Haywood, CA: Alemany Press.

———. 1992. *Fundamentals of Language Education*. Beverly Hills, CA: Laredo Publishing.

———. 1996. *Under Attack: The Case Against Bilingual Education*. Culver City, CA: Language Education Associates.

Krashen, S. D., L. Tse, J. McQuillan. 1998. *Heritage Language Development*. Culver City, CA: Language Education Associates.

Kucer, S. B., C. Silva, E. Delgado-Larocco. 1995. *Curricular Conversations: Themes in Multilingual and Monolingual Classrooms*. York, ME: Stenhouse.

Larsen-Freeman, D., and M. Long. 1991. *An Introduction to Second Language Acquisition Research*. New York: Longman.

Levinson, R. 1985. *Watch the Stars Come Out*. New York: Dutton.

Lindfors, J., ed. 1982. *Exploring in and Through Language*. "On TESOL '82: Pacific Perspectives on Language Learning and Teaching." Washington, DC: TESOL.

Lindfors, J. 1987. *Children's Language and Learning*. Englewood Cliffs, NJ: Prentice Hall.

―――. 1989. "The Classroom: A Good Environment for Language Learning." *When They Don't All Speak English: Integrating the ESL Student into the Regular Classroom*, ed. P. Rigg and V. Allen, 39–54. Urbana, IL: National Council of Teachers of English.

Long, M. 1983. "Does Second Language Instruction Make a Difference? A Review of the Research." *TESOL Quarterly* 14(1): 378–90.

Lucas, T. 1997. *Into, Through, and Beyond Secondary School: Critical Transitions for Immigrant Youths*. McHenry, IL: Center for Applied Linguistics.

Marasco, L. 1993. "Parent Empowerment Through Involvement." *TIPS (Teacher Inspired Practical Strategies)*, NCTE/ESL Assembly Newsletter 21(1): 6–7.

McGroarty, M. 1993. "Cooperative Learning and Second Language Acquisition." *Cooperative Learning: A Response to Cultural and Linguistic Diversity*, ed. D. Holt. Washington, DC: Center for Applied Linguistics.

McQuillan, J., and L. Tse. 1997. "Does Research Matter? An Analysis of Media Opinion of Bilingual Education, 1984–1994." *Bilingual Research Journal* 20(1): 1–27.

McWhorter, J. 2000. *Spreading the Word: Language and Dialect in America*. Portsmouth, NH: Heinemann.

Mercuri, S. 2000. "Supporting Preliterate Older Emergent Readers to Become Bilingual and Biliterate." *Talking Points*. 12 (1): 8–13.

NCBE (National Clearinghouse for Bilingual Education). 2000. *The Growing Numbers of Limited English Proficient Students*. Washington, DC: National Clearinghouse for Bilingual Education.

Nunan, D. 1993. "Action Research in Language Education." *Teachers Research Teachers Develop: Papers on Classroom Research and Teacher Development*, ed. J. Edge and K. Richards, 39–50. Oxford: Heinemann International.

Ogbu, J. 1991. "Immigrant and Involuntary Minorities in Comparative Perspective." *Minority Status and Schooling: A Comparative Study of Immigrant and Involuntary Minorities*, ed. M. Gibson and J. Ogbu, 3–33. New York: Garland.

Olsen, L., and N. Mullen. 1990. *Embracing Diversity: Teachers' Voices from California Classrooms*. San Francisco: California Tomorrow.

Ouk, M. 1993. "Cambodian Proverbs Help U.S. Educators Understand and Respond to Children and Their Parents." *BEOutreach* 4(2): 5, 6.

Ouk, M., et al. 1988. *Handbook for Teaching Khmer-Speaking Students*. Folsom, CA: Folsom Cordova Unified School District.

Palinscar, A. S. 1986. "The Role of Dialogue in Providing Scaffolded Instruction." *Educational Psychologist* 21: 73–98.

Paulsen, G. 1995. *The Tortilla Factory*. New York: Harcourt Brace.

Pérez, T. 1991. *Portraits of Mexican-Americans: Pathfinders in the Mexican American Communities*. Carthage, IL: Good Apple.

Peyton, J. K., ed. 1990. *Students and Teachers Writing Together: Perspectives on Journal Writing*. Alexandria, VA: TESOL.

Phillips, S. 1972. "Participant Structures and Communicative Competence: Warm Spring Children in Community and Classroom." *Functions of Language in the Classroom*, ed. C. Cazden, V. John, and D. Hymes, 370–94. New York: Teachers College Press.

Piaget, J. 1955. *The Language and Thought of the Child*. New York: Meridian.

Pinker, S. 1994. *The Language Instinct: How the Mind Creates Language*. New York: William Morrow.

Power, B. 1999. *Parent Power: Energizing Home-School Communication*. Portsmouth, NH: Heinemann.

Power, B., and R. Hubbard. 1999. "Becoming Teacher Researchers One Moment at a Time." *Language Arts* 77 (1): 34–39.

Radford, A. 1981. *Transformational Syntax: A Student's Guide to Chomsky's Extended Standard Theory*. Cambridge, England: Cambridge University Press.

Rigg, P., and V. Allen, eds. 1989. *When They Don't All Speak English: Integrating the ESL Student into the Regular Classroom*. Urbana, IL: National Council of Teachers of English.

Rigg, P., and D. S. Enright. 1986. *Children and ESL: Integrating Perspectives*. Washington, DC: Teachers of English to Speakers of Other Languages.

Rigg, P., and V. Allen. 1989. Introduction. *When They Don't All Speak English*, vii–xx. Urbana, IL: National Council of Teachers of English.

Robinson-Flint, J., E. Manilton, D. Kirka, R. Rense, G. White. 1992. "The Stereotyping Habit: Young People Try to Fight It." *Los Angeles Times*, 30 November, D4–D5.

Rojas, J. 1993. "Book Bags: Literacy at Home." *TIPS (Teacher Inspired Practical Strategies)*, *NCTE/ESL Assembly Newsletter* 21:8.

Samway, K., and G. Whang. 1996. *Literature Studies in a Multicultural Classroom*. York, ME: Stenhouse.

Samway, K., G. Whang, M. Pippitt. 1995. *Buddy Reading: Cross-Age Tutoring in a Multicultural School*. Portsmouth, NH: Heinemann.

Saunders, W., and C. Goldenberg. 1997. *Identifying Salient Elements of a Successful Transition Program*. Santa Cruz: University of California Center for Research on Education, Diversity, and Excellence.

Scarcella, R. 1990. *Teaching Language Minority Students in the Multicultural Classroom*. Englewood Cliffs, NJ: Prentice Hall Regents.

Scarcella, R., and R. Oxford. 1992. *The Tapestry of Language Learning: The Individual in the Communicative Classroom*. Boston: Heinle and Heinle.

Schumann, J. 1978. *The Pidginization Process: A Model for Second Language Acquisition*. Rowley, MA: Newbury House.

Seliger, H. 1988. "Psycholinguistic Issues in Second Language Acquisition." *Issues in*

Second Language Acquisition: Multiple Perspectives, ed. L. Beebe, 17–40. New York: Newbury House.

Skinner, B. F. 1957. *Verbal Behavior*. New York: Appleton.

Skutnabb-Kangas, T. 1983. *Bilingualism or Not: The Education of Minorities*. Clevedon, England: Multilingual Matters.

Smith, F. 1983. *Essays into Literacy: Selected Papers and Some Afterthoughts*. Portsmouth, NH: Heinemann.

———. 1988. *Joining the Literacy Club: Further Essays into Literacy*. Portsmouth, NH: Heinemann.

Snow, M., and D. Brinton, eds. 1997. *The Content-Based Classroom: Perspectives on Integrating Language and Content*. White Plains, NY: Longman.

Socios. 1996. *Poemas de nuestros hijos*. Merced, California.

Sue, S., and A. Padilla. 1986. "Ethnic Minority Issues in the United States: Challenges for the Educational System." *Beyond Language: Social and Cultural Factors in Schooling Language Minority Students*, 35–72. Los Angeles: California State University Evaluation, Assessment, and Dissemination Center.

Swain, M. 1985. "Communicative Competence: Some Roles of Comprehensible Output in Its Development." *Input in Second Language Acquisition*, ed. S. Gass and C. Madden, 235–53. Rowley, MA: Newbury House.

Terrell, T. 1991. "The Role of Grammar Instruction in a Communicative Approach." *Modern Language Journal* 75: 52–63.

Thomas, W., and V. Collier. 1997. *School Effectiveness for Language Minority Students*. California Association of Bilingual Education (CAB) conference, San Diego.

Valdés, G. 1996. *Con respeto: Bridging the Distances Between Culturally Diverse Families and Schools*. New York: Teachers College Press.

Van Lier, L. 1988. *The Classroom and the Language Learner*. New York: Longman.

Villaseñor, V. 1991. *Rain of Gold*. New York: Dell.

Vopat, J. 1994. *The Parent Project: A Workshop Approach to Parent Involvement*. York, ME: Stenhouse.

Vygotsky, L. 1978. *Mind in Society: The Development of Higher Psychological Processes*. Cambridge, MA: Harvard University Press.

———. 1981. "The Genesis of Higher Mental Functions." *The Concept of Activity in Soviet Psychology*, ed. J. V. Wertsch. Armonk, NY: M. E. Sharpe.

Wallerstein, N. 1987. "Problem Posing Education: Freire's Method for Transformation." *Freire for the Classroom*, ed. I. Shor, 33–44. Portsmouth, NH: Heinemann.

Waters, K. 1989. *Sara Morton's Day: A Day in the Life of a Pilgrim*. New York: Scholastic.

Wells, G., and G. Chang-Wells. 1992. *Constructing Knowledge Together*. Portsmouth, NH: Heinemann.

Whitmore, K. F., and C. G. Crowel. 1994. *Inventing a Classroom: Life in a Bilingual, Whole Language Learning Community*. York, ME: Stenhouse.

Widdowson, H. 1978. *Teaching Language as Communication*. Oxford: Oxford University Press.

Wink, J. 1993. "Labels Often Reflect Educator's Beliefs and Practices." *BEOutreach* 4: 228–29.

———. 2000. *Critical Pedagogy: Notes from the Real World.* Reading, MA: Addison-Wesley Longman.

Wolfram, W. 1991. *Dialects and American English.* Englewood Cliffs, NJ: Prentice Hall Regents.

Wolfram, W., and D. Christian. 1989. *Dialects and Education: Issues and Answers.* Englewood Cliffs, NJ: Prentice Hall Regents.

Wong, S. 1992. "Contrastive Rhetoric: An Exploration of Proverbial References in Chinese Student L1 and L2 Writing." *Journal of Intensive English Studies* 6: 71–90.

Yang, L. 1992. "Why Hmong Came to America." *The Fresno Bee*, 27 December, B9.

Zanger, V., ed. 1996. *Math Story Book.* Boston: Joseph Hurley School.

Index